PASTOR

Pastor

The Theology and Practice of Ordained Ministry

William H. Willimon

Abingdon Press
Nashville

PASTOR
THE THEOLOGY AND PRACTICE OF ORDAINED MINISTRY

Copyright © 2002 by Abingdon Press

This book is printed on recycled, acid-free, elemental-chlorine–free paper.

Library of Congress Cataloging-in-Publication Data

Willimon, William H.
  Pastor : the theology and practice of ordained ministry / William H. Willimon.
    p. cm.
  Includes indexes.
  ISBN 0-687-04532-0 (alk. paper)
  1. Pastoral theology. 2. Clergy—Office. I. Title.

  BV4011.3 .W55 2002
  253—dc21
                                                          2001053531
ISBN 13: 978-0-687-04532-7

Scripture quotations, unless otherwise indicated, are from the *New Revised Standard Version of the Bible,* copyright 1989, Division of Christian Education of the National Council of the Churches of Christ in the United States of America. Used by permission. All rights reserved.

Scripture quotations marked (RSV) are from the *Revised Standard Version of the Bible,* copyright 1946, 1952, 1971 by the Division of Christian Education of the National Council of the Churches of Christ in the United States of America. Used by permission. All rights reserved.

Scripture quotations marked (NIV) are taken from the HOLY BIBLE, NEW INTERNATIONAL VERSION ®. NIV ®. Copyright © 1973, 1978, 1984 by International Bible Society. Used by permission of Zondervan Publishing House. All rights reserved.

"Words We Tremble to Say Out Loud" copyright © 1993 by Barbara Brown Taylor. All rights reserved. Excerpt is reprinted from *The Preaching Life* by Barbara Brown Taylor, published by Cowley Publications, 907 Massachusetts Avenue, Cambridge, MA 02139. www.cowley.org (800) 225-1534.

Prayer "Ash Wednesday" from *The United Methodist Hymnal.* Copyright © 1989 by The United Methodist Publishing House. Used by permission.

Excerpt from "The Great Thanksgiving" in *A Service of Word and Table I.* Copyright © 1972, 1980, 1985, 1989 by The United Methodist Publishing House. Used by permission.

Excerpts from *Treatise Concerning the Christian Priesthood* in *A Select Library of the Nicene and Post-Nicene Fathers of the Christian Church,* vol. 9, Philip Schaff, ed. copyright © 1956 by William B. Eerdmans Publishing Company. Used by permission.

Excerpt from "East Coker" in FOUR QUARTETS. Copyright 1940 by T. S. Eliot and renewed 1968 by Esme Valerie Eliot, reprinted by permission of Harcourt, Inc.

Excerpts from *The Intrusive Word: Preaching to the Unbaptized* by William H. Willimon © 1994 Wm. B. Eerdmans Publishing Company, Grand Rapids, MI. Used by permission.

07 08 09 10 11–20 19 18 17 16 15 14 13 12 11

MANUFACTURED IN THE UNITED STATES OF AMERICA

To

Patricia Parker Willimon

Companion in Ministry

Acknowledgments

My thanks to David Wood and the Louisville Institute for a generous grant that enabled me to bring this work to completion and to convene a group of distinguished colleagues in ministry to offer me critique and correction as this work was in progress. Martin Copenhaver, Sam Lloyd, Peter Marty, David Byrum, Nicholas Hood, Frank Brosend, Michael Turner, Tripp York, David Hansen, David Dragseth, Kathryn Bannister, Wes Avram, Jim Antal, Allan Poole, Nancy Sehested, John Cook, Thomas Frank, C. G. Newsome, Martha Forrest, William Trexler, Robert Ratcliff, Nancy DeVries, Charlene Kammerer, Kelly Clem, and Luonne Rouse participated in two national convocations on the manuscript. I also owe a debt of thanks to my faculty colleagues at Duke Divinity School: Gregory Jones, Jackson Carroll, Willie Jennings, Richard Heitzenrater, Albert Mosley, Keith Meador, Nancy Ferree Clark, and Jenny Copeland. I am especially indebted to my able graduate assistant, Jason Byassee, for his extensive help in the research and writing of this book.

Contents

Introduction

ask if they use these

Take a Christian, a follower of Jesus by virtue of baptism. Put a stole around the neck of this Christian and you are on your way to making a pastor. This stole, once the necktie of Roman nobility, becomes now, in the hands of the church, a sign that reminds of the yoke put around the necks of oxen or other beasts of burden. Of course, Jesus reassured us that his yoke was easy and his burden light (Matt. 11:28-30). Still, by this world's standards, having a yoke hung around your neck is an odd way to begin a job.

Before the altar of God, at the bedside of the sick, in conversation with troubled souls, befuddled before the biblical text, there is the pastor. Standing in that fateful intersection between God's people and God, at that risky transaction between Christ and his Body, the church, stands the priest. It is no small thing to be in mediation *how does this relate to Hebrews?* between God and humanity, to offer the gifts of God's people, to intercede for the suffering of the world in prayer, rightly to divide the Word of God. With trembling and with joy, the pastor works that fateful space between here and the throne of God. This yoke, while not always as easy as Jesus implies, is often quite joyful. It is a joyful thing to be a pastor, to have one's life drawn toward dealings that are divine; to bear burdens that are, while not always light, at least more significant than those that the world tries to lay upon our backs. It is a joy to be expended in some vocation that is greater than one's self.

This book is the fruit of my now thirty years of pastoral ministry and almost as many years preparing people for that ministry in seminary teaching. This is my loving, grateful, but not uncritical meditation upon the ministry of the ordained. For experienced pastors, I hope that this will be a remembrance of the origins, a recalling to the blessings and the high adventure of ministry. For those preparing to be pastors, may this be a sort of textbook, a kind of manual that will guide in their preparation. For all, I pray that this book will be part of what Paul might call "a ministry of encouragement" (Rom. 15:5; 1 Thess. 5:11).

how is he using this?

The pastoral ministry is a gift of God to the church. It is not an easy vocation, this calling full of peril. Yet it is also a great gift to have one's life caught up in such a pilgrimage. This book hopes to do justice both to the difficulties and to the joys of ministry.

(1) We begin with investigation of who pastors are, as a means of understanding what pastors do. At its best the church believes that the most secure basis for the pastoral ministry is theological rather than personal or social. It all begins in the vocation of God and the church, and ends there too. Therefore this book begins with theology and with history, in the confidence that if pastors know whose they are, where they come from, and why they are here, they will better know what to do, here, now.

Because of its nature, pastoral identity is never secure. In every age the church must ask, What are pastors for? Reflecting upon an earlier crisis of ministerial identity, H. Richard Niebuhr wrote:

> Whenever in Christian history there has been a definite, intelligible conception of the ministry, four things at least were known about the office: what its chief work was and what was the chief purpose of all its functions; what constituted a call to the ministry; what was the source of the minister's authority; and whom the minister served.[1]

This book attempts to raise and to answer each of Niebuhr's criteria, though in a somewhat different way from Niebuhr. We shall conduct our reflection upon the pastoral ministry in tandem with a reading of the Acts of the Apostles, which I interpret as an early Christian narrative of the challenges of church leadership. There will be "Interludes," short reflections upon selected topics of the pastoral ministry. There will also be periodic celebrations of the witness of those who have preceded us in this vocation.

Here, at the beginning, are my guiding assumptions for this exploration of Christian ministry:

1. Ministry is an act of God. Service, self-giving love, is God's idea before it is ours. Ministry is one aspect of God's determination to have a human family, then to maintain that family into eternity. The Scriptures bear eloquent testimony: God will have a family of priests, a holy nation that shall be a blessing to all the nations, no matter what it costs God to get it.

It is of the nature of the Trinity to be creative, communicative, to evoke a world out of nothing, a family out of nobodies. One thinks of how Luke begins the story of Jesus, not with Jesus, but with John the Baptist, who comes to "prepare the way of the Lord" (Luke 3:4). "Get ready, God is coming!" is John's laconic message. To those who took comfort in the securities of the old order, saying, "We have Abraham as our ancestor" (Luke 3:8), "My family founded this church," "I tithe," John warned, "God is able from these stones to raise up children to Abraham." God will have a family, one way or another. If God must raise up a family out of the stones in the Jordan River, God is able.

God had done it before. From those as old and unfutured as stones, Sarah and Abraham, God announced, "Look toward heaven and count the stars. . . . So shall your descendants be" (Gen. 15:5). From out of nothing, God promises a people. This is the way God gets a family, through promise, vocation. This is the way, you will recall, God got a world, through nothing more than a word; "Let there be light" (Gen. 1:3), and there was. Other gods get what they want through war, or procreation, or violence. This God works through the Word, in call, by vocation.

> And because [God] loved your ancestors, [God] chose their descendants after them. (Deut. 4:37)

> It was not because you were more numerous than any other people that the LORD set [the Lord's] heart on you and chose you— for you were the fewest of all peoples. It was because the LORD loved you and kept the oath that [the Lord] swore to your ancestors. (Deut. 7:7-8)

> You did not choose me but I chose you. And I appointed you to go and bear fruit, fruit that will last. (John 15:16a)

Divine creativity is the basis for both the church and its leaders. Thus one story of vocation has been paradigmatic for Christians: Luke's account of the call of Saul in Acts 9. Saul, the very one who breathed "threats and murder against the disciples of the Lord" (9:1) is knocked down on the road to Damascus, blinded by light, must be led by the hand (9:1-9), and for three days is entombed as one who can neither eat nor drink.

"Saul, Saul, why do you persecute me?" asks the voice (9:4). Saul has been persecuting the church, not Jesus. Yet there seems to be such an intimate connection between the risen Christ and the church that an injury against one is an insult to the other. Saul's is a story of conversion and vocation. In biblical narratives of vocation, usually someone's name is called at least twice, for the call of God is rarely self-evident. In a world determined to listen to other voices, God must get our attention: "Saul, Saul . . . "

The story turns to a disciple named Ananias (9:10-17). He is called by God to go to Straight Street and there to greet one named Saul. "Did you say 'Saul'? Not the same murdering persecutor who has ravaged the church?"

The voice says to Ananias, "Go!"

So here we have two call stories in succession. The Lord explains to Ananias the rationale for going to this church enemy number one:

"Go, for he is an instrument whom I have chosen to bring my name before Gentiles and kings and before the people of Israel" (9:15). Saul has been called for a mission. Then God says, "I myself will show him how much he must suffer for the sake of my name" (9:16).

Those who think the call of God is for privilege or prestige, think again. Saul may think that he knows suffering. But no, he is called for suffering that was previously unknown to him, for it is suffering in service to the crucified Christ (9:16).

These two vocation stories from Acts 9 are thick with meaning for those of us who are called to ordained leadership. Let us simply say, here at the beginning, that ministry is at the Creator's initiative, God's evocation, and is strategic for the way God intends to win back what belongs to God. Some have suggested that Acts should more aptly be named "Acts of the Holy Spirit." Thus, when Charles Williams wrote his classic history of the church, he named it *Descent of the Dove*.[2]

This is all meant to remind us that ministry is not a profession. It is a vocation. One could not pay pastors for what is routinely expected of them. One must be called in order to do it.[3] Although pastors may struggle with exactly what it means to be called by God to lead a church, they must have some sense that they are in ministry because God wants them to be. Time and again, amid the challenges of the pastoral ministry, this divine, more-than-subjective authorization is a major means of pastoral perseverance. To know that our ministry is first and finally validated not by our feelings, or even by the judgments of the bishop, but by God; this is great grace. To assert that, in our ministry, we are representatives of something more significant than the denomination, that we are accountable to some criterion of judgment higher than our personal opinion; this is empowerment. To believe that we are in ministry as God's idea, rather than our own sense of occupational advancement; this is the submission, the yoking that is the source of true freedom (2 Cor. 3:17). Time and again, the main thing that keeps our ministry specifically *Christian* is to be able to assert with conviction, "We must obey God rather than any human authority" (Acts 5:29).

We fear loss of control. We have anxiety over what life is like to [*ruled by God*] be accountable to someone other than ourselves. It is somewhat frightening to construe our lives in such a theonomous cast, to have our lives lived in constant reference to the purposes of God. But it is also invigorating to receive the freedom and the dissonance of living the called life in a world where too many people are answerable to nothing more than their own ill-formed desires.

Sometimes the call comes early. Jeremiah felt it from his time in the womb ("Before I formed you in the womb . . . before you were born" [Jer. 1:5]). Sometimes it comes late as with Abram and Sarai (Gen. 17). Whenever the call comes, in saying yes to the summons we begin to march to the beat of a different drum, to the "drawing of this Love and the voice of this Calling."[4] We yield to the adventure of a life free of the ideology of personal autonomy that so enslaves this culture.[5] We are owned, commandeered for God,[6] yoked to a manner of service wherein is perfect freedom.

2. Ministry is an act of the church. The Acts of the Apostles begins rather dramatically with the ascension of the risen Christ into heaven (1:6-11). But then the very next episode is a rather humdrum description of the election of Matthias as a replacement apostle (1:15-26). Perhaps this ecclesial business meeting seems anticlimactic after so wonderful an event. Yet here is testimony that there is no church without leadership. From the first, leaders were needed in order for the church to be faithful to its divine vocation to be "my witnesses in Jerusalem, in all Judea and Samaria, and to the ends of the earth" (1:8).

Ministry arises from the top down, from the action of God through the Holy Spirit in calling us. Yet the story of the selection of Matthias also demonstrates that ministry arises from the bottom up, through the call of God working through the church.[7] As John Calvin noted, God calls, but the church also must call for there to be leadership in the name of Christ.

At times in the history of the ordained ministry there has been a tendency to disjoin the pastoral vocation from the community—as if the call to ministry were a personal possession of the pastor, as if the work of pastors is intelligible apart from the work of the church that necessitates pastoral work. This is a singular perversion of the pastoral vocation. The call to be clergy has more in common with the call of Paul in Acts 9, in which someone is summoned for a specific task within the church's mission ("Go, for he is an instrument whom I have chosen to bring my name before Gentiles and kings and before the people of Israel" [Acts 9:15]), than with the call to Cornelius to be a disciple (Acts 10). Damage is done to the unique quality of the pastoral vocation when it is conflated with the vocation of all Christians to follow Jesus. Thus we have those who come to seminary not because they are called there to train to be pastors, but rather because they have received a call to be a more thoroughly committed Christian. Sadly, the church often does such a poor job of fostering the ministry of all Christians that there is nowhere to take a sense of vocation except to seminary. This is a judgment upon a church that seems not to know what to do with those who desire more faithful commitment to their baptism.

All Christians, by virtue of their baptism, are called by God to witness, to teach, to heal, and to proclaim. All Christians are amateurs so far as their relationship to God is concerned.[8] Yet from the ranks of the baptized, some are called to lead. As Luther noted, because not every Christian can do all the church's tasks every time the church gathers, for the sake of good order the church has found it helpful to ordain some from among the baptized to witness, to teach, to heal, and to proclaim to the church on Sunday so that all the baptized may witness, teach, heal, and proclaim during the rest of the week. Those who are called by God and the church to lead us in this way are called *pastors, priests, ministers.* Therefore, you

[handwritten margin note: I wonder]

will note in this book a preference for referring to clergy as "pastors" or "priests," rather than simply "ministers," in order to differentiate between the ministry of all baptized Christians and pastoral leadership that exists "to equip the saints for the work of ministry, for building up the body of Christ" (Eph. 4:12).

The ordained ministry is a species of a broader genus called *Christian*. The pastoral ministry is always a function of what needs to happen in the church in order for the church to be faithful to its vocation. The *Discipline* of The United Methodist Church defines the pastoral vocation as a particular elaboration of the vocation of all Christians:

> Ministry in the Christian church is derived from the ministry of Christ, who calls all persons to receive God's gift of salvation and follow in the way of love and service. The whole church receives and accepts this call, and all Christians participate in this continuing ministry. Within the church community, there are persons whose gifts, evidence of God's grace, and promise of future usefulness are affirmed by the community, and who respond to God's call by offering themselves in leadership as ordained ministers.[9]

Sometimes there are candidates for ordination who resist the notion that the church has a responsibility to examine their call. Their attitude is, "If I really believe that God has called me into the ministry, what right have you to question my vocation?"

Although we may rejoice at the personal inner "call" of someone into the ministry, historically such personal inner calls from Christ have more in common with the call to the monastic life than to the ancient presbyterate. Pastors are called by the church for specific communal leadership, therefore the community has a responsibility to prayerfully examine those who come forward to be considered for ordination. Those churches in the congregational tradition always celebrate their rites of ordination within the congregational context—thereby stressing the communal congregational responsibility within the call to ordained leadership.

During an ecclesiastical ruckus in Milan, young Ambrose, a rapidly rising attorney in the city, entered the cathedral to observe the fray. During the confused debate, someone—it was thought to be a little child—shouted, "Ambrose, bishop!" This refrain was picked up by others who began to chant, "Ambrose, bishop!"

He protested. He was not even baptized. In quick succession, Ambrose was baptized then ordained a bishop, and went on to become one of the early church's most gifted leaders, the teacher of Augustine. God graciously works through the church, sometimes (as in the case of Ambrose) through the church's children, to call people to pastoral ministry.

Martin Luther King Jr., when asked as a new seminarian to write an account of his vocation into the ministry, admitted that he had felt no dramatic call to ordination. Rather, his father was a pastor and wanted him to be one too. He hoped to please his father by his entrance in seminary.

He was a good student, bookish and conscientious. King hoped to teach in college, perhaps one day to be president of Morehouse College. Biding his time, he was called to serve a rather forlorn little church in Montgomery, Alabama.[10] Shortly after he arrived, an African American woman was ordered off a city bus because she violated the city's laws for racial segregation. A meeting was held at one of the city's black churches. The crowd that night was confused, angry, disheartened. No one knew for sure what to do, though all agreed something ought to be done. Toward the end of the meeting, someone thought it might be good if the new young preacher in town would speak.

King rose, began hesitatingly, worked into a rhythm; the congregation joined in, the Spirit descended. Someone said later, "We gathered as a confused crowd; we left as a movement." [11]

Ordination is a gift of God, to be sure, but a gift of God through the church, for the church, that the church might be the church of God. One of our greatest challenges in seminary is to take people— many of whom may have been rather poorly formed by their home congregations, many of whom have had little experience in actual congregations—and form them into leaders of congregations, officials of the church, bearers of the church's faith rather than merely of their own.

Elsewhere I have spoken of clergy as "community persons."[12] The clergy are not a patrician upper crust set over the plebian laity. The essence of the priesthood is primarily relational (whom it serves) and functional (what it does) more than ontological (what it is). Clergy arose because of the church's need for leaders. The difference between a pastor who visits, preaches, and baptizes, and any other skilled layperson who performs these same functions is in the pastor's "officialness." The pastor functions at the authorization of the whole church. The pastor's acts are "read" by the whole church in a way that the individual Christian's are not.

We work within a culture of rugged individualists and fragmented communities. We are officially schooled in the notion that we are most fully ourselves when we are liberated, autonomous, on our own. We live under the modern myth that it is possible, even desirable, to live our lives without external, social determination. Ironically, that we think it desirable to live our lives without external, social determination is proof that our lives have been externally, socially determined by the culture of capitalist consumption. I did not on my own come up with the notion that I am a sovereign individual who has no greater purpose in life than to live exclusively for myself. Rather, this culture has formed me to believe that I have no other purpose in life other than the purpose I myself have chosen. The irony is that I did not choose the story that I have no purpose in life other than that which I have chosen.

The issue is not, Shall I be externally determined by some community of interpretation and authorization? The issue is, Which community will have its way with my life? Or perhaps more accurately, Will the community that determines, interprets, and authorizes me be worthy of my life?

3. To be a pastor is to be tied in a unique way to the church, the believing community in Christ. Part of the joy of being a Christian is to be tied to someone and something more important than you. For pastors, this communal attachment is especially significant. Despite my misgivings against characterizing the pastor as a "professional," in one sense ministry is a profession. The pastoral ministry is a profession in the original sense of that designation. Pastors, as the first "professionals," are people who *profess* something, who are tied to and who receive authorization from a body of belief. From the earliest writing on ministry, there was a stress upon the representative function of the pastoral ministry. It may be enough for individual Christians to live out their personal relationships with Jesus Christ, not too troubled by the state of the church. Something different is expected of the pastor. The pastor is expected to profess the faith of the church, to represent the church's account of what is going on in the world, to bear the burden of the church's tradition before the congregation, to help contemporary disciples think critically about their faith, to test the church's current witness by the canon of the saints.

One of the great tragedies of the practice of contemporary professions like law and medicine is that too many doctors and lawyers have so little to profess. They are primarily accountable to their clients or patients, rather than to jurisprudence or public health. The pastor professes God, and is accountable to more significant criteria than the praise even of the congregation.

Although vocation is a primary matter for clergy, expertise is also required. Clergy must know the historic, orthodox, ecumenical faith of the church in order to bear witness to, and to interpret, that faith. Pastoral counseling, church administration, and biblical interpretation require competence. Thus adequate theological training is an aspect of the clergy's peculiar vocation, an aspect of the service that we render to the church. Careful preparation for pastoral leadership is a moral matter of the need for clergy to submit themselves to the leadership needs of the church. A warm heart and good intentions are not enough to fulfill the requisites of this vocation.[13] Thus, James Gustafson says:

> A "calling" without professionalization is bumbling, ineffective, and even dangerous. A profession without a calling, however, has no taps of moral and human rootage to keep motivation alive, to keep human sensitivities and sensibilities alert, and to nourish a proper sense of self-fulfillment. Nor does a profession without a calling easily envision the larger ends and purposes of human good that our individual efforts can serve.[14]

Recently, a friend who is a high school teacher said to me, "I believe that the profession of teaching has lost respect, and has difficulty finding its way because we have lost anything really important to teach. Once teaching was about human transformation. Now we teach an assortment of facts, deliver data, but why give a life to that?"

One of the sources of clerical self-respect and empowerment is the content of what we profess—Jesus Christ and him crucified. Preachers deserve a hearing when we have something significant to say. Thus we pastors are expected to master those concepts, insights, and grand narratives that are the means of rendering the way, the truth, and the life that is Jesus Christ.

The clergy's representative burden can also be a great blessing, a source of pastoral wisdom and power. A parishioner emerged from a little church on a Sunday, muttering to her pastor, "You are not even thirty, what could you know?"

Her pastor drew himself up to his full height, clutched the stole around his neck, and said, "Madame, when I wear this and I climb into that pulpit, I am over two thousand years old, and speak from two millennia of experience."

The man may have been somewhat of an ass, but still his point was well taken, ecclesiastically speaking. It is not my task primarily to "share myself" with my people, certainly not to heed the facile advice of those who say, "Just be yourself." As Mark Twain said, about the worst advice one can give anybody is, "Just be yourself."

Fortunately, as I enter into the struggles of my people, I have considerably more to offer than myself. I have the witness of the saints, the faith of the church, the wisdom of the ages. A pastor must therefore be prejudiced toward the faith of the church. One does not have to be a traditionalist to be a pastor, but it helps, particularly in a culture of "neophiles" (as Margaret Mead once called us), incurable lovers of the new who believe that old is bad and new is good. The frequent reference in this book to dead people is my way of witnessing that the church lives by the lives of the saints.

I am not free to rummage about in other texts before I have submitted to the biblical text. I am not at liberty to acknowledge as source of ultimate truth those contemporary, culturally sanctioned sources such as psychology, sociology, economics, and so forth before I have done service to the historic faith of the church. It is fair to have a lover's quarrel with the tradition of the church, to wrestle with and to question which tradition is sanctioned by God and which is spurious irrelevancy. Yet it is not fair to place oneself or one's culture above the story of Jesus of Nazareth as represented in the creeds, councils, and faith of the church.[15]

Ironically, it is powerful freedom to know who claims your ultimate allegiance, to whom you are finally accountable, who has the last say in the validation of your ministry. One of the great challenges of contemporary pastoral ministry is having something more important to do in our ministry than simply offering love and service to our people.[16] Too many pastors never rise above simple congregational maintenance, never have any higher goal in their ministry than mushy, ill-defined "love" or "service." To find ourselves yoked, bound to our profession of faith, namely, that Christ really is present in Word and Sacrament, overturning the world through us; this is great grace.

4. Ministry is difficult. Gregory Nazianzen was a reluctant enlistee to the ordained ministry. The task of being a pastor, he wrote, was "too high" for him. He was ill suited to bear "the commission to guide and govern souls . . . especially in times like these." Shortly after his ordination on Christmas, Gregory completely lost heart, deserted his congregation, and headed for the hills. His people begged him to return to his parish. By the time he relented and returned to his church at Easter, his people were so angry that they refused to come hear him preach.

Just after Easter, in 362, Gregory wrote a letter in which he explained to his people why he had run away. He pled that he was unqualified for so high a task as the priesthood. Pastors, he said, are like sailors "who cross the wide oceans and constantly contend with winds and waves," whereas he much preferred to "stay ashore and plow a short but pleasant furrow, saluting at a respectful distance the sea and its gains." In the end, Gregory came back, he said, because his people needed him and because he was more afraid of disobeying God than he was of being a pastor.[17]

In so many ways, ministry is difficult because it is about the construction, the evocation, the invocation of another world. In the most unassuming manner, Christian ministry provokes a collision with so many of the values held dear in this society. That which we are taught to name as the kingdom of God is at odds with our kingdoms. Although I in no way mean this as justification of low clergy salaries, that many ministers are highly trained and often poorly paid is itself an affront to a culture that believes that a person's worth is measured in money.

Seminarians are forever complaining about the gap between their expectations for the church, as engendered in seminary, and the reality of the church they experience as new pastors. That gap between the sociological reality of the church and the theological vocation of the church is necessary and even admirable. It is part of the pastor's vocation to keep working that space, to keep noting that gap between who the church is and who the church ought, by God's grace, to be—and will, by God, be someday.

Note the way that Acts underscores this gap between the theological vocation and the sociological reality of the church. Acts follows the depiction of the Ascension of Christ with the reminder of the betrayal of Judas (Acts 1). If one is looking for the crucifiers of Jesus, look first among those who gathered with Jesus at the table. The glory of Pentecost and the descent of the Spirit upon the church (Acts 2), as well as the astounding homiletical success of Peter (Acts 3), are followed by the arrest of Peter and Paul. Then there is the nasty business of Ananias and Sapphira (Acts 5), and the martyrdom of Stephen (Acts 6–7). The church has enemies, within and without. Jesus is the triumph of the kingdom of God, but not yet. What they did to Jesus, they continue to do to Jesus' people.

Some have accused Luke of triumphalism. The author of Acts does enjoy reports of the success of the apostles, as "the Lord added to their number those who were being saved" (Acts 2:47). Yet for nearly every astounding evangelistic success, Luke follows with an account of miserable evangelistic failure. Ministry in the name of Jesus is tensive, in constant conflict with the powers that be, at times triumphant, but often beset by defeat.

The pastoral ministry requires a wide range of sophisticated skills—public speaking, intellectual ability, relational gifts, self-knowledge, theological understanding, verbal dexterity, management acumen, sweeping floors, moving folding metal chairs, serving as moral exemplar, and all the rest. No wonder failure is always crouching at the door.

Again, Acts warns of this by recounting the story of Judas, betrayer of Jesus, before the end of the first twenty verses of the first chapter of Acts (Acts 1:15-20). Jesus' most notable betrayal came from the ranks of the inner circle of his disciples.

Yet some of our ministerial "failures" are due, not just to our lack of intelligence and skill, but to Jesus himself. Jesus' ministry ended upon a cross, and he warned us well that ours will, even ought, end there too (Mark 8:34-38). Luke makes Jesus' first act of ministry a visit to his hometown synagogue where, after his sermon, his own

must not bypass Calvary

friends and family try to murder him (Luke 4:16-30). In our ministry, we are no better than Jesus. That is, there is no magic formula that will keep us safe from the cross. In fact, Scripture teaches us to be particularly suspicious when our ministry appears to be successful in somehow bypassing Calvary.

In calling us into gospel service, God promises us that nothing worse shall happen to us than happened to Jesus. Therefore, we do well to reflect upon the practice of ministry, to work diligently to acquire the skills necessary to be faithful to this high vocation. The virtues required to be a good pastor—wisdom, truth telling, courage, compassion, study—do not come naturally to most of us. So our first duty is to work. Our second duty is to pray daily that God will give us what we need to fulfill the vocation to which God has called us. Work and pray. *Labor et Orans.* We work under the prayerful conviction that God is able to provide what God demands.

Sometimes seminarians complain that the seminary's expectations of them are too demanding, that the course is too difficult, or that it is placing academic burdens upon them that they cannot bear. Perhaps they feel that their sincerity and their sense of vocation are enough to sustain them in their ministry. They are wrong.

I remind them that I did not call them into the ministry. I am sorry if they have been misled, but the pastoral ministry is a very difficult way to earn a living, and our Master can be very demanding, despite his reassurance of a light burden and an easy yoke. Then I tell them something that happened to me.

One day the dean casually commented to me that a member of my Annual Conference once wrote him a particularly moving letter. Did I know him? Before I could answer, the dean continued, "He wrote to tell me that he had been called into the ministry some years ago. He commuted to a seminary not far from his home, doing just enough work to get by. He said that he got along well with people and knew how to please a congregation. For four years at his first church, he delivered this 'package,' and it worked. Then he delivered the same package of pleasing sermons and caring concern at his next congregation and, for four years, it worked there too. He is now at his third congregation and he said that his 'well has run dry.' He needs renewal, but he doesn't know where to find it. He doesn't know enough theology to be able to read his way back into ministry. He wrote me this letter, asking if he could come here for a sabbatical and spend time working back through all the theology that he had missed. We tried to help him, but with his family and all, he just couldn t swing it. Do you know what ever happened to him?"

I told the dean, "He had been on a year's leave of absence to receive treatment for his alcoholism. Last week, he was found dead in his kitchen, drowned to death in his own vomit after a bout of drunkenness."

And the dean and I stood there for the longest time in silence. Then he said, "We really have our work cut out for us here, in preparing people for ministry. The stakes are at times unbearably high. Let's get back to work."

William H. Willimon
Duke University Chapel
Pentecost 2001

CHAPTER ONE

Ordination: Why Pastors?

New Creation by Water and the Word

In the living room of my grandmother's rambling house, after a large Sunday dinner, the family and its friends gathered. Lifting a silver bowl filled with water, the preacher said some words, made some promises, and then baptized me—made me Christian. There is much about this originating faith event that I would have done differently. (Baptism properly belongs in a church, not in a living room.) Yet God manages to work wonders despite the ineptitude of the church. And part of the point of becoming a Christian is that it is something done to us, for us, before it is anything done by us. What we might have done differently, had it been our action alone, is not as important as what Christ and his church does for us in baptism. As an infant, I was the passive recipient of this work in my behalf. Someone had to hold me, had to administer the water of baptism, had to tell me the story of Jesus and what he had done, had to speak the promises of what he would do, had to live the faith before me so that I might assume the faith for myself. In other words, by water and the Word, it was all gift, grace.

Thus I began as a Christian by water and the Word. Thus the whole world began (Gen. 1). Brooding over the primordial waters, God speaks, and a new world springs forth. My world as a Christian began in baptism, that strange, deep, formative, and indicative rite of the Christ and his church. It is up to God, in each generation, to make the church, to call by water and the Word a new people into being, or there is no church.

Jesus' baptism in the Jordan by John was the beginning of his ministry. When Jesus was baptized, the heavens opened and there was a voice, "You are my Son, the Beloved; with you I am well pleased" (Luke 3:22b). It is a scene reminiscent of the Spirit of God brooding over the primal waters of Creation, creating a new world, then pronouncing it all "very good" (Gen. 1). Luke follows this

dramatic baptismal descent of the Spirit with an unexciting genealogy of Jesus (Luke 3:23-38), taking Jesus' paternity all the way back
to Adam. I suppose this is Luke's way of reiterating the gifted quality of the Beloved. True, he is a gift from heaven, the descent of the
Holy Spirit, yet he is also the bequest of the ages, of a gaggle of
ordinary folk like Peleg, Eber, Shelah, Noah, and Adam. He is here
as gift of God from above, and also of Israel from below. God calls,
but we must respond.

In my baptism, I was the product of a human family, a people
who had clung to the promised land of upcountry South Carolina
for five generations, scratching out a living in cotton and cows until
my nativity into a new generation who would rather live off of
schools, churches, and hospitals than work the land. It was a human
family, with all the goodness and badness of most any family.

Yet I was, as signified that day in my baptism, also a gift of God.
Heaven was mixed up in who I was, and was to be. In my beginning was also some divine condescension enmeshed in my humanity; some incarnation. From that day on, in ways that I am still
discovering, you could not explain me without reference to my
baptism, to the water, the promises, the story, the hands laid upon
my head. Criticize what you will about the mode of my baptism—
whether or not it should have occurred so early, or if there should
have been instruction, or a different location, or more informed
intention—you at least must admit that it worked. Here I am
telling the story of the story that was told to me, the story that I did
not devise on my own, the story that I am still learning to tell—a
story named *discipleship.*

As soon as Luke is done with Jesus' genealogy, the story of Jesus'
ministry begins. "Jesus, full of the Holy Spirit, returned from the
Jordan and was led by the Spirit to the wilderness" (Luke 4:1). Now
his work commences. Ministry is a gift of baptism. This gift of
water and the Word, this act of a descending Holy Spirit, is also an
assignment. First the baptismal gifts. Then the baptismal vocation.
"Then Jesus, filled with the power of the Spirit, returned to Galilee,
and . . . He began to teach in their synagogues" (Luke 4:14-15).

Yet if you know the story, you know that between his baptism
and his ministry in Galilee there is his temptation (Luke 4:1-13). In
the wilderness, during his forty days there, the devil offers Jesus
some tempting, even noble, alternatives—stones to bread, political

power, miracles—all good in themselves. Jesus rejects them all. Somehow these good works do not fit the ministry to which Jesus has been called. Right at the start of Jesus' work, Luke reminds us that ministry is, from the beginning, a choice between God's work and our own. Vocation and temptation seem to go together. If we lack clarity about our proper work, the devil is quite willing to tell us what to do.

Therefore this book's exploration of ordained leadership assumes the originating baptismal call, then moves to the peculiar nature of the clerical vocation, expending much effort to gain clarity about that vocation and its duties. Ministry is always both gift and assignment. All this reflection upon the ordained life is carried out against the background assumption, instilled in us by Luke 4:1-12, that among pastors it is always possible to get things wrong, that temptations abound, and the devil is ever eager to substitute his work for God's.

Ordination: A Theological and Historical Commentary

We search the New Testament in vain for much stress on continuity of *structures* of Christian leadership. Continuity of faithful witness (2 Tim. 2:2) is the main concern rather than continuity or uniformity of ecclesiastical structure. The New Testament sources are notoriously inconclusive on precisely which structures of leadership were in place in the New Testament churches. Some churches seem to have been led by "bishops" (*episkopoi*, "overseers"), also called "pastors." In other churches, there seems to have been a council of "elders" (*presbuteroi*), with different elders assuming different duties in the congregation. This form of congregational governance surely came out of the synagogue and its structures of authority.[1]

Eventually, these two patterns seem to have merged into one in which bishops presided over a number of congregations, with elders becoming priests who presided over individual churches. What emerges in the time right after the apostolic era, even as early as the Catholic epistles, is a threefold picture of ministry—bishop, elder (nowhere is "priest," *hieros*, used by the New Testament to designate a Christian leader), and deacon (*diakonoi*). Deacons were congregational social workers who assisted in the care of the needs both within and outside the congregation.[2] But the picture, in the first centuries, was not nearly so neat. In many places within his Epistles, Paul addresses the problems caused by free-floating evangelists, prophets, healers, and spiritual gurus who wander through the churches. What is significant, in comparison with today's church, is that the church then seemed to recognize the possibility of a wide array of leadership gifts.

All present forms of ministry, among both Protestants and Catholics, appear to be considerably more rigid, formalized, and uniform than ministry in the New Testament. In the earliest time of the church, the community showed admirable ability to adapt and to create new forms of leadership to serve new challenges of the church (Acts 6:1-7). Furthermore, there seems to have been more spontaneous recognition, on the part of the community, of the *charismata*, the spiritual gifts, of those who were called to leadership. In our contemporary ecclesiastical structures, are we in danger of stifling some spiritual gifts? It is certainly true that in the last century the more charismatic and pentecostal churches were among the first to recognize women as pastors. Paul, whose churches had their share of problems with disordered leadership, still affirms a diversity of gifts for the guidance and upbuilding of the congregation. "Now there are varieties of gifts, but the same Spirit; and there are varieties of services, but the same Lord" (1 Cor. 12:4-5). So in the early church, with leaders such as "exorcist" and "reader," ministry was much messier than today.

Who are pastors? What are they for? Those questions are answered when the church makes its leaders—the Service of Ordination. In these rites, the church says and shows what it believes about its clergy. For twenty centuries the church has called some from among the baptized to serve as leaders, to fulfill the role of pastor. Theological reflection upon these rites reveals much to contemporary pastors about who they are and what the church means when it designates them as leaders.

We will use, as a basis for thinking about who clergy are and what they are to do, the Liturgy for the Ordination of Bishops that is found in the *Apostolic Tradition* of Hippolytus, from the church of early third-century Rome. Hippolytus gives our first full account of the ordination of a bishop, a presbyter (elder), and a deacon—an account that has been popular as a model for the ordination prayers of subsequent revisions of many ordination rites.[3]

The Ordination of a Bishop in the *Apostolic Tradition* of Hippolytus

Let the bishop be ordained being in all things without fault chosen by all the people.

And when he has been proposed and found acceptable to all, the people shall assemble on the Lord's day together with the presbytery and such bishops as may attend.

With the agreement of all let the bishops lay hands on him and the presbytery stand by in silence.

And all shall keep silence praying in their heart for the descent of the Spirit.

After this one of the bishops present at the request of all, laying his hand on him who is ordained bishop, shall pray thus, saying:

O God and Father of our Lord Jesus Christ, Father of mercies and God of all comfort, "Who dwellest on high yet hast respect unto the lowly," "who knowest all things before they come to pass";

Who didst give ordinances unto Thy church "by the Word of Thy grace"; Who "didst foreordain from the beginning" the race of the righteous from Abraham, instituting princes and priests and leaving not Thy sanctuary without ministers; Who from the foundation of the world hast been pleased to be glorified in them whom Thou hast chosen;

And now pour forth that Power which is from Thee of "the princely Spirit" which Thou didst deliver to Thy Beloved Child Jesus Christ, which He bestowed on Thy holy Apostles who established the Church which hallows Thee in every place to the endless glory and praise of Thy Name.

Father "who knowest the hearts" grant upon this Thy servant whom Thou hast chosen for the episcopate to feed Thy holy flock and serve as Thine high priest, that he may minister blamelessly by night and day, that he may unceasingly propitiate Thy countenance and offer to Thee the gifts of Thy holy church.

*And that by the high priestly Spirit he may have authority "to
forgive sins" according to Thy command, "to assign lots"
according to Thy bidding, to "loose every bond" according to the
authority Thou gavest to the Apostles, and that he may please
Thee in meekness and a pure heart, "offering" to Thee "a sweet-
smelling savour,"*
   *through Thy Child Jesus Christ our Lord, through Whom to
Thee be glory, might and praise, to the Father and to the Son
with the Holy Spirit now and world without end. Amen.*[4]

The central liturgical gesture for ordination is the laying on of
hands *(epitithenai tas cheiras)*, a symbolic act that was probably
derived from rabbinic custom (1 Tim. 4:14; 2 Tim. 1:6). This act both
symbolizes the gift of the Holy Spirit and the bestowal of authority by those who have preceded the candidate in ministry. Ministry
is interior—the call that a person feels within. And ministry, in the
laying on of hands, is shown to be exterior—an act of the church
upon the life of the ordinand.

In Hippolytus's account of the ordination of a bishop, we detect
a pattern that was to inform all later rites of ordination in the
Western Church: (1) The entire community and its presbyters
choose the bishop. (2) The candidate must respond in free will.
(3) The local congregation tests the faith of the person to be sure
that his faith is apostolic. (4) Episcopal laying on of hands with a
prayer for the Holy Spirit *(epiclesis)* shows that, though the community chooses, this is not solely a congregational choice. (5) The
new ministry is interpreted as a gift of the Holy Spirit, because of
the choice of the community. Little is said in this earliest of ordination rites about alleged special characteristics of the clergy, which
were ascribed in later rites. Rather, the church needs leadership,
and through God and the church leadership is given as a gracious
bestowal of the Holy Spirit.

Using this prayer and its setting as a basis of thinking about ordination, we make the following observations that are relevant to a
theology of ordination:

1. Ordination is an act of Christ and his church.

*O God and Father of our Lord Jesus Christ, Father of mercies
and God of all comfort, "who dwellest on high yet hast respect*

unto the lowly," "who knowest all things before they come to pass";

Who didst give ordinances unto Thy church "by the Word of Thy grace"; Who "didst foreordain from the beginning" the race of the righteous from Abraham, instituting princes and priests and leaving not Thy sanctuary without ministers; Who from the foundation of the world hast been pleased to be glorified in them whom Thou hast chosen.

God is called "Father," which signifies a relationship to the Son, and has an office, which is Creator, the one who makes worlds, who sits on high, yet reaches down toward the lowly; who created not only the world but also a "race of the righteous" out of nothing; who knows, gives, institutes, and chooses. Thus ordination, in this prayer, is linked to God's creating and ordering of the world. Ordination is *a creative act of God*, not unlike the creation of the world or the call of Israel, that brings order out of the chaos, a world out of the void.

The prayer is prayed in *the presence of the gathered community.* At the service, the church gathers to thank God for the gift of new leadership and to designate one of its own for ministry to Christ and his church. God gives us the gospel, then the church, and then the church's leaders. The logical sequence is significant because pastors serve the church so that the church might better serve the gospel's Lord. That which makes church *church* is the presence of the living Christ. The church is thus the fulfillment of Christ's promise, "For where two or three are gathered in my name, there am I in the midst of them" (Matt. 18:20 RSV). Jesus is "Emmanuel," meaning "God with us" (Matt. 1:23 RSV). The peculiar way God has deemed to be with us is called the church. "God is really among you" (1 Cor. 14–15), Paul exclaimed before one of his congregations. The leaders of the church are subsequent and subservient to the church—the laity—and derive their significance from what Christ has promised, and what Christ intends to do in the world through the *laos*, the people of God.[5] It is not the congregation's clergy, but the congregation, gathered around the table of the Lord, who is the chief manifestation of the presence of Christ in the world. Church is prior to its leadership.

> Let the bishop be ordained being in all things without fault chosen by all the people.

And when he has been proposed and found acceptable to all, the people shall assemble on the Lord's day together with the presbytery and such bishops as may attend.

By the second century, *a bishop presides at ordinations.* Ignatius of Antioch, writing in the early second century, asserts the role of the bishop in the designation of new elders for the church. Ignatius interprets the bishop's leadership as ensuring the unity and harmony of the church—someone who, in his physical presence, represents the unity and continuity of the congregation with the church as a whole.[6] A bishop is an elder, or presbyter, who is designated by the elders to convene and to lead the elders, and to symbolize and to work for the unity and harmony, the apostolicity and the catholicity, of the church.

> *Who didst give ordinances unto Thy church "by the Word of Thy grace"; Who "didst foreordain from the beginning" the race of the righteous from Abraham, instituting princes and priests and leaving not Thy sanctuary without ministers.*

The church claims *leadership as a gift of God to the church,* as due to the leading of God. Jesus did not accomplish his work in the world on his own, but appointed the Twelve to aid him in forming his followers and doing the work of the kingdom of God. There is no evidence anywhere in the New Testament that there are communities without leadership. It is theologically impossible for there to be a shortage of priests or a paucity of vocations in the church because of the conviction, so apparent in places like Acts, that God graciously, and sometimes quite surprisingly, provides the leadership needed by the church. Where there is a shortage of leadership, that shortage is probably due more to the unfaithfulness of the church, or to the shortsightedness of those in authority, than to the parsimony of the Holy Spirit.

what do you think of this?

> *Which Thou didst deliver to Thy Beloved Child Jesus Christ, which He bestowed on Thy holy Apostles who established the Church which hallows Thee in every place to the endless glory and praise of Thy Name.*

It was Jesus' nature to give away authority, first to his "holy Apostles," then to all whom he called to himself (Acts 2:39).

Leadership in this community is not due to the natural attributes of those who lead, nor primarily due to the adulation of those who follow, but rather *due to the gift of Christ who condescends to be present* in the lives and deeds of those on whom he bestows this task.

2. Ordination is for service to Christ and the church.

Grant upon this Thy servant whom Thou hast chosen for the episcopate to feed Thy holy flock and serve as Thine high priest, that he may minister blamelessly by night and day.

Those whom we designate as "ministers" are, in the New Testament, *diakonoi*, Paul's favorite title for Christian leaders, derived from the Greek word for "service" (1 Cor. 12:4-30). Significantly, it is the same word that is the root for "butler" and "waiter," terms that have a greater edge to them than "ministry." How odd of the church to designate its leaders by so mundane and lowly a term. No pastor rises much higher than being a butler. Yet, in the topsy-turvy ethics of the Kingdom, this is as high as anyone rises—*a servant of the servants* at the Lord's Table (cf. John 13).

That the table being waited upon is the Lord's, and those gathered are none other than the Body of Christ, makes all the difference for the *diakonoi*. For Paul, the whole church is the Body of Christ (1 Cor. 12) and *all the baptized are engaged in "ministry," though there are apostles, teachers, prophets, and others who have special gifts recognized by the community that are helpful for the upbuilding of the community.*

Jesus, the one who modeled leadership with a basin and towel, admonished his followers that they ought not behave like power-grubbing Gentiles. "But it is not so among you; but whoever wishes to become great among you must be your servant *(diakonos)*, and whoever wishes to be first among you must be slave *(doulos)* of all" (Mark 10:43-44). Servant. Slave. What peculiar definitions of leadership. Compare the ordination of a pastor with the inauguration of the president. As the great P. T. Forsyth put it many years ago, "The ideal minister is three things at least. He is a prophet, and he is a pastor, but he is just as much priest. What he is not is a king."[7]

In 1 Corinthians 4:1, Paul speaks of himself, and those who lead with him, using the words *huperetes* ("servant") and *oikonomos* ("steward"). *Huperetes* is the word by which Greeks designated a slave who is chained in the galley of a ship, a striking image of the tetheredness of Christian ministry. *Huperetes* could also mean someone who serves under an authority and is charged with speaking on behalf of the authority. A physician's assistant was also called a *huperetes*. The historian Josephus calls Moses God's *huperetes* in leading Israel to the Promised Land, and interpreting to Israel the commandments of God. As God's *huperetai*, Paul says that he and Apollos faithfully conveyed the gospel of Christ.

Later, when Ephesians speaks of the church's leaders as "apostles," "prophets," "evangelists," and "pastors and teachers," it says that all of these share the servile function "to equip the saints for the work of ministry *(diakonia)*" (Eph. 4:11-12). These ministers have as their purpose "to equip the saints," that is, the whole church, so that the church can be about "the work of ministry." The significance of pastors is derived from what needs to happen among the ministers; that is *church*. These equippers of the saints are called "pastors." Even First Timothy's rather high view of bishops is based on their function to "take care of God's church" (1 Tim. 3:5).

The peculiar quality of church leadership was sorely tested in events that occurred during the fourth century.[8] Imperial persecution suddenly ceased. Christian clergy, once the leaders of small communities that made up a subversive, sometimes persecuted, and often just ignored sect on the fringes of the empire, were about to become representatives of the state. The earlier tensive relationship between church and culture was relaxed. There were some, it was said, who sought ecclesiastical office (leadership was becoming an office, in addition to being a vocation) for economic or political advancement. Clergy adopted the dress of Roman patrician men. The stole, a sort of Roman necktie worn by well-bred Roman men on the street, symbol of culture and authority, became common among clergy in the west. Processions, so dear to imperial culture, in which social rank and political position were demarcated, became a distinguishing characteristic of Christian worship. These and similar events of the fourth century were to be repeated in the history of the ordained ministry as pastors struggled to be faithful to the peculiar designation of Christian leaders (in Gregory the Great's term) as *servus servorum Dei*, servant of the servants of God.

3. Ordination arises "from above," as a gracious gift of the Holy Spirit.

And all shall keep silence praying in their heart for the descent of the Spirit.

And now pour forth that Power which is from Thee of "the princely Spirit" which Thou didst deliver to Thy Beloved Child Jesus Christ, which He bestowed on Thy holy Apostles who established the Church which hallows Thee in every place to the endless glory and praise of Thy Name.

Hippolytus shows that episcopal laying on of hands with *epiclesis*, or prayer of the community for the outpouring of the Holy Spirit, was the chief symbolic gesture related to ordination. Paul writes to Timothy: "I remind you to rekindle the gift of God that is within you through the laying on of my hands" (2 Tim. 1:6).[9] Through this pattern of ordination, *the choice of this new leader was experienced both as a gift of an effusive Spirit and as the designation of the Spirit-filled community.* The ancient hymn *Veni Sancte Spiritus,* "Come, Holy Spirit," was an important part of ordination rites, including Luther's reformed rite,[10] though sadly it is optional in the service of the United Methodists.[11]

The leadership of the church is functional. Pastors do those things that need to be done to enable the church to be the church.

And that by the high priestly Spirit he may have authority "to forgive sins" according to Thy command, "to assign lots" according to Thy bidding, "to loose every bond" according to the authority Thou gavest to the Apostles, and that he may please Thee in meekness and a pure heart, "offering" to Thee "a sweet-smelling savour."

Ministry is also charismatic, something that God gives and demands. Leadership in the church is an institution, but it begins as an event. If God should withdraw this gift, then ministry would collapse and all efforts to make ministry make sense, apart from the gifts of the Holy Spirit, would be futile. If this book becomes my attempt to list all of the important, skilled deeds that pastors do, without constant dependency upon the Holy Spirit, then this is not a text about ordained leadership, but rather one more blasphemous attempt to have leaders in the church without the Spirit's gifts.[12]

Here we suspect tension in maintaining the stress between ministry being "from above," as a gift of God, as special charisma, and ministry being "from below," arising out of the needs and expectations of the community.[13] An exclusive stress upon ministry as a gift of God can lead to vocation being private, personal, and detached; an event that too easily evaporates over the long term. On the other hand, too great a stress upon ministry as a mere function of the needs of the community, arising "from below," makes ministry vulnerable to being institutionalized, formalized, fossilized, and merely subservient to organizational maintenance.

I have felt this tension within my own teaching at the seminary. We have a responsibility to form seminarians into institutional leaders—those who function at the authorization of, and in service to, the church. Yet in this process, are we in danger of grinding them down too smooth, forcing them to fit into the preconceptions of the current church? My own church, caught in decades of decline, seems now to need most the sort of persons who abrasively criticize, judge, and then help lead the present church toward greater fidelity and vitality. The gesture of laying on of hands, still the heart of the rite of ordination, continues to be a powerful sign in which the church acknowledges the charismatic gifts of ministry as well as the communal authorization of ministry. To be a pastor is to hold these often conflicting tendencies in some tension.

4. Ordination arises from below, from the church's need for, and wisdom in designating, leadership.

David Bartlett, after examining the New Testament material on ministry and comparing it with contemporary discussions, says that he suspects that in the church today two quite different views of the pastor vie with one another. In one view, the pastor is sent from God to fill the pulpit, or appointed by Christ to take Christ's place as host at the table. In the other view, the pastor is called out from among the people to help interpret scripture by preaching, and to help serve at a table where Christ alone is host.[14]

The implication of Bartlett's generalization is that the first view leads to a "high" theology of ordination in which the minister is "appointed by Christ to take Christ's place as host at the table." The other view leads to a "low" theology of ministry where someone is merely "called out from among the people to help."

We need not choose between the two. Both views have scriptural basis and historical precedent. The first stresses the gifted, grace-filled quality of ministry as a special gift of God to the church. The second asserts the functional, community-derived quality of Christian ministry. Both emphases are found in the prayer of Hippolytus.

Thus, in their *Book of Discipline*, the United Methodists say that their clergy are ordained for a twofold task: "sacramental and functional leadership."[15]

> Let the bishop be ordained being in all things without fault chosen by all the people.
> And when he has been proposed and found acceptable to all, the people shall assemble.

Though ordination is an act of God, *the church chooses and proposes the candidate.* In the introduction to their ordinal, the United Methodists say:

> Ordination is a public act of the Church which indicates acceptance by an individual of God's call to the upbuilding of the Church through the ministry of Word, Sacrament, and Order and acknowledgment and authentication of this call by the Christian community through prayers and the laying on of hands.

All ordination rites are at some pains to demonstrate this twofold call of the clergy. God calls and the church recognizes, examines, and validates that divine vocation.[16] The twofold quality of the clerical vocation has proved to be difficult for the church to hold in proper relationship. Not everyone whom God calls may be recognized by the church as a leader. Not everyone whom the church calls to leadership may have the God-given *charismata* for leadership. The call of God, the call of the church, gifts for ministry, and (for some churches) educational preparation for ministry are the qualifications for ordination throughout the church.

Richard Niebuhr provided a good differentiation of the various aspects of the pastoral vocation:

> (1) *The call to be a Christian*, which is variously described as the call to discipleship of Jesus Christ, to hearing and doing the Word of God, to repentance and faith, et cetera; (2) *the secret call*, namely, that inner persuasion or experience whereby a person feels himself directly summoned or invited by God to take up the work of the ministry; (3) *the providential call*, which is that invitation and command to assume the work of the ministry which comes through the equipment of a person with the talents necessary for the exercise of the office and through the divine guidance of his life by all its circumstances; (4) *the ecclesiastical call*, that is, the summons and invitation extended to a man [or woman] by some community or institution of the Church to engage in the work of the ministry.[17]

The Christian ministry is multivocal. God calls and the church calls. The inner, personal call must be tested and confirmed by the outer call of the church.

Among the Baptist and Congregationalist churches, there is the conviction that a person is called by God into the ministry and demonstrates gifts and graces that justify setting this person apart as a pastoral leader of that congregation. Among these churches, ordination tends to be recognition by the laity of a call, rather than their approbation. Nevertheless, churches within this tradition have some form of systematic examination and approval of candidates for the ministry beyond the individual congregation to link the congregational call of a pastor to the whole church.[18]

Keeping ordination tied to the call of the congregation has been difficult for the church down through the ages. Although leadership of the church was characterized by fluidity and much local variation throughout the first three centuries, by the time of the Council of Chalcedon (451) it is obvious that the church is trying to bring some degree of official standardization to the church's leadership. Chalcedon found it necessary to assert that ordination is linked to the ministry of a congregation rather than simply a personal attribute that is held apart from service to a congregation.

Canon VI of Chalcedon, which deals with leadership, notes that no one can be ordained priest or deacon (note the first official, standardized, conciliar use of the term "priest") unless some church is clearly assigned to him. Only someone who has been called by a particular community can be ordained as a leader of the church. The church appears to be trying to end the possibility of free-floating ministry, in which ordination is a possession of an individual rather than tied to the leadership of a congregation.

At Chalcedon we see further evidence of the clericalization of the ministry, because ministry is referred to as an order. The Romans spoke of the *ordos cenitorium*, the upper class that was permitted to rule, as opposed to the order of the plebes, or the people in general. It is significant that this sort of imperial interpretation is now laid over the ministry. People are being ordained to membership in an order, a class. The tendency to think about clergy in this fashion goes back as far as Ignatius, but now that tendency has been solidified in the practice of the church.[19]

Chalcedon took pains to define ministry as essentially corporate, public, attached to a congregation rather than detached from communal accountability, private. At the same time ministry was already moving from a matter of local congregational prerogative to a larger church matter, something that bishops authorized rather than something that arose from the leadership needs of the church. A little later, Pope Leo I said, "Candidates for ministry ought to be chosen by the clergy, but wanted by the people." This was clearly a move away from the primacy of the community toward ordination being a matter of selection by a college of clergy.[20]

5. Ordination forms those who are to serve as priests to the priests.

In places like Hebrews, Jesus is designated as the "Great High Priest." Yet in places like First Peter, the church—all the baptized—are depicted as "a holy people," "a nation of priests." *All the baptized share in Christ's priesthood to the world.* There are not laity presided over by priests, but rather all are priests by virtue of baptism.

Yet we see, even as far back as Hippolytus and his *Apostolic Tradition,* what was to become a troublesome tendency.

> *Father who "knowest the hearts" grant upon this Thy servant whom Thou hast chosen for the episcopate to feed Thy holy flock and serve as Thine high priest, that he may minister.*

Hippolytus speaks of the ministry as related to "that Power which is from Thee of 'the princely Spirit.' " In other words, Hippolytus's *Apostolic Tradition*, our oldest surviving liturgy of ordination, linked Christian ministry to the Old Testament priesthood. This typology, found in Athanasius, Tertullian, and the writings of other early Fathers, became a major way of thinking about clergy in the medieval period.[21] It contributed to a sacredotalizing and distancing of the role of clergy, eventually making them primarily those who concoct the Christian liturgy rather than those entrusted with the community that is formed through the liturgy.

In the Third and Fourth Lateran Councils of 1179 and 1215, there was a radical disjunction of clergy from the community. Formerly, only men who had been put forward by a particular community to be a minister could be ordained. All "absolute ordinations," ordinations that were not tied to the leadership of some congregation, were invalid, according to Chalcedon. But after the Lateran Councils, only those people who can be placed by a bishop are ordained. The ordained must wait until a bishop finds a ministerial appointment for them.[22] The claim of the community, which as we have seen in Hippolytus was originally the essential originating element in ordination, is beginning to recede into the background. Ordination becomes an office held by an individual, passed down by a duly appointed bishop.

Also in the Fourth Lateran Council there emerges a claim for a mysterious *sacramental character of ordination.* There is much more talk about ministerial "character," linking that character to the elaborate requirements for priests in the Old Testament. This would contribute to an ontological (as opposed to functional) sacredotalizing of the priesthood. Now priests are those who are different because of something sacred that is given to them in the sacrament of ordination. *Sacramentum* relates to the stamp of the emperor on something. The word *character* originally referred to the indelible brand or stamp with which a Roman soldier was branded when he joined the army. Augustine had used this image in discussing the permanence and imperviousness of baptism. Now it is applied as well to ordination.

The priesthood tended now to be seen as a personal state of life, a status, rather than a function in service to the community, and thus was personalized and privatized.[23] Now ordination became a sacred rite, a sacrament of the church. A man was ordained as a priest apart from designation by and service linked to a particular community. What Chalcedon had condemned as "absolute ordination" was to become the norm in the West. In ordination, a person was given a new character, a *character indelibelis,* an indelible stamp making the priest ontologically different. One is ordained as a "priest for ever, after the order of Melchizedek."[24]

> For every high priest chosen from among men is appointed to act on behalf of men in relation to God, to offer gifts and sacrifices for sins. He can deal gently with the ignorant and wayward, since he himself is beset with weakness. Because of this he is bound to offer sacrifice for his own sins as well as for those of the people. And one does not take the honor upon himself, but he is called by God, just as Aaron was. . . . Thou art a priest for ever, after the order of Melchizedek. (Heb. 5:1-6 RSV)

These words from Hebrews, applied to Christ and his high priesthood, were now applied to Christian clergy, thus linking the *cleros* alone to the priesthood of Christ, and undercutting the priesthood of the *laos* of God. Hebrews asserts that because Christ has made the perfect sacrifice, there is now an end to sacrifice and no "priest" but Christ, the High Priest, which makes all the more odd the use of this passage to talk about Christian clergy as leaders of the cultic aspects of the church.

The Protestant Reformation sought to restore all the baptized to the priesthood of Christ. Luther says that every Christian is preacher, evangelist, teacher (parents must preach to children, husbands and wives ought to preach to one another). There is a "universal priesthood," says Luther, but it is not the order of priests, it is the "priesthood of believers." As Luther says:

> Whoever comes out of the water of baptism can boast that he is already a consecrated priest, bishop, and pope, although of course it is not seemly that just anybody should exercise such office. . . . There is no true, basic difference between laymen and priests. . . . except for the sake of office and work, but not for the sake of status.[25]

All Christians are baptized to share in the high priesthood of Christ. The "priesthood of believers" doctrine does not mean, as is sometimes asserted, that each person is his or her own priest, but rather that each person is a priest to his or her neighbor, one who shares in Christ's priesthood to the world.[26] Perhaps this is why, in our own day, Protestants were the first to ordain women. After all, according to Reformation theology, baptized women were "priests" already.

For the sake of good order, when the church gathers, some from among the "priests" are to serve as "priests" or "servants of the servants of God." These are called *pastors.* "We are all priests, as many of us are Christians. But the priests, as we call them, are ministers *(diener)* chosen from among us, who do all that they do. And the priesthood is nothing but a ministry," says Luther. Of the "priesthood of believers," Luther said, "As many of us as have been baptized are all priests without distinction. . . . for thus it is written in 1 Peter 2, 'Ye are a chosen generation, a royal priesthood, and a priestly kingdom.' Therefore we are all priests, as many of us are Christians."[27]

The Reformers were able to stress, in effect, that the question for each Christian is not, "Am I called to ministry?" but rather, "To which ministry am I called?" In the Reformation tradition, pastors are called to preach to the congregation, in the name of Christ, so that the congregation may preach to the world in the name of Christ.

The Reformation was, to a great extent, a movement to reform the leadership of the church. The Reformers were able to stress in doctrine, if not always in practice, a number of clerical values that were to have great implications for the history of the ordained ministry. Particular stress was put on the education of clergy. (Protestant clergy tended to eschew liturgical garments, wearing instead the black Geneva gown, which was academic rather than clerical attire.) In reaction against the intellectual laxity of many medieval clergy, Protestant clergy were expected to be well schooled in the scriptures, in order to be servants of the Word.

Marriage was permitted for Protestant clergy. Luther made marriage and childbearing virtual necessities for clergy. Clergy were thereby to demonstrate that the gospel was meant to be lived here, now, in this world, amid the daily concerns of this life.

explain

The gathered congregation was linked again to the making and function of clergy. Care of the congregation rather than leadership of the cult became the pastor's chief concern. Protestant ordination rites stressed the pastor as shepherd, as the one who kept the flock, as the one whose ministry arose from and was focused upon the gathered people of God.

Clergy were again seen as *collegial,* colleagues with other clergy who helped train and oversee their fellow clergy. Some Protestants, such as the Reformed, abolished the episcopacy but sought to continue the traditioning and ruling functions of the episcopacy through a college of clergy.

6. Ordination sets apart those who are to serve as exemplars to the congregation, being in all things without fault.

That he may minister blamelessly by night and day.

Pastors are expected, from the earliest days, to be exemplary Christians. A pastor's *exemplary moral life is an aspect of the pastor's service* to the people of God.

First Timothy makes explicit mention of the moral qualities of Christian leaders:

> Now a bishop must be above reproach, married only once, temperate, sensible, respectable, hospitable, an apt teacher, not a drunkard, not violent but gentle, not quarrelsome, and not a lover of money. (1 Tim. 3:2)

It is not that the pastor is expected to be a morally more exemplary Christian than other Christians, but rather that pastors are expected to act in a way that befits their public and communal, that is, churchly, obligations. Note that 1 Timothy has no qualms about linking a pastor's public, congregational role with the pastor's responsibility toward marriage and family. Clearly, pastors are to be role models for the church, without that troublesome modern separation between public and private, social and personal, behavior. Later in this book, we will examine in more detail what it means for the pastor to be "a faithful example for all God's people."

The pastoral yoke of obedience is not easy. There is a long and honored tradition of those who fled the call to be a pastor. In a sermon on Isaiah, Origen compared Isaiah's youthful and exuberant, "Here am I, send me!" to Jonah who did everything he could to flee the call of God. Jonah was smarter, says Origen:

> As we have compared Isaiah and Moses, let us make another similar comparison of Isaiah and Jonah. The latter is sent to foretell to the people of Nineveh its fall after three days, and he is reluctant to set out and become the unwilling cause of calamity to the city. But Isaiah, without waiting to hear what he was bidden to say, answers, "Here am I, send me." It is a good thing not to rush eagerly to those honors, high positions, and ministries of the church which are from God, but to imitate Moses and with him to say, "Secure someone else to send." The one who wishes to be saved takes no steps to high position in the church, and, if appointed, takes office for the Church's service. If we are to use also the words of the Gospel, "The princes of the Gentiles have lordship over them, and they that have authority over them are called officers. But it shall not be so with you."[28]

It is clear in Hippolytus that Christian leaders are visibly to represent a manner of life and a style of leadership in marked contrast to that of the world. True, the basic identity of the minister is that of any Christian—one who has been baptized—with ordination being but an elaboration or further implication of the pastor's baptism. Yet leaders of the church are to be, in Hippolytus, "without fault" and "blameless." The exemplary character of clergy is asserted from the first.

The role of clergy as moral exemplars was undercut somewhat in debates during the time of Pope Innocent III (1198–1216). Ordination became formally defined as a person who had experienced the rite of laying on of hands "by a duly consecrated bishop." It is the work of a duly consecrated bishop that makes clergy. Thus the ordained ministry, after Innocent III, is linked to *opus operatum*—the ritual act itself is the source of that which is signified.

Nearly a thousand years before, during the Donatist controversy, Augustine had argued that ordination carries with it the grace of God, despite the personal failings of the priest. Even though the individual may be a person of some disrepute, ordination enables God's grace to work through that individual, despite the failings of the individual.[29] From my own experience as a pastor, unworthy as I am, I know Augustine's claim to be true. Yet in the Middle Ages, Augustine's pastoral argument is taken to the extreme, as if the character of the individual, or the community's need for and response to that individual, were of little consequence.

The old relationship between ministry and church now shifts to a relationship between certain liturgical powers and sacramental functions. The priest is the one who has the power to make a mass. Only the duly ordained priest can speak the "words of consecration." The priesthood is defined by its relationship with the cult, more than with the community. A mass is "valid" when it has been consecrated by a validly ordained priest, regardless of the participation or lack thereof by the community. Priests are now an order of special persons. The Old Testament Laws for priests on such things as celibacy and virginity are now passed on to priests.

Thus many of our current notions of the ordained ministry rest upon an innovation that occurred within the first two centuries of the church, and which was brought to fulfillment in the first thousand years—*the creation of the laity.* The historian Faivre has it right: The most significant change in church order in the first centuries of the church was not the creation of leaders, but rather the creation of the laity. In later rites of ordination, those virtues that were once gifts given to all Christians at baptism are now read solely upon the priests at ordination. The laity, commonly considered as the elect, are, in effect, declared to be a people *not* set apart, a people who no longer share in Christ's high priesthood.[30] Christ's priestly attributes are now read onto only one group of the baptized—the clergy. This is a sad development for the baptized.

By the way, I find nothing in the prayer of Hippolytus that would lead to an exclusion of women from ordination. Sexual orientation is not mentioned. As Paul taught, the gospel transcends our social, racial, and economic divisions (Gal. 3:27-29).

(7.) Ordination is an act of collegiality.

In Hippolytus, *the ministry of the church is also characterized by collegiality,* that is, admission to a group of colleagues, the elders of the church who sit in council and decide on matters related to the governance of the congregation.

> With the agreement of all let the bishops lay hands on him and the presbytery stand by in silence.
> After this one of the bishops present at the request of all, laying his hand on him who is ordained bishop, shall pray thus, saying:

From the first, Christian leadership seems to have been collegial.[31] Paul speaks about how he and Apollos, in their leadership at Corinth, complemented each other, with Paul planting the seed and Apollos nurturing the young plants of faith. Through such collegiality, God gave growth (1 Cor. 3:5-9). The garden is God's, the building being built is God's, though God requires a number of farmers to work the field, and carpenters to build the building (1 Cor. 3:9).

When Cyprian, bishop of Carthage during the Decian persecution, was asked to rule on a sensitive matter under dispute, he refused, saying "From the first commencement of my episcopacy, I made up my mind to do nothing on my own private opinion, without your [his fellow clergy's] advice and without the consent of the people."[32] Christian leadership is collegial.

8. Ordination is effected through the laying on of hands and prayer.

With the agreement of all let the bishops lay hands on him and
the presbytery stand by in silence.
*   And all shall keep silence praying in their heart for the descent*
of the Spirit.
*   After this one of the bishops present at the request of all, lay-*
ing his hand on him who is ordained bishop, shall pray thus.

The *central liturgical gesture of ordination is the laying on of hands,* a sign that is full of significance for clergy. There is in this gesture a conferral of power and authority from those who have borne this burden to those newly called to lead. Any authority and power that clergy have is never our own; it is a gift, a bestowal from the Holy Spirit and the church. Though most of us today associate the laying on of hands with ordination, it is a *baptismal gesture.* When used in ordination, the laying on of hands is a sign that the call to ministry is preceded by the baptismal call and arises out of the general ministry of all Christians in baptism.

Little wonder, then, that in the history of the church there have been churches (such as the Society of Friends, or Quakers) who have radically called into question the institutional ministry. Ulrich Zwingli called ordination a "human invention."[33] It is difficult to embody the distinct tensions within ordained leadership, difficult to affirm the necessary role of leaders without having those leaders assume the ministry that rightly belongs to all Christians. No wonder there have been some who have attempted to avoid those tensions by avoiding ordination altogether. I agree with Geoffrey Wainwright that these groups have served as "a critical irritant in the history of Christianity."[34] They keep reminding us that Christian leadership is a gift. Their churches keep judging the (in Wainwright's words) "institutional sclerosis" of our larger communities of faith. Like the martyrs, their ministry reminds the rest of us that all of God's people—not just the clergy—are called forth by God to be priests and prophets.

Yet, in my interaction with these communities, I have found that they also demonstrate that leadership is not an optional matter for the church. There must be some from the baptized who assume the burdens of guidance, teaching, correction, care, and community concern in a way that edifies and calls forth the ministry of all Christians. These communities may be loathe to call their leaders "priests," but among them are those who function in priestly ways all the same. I expect the perennial issue for the church is not *if* we shall have some from among the baptized who exercise leadership, but rather *how* will their exercise of leadership be peculiarly Christian?

The prayer with laying on of hands signifies the distinctiveness of Christian leadership. It not only shows the gifted quality of church leadership, but also symbolizes the *handing on of the apostolic faith from one generation of its guardians to another.* The pastor is to be a witness, bearing testimony to the received faith of the church. The pastor is not ordained to share his or her personal or idiosyncratic theology, but rather to bear the burden of the whole faith of the whole church, the testimony of the saints, the witness of Scripture. Thomas Merton begins his spiritual classic *Seeds of Contemplation*

by bragging that all of his thoughts therein are completely unorig-
inal and about the same as might be written by any Cistercian
monk writing down his thoughts in the year 1000 or in the 1940s.
Christians are distinguished by our effort to think as the church has
thought down through the ages. Among us, a truly "original idea"
is what we usually call heresy.[35]

Jews and Christians are folk who practice *anamnesis*, the refusal
to forget, the earnest effort to remember. Much of our Sunday worship tends to be acts of remembrance. Thus the laying on of hands
signifies one of the major New Testament functions of Christian
leadership, particularly as it is depicted in Acts—to ensure *continuity*. In Acts 1:21-26 it is important for the apostles to select someone
to replace the betrayer Judas who "accompanied us during all the
time that the Lord Jesus went in and out among us . . . a witness
with us to his resurrection" (1:21-22). Ministry has, as one of
its responsibilities, to ensure that there is continuity between
the gospel preached today and the gospel as it has always been
proclaimed.

In all New Testament discussions of Christian leadership, there
is stress upon the principle of continuity in the apostolic tradition.
As Titus 1:5-9 says, ministry is necessary to keep the community as
"the community of Jesus." Therefore a major function of the
church's ministry is *preservation of Christian identity*. We look to our
clergy to ensure that the procession in which we march moves
along the same adventurous path walked by the saints.

> *Through Thy Child Jesus Christ our Lord, through Whom to Thee be
> glory, might and praise, to the Father and to the Son with the Holy
> Spirit now and world without end. Amen.*

Servant of the Servants of God

The sacrament administered in my grandmother's living room
that Sunday afternoon a long time ago worked. I stayed Christian,
defined by God through my family and the church. There were
adolescent doubts and wanderings not interesting enough to
recount. In college, somewhat to my surprise, I found myself
drawn back to where I had always really been. I found myself willing to admit that I was thinking about going to seminary; considering becoming a pastor. The thought was too strange to have come

to me on my own. It must have come to me as a gift of God and the church.

I had always enjoyed the church. I was active in my church youth group. In college, the religion courses were wonderfully challenging. As a teenager, I had been close to a couple of our church's pastors. Some of the courageous young pastors in the then current Civil Rights movement in the South impressed me with their courage and conviction.

But mostly I was feeling called. An old preacher had told me, "Don't even try being a pastor unless you are called, unless you have no way of avoiding the summons." And I believed him.

Gradually I gained the courage to tell people that I was going to "try seminary," maybe just for a year. My days at Yale Divinity School, my courses there, my positive experiences in field work in an inner-city parish, all confirmed my sense of vocation. Wonder of wonders, all evidence to the contrary, even against the advice of some reliable friends, God was calling me into the pastoral ministry.

Then one night, in early summer, in a little town in South Carolina, the church gathered and songs were sung—Samuel Wesley's "The Church's One Foundation," and Ralph Vaughan Williams's *Sine Nomine*, "For All the Saints." Family and friends were there, even a couple of my old Sunday school teachers. And a bishop preached, then called me before him, and after questions and answers and a charge to me, Bishop Tullis summoned all elders to come forth. Hands were laid upon my head.

I felt upon my head two score of hands, and the weight of the centuries. All the doctrine of the church, everything the church had believed and said and done, the witness of the saints, all the good work of those "soldiers, faithful, true, and bold," as the hymn has it—all that was laid upon me. Strange, but the hands laid upon my head felt both like a huge burden and a strong support. Hands were pressing down upon me, loading upon me the weight of the church's faith, but those hands were also holding me up, giving me that which I did not have through education or natural inclination. I was too young at the time, too inexperienced. Even after years in seminary, I had little idea of what lay ahead for me or for the church. And the church surely knew this, for it seemed to pray with particular earnestness when the bishop asked for the gifts of the

Holy Spirit, that I might be the person whom God and the church had called me to be. And it worked. By the end of the service and the final "Amen," I was sure that God had given, *would* give me, what I needed to do joyous things. My church, for various good reasons, does not believe that ordination is a sacrament, a particular means of grace. But that night, at Broad Street United Methodist Church in Clinton, South Carolina, for me, it was.

The next day, strolling down the street on my way from the church to the post office, a kid—one of the teenagers in the church—whizzed by me on his bike. He was whistling a tune. *Sine Nomine!* I took it as a sign, a divine benediction upon the work of the church the night before. Thirty years later, the wonder of it all still manages, on most days in the ministry, to amaze me—thank God. The Holy Spirit really does give those gifts that ministry demands. Thereby, God's Word is preached, the sacraments duly administered, and the sheep are fed, despite us, through us. The Holy Spirit is amazing.

The history of the ordained ministry shows the challenge of living out Jesus' warning that leadership in the Body of Christ ought to be different from those forms of leadership so popular among "the Gentiles." From the first, leadership in the name of Jesus Christ is inherently countercultural, subversive to current secular understandings of power and authority, and difficult to embody. The vocation is too grand for us. Perhaps the great wonder is that so many have so faithfully, for so many centuries, answered the call with courage and grace to the great glory of God, for the preservation of the church, and for the redemption of the world.

The vocation of pastor is difficult, not only because it is leadership within the church (church people can be difficult), but also because it is leadership in the name of Jesus (Jesus can be difficult too). Jesus modeled leadership with a basin and a towel. His high point as a leader came when he stooped down and washed his own followers' feet (John 13:12-20). Thus Hippolytus's prayer ends in Christology, with reference to "Jesus Christ our Lord," the one who is the model for all ministry.

On the virtual eve of his death, Martin Luther King Jr. stood in the pulpit of Atlanta's Ebenezer Baptist Church, his own congregation, and preached a sermon that was full of premonition of the impending end of his ministry. King was not standing before great multitudes on the Mall in Washington, or before a crowd of civil rights protestors in Mississippi. He was within the church that had called and commissioned him, the church that had formed him and given him his voice, the church he had faithfully served. When it came time to judge his life and his ministry, King said that he wanted to be remembered in a way that is congruent with the diaconal nature of Christian leadership:

> If any of you are around when I have to meet my day, I don't want a long funeral. And if you get somebody to deliver the eulogy, tell them not to talk too long. Every now and then I wonder what I want them to say. Tell them not to mention that I have a Nobel Peace Prize, that isn't important. Tell them not to mention that I have three or four hundred other awards, that's not important. Tell him not to mention where I went to school. I'd like somebody to mention that day, that Martin Luther King, Jr., tried to give his life serving others. I'd like for somebody to say that day, that Martin Luther King, Jr., tried to love somebody.[36]

The ordained ministry is one of the ways in which Christians love somebody, and through that attempt, Christ loves the church.

CHAPTER TWO

Ministry for the Twenty-first Century: Images of the Pastor

The Acts of the Apostles depicts the life of the early church most-ly through the story of the church's leaders: Paul, missionary to the Gentiles; Peter, leader of the church at Jerusalem and the first apos-tle; Barnabas, Silas, Priscilla and Aquila, Damaris, and Mary. From the first, the leadership of the church seems linked to the images of the saints, who enable pastors to see who they are and to whom they are accountable. Contemporary ministry has been the victim (or the beneficiary, depending on how one reads our history) of images of leadership that are borrowed not from scripture, but from the surrounding culture—the pastor as CEO, as psychotherapeutic guru, or as political agitator. One of the challenges of the ordained ministry is to find those metaphors for ministry that allow us appropriately to embody the peculiar vocation of Christian leader-ship. Uncritical borrowing from the culture's images of leadership can be the death of specifically *Christian* leaders.

Modern-day pastors work, whether we know it or not, out of a reservoir of received images of Christian leadership. The powerful national pulpit presence of Henry Ward Beecher, the social critic embodied in Washington Gladden and his heirs Walter Rauschenbusch and Reinhold Niebuhr, the oratorical and organi-zational genius of Charles G. Finney with his citywide revivals and his heir Billy Graham all have served as models for ministers. We have Martin Luther King Jr., the prophet and martyr, as well as Harry Emerson Fosdick, urbane interpreter of the faith to skeptical modern people; Georgia Harkness and Carter Heyward, pioneers; and Fulton Sheen, first of the television preacher celebrities.[1] Every time I enter a pulpit or a hospital room as a pastor, for good or ill, I bear memories of those who lived out this vocation before me. Knowledge of their sacrifices and achievements, their stumblings and mistakes, can help inspire and encourage me, correct and judge me in my ministerial work today.

Clerical biography and autobiography can be nourishing read-ing for the contemporary pastor. As a young pastor, I well remem-ber being inspired by Fosdick's *The Living of These Days*, as he honestly admitted his struggles with depression as a young man and detailed his fight with the fundamentalists.[2] I recall reading William Sloane Coffin's *Once to Every Man*, and marveling at how small a place theological commitment seemed to play in his own vocation and practice of ministry, and wondering how that shaped his own witness.[3] The raucous account of the life of Aimee Semple McPherson, *Sister Aimee*, describes a woman whose ministry evoked an entire denomination.[4] Barbara Brown Taylor's *The Preaching Life* is an engaging reminder of the difficulty and the delight of being a preacher.[5] Above all, I remember Reinhold Niebuhr's *Leaves from the Notebook of a Tamed Cynic*, which con-vinced me that the parish ministry was a wonderful way to expend one's life—a vocation that required a lifetime of hard intellectual work combined with the grace of God—even though neither Niebuhr nor I spent all our ministry in the parish.[6] Will Campbell's *Brother to a Dragonfly* demonstrated that joy of not fitting in, of remaining a truth-teller all of one's life.[7] In their heights and depths, in their ability to embody the gospel or to betray it, these preachers, these predecessors in ministry, serve as models for us of the promise and the pitfalls of ministry.

Contemporary Images of Ministry

We cannot easily know where we ought to be going until we know where we have been. I am no great prognosticator of the future of the ordained ministry. However, we can obtain some sense of future direction through a brief survey of some of the images that have held sway over our ministerial imaginations dur-ing the later half of the twentieth century.[8]

Here are some of the chief ministerial metaphors of our time.

Media Mogul

This is the image of Christian leadership that first comes to the minds of millions when they hear the term, *Christian minister*. Pat Robertson, Oral Roberts, Billy Graham, and Robert Schuller have touched the lives of more people than any other pastors in history. In the twentieth century, television was the great invention. We live in a media-saturated, media-addicted, media-sanctioned culture. These preachers have sought to exploit this medium to reach others with the gospel.

For the critics of these pastors of mass media, the image of Sinclair Lewis's *Elmer Gantry* has been difficult to shake. We ought to remember that the Protestant Reformation was tied to the invention of the cheap book, thanks to the technological advance of the printing press. Why should ministry be the foe of advances in technology? The media moguls have often justified their television ministry with appeals to, "If Jesus had had television, he would have used it to reach people too. The greatest good to the greatest number."

But mass communication requires millions of dollars, so media ministries have often been consumed with financial appeals and financial woes, and for some of them, periodic charges of financial impropriety. To turn the church into a television studio, as Robert Schuller has done at his Crystal Cathedral, seems to some like a gross capitulation to the spirit of the age. Of course, television preachers plead that TV is only a tool, a neutral device to get across the age-old message of the gospel in a new way.

We are learning that no medium is neutral. The medium shapes and reforms the message, transforming the message even as it purports to be delivering it. An entertainment culture tends to consume Christian worship. The sincerity and concern conveyed by the media preacher are only apparent. Among the media mogul's failings is an inadequate ecclesiology. The virtual church made through electronic media is less than church, where, to extend Paul's corporeal analogy, the eye has no opportunity ever to meet the foot. There is no flesh for incarnation. The fundamental form of the Christian church as a participatory body, the character of the pastor as one who knows the flock and is known by the flock, is changed by immersion in the modern "entertainment culture."[9] The primary function of television is entertainment, whereas the purpose of the gospel is transformation. Furthermore, when we are holding the TV remote control, we are in control of what can be said and shown to us. There is thus little opportunity to be jumped from behind by grace.

Because this image of the media mogul is so pervasive, parish pastors unconsciously take on the mannerisms and style of the television preacher, particularly in their leadership of public worship. The pastor as performer, as grinning personality, supersedes the roles of pastor as teacher, priest, and leader of the congregation.

Political Negotiator

Martin Luther King Jr. is probably more widely remembered as the leader of a political movement than as pastor of a Baptist congregation. In a recent television dramatization of the life of Dietrich Bonhoeffer, the great theologian and teacher was portrayed more as a political opponent of the Nazis than as a teacher of the church. These ministers left us the legacy of the pastor as the embodiment of "public theology," an image of ministry in which the pastor is seen as negotiating between the demands of the gospel and the realities of the political and economic power structures.[10]

Jesse Jackson has been a political organizer, television talk-show host, negotiator, and statesman in addition to his pastoral roles. J. Philip Wogaman became the counselor and public defender of President Clinton, even as Billy Graham before him was the court preacher to Richard Nixon.[11] Tony Campolo was asked to help the president repent of his sexual sin, and was severely criticized by some of his fellow Evangelicals for being "used" by the president. Yet the possibility, even the likelihood, of a pastor being used by the powerful is a danger that prophets to the powerful have always thought worth the risk. Even the king requires a confessor.

Sometimes these public, political pastors give the impression that real ministry is somewhere other than at church. As they move confidently among the powerful, how can they know that they are not being used and abused by the politicians they are purporting to counsel?

When Girolamo Savonarola told Lorenzo the Magnificent what God demanded, the troublesome friar was promptly tried and burned at the stake. Hugh Latimer pled the plight of the poor and pressed the boy king Edward VI to be faithful to his religious vocation as defender of the faith, dismissing those who challenged his sermons to the king as "flatterers and fibbergibs." Though court preachers like Savonarola sometimes had a short tenure, the role of the chaplain to the court has a long, though mostly dubious, history. Attempting to use the political powers that be to accomplish good in a society where imperial politics is everything, how do these court preachers avoid selling out to solutions and strategies that compromise and deface the gospel they are ordained to serve? These are among the struggles of the court preacher.[12] Although King Henry II was eventually moved to repentance through the courageous ministrations of Thomas à Becket, it cost Thomas his head.

No doubt these public figures would remind us that there is also a price being paid by the pastor who settles down to tend the flock, focusing ministerial energies exclusively upon the congregation without contact or concern with the "wider world." Yet who defines which world is the one worth having? A crucified God wins victories, not through the savvy balancing of power or through well-crafted compromises, but rather through the cross, which is the normative Christian means of "politics."[13]

Therapist

Many have noted that we live in a therapeutic culture where all human problems are reduced to sickness. We want not so much to be saved or changed, but rather to feel better about ourselves. Harry Emerson Fosdick once called preaching "counseling on a group scale."[14] The pastor becomes not the teacher or the preacher or the moral guide, but rather the therapist who helps evoke spiritually-inclined sentiments in individuals—soothing anxiety, caring for the distressed, and healing the maladjusted.

Certainly, the pastor is to care for people. But the pastor cares "in the name of Christ," which may give a different cast and set different goals for the pastor's care than for that of a secular therapist. What the Christian faith might define as "a well-functioning personality" might be considerably at odds with contemporary definitions of mental health.

I recall a contemporary historian, recounting in some detail Martin Luther King Jr.'s rather persistent attempts to win the praise of his father, "Daddy King." So much of the younger King's life can be explained, said the historian, as his tortured efforts to please a father who was very difficult please.

"Well, then, thank God Martin never got well adjusted," shouted an old preacher from the rear of the room. Thank God, indeed. A certain dissonance with the world, a holy kind of discontent, seems to be fertile ground for God's prophets. Truth is superior even to mental health.

Lacking theological control on our "care," we lapse into secular goals and techniques of care. We offer the church care that is not too different from that which might be received from any well-meaning secular therapist. The pastor is reduced to the level of the soother of anxieties brought on by the dilemmas of affluence, rather than the caller of persons to salvation. *discuss*

My colleague Stanley Hauerwas has accused the contemporary pastor of being little more than "a quivering mass of availability."[15] Practicing what I have called "promiscuous ministry"—ministry with no internal, critical judgment about what care is worth giving—we become the victims of a culture of insatiable need. We live in a capitalist, consumptive culture where there is no purpose to our society other than "meeting our needs." The culture gives us the maximum amount of room and encouragement to "meet our needs" without appearing to pass judgment on which needs are worth meeting. The capitalist, big-is-better mentality infects our pastoral work as we labor to increase the size of our congregation through our care, to move up the ladder of pastoral appointments, to be a "success" as this culture defines it. In this vast supermarket of desire, we pastors must do more than simply "meet people's needs." The church also is about giving people the critical means of assessing which needs give our lives meaning, about giving us needs we would not have had if we had not met Jesus.

One reason many pastors become so exhausted by the demands of ministry is that they enter ministry with little basis for it other than "meeting people's needs." That is dangerous in a society of omnivorous desire, where people, not knowing which desires are worth fulfilling, merely grab at everything. The pastor's ministry ends in fatigue and resentment at having given one's life for a bunch of selfish people who have no other purpose in their lives than the fulfillment of an unexamined, inexhaustible set of false "needs."

Years ago, my own teacher of pastoral care, James Dittes, noted that alumni of Yale Divinity School, when asked what courses in clergy continuing education they desired, tended to put "Pastoral

Counseling" at the top of their list. Dittes said that although such interest in pastoral counseling ought to cheer him, as a professor of the subject he was suspicious.

"I fear that in a therapeutic culture, pastoral counseling is the last socially approved activity left for pastors," said Dittes. We live in a culture with an extravagant faith in the potency of counseling combined with a relentless interest in self-help techniques for human betterment. In such a culture, the pastor as therapist is a risky image for pastoral work—a possible capitulation to the infatuations of capitalist, bourgeois concerns rather than specifically Christian ones. We are not only often sick, we are always sinners, says the orthodox Christian faith. Pastoral care without a strong sense of human sinfulness puts pastors as well as their parishioners in peril.

Manager

A pastor is a leader of a complex volunteer organization. Pastors sometimes complain that their greatest weakness in moving from seminary to parish is lack of administrative ability. They grumble that an inordinate amount of their time is consumed with petty, inconsequential, administrative routine. Admittedly, we live in an anti-institutional age, when people tend to be suspicious of organizations. We have a romantic notion that it is possible to have religious experience without religious community.[16]

Yet Christianity is an incarnational faith. As we have said, the pastor is the "community person," the one who is ordained by the church to worry about internal, congregational concerns. So the issue is not, Should I be concerned with internal administration? but rather, *How should I be concerned with administration?*

In a business culture, where efficiency and productivity, competitive advantage and technical expertise are valued, where time becomes a commodity and the expert becomes the high priest of competence, the pastoral ministry can appear hopelessly inefficient and archaic.[17] By standards external to the church, so much of a pastor's time can appear wasted. The afternoon spent visiting in a nursing home or the hours spent in preparation for Sunday's sermon may not be an efficient use of time as the world judges these matters.

Much of ministry ought to be spent resisting the world's judgments of efficiency. Efficiently administrating and coordinating volunteers—with briefcase in hand, laptop nearby, schedule closely watched, agenda always followed—may not be the most fruitful deployment of a pastor's gifts, or the most faithful way to do ministry, judged by the historic metaphors for ministry.

I have always been grateful for the delightful diversions that occur in the Gospels as Jesus is on the way somewhere and gets sidetracked, diverted by someone in need, or by some odd occurrence. These digressions remind me that much of my best ministry is when I am open to surprise and interruption, and willing to submit my plans to God's plans or to people's needs.

Jesus was out in Tyre and Sidon, attempting to get away from the crowds, when a woman whose daughter was ill entered the house, fell at Jesus' feet, and demanded attention. She was a "Syrophoenician by birth." Thus, out in Gentile territory, on his way to minister to his own, Jesus is intruded upon by a woman—a Gentile woman. Yet this unplanned, unsought interruption becomes a moment for a marvelous demonstration of Jesus' power and compassion as he heals her little girl (Mark 7:24-30). Through such "interruptions" we find occasion for some of our best ministry.

Certainly, we pastors could be more efficient administrators. Good time management is a theological issue, a matter of what we deem to be essential in our ministry. As I heard Henri Nouwen say to us pastors, "If you do not know what is absolutely essential in ministry, then you will do the merely important." Because so much of what a pastor could do is important, it is easy to become bogged down, sidetracked by the merely important to the neglect of the absolutely essential, unless one keeps ever before oneself the essential theological rationale for ministry.

The pastor as manager can be a positive image as the pastor empowers and coordinates the ministry of the laity, rather than taking over all ministry from the laity. Some time ago, Lyle Schaller maintained that the lone "shepherd" ought to become the resourceful "rancher" if a congregation is to be more than 150 to 200 members in attendance on Sunday. "The responsibility of the rancher . . . is to see the total picture, to make sure that everything gets done, rather than attempt to do all the work singlehandedly. . . . The rancher's . . . responsibility is to delegate to others and to trust *but delegating doesn't honor the calling of the other*

the people to whom specific responsibilities have been delegated."[18]
The pastor who cannot delegate, who cannot work well with a
church staff, who insists on being the sole proprietor of all ministry
of the congregation, who does not use time well, is not only a poor
manager but also theologically confused. Skillful administration by
a pastor is important in order that a pastor may quickly perform the
more mundane management duties of the job and get on to more
invigorating activities such as reading books, preparing sermons,
visiting the sick, counseling the troubled, and being in prayer.

More could be done in seminary to train future pastors in the arts
of peculiarly *pastoral* administration, to help pastors not become the
victims of secular images of the efficient administrator that are detrimental to the nature and goals of the church. Good organizational
management is leadership that is congruent with the goals and purposes of a specifically ecclesial organization, that helps that organization do the work that it is specifically called to do. As historian
Brooks Holifield had shown, the history of pastoral care in America
is a history of the adoption of inappropriate models of leadership
by the clergy.[19] This stands as a warning to us of the perils of uncritical adoption of secular techniques and models of leadership.

The pastor as manager can be an all too appealing image for pastors who lack the creativity and the courage to do more than simply
maintain the status quo of the church—to keep the machinery oiled
and functioning rather than pushing the church to ask larger, more
difficult questions about its purpose and faithfulness. Pastors are
called to lead, not simply to manage. Many of us serve churches that
have become dysfunctional, unfaithful, and boring. Having lost a
clear sense of our mission, we diffuse ourselves in inconsequential
busyness. Lacking a sense of the essential, we do the merely important. Any pastor who feels no discontent with the church's unfaithfulness, who is too content with inherited forms of the church, is not
just being a bad manager, but has made the theological mistake of
surrendering the joyful adventure of pastoral ministry for the theologically dubious office of ecclesiastical bureaucrat.

Resident Activist

Although this image of ministry was most appealing three
decades ago, when I was exiting seminary, it now seems rare. The

coming maybe back

pastor as the community prophet—moving about town agitating for reform, speaking out on justice issues, engaging the powers that be—was an attractive vocation for us 1960s activists.

But the sixties faded and most of us quickly settled in to more personal, therapeutic, narcissistic concerns. Few pastors are viewed today as community leaders who have a responsibility to help make the whole town work better. There was a day when the political activist pastor who "mixed religion with politics" was usually a theological liberal. Today, the political pastors tend to be evangelical conservatives, a curious exchange of theological bases for political engagement.

I must confess a certain sadness at the fading of this metaphor for ministry. Part of my sadness is my own grief at the demise of mainline Protestantism. The churches that many of us serve are no longer sleeping giants awaiting awakening by a committed pastor, ready to change the world. Few pastors today are considered to be community opinion makers and community consciences. Exceptions include some rural pastors who, of necessity, must be power brokers and community leaders in areas where there are no others to perform these roles. Also, pastors in some urban areas where there has been a breakdown of social services for the poor must become care brokers and advocates for those who have no one else to speak for them. Sadly, most of us pastors today see ourselves as maintainers of equilibrium in the congregations that we serve; controllers of damage, soothers of ruffled feathers, rather than agents of social change.

We ought to admit that there was a touch of Constantinian imperialism in the image of the pastor as resident social activist. It was perhaps the last gasp of the old hegemony that mainline Protestantism once enjoyed over American life. As the largest denominations in the country, we felt a responsibility to help make America work through the only means that most Americans recognized as path to power—secular politics. There is more than a touch of arrogance, if not self-delusion, in a pastor's self-image as ordained to lead the whole town, rather than ordained for the arduous task of working with God to form the Body of Christ.

However, I regret the loss of the pastor as an instigator of holy discontent, righteous indignation, disease with the powers. Some of my guiding images for ministry were provided by people such as William Sloane Coffin, Will Campbell, William Stringfellow, and Martin Luther King Jr.—people who did not mind causing a stir, who relished the role of speaking truth to power—prophets who knew that Jesus provokes conflict. These gadflies respected the power of the gospel over the narcotic appeal of the status quo. Too many of us contemporary pastors are far too easily pleased with present arrangements, less critical than we ought to be, too deferential to Caesar and his accomplices.

Remembering the witness of Bishop Gerald Kennedy's pacifism in World War II, and recalling how many clergy spoke out against the war in Vietnam in the 1960s, some of them paying dearly for their preaching, it was with sadness that I noted how few of us preachers seemed to have any discomfort with the Gulf War with Iraq in the 1990s. Vietnam involved many American casualties, whereas mostly Iraqis died in the later war, which may explain some of the pulpit silence. An equally disturbing explanation is that preachers had moved into more limited, parochial, personal concerns in their preaching.

I cannot decide whether the current interest in "public theology" is the last gasp of a dying and dated image of prophetic ministry, or a new form of accommodation to the powers that be. Much stress upon the need for the church to be in service to the "wider world" rests upon the assumption that the church is basically strong and vital already and only needs to get out, go public, and help North American democracy work a bit more efficiently. I feel this is a misreading of both the situation of the church and of the culture, giving far too much deference to the culture and far too little attention to the need to form a distinctive alternative polis called *the church*.

For instance, in his book on pastoral care, Charles Gerkin says that "pastoral care . . . involves the pastor in giving caring attention to concerns that reach beyond the individual to the community of Christians and the larger society."[20] Although this of course is true, one is suspicious that his reference to the "larger society" somehow implies that the church is a "small society," whereas the state, the capitalist economy, the dominant culture is where the real action lies. From a peculiarly Christian point of view, "small" is the United States of America, which builds national borders between people and then defends those borders and national interests with murderous intensity. "Large" is the Catholic Church, which embraces people of all races and nations without regard to Caesar's borders and whose pope believes that he is more important than the president.

With the prevalence of strong temptations for pastors to do something "useful" or "effective," as the world measures these matters, pastors must guard against being surrogate social activists. The pastor ought to spend more effort in equipping the saints to speak truth to power than in being the free-floating, carping social critic. As Acts 2 depicts it, the glory of Pentecost is that the Spirit descended making prophets of the whole church, not just the church's leaders. Now everyone—old men and women, young people, maids, and janitors—are prophets.

Pastors ought not to be distracted from the more mundane and often more difficult work of forming an entire prophetic community in the church by their sometimes more visible and appealing work of roaming about the community and appearing as prophets before the media to pontificate on various "justice issues."[21]

Preacher

I have talked to older pastors who remember the day when ministerial duties consisted of little more than preparing sermons and visiting the sick. In my own denominational tradition, pastors were most often referred to as "preacher." During the last century, pastors, perhaps groping about for some socially approved work to do, took on a host of roles that were new to ministry—coordination of volunteers, management of social service agencies, counseling, financial administration, community activism.

I sense a return to the pastor as preacher as a guiding metaphor of ministry. A major factor in this recovery has been the rediscovery of preaching after the Second Vatican Council in the Roman Catholic Church. In the megachurches of American Protestantism, there is little means for the pastor to be the congregational visitor or the resident counselor when the congregation is made up of over two thousand souls.[22] Furthermore, through the influence of the entertainment industry, there is a lure to the image of pastor as entertainer, as celebrity. Therefore it appears that many pastors, for a mix of good and bad reasons, are returning to the image of the pastor as preacher as the dominate focus of their work—the older "pulpit prince" *redivivus*.

This emphasis upon preaching is not only, in many of its aspects, a historically and theologically defensible role for the pastor, but it is also a good use of the pastor's time. The pastor can be with many parishioners during the course of a week, in a variety of pastoral settings, and not be with as many people in as intentional a way as when the pastor ascends the pulpit to preach on Sunday. Focus on the preaching ministry is simply a wise use of the pastor's time.

The preaching ministry also has a way of keeping the pastor in touch with the basic stuff of the faith—that theological material that is the rationale for all ministry. The pastor who expends much time and effort in preaching is thus kept in contact with the well-springs of the faith, engaging in that pastoral act that tends to provide the theological context for all other acts of ministry.

In my own denomination, where pastors are usually appointed by bishops who have never heard them preach, the preaching ministry can be neglected. There are few obvious rewards for good preaching. Preaching takes time. Most of the labor that goes into sermon preparation is invisible to the congregation. Therefore, the pastor as preacher can be a difficult focal image of ministry to maintain.

Preaching derives part of its power because it is done by *pastors.* The one who stands in the pulpit to speak on Sunday is the one who has been with the flock, in a variety of settings, throughout the week and over the years. The lonely, detached preacher, cloistered away in the pastoral study for much of the week, is not the most fruitful image for faithful preaching. It is the pastor who stands at that fateful intersection between the biblical text and the congregational context, the one who rises each week in service to the congregation's, "Is there any word from the Lord?" A sermon is not a perfectly prepared and delivered oration suitable for later publication. The sermon is an act of corporate worship within the gathered congregation. The pastor engages (in the words of Leander Keck) in "priestly listening," listening to the biblical text on behalf of the congregation, so that the congregation may better hear the text.[23] Therefore, the metaphor of the pastor as preacher is best employed within the context of the pastoral work within a parish where it is clear that the preacher is also pastor.

Servant

Pastors take Jesus as a model for their ministry. At the end of his earthly ministry, Jesus gathered with his disciples at a table for a meal in which Jesus was the host (Luke 22). There, while Jesus was serving them food, "A dispute also arose among them as to which one of them was to be regarded as the greatest" (22:24), a supreme irony considering what Jesus was doing for them at that very moment. Jesus then contrasted the leadership of the Gentiles, who love to lord over people, with that of his followers. "The greatest among you must become like the youngest, and the leader like one who serves. . . . I am among you as one who serves" (22:26-27).

After a popular book by Robert K. Greenleaf, *Servant Leadership: A Journey into the Nature of Legitimate Power and Greatness*, "servant leadership" has become popular as a description of the leadership of pastors.[24] Although the image of pastor as "servant of the servants of God" has much to commend it, recent thought on the pastor as servant has received some severe criticism. Some feminist commentators have charged that the image plays into the hands of a dominant traditional role for women in our society—women as servants of men.[25] Theologian Edward C. Zaragoza has exposed the ways in which the servant leader model often masks a subtle temptation to have authority and power over others while at the same time publicly denying power and authority. Greenleaf's book is not only about service, but also about "power and greatness." Zaragoza reminds us that Jesus told his followers that they were no longer servants, but friends (John 15:12-15).[26] "Servant" is the name Jesus gave to himself and his work on our behalf, not the all-encompassing model for all of his followers.

Manipulation of others can come in many forms. Sometimes the humble servant leader, going about simply serving others, can be a cover for manipulating the laity to serve the servant's needs for adoration, appreciation, and affection. Servant leadership is but the most recent means of centering the effectiveness and power of ministry in the person of the minister, says Zaragoza, rather than in the active work of the Holy Spirit. Servant leadership continues to misunderstand ordained leadership by situating the source of ministry in the person and self-understanding of the pastor rather than in the nature and work of the church.

I confess that I am troubled by the way that Zaragoza seems so willing to dismiss the biblical image of servant in the face of some feminist criticism of the metaphor. Jesus constantly took problematic words like "poor," or "child," or "father," and in his life and teaching reinterpreted those words. His peculiar service was not that of a divine doormat. His subservience was to the truth of God rather than to the dominance of other people. I would be loath to call the service of Dorothy Day, leader of the Catholic Worker movement, that of servility to culturally controlled attitudes about women.[27]

A better basis for our ministry, asserts Zaragoza, is the Trinity—that free, self-communication of a God who is constantly reaching out to humanity, constantly seeking to make us friends. The Trinity is our recognition that God exists as community and mutuality in the three persons of the Trinity, not as master-servant. Yet despite the difficulties of the metaphor of servant, as Maria Harris says, the concept of ministry as servanthood "remains critical in the life of the church and a constitutive part of the Gospel."[28]

A Fitting Metaphor for Our Ministry Today

Gregory and Basil, the great Cappadocian fathers, were childhood friends during the mid- to late-fourth century. Gregory was by inclination a retiring personality, fleeing when his father insisted that he become ordained. During the struggle with the Arians, he was forced out of the monastic life and eventually became a bishop who championed the Orthodox cause through his brilliant preaching. Yet in his letters he constantly complains about the distracting and sordid politics that are required to be an active leader of the church.

Basil, on the other hand, was a man of action, a decidedly activist bishop who not only relished running his episcopate but also founded many hospitals and orphanages. He reorganized the administration of the church and even reformed the liturgy, a liturgy still in use in the Orthodox churches. Although he was also a great preacher, his tireless work in the face of severe political pressure greatly contributed to the eventual triumph of Orthodoxy over Arianism.

My point, in recounting the examples of Basil and Gregory, is to remind us that the Christian ministry is heir to a rich legacy of patterns for leadership. Each of us is suited, by inclination, to certain patterns. Scripture has a rich diversity of church leaders. Different ages call forth different styles of leadership. There is therefore no single and normative style or focus for pastoral work. My impression is that contemporary ministry is groping for an appropriate metaphor for our pastoral work. Perhaps there has always been a certain tension in the guiding images for what we do. It is the nature of the Christian ministry to be multifaceted and multidimensional. The gospel does not change, but the contexts in which the gospel is preached and enacted *do* change. A predominate pastoral image that might have been fruitful in one age may not be so in the next.

I would venture these generalizations in regard to the guiding images of our ministerial work today:

1. Because the Christian ministry is significantly *countercultural*, at some odds with the predominate culture, including the very first cultures of Israel and Rome in which we found ourselves, we must guard against styles of Christian leadership that are essentially accommodationist. To be sure, we can never escape our culture. Yet all cultures stand under the judgment of God, including the "culture" called *the church*. Therefore, pastors ought always to expect some dissonance, a degree of abrasion with the culture—both social and congregational—in which they work. In attempting to be "relevant" to the world, we have sometimes been guilty of offering the world little that the world could not have had through purely secular leadership. First Peter 2:11 encourages us to live "as aliens and exiles." I believe that the contemporary North American church finds itself in a situation akin to exile, missionaries in the very culture that we thought we had created and made safe for Christianity. Therefore, I find much to be commended in the image of the pastor as a missionary, or more accurately, a lead missionary or equipper of the missionaries. We are no longer keeping house in an essentially hospitable and receptive culture, if we ever were. The African American church could tell the rest of us a thing or two about what it means to live as "strangers in a strange land." Today, even those of us pastors in mainline Protestantism are beginning to feel like the leaders of an outpost, an enclave of an alien culture

within a majority, non-Christian culture.[29] I therefore predict more of a pastor's time will be spent in the education, formation, and enculturation of the members of the congregation to be people who know how to analyze the corrosive acids within the surrounding and essentially indifferent—at times openly hostile—dominant culture. More of our efforts will need to be expended in giving our people the means to resist, to live by, and to creatively communicate the gospel in a world where Christians are a cognitive minority.[30] Just the other day I was talking with a pastor who has formed a "Public School Teachers' Prayer Breakfast" for the teachers in his congregation. At this weekly breakfast, the teachers present case studies from their work that challenge their Christian faith. They share a meal, have prayer, and venture forth better equipped to live their faith in the public-school setting.

2. There is much to be said for the pastor being educated in the *classical forms of Christian ministry.* The church has much experience as a minority movement. We need to draw from that experience today. In that regard, I predict a recovery of the classical shape of ministry: to teach, to preach, and to evangelize through *the ministries of Word, sacrament, and order.* I sense the end of a proliferation of ministerial duties and a reclamation of the essential classical tasks of Christian ministry. Because so many of our people have not been well formed in the faith, pastors must now stress doctrine, the classical texts of our faith, our master narratives, the great themes. The culture is no longer a prop for the church. If we are going to make Christians, we must have a new determination to inculcate the faith.[31] In some ways our age parallels that of the Reformation, in which the church was faced with a vast undereducated, uninformed, unformed laity and clergy. Pastors must be prepared to lead in catechesis, moral formation, and the regeneration of God's people.[32]

3. We need a *continuing critical assessment* of our present needs within each of our denominational families. Jackson W. Carroll has cited research that shows how different denominations appear to value different qualities in their pastoral leaders. For instance, it appears that Presbyterians desire thoughtful, well-informed, scholarly pastors, whereas United Methodists value interpersonal skills and personal warmth in their clergy.[33] We pastors ought not uncritically accept the ethos of our denominations. We must join with the

laity in asking, Are we in need of managers or leaders, or some creative combination of both? Is our church most in need of reconcilers of warring factions, or do we need those who can provoke conflict, change, and renewal? Do we need those who help keep the present system functioning, or do we need those who enter the fray in order to disrupt the present system? My hunch is that my particular ecclesiastical family is in dire need of the latter. We are a graying, moribund, overly organized system that badly needs disruption from new ideas, younger people, and greater attentiveness to the leadership of the Holy Spirit. When I entered the ministry, much was being said of the pastor as "enabler"—the one who humbly stands in the wings, coaxing the laity out onto the stage of ministry, giving them the tools that they need to be in ministry. Although I had difficulty being humble or waiting patiently in the wings, I was much attracted to this image of the pastor. I eventually learned that the enabler metaphor presumed a well-formed, potentially powerful church—a church full of people who knew what they were to do as disciples if only they had the leaders to provide them proper motivation and encouragement. The churches that I served seemed to me anything but that. They were full of people hanging on for dear life, tentative, unsteady; needing, I thought, a pastor to step out and model for them the moves of ministry. They needed more than reticent "servant leadership" (a more contemporary variation of this theme).

I noted that in congregations of my acquaintance where there was strong lay leadership, there was often quite strong pastoral leadership as well. The laity seemed to be energized, evoked by the ministry of a strong pastor, rather than intimidated. One of the skills needed for the future ministry of the ordained will be the constant ability to be critical—to be diagnostic of the present context for clerical leadership—and adaptive to the particular needs of the church in our particular time and place. More of our pastoral time, in this missionary situation, will be spent in catechesis, the formation of Christians who have the equipment they need to survive as Christians.

I was invited to preach in a congregation being led by a friend of mine. The church is a predominantly African American congregation, located in one of the poorest parts of the city. I arrived at the service a few minutes before eleven on Sunday. We did not really begin until a quarter after the hour. Then we had four anthems by the choir, assorted praise songs with the congregation, spirituals, and *two* offerings. I did not begin to preach until just after noon. After I preached, my friend had "just a few things to add," which took us until nearly one o'clock. After the service, standing in the parking lot, I asked my friend, "Why do your people take so long to worship?"

He laughed and replied, "Why does worship take our folk so long? Well, I'll explain it this way. Male unemployment is running about 20 percent in this neighborhood; young adult unemployment is higher. That means that when my people get on the street, everything they hear is, 'You are nothing. You don't have a big car or a great job. You are nobody.' So I get them in here on a Sunday and, through the words of the hymns, the prayers, the sermon, the Scripture, I try to say, 'That's a lie. You are royalty. You are God's own people. You were bought with a price.' It takes me about two hours to get their heads straight."

I predict that more of us pastors will need more time to get our congregations' heads straight. In the book of Acts, as the church is experiencing its first days, there is a need for a critical assessment of the leadership needs of the church.

> Now in these days when the disciples were increasing in number, the Hellenists murmured against the Hebrews because their widows were neglected in the daily distribution. And the twelve summoned the body of the disciples and said, "It is not right that we should give up preaching the word of God to serve tables. Therefore, brethren, pick out from among you seven men of good repute, full of the Spirit and of wisdom, whom we may appoint to this duty. But we will devote ourselves to prayer and to the ministry of the word." And what they said pleased the whole multitude, and they chose Stephen, a man full of faith and of the Holy Spirt, and Philip. . . . These they set before the apostles, and they prayed and laid their hands upon them. (Acts 6:1-6 RSV)

The Spirit-led community is willing to adapt and innovate in order to be obedient to the Spirit's leadings. Distribution to the widows, a growing group with the persecution of the church in Acts, has become unmanageable. The apostles do not disparage such distributive work, rather it is their concern that it be done efficiently that necessitates a new order of Christian leadership. Though Luke does not use the word *deacon*, this does seem to be an account of the origins of the diaconate. Christian leadership arises from what needs to be done within the Christian community, and is involved in such mundane activity as that which Luke describes.

However, leadership is a gift, thus the church prays as it lays on hands (Acts 6:6), a sign that leadership is the result of God's continuing graciousness toward the community. That all of those chosen have Greek names may imply that leadership is being drawn from the ranks of the oppressed, those on the bottom of the social order, who ought to know best from personal experience how to care for those in need. One of those chosen will, in the next episode in Acts, lead with his life. Stephen is the first martyr, embodying in his death, and in his forgiveness of his killers, the death of Jesus (Acts 6:8–7:59).

Stephen reminds us that leadership in the church is cruciform. It is also eschatological, a matter of what God is doing more than what we ought to do. The cross and resurrection of Jesus serve as a critique of all our models of ministry. For us to adequately embody the risk and the obedience of the cross, the shock and the power of the Resurrection, we pastors must be willing to forsake and to embrace all our models of ministry for the good of Christ and his church. It is well for pastors to struggle for appropriate, biblically sanctioned metaphors and focal images for pastoral work. The struggle to be transformed by Christ rather than conformed to the dominant culture is a constant one for pastors. We work in the confidence that God is able to give us the gifts and graces needed for ministry in our time and place.

CHAPTER THREE

The Pastor as Priest: The Leadership of Worship

When, in the beginning of Acts, just after the risen Christ has promised his followers that "you shall receive power when the Holy Spirit has come upon you; and you shall be my witnesses in Jerusalem and in all Judea and Samaria and to the end of the earth" (Acts 1:8 RSV), the first thing the disciples do is gather in an upper room. There, they engage in what some might regard as a pious triviality. "All these with one accord devoted themselves to prayer" (Acts 1:14 RSV).

After so stirring a promise of pentecostal power, and spread of their witness into all the world, one might have expected a more activist, pragmatic response from the apostles. Is this any way for the Jesus revolution to begin? Apparently, the activism demanded of the church is something more than mere breathless busyness and strenuous human effort. These are the disciples who have been told that they ought to "pray always and not to lose heart" (Luke 18:1). Prayer is a major activity of the church in Acts, an act that is primary to all other activity, the source of the church's power to witness in word and deed to what has happened in the world because of Jesus Christ. Prayer is not so much an "activity" as a way of life for the church. We worship God, not for utilitarian or pragmatic purposes, but rather because we have been loved. God, being God, is to be adored, not used. We do not worship God in order to get things from God, though in worship we often experience the grace of God in ways too wonderful for words. Worship is a way of being in love. As Marva Dawn so well puts this matter of Christian worship, it is "a royal waste of time."[1]

In worship, says Luther, the Holy Spirit "calls, gathers, enlightens, and sanctifies the whole Christian Church on earth, and keeps it with Jesus Christ in the one true faith."[2] *Lex orandi, lex credendi*, the rule of prayer is the rule of belief; this is how the church has historically prioritized its work. Our praying precedes our believing;

75

our liturgical work on Sunday is prior to our theological reflection and the lives we live on Monday. Liturgy means literally, in the Greek, "the work of the people." Our worship in the church is a prelude to and the source of our work in the world. When the pastor presides at the Lord's Table in divine service, the pastor is visibly signifying the source of all the pastor's work in the congregation. Therefore, liturgical leadership is the round for all ministry.

Pentecost means not only the miracle of ecstatic, strange speech and hearing, but also the miracle of corporate worship:

> And day by day, attending the temple together and breaking bread in their homes, they partook of food with glad and generous hearts, praising God and having favor with all the people. And the Lord added to their number day by day those who were being saved. (Acts 2:46-47 RSV)

The charge against Jesus, in Luke's Gospel, was that "this man receives sinners and eats with them" (Luke 15:2 RSV). That charge is well documented in all the Gospels in the many meals where Jesus is a guest, and the last meal where Jesus is host. Now, in Acts, the meals with Jesus and sinners continue as a visible sign that the prophetic promise, uttered by Isaiah, is now being fulfilled. When the Messiah came, there would be a great feast of the Lord for all the hungry and dispossessed:

> Ho, every one who thirsts,
>   come to the waters;
> and he who has no money . . .
> Come, buy wine and milk
>   without money and without price.
> (Isa. 55:1 RSV)

The great signal that the long-promised messianic age has begun is Jesus' table fellowship. The Kingdom begins where the hungry are being blessed and filled (Luke 6:21). His high priesthood (Hebrews) is most vivid as he serves as host at the table for the hungering and thirsting. Our priesthood is likewise most vivid as we preside, in his name, at the table.

A Pattern for Sunday Worship

Here is one of the earliest accounts, outside of glimpses inferred from those passages in Acts (20:7) and some of Paul's Letters such as First Corinthians, of the church at worship on Sunday. This is from the *First Apology of Justin Martyr,* a portrait of the church about A.D. 90:

> [1] On the day which is called Sunday, all who live in the cities or in the countryside gather together in one place. [2] And the memoirs of the apostles or the writings of the prophets are read as long as there is time. [3] Then, when the reader has finished, the president, in a discourse, admonishes and invites the people to practice these examples of virtue. [4] Then we all stand up together and offer prayers. [5] And, as we mentioned before, when we have finished the prayer, bread is presented, and wine with water; [6] the president likewise offers up prayers and thanksgivings according to his ability, and the people assent by saying, Amen. [7] The elements which have been "eucharistized" are distributed and received by each one; and they are sent to the absent by the deacons. Those who are prosperous, if they wish, contribute what each one deems appropriate; and the collection is deposited with the president; and he takes care of the orphans and widows, and those who are needy because of sickness or other cause, and the captives, and the strangers who sojourn amongst us—in brief, he is the curate of all who are in need.[3]

We detect here a basic pattern for the church's Sunday gatherings. At this point in our history, there is no set ritual of words. Rather, there is a set pattern of actions. Moving through Sunday, as Justin describes it, we see these common acts:

1. *The church gathers.* As we noted earlier, one of the earliest designations of the church is *ekklesia*, the "called out." There is a difference between the church and the world. The church is the church by virtue of the vocation of God to, at least in our worship, "come out . . . and be separate" (2 Cor. 6:17). Christian worship has about it an exclusive quality, for the danger is not godlessness, but idolatry. We gather as those who have been summoned to worship "in spirit and in truth" (John 4:24).

2. *The church remembers* by encountering the "writings"—the Scriptures that evoke, form, and critique the church. At this point

in the liturgy, the Service of the Word, the service of Christians is remarkably similar to gatherings in the synagogue (a word that means literally, "the gathering"), which were decidedly services of the Word. In the synagogue, Israel gathered around its sacred writings for proclamation, recollection, study, and teaching.

3. *The church listens and then speaks.* At some point, the sacred writings are enacted, contemporized, contextualized, expounded by the "presider," as the church moves from reading to speaking, from listening to interpretation.

4. *The church prays;* interceding to God for the needs of the church and the world. All of the church's listening to Scripture and to preaching moves the church toward responsive speaking to God in prayer. The church shares in Christ's high priestly ministry of intercession to God for the world (John 17).

5. *The church offers;* giving back to God from the bounty of gifts that God has given us. Here, the material becomes spiritual, the daily stuff of life is given liturgical significance, the produce of our hands is sanctified, and bread and wine are laid upon the table as a sign of the sacramentalizing of all of life.

6. *The church gives thanks;* "eucharistizing" the offering, that is, giving thanks (*eucharistia*, "thanksgiving") to God. Israel has a theologically reflective mode of "think-thank." At the gathering of the people of God, God's people think of all the ways that God has blessed and is blessing them, through the mighty acts of God in the past, through the mundane acts of beneficence in daily life. In remembering God's graciousness, we thank God as we enact the whole sweep of the story of our salvation. All of life becomes sacramental, a means of grace, bearer of the holy through God's gracious acts and our gratitude. Our custom of saying grace before meals is a gift of Israel. In this faith, one need not, like Moses, go up some sacred mountaintop to meet God. God is to be encountered in grateful remembrance at the daily dinner table when we give thanks. Something so ordinary, so mundane as bread, becomes the very presence of Christ, the bread of heaven that is the bread of life.

7. *The church distributes the gifts of God* to the people. The church shares a meal together in the name of Christ. Remembering all of the times that Jesus ate and drank with sinners, enacting the kingdom of God through the shared gracious meal, the church eats and

drinks with Jesus as a sign of God's inbreaking kingdom. Christian worship is inherently sacramental, symbiotic of the stuff of every-day life. Here, in the Communion, is the church's most vivid, most beloved and frequent experience of the presence of Christ, our fore-taste of the "Communion of the Saints," of that great banquet table promised when God's kingdom has come in its fullness.

8. *The church scatters into the world.* The church that gathers, lis-tens, and prays, is nourished not in order to keep that nourishment closed within the church. The church is strengthened and enlivened in order that the church might scatter into the world as salt, light, God's heralds of a new order, bearers of an invitation to a new social configuration called the kingdom of God.

Justin's pattern for Sunday seems to be an amplification of the earlier account in Acts where "they devoted themselves to the apostles' teaching and fellowship, to the breaking of bread and the prayers" (Acts 2:42). This is the normal, catholic (i.e., universal) Sunday pattern for the majority of the world's Christians since the earliest days of the church.[4] Let us take these eight acts of ministry, as gleaned from Justin's account of Sunday, and draw out from them insights for the role of the pastor as priest. Because Justin's account is the norm, the basic historic shape for Sunday worship throughout the church, throughout the ages, we detect here a basic shape of Christian ministry. The acts within this pattern remind us that here is a normative shape for all pastoral work, not just on Sunday when we preside at the Lord's Table, but in all forms of ministry.

A Pattern for Priestly Ministry

How does the pattern inform the priestly ministry of pastors?

1. The pastor is the one who, in the name of Christ, leads the church by gathering the congregation, calling out people from their other social attachments to be members of this distinctive group. In a mobile society, there is some reason to believe that this particular pastoral function needs special attention. Although the church is not an escape from the world, it is not *of* the world. There will be a necessary separation from the world in order that the church may be constituted, attentive, and submissive to the church's account of what is happening in the world in the light of the gospel.

Sometimes the church is accused of archaic escapism because we withdraw from the "real," everyday, workaday world into the antique dream world of the church. No. The church withdraws from what the world calls "real" in order to better discern the world as God intends—the new heaven and new earth (Rev. 21:1) of which the church is the foretaste, a world more "real" than what the world calls reality, that which C. S. Lewis once called, "the great divorce."

Reality, the world as intended by God in Creation, is now taking visible form in the re-creation called the church. God is by nature communal, mutual, as we learn God's nature as Trinity. God's world is therefore inherently communal. The earliest apostles, after Pentecost, "devoted themselves to the apostles' teaching and fellowship, to the breaking of bread and the prayers" (Acts 2:42). Fellowship, *koinonia*, is a principle criterion for worship that is truly Christian. In 1 Corinthians, Paul tells the Corinthians that their congregational divisions have negated the power of the Lord's Supper, telling them, "When you meet together, it is not the Lord's supper that you eat. For in eating, each one goes ahead with his own meal, and one is hungry and another is drunk" (1 Cor. 11:20 RSV). Interestingly, Paul does not tell them that it is not the Lord's Supper because they have not followed proper ritual or failed to say the right words. Rather, it is not the Lord's Supper, the *kurakon diepnon*, but the *idion diepnon*, "your own supper," that they eat because of their sinful social divisions at the table. They thereby profane the body and blood of the Lord (11:27). For Paul, the Body of Christ is none other than the church gathered about the table. To profane that Body with divisions is nothing less than an offense against Christ and that which makes a mockery of Christian worship.

I recall a fierce debate that erupted at an ecumenical gathering of clergy when it was suggested that we end the gathering by celebrating Holy Communion. Some objected to this intercommunion saying, "My church has a very high theology of the Eucharist and therefore I am not allowed to partake with those who are members of churches where there is a low eucharistic theology. I have such a high view of the Eucharist that I cannot celebrate the meal with those who have another theology of the sacrament."

But based upon Paul's corporeal reading of the Lord's Supper, it would seem that a "high" view of the Eucharist is that view that stresses the unity of Christians about the table of Christ. A "low" eucharistic theology is that which uses the table to draw lines of division between Christians.

My sense is that pastors will need to expend more of their pastoral energies, in a rootless, mobile society, pondering the requirements for truly Christian *koinonia*. On Sunday, those elements of worship, those rituals that help unite us, are to be emphasized. Those that fragment and isolate believers from one another are to be avoided. Individual glasses of wine at Communion, individual bits of bread, individual worshipers in silent meditation, solos rather than congregational hymns, are all questionable acts of communal worship in the light of this *koinonia* principle. Indeed, private meditation is best on other days, in other services of worship. Sunday is a day to get together, and the pastor, as the leader of worship, bears primary responsibility for gathering the church.

2. The church is a community gathered around the story of God in Jesus Christ as recounted in Scripture. The pastor bears the chief burden of lifting up that story to the church on a weekly basis, to "open the Scriptures" to those who, in baptism, are called to align their lives to this story. We will say more about this crucial pastoral task in our reflection upon the pastor as interpreter of Scripture and the pastor as preacher. For now, let us note that the normative scriptural encounter for the church is in Sunday worship. Think of the church as primarily a place where we are taught to read in a way that is Christian. Christian reading of Scripture ought to be communal, public, in the context of those who prepare for the challenges of faithful reading by confession of sin, by forgiveness, by praise, and by daring to read in common with fellow Christians, including the saints down through the ages. All of this is necessary for the arduous task of listening to God's Word in a world where we are taught to submit to no other word than that which is contemporary (literally, "with the times") and self-derived.

I love the way that among some Anglicans, at the time of the reading of the Gospel, the Scripture is borne into the congregation in the Gospel Procession. I think that the lessons ought to be read by a layperson, thus signifying the Word dwelling in us richly (Col. 3:16), having its way in the congregation.

The oral reading of Scripture, within the congregation, is a special ministry that ought to be entrusted to those who have gifts for oral reading. In simply hearing the Word read aloud, within the Body of Christ, Scripture is being interpreted, is thriving in its native habitat. The main justification for using the Common Lectionary with its three-year cycle of readings from the Old Testament, Gospels, and Epistles is that God's people ought to hear the full sweep of God's Word read aloud on Sunday.

3. Scripture is interpreted, proclaimed, and expounded upon. Scripture for us is not some passive, inanimate object. Scripture is meant to speak, to transform. The church's contemporary interpretation of Scripture is our continuing attempt to embody Scripture, not only to understand the Bible, but also to stand under the Bible. The church does not sit passively and quietly, merely receiving the Word, the church works with the Word, prays for the power of the Holy Spirit rightly, not only to revere, but also to embody the Word. Jesus, tempted in the wilderness, tells Satan that we are meant to live not by bread alone, but also "by every word that proceeds from the mouth of God" (Matt. 4:4 RSV). Jesus' words are themselves a demonstration of the power of Israel's encounter with the Word, for the words Jesus uses to resist Satan are not original with him, but are his citation of Israel's testimony, a testimony known by heart by those schooled in the synagogue. "It is written. . . ." Through such inculcation of the Word—handed down from generation to generation, lovingly repeated to the young, recalled by the church in different times and contexts, the whole process enlivened by the Holy Spirit—the church receives its life. As preacher, the pastor bears the responsibility of embodying Jesus' great (and not altogether well received!) announcement in the synagogue in Nazareth, "Today this scripture has been fulfilled in your hearing" (Luke 4:21).

4. It is as if all that has preceded, in gathering around the Word and in listening to the Word read and proclaimed, has prepared the church for the rest of the service. All of the church's work and worship could be construed as response to the Word read, heard, and proclaimed. Having listened to God, the church now joins in Christ's high priestly ministry and dares to speak to God in prayer. As is sometimes the custom to say as we begin to pray the Lord's Prayer, "We are bold to say, 'Our Father. . . .' " Of course the pastor

is not the only one in the church who may address God in prayer, but when the pastor prays, the pastor prays on behalf of, and at the authorization of, the whole church. The pastor's prayers, particularly in common worship on Sunday, ought to be clearly communal, informed by the prayers of the saints down through the ages, cognizant of all those concerns and needs felt throughout the church, not only in the congregation, but at all times and places.

Whereas prayer is the church's speech to God and not to the congregation, it is undeniable that the pastor teaches the congregation about prayer in the pastor's leadership of the Sunday prayers. Do our prayers ever reach beyond the confines of our congregation? Have we prayed for our enemies? Are our prayers only petition, or do they also include confession, praise, adoration, thanksgiving, and the full range of notes that we find in biblical prayer, such as in the psalter, the prayer book, and hymnbook of Israel? The pastor's ministry of public prayer will be based in great part on the pastor's own prayer life, the pastor's continual practice of the presence of God in prayer. In prayer, the pastor does most explicitly and publicly what a pastor does throughout the week—lift the congregation and its needs, the world and its needs, before the throne of God. Thus the pastor's leadership of prayer is a wonderfully formative aspect of the pastor's total ministry. Our pastoral leadership ought to have as its goal the enabling of the congregation to speak and to listen to God. Pastoral prayer on Sunday ought to be more like a hymn than a sermon. Note that Justin says, "We all stand up together and offer prayers."

5. When the church offers its gifts to God in the offering, the church is engaging in much the same activity that ought to characterize the prayers of the church. Here is the church's oblation, that laying of ourselves upon God's altar. When the offering is received, Christian worship becomes very material, incarnational. This faith does not demean the labors of human hands, does not detach itself from the material and the bodily. Serving a Savior who entered the flesh and dwelt among us (John 1), the church sanctifies the fleshly and the material by asking God to transform our possessions and achievements into God's gifts.

On the Sunday after Easter, the lectionary has us read this portrait of life in the post-Easter church:

> Now the company of those who believed were of one heart and soul, and no one said that any of the things which he possessed was his own, but they had everything in common. And with great power the apostles gave their testimony to the resurrection of the Lord Jesus, and great grace was upon them all. There was not a needy person among them, for as many as were possessors of lands or houses sold them, and brought the proceeds of what was sold and laid it at the apostles' feet; and distribution was made to each as any had need. (Acts 4:32-35 RSV)

Here is the church's strongest visible evidence of the truth of resurrection—a resurrected community in which old, deadly economic and social arrangements have been overturned. Here is truly "testimony to the resurrection" in this transformed people. Here is the world recreated as God meant it to be, where "there was not a needy person among them," and all things are seen as gifts entrusted to us by God rather than possessions to be tightly grasped. Each Sunday's offering is meant to be a revolutionary, countercultural, and prophetic act for the church. There are few more inflammatory and potentially disruptive acts than when the pastor stands and announces to the congregation that it is now time for the offering. Here embodied before the congregation on Sunday is what the pastor ought to be doing all week—demanding that we give God what is rightly God's, that we show that our money is where our hearts are (Matt. 6:21), and that by God's grace we are able to feel the needs of someone other than ourselves, that we are being transformed from takers into givers, that we give material, visible, monetary testimony to the Resurrection.

At the conclusion of his speech to the Ephesian elders, Paul speaks of the centrality of oblation in the leadership of the church:

> In all things I have shown you that by so toiling one must help the weak, remembering the words of the Lord Jesus, how he said, "It is more blessed to give than to receive." (Acts 20:35 RSV)

Paul spoke these words on his way to make his own "oblation" in offering his life for Christ in martyrdom in Rome.

The offering is a prophetic, deeply revealing activity in our worship. Early in my ministry, our church sought to raise a large amount of money to build a service center for the poor in our city.

We engaged a church fund-raiser to help us manage the campaign. At his first meeting with me, he asked me to make a list of the top twenty givers in the congregation, along with a list of those who were not giving up to their potential. Taking offense, I told him that I was proud that I knew nothing of the specific giving patterns of my congregation. He replied, "That is irresponsible. You are the pastor. If I were to ask you to name the ten model marriages in your congregation, or the ten marriages in the most trouble, couldn't you tell me?"

I answered that I could.

"Well, Jesus put much stress upon the potential dangers of money. You ought to hold up before your congregation the opportunity to respond to Jesus' teachings upon wealth."

Wealth is a spiritual issue in the New Testament. In Acts, Judas betrays Jesus for cash (1:18), Paul and Silas are jailed when they interfere with business among the Philippians (16:16-24), and the silversmiths of Ephesus riot when the gospel disrupts their income (19:23-41). The congregation at Antioch sends famine relief to the impoverished in Judea (11:19-30). No wonder Antioch was the first place we were called "Christians" (11:26).

In Acts 16 we meet Lydia, a rich woman who opens her heart to the gospel and her home to the church. Throughout Acts, the wealthier members of the church give to those who have less (2:44-45; 4:32-35). Cornelius, first Gentile convert, is presented as a philanthropist (10:2). By the way, if pastors are to be "examples to the flock," as we noted in chapter 1, then our stewardship, our financial commitment to the work of the congregation, ought to be exemplary.

At this point in the service, with the offering, the Christian faith appears more material than spiritual, and well it should. Jesus wants all of us. In calling for and in receiving the offering on Sunday, in placing the gifts of the people upon the altar of God, I am participating in one of the most prophetic of pastoral tasks.

6. The church remembers God, recollecting the mighty acts of God, in its prayer of thanksgiving. Our worship is responsive, our fitting response to the actions of a gracious God. In making Eucharist, in giving thanks, the church names the source of the blessings of this life, narrates the story of our salvation, and proclaims to the world who is in charge and where history is heading.

The priest is the one who keeps pointing the congregation to the presence of Christ in our midst; keeps narrating our lives in a manner quite different from that of the world. The world tells us that we are our own creations, that we are masters of our fate, captains of our souls. The church offers a counteraccount of what is going on in the world that helps us see our lives as part of the adventure of God become flesh, the story of our salvation, the story which, in the very telling of it, is our salvation. Historic eucharistic prayers narrate the full sweep of salvation, beginning with Genesis and going all the way toward the acclamation, "Christ has died, Christ is risen, Christ will come again!" In a consumerist society, doxology becomes one of the most radical, countercultural activities of the church. Our possessions are not ours. All that we have has come as a gift—a trust—from God. Even something so ordinary as bread becomes, in the light of the prayer of thanksgiving, a sign, signal, sacrament of the full sweep of God's saving love for us. Jesus was only doing at the table with his disciples that which he did in teaching, healing, and dying on our behalf. Every time we make Eucharist we take back some enemy territory in the name of Christ. We pastors give the congregation training in viewing all of their lives as sacramental, as that sphere where even something so ordinary as bread and wine can be a vehicle of God's revelation, Christ's very presence.

7. The church eats together in the name of Jesus. The great high moment of this movement's worship is a communal meal among friends. The priest serves as a representative of the host, Jesus. A good model for the demeanor of the one who leads Christian worship is that of the gracious host at a meal. To be a pastor is to be the person who invites people to eat and drink with Jesus and with those whom Jesus has invited to his table. The pastor who practices the gestures of hospitality at the Lord's Supper then keeps inviting, keeps opening the congregation to new participants, keeps welcoming people to the feast of God in evangelistic graciousness. A church where members walk to worship past homeless people asking for food ought to see what a gift God has given us—to enable us to recover the church as a place where the poor are fed at the Table of the Lord. The Eucharist is a foretaste of what God intends to do for the poor always, in God's promised kingdom. Church is an invitation to the table.

In that curious sea journey toward the end of Acts (Acts 27), after fourteen days of darkness and horrible seas, before his terrified shipmates, Paul takes charge. Just about dawn, Paul reassures those on board and urges them to take food. Then Paul takes bread, blesses bread, breaks bread, and gives bread to those on board. In this familiar fourfold action—this eucharistic gesture of taking, blessing, breaking, and giving bread—Paul feeds the frightened multitudes in much the same way that Jesus fed the multitudes before him. Whether Luke meant this as the Eucharist or not, it is clear that this meal at sea is meant to remind the church of the heart of its witness at the table. A new day is breaking. The church stands at dawn, a new creation, as we break bread in the darkness, in the storm, in order for there to be a new day for the sake of the world.

Wondrous transformation is God's gift at the Eucharist. The gifts of God—bread and wine—are transformed as signs of Christ's real presence among us. The church—ordinary people of flesh and blood—is changed into the Body of Christ. Women and men are transformed into Christ's ministers in the world. A meal of only bread and wine becomes a stunning victory banquet for God's triumphant kingdom. As is prayed in the *Epiclesis* (that portion of the prayer that invokes the Holy Spirit) in the prayer of thanksgiving:

> Pour out your Holy Spirit on us gathered here,
>   and on these gifts of bread and wine.
> Make them be for us the body and blood of Christ,
>   that we may be for the world the body of Christ,
>   redeemed by his blood.
> By your Spirit make us one with Christ,
>   one with each other,
>   and one in ministry to all the world,
> until Christ comes in final victory
>   and we feast at his heavenly banquet.[5]

As we have noted, the church in Acts concerned itself with the efficient and fair distribution of the offered gifts to those in need within the congregation (Acts 6). The ministry of pastoral administration has its roots here. Administration with integrity, honesty, efficiency, and compassion is also an act of worship, a mode of ministry that flows from the church's ancient concern for faithful distribution of the gifts that have been given to God.

8. The church, having gathered, having listened to the Word read and proclaimed, having prayed to God on behalf of itself and the world, and having been strengthened by the sharing of a meal with Jesus, now scatters into the world. The church gathers, listens, prays, is nourished, not in order to stay forever at church. The purpose of church is not to hunker down with people like us behind our theological barricades. Jesus has commanded us to, "go therefore and make disciples of all nations..." (Matt. 28:19). Admittedly, most of Acts appears more concerned with the church's scattering than with its gathering. The Word of God spreads like wildfire throughout the world by the work of a group of energetic apostles who will talk with anyone, anywhere, anytime. As Acts shows, you have to kill an apostle to shut him or her up. In the great persecution that ravaged the church after the death of Stephen, "they were all scattered throughout the region of Judea and Samaria" (Acts 8:1 RSV), the church's very life was under threat. Yet even then, "Now those who were scattered went about preaching the word" (Acts 8:4). One might think that the persecuted church would keep its head down, hide for safety, and keep quiet. But not this church. Even some evil such as persecution becomes itself an occasion for the goodness of God because of the church's willingness to speak. Thus begins the evangelistic thrust into Samaria; thus there was "much joy" even among the once excluded Samaritans (Acts 8:8). This church loves to scatter.

The pastor nourishes the church so that the church might move beyond the confines of the congregation, might be in the world proclaiming the Word in word and deed. Although the pastor's priestly ministry means that the pastor's primary duty will be within the congregation, equipping the saints for the work of ministry in the world, the pastor's work will not be exclusively there. The pastor, like all Christians, is to be in the world as witness, evangelist, missionary, and apostle, enjoying the inventiveness of God's determination to get back the world. Of course, the church and the world are not neatly divided. There is much "world" within the church on any Sunday morning, so the pastor need not look far in order to encounter the world. The line between church and world cuts through our own hearts.

Our scattering into the world in the name of Christ is our great act of confidence in the power of the gospel. The gospel is able to hold its own, even to triumph in confrontation and conflict with the world. We need not protect Jesus from the world, for the world is his and he intends to have it all. A friend of mine who teaches religion in a public university says that, in teaching theology to students, he must first overcome the notion that theology has to do with religion, with spiritual things. No, he tells them, theology deals with *everything*. Our model ought to be the church in Acts, a church that is unafraid to make its testimony before the authorities, religious and political, unafraid to scatter throughout the world in the name of Christ.[6] And God will finally have what belongs to God.

> "See, the home of God is among mortals.
> He will dwell with them;
> they will be his peoples,
> and God himself will be with them."
>
> (Rev. 21:3)

Philip's encounter with the Ethiopian occurs because Philip is obedient to the angel's order to go, of all places, to the desert, at of all times, noon, the most hostile time of the day (Acts 8:26-40). Philip speaks to the Ethiopian, who immediately asks to be baptized. Of course, Philip is not working alone. Already the Holy Spirit, which has summoned Philip out to the desert, has prepared the way for him in the heart of the Ethiopian. The church ventures nowhere that the Holy Spirit has not preceded us.

Thus the pastor's priestly ministry is a necessary rehearsal of the church's mission to go into all the world. Through our ministry at the altar, we pastors are reminded of who we are and the source of our authority, the ultimate goal of our ministry: that we all might feast with the risen Christ here on earth, today; that we might feast with him in eternity, forever.

As Karl Barth puts it, all ministries are essentially prompting in praise:

> All ministries, whether of speech or action, are performed well to the extent, that they all participate in the praise of God. The praise of God which constitutes the community and its assembly, seeks

to bend and commit and therefore to express, well up and surge in concert. The Christian community sings from inner material necessity. What we can and must say quite confidently is that the community that does not sing is not the community.[7]

In all acts of ministry the pastor is priest, the one who constantly looks for ways in which all of our meetings with one another might also be meeting with the living Christ, in which every activity of the church might be sacramental, a means of grace, a human act whereby we sign, signal, and point to the outbreak of the kingdom of God among us.[8] The church thus wants all of its life to mirror Sunday, and we as pastors ought to want all of our pastoral activity to be priestly, the mediation of God to humanity, the representation of humanity to God.[9]

A Catholic priest, in a large and sprawling suburban parish, began his Sunday worship saying, "First, let's all introduce ourselves to one another. Turn to those who are seated near you and tell them who you are and find out who they are, for it would be a great shame to gather and not meet one another."

There was pandemonium as the congregation greeted one another. When their greeting was subsiding, the priest said to them, "Of course, it would be an even greater shame for us to gather and not meet God!"

The place exploded in exuberant praise.[10]

CHAPTER FOUR

The Priest as Pastor: Worship as the Content and Context of Pastoral Care

He does some critique of a therapeutic culture here

We have noted that the "Service of the Lord's Day" in Justin Martyr's account ends with food being gathered by the deacons and taken to those who are in need. Acts reports that creative leadership adaptation whereby seven are chosen as the first deacons to ensure that none of the widows are "neglected in the daily distribution of food" (Acts 6:1-5). There is thus from the first a link between our worship and work, the work of the people of God on Sunday and their work throughout the week, the pastor's leadership at the Lord's Table and the pastor's care for the congregation. We call pastors "shepherds." All of the pastor's shepherding and care takes its purpose and content from the pastor's leadership of worship. Think of pastoral care as our clerical attempt to help the congregation worship the true and living God in every aspect of their lives.

For many centuries, pastors were called "curates," derived from the Latin *cura animarum*, the cure, or care of souls. Pastoral care would not be such a challenge were it not for the requirement that our care be *pastoral*. It is not our vocation to "care for people." Pastors care for people *in the name of Jesus*. The shepherd is responsible not only to the flock, but also to God for the flock. We worry not only about the health and happiness of our people, but about their salvation as well. And that makes all the difference.

Pastors were also called "parson," derived from the Latin *persona*, or "person." The pastor is that person among persons in the congregation who cares for the congregation. We have a treasure that we offer to the congregation, but it is a treasure in earthen vessels. Some say that pastors get into trouble when they forget that they are persons among other persons, when they lose sight of *—discuss* their humanity with all their human strengths and weaknesses. I feel that a greater problem for us pastors is when we forget that we are called to be curates, those who care for souls. We are earthen vessels, but to us has been entrusted a treasure—the treasure of the gospel, the treasure of those convened by the gospel.

This was impressed upon me in my own practice of pastoral care. A woman in my church suffered from periodic bouts of depression. These were described to me as times when she felt "down and depressed." During such times, she would often call me to come by her house for a visit. I would have conversation with her, offer a prayer, and often she would say that she felt better.

One day she called me to come to her house because, she said, "I'm feeling kind of down today." As Providence would have it, I was reading Walter Brueggemann's commentary on Jeremiah.[1] I told her that I would be by that afternoon. After speaking with her, I returned to my study of Jeremiah. Brueggemann comments that the prophets of Israel are best described, not as carping social critics, or as political activists, but as poets. He also says that, among the prophets, one can discern a number of typical prophetic moves. And the first prophetic move is tears. The prophet attempts a public expression of grief, a public processing of pain. The prophet does this, not to leave people in tears, says Brueggemann, but rather so that people, through their grieving, might learn to relinquish their commitment to the status quo, and try to be open to new arrangements of reality, to the will of God. Vision—revision—is dependent upon letting go, and in the relinquishment there are tears.

When I appeared at this parishioner's house that afternoon, I had a different mode of care to offer. I said to her, "I want to apologize. I have been treating you as if you had some sort of illness. But how do I know that? Here you are, sitting in your half-million-dollar house, all that the world has to offer around you, and yet this doesn't appear to be enough. You seem to be in grief, as if you were expecting more. I wonder why you think you deserve more, that life could be even better for you than it is. Many people think Greenville is a great place to live. I wonder why you look for more."

This led to a wonderful conversation about her life. We came to the conclusion that afternoon that God was indeed pushing her to some new place. Her grief did appear to be a kind of prelude to a more abundant life, a wider world. *unpack his implicit message*

Where did we get the word *depression?* Not from the Bible. We live in a relentlessly therapeutic culture, where all human need is reduced to illness. In this climate, the historic "care of souls" becomes reduced to merely secular therapy. One of the challenges of being a pastor is offering people care that is worthy of the name *Christian*.

The Naming of a New World

interpretive leadership

Elsewhere I remember Walter Brueggemann saying, "You pastors are world makers." Like the prophets of Israel, we render a new world through nothing but words. The world belongs to those who can describe the world truthfully, those who are able to name rightly what is going on among us. Thus, the pastor works with words faithfully to describe the world as God's world, the sphere of the activity of the Holy Spirit, that beloved but troubled realm for which Jesus died. There must be a harmonious convergence between the words we are using in the pulpit when we preach, and the words that we use as we offer care in the pastoral counseling session.

I also recall Brueggemann saying to us pastors, "And if you won't let God use you to make a new world, through faithful words, then all you can do as a pastor is service the old one. And that's no fun." Our care is concerned not to enable people to adapt and to adjust to the received world, but rather to let God move them to a new and different world.

A distinguished psychotherapist began a lecture on the history of psychotherapy by saying, "Psychotherapy is an attempt to help people through words." So is pastoral care, and we ought to choose our words carefully. Our basic struggle, on a Sunday morning, revolves around the questions: Who gets to name the world? Who is authorized to tell the story of what is going on among us? This is why I believe that our preaching is primary, even to our care. In our preaching ministry, our pastoral care is set in context. We are given the master story called *gospel*, to which we are attempting to align our contemporary stories. We do not know what "care" is until the gospel tells us. We have some very different notions of care from those of the world.[2] True, Acts characterizes the ministry of Jesus as one of healing:

> You know . . . how God anointed Jesus of Nazareth with the Holy Spirit and with power; how he went about doing good and healing all that were oppressed by the devil, for God was with him. (Acts:10:36-38)

Now this same Jesus authorizes his own followers to engage in "doing good and healing all that were oppressed." Earlier, when the seventy were sent out (Luke 10:1-16), they returned with joy because "even the demons are subject to us in your name!" (Luke 10:17 RSV). Right after Pentecost, Peter miraculously heals, in the name of Jesus, a man who is lame (Acts 3:1-10).

Yet the church's healing work has become problematic in our cultural context. If our therapists were willing to merely miraculously cast out a demon or two, then our quarrel with the therapeutic might not be so great. In a voraciously therapeutic culture, it is not that Christianity has a primitive notion of what it would take for people to get better and psychotherapy has a more modern view of the human being. It is rather that Christianity has a different notion of who human beings are and for what we are destined, based on our attentiveness to the Christian story. When Peter heals the man who is lame (Acts 3:1-10), he must immediately instruct the man in the meaning of the healing. Furthermore, Peter's healing of the man immediately lands Peter and John in hot water with the authorities, who want to know why these "uneducated, common men" are engaging in unlicensed, unauthorized healing (Acts 4:1-22). At least the authorities have the insight to see that healing and care by noncredentialed, unauthorized persons is a threat to who is in charge. There is a link between healing and power. Christians do not only believe in healing. Health and wholeness are not the supreme virtues. We believe in healing in the name of Jesus, which sometimes brings us into some degree of conflict with the established, authorized health care delivery systems.

As Augustine pointed out so long ago, it all depends on one's view of ultimate happiness, the *telos*, or purpose, for which we were created. A comfortably domesticated church tends to abandon its theological language and replace it with the language of secular therapy, for that is the mode of salvation currently affirmed by the dominant culture—the goal of self-fulfillment.[3] As Robert Bellah and his associates observed, at some point we stopped worrying about whether we were "sinful," or whether it was possible to be "righteous," and instead sought to avoid being "unhealthy" and to be "healthy."[4] Or as someone else has said, we Americans stopped naming our children "Charity," or "Grace," and began naming them "Tiffany," and we forgot why.

Thus I am troubled when a seminarian tells me that she or he is going into the Christian ministry because, "I like helping people." "Helping people," may be a satisfactory basis for ministerial work, if ministry is practiced in a place like Honduras, the second poorest country in the Western Hemisphere. In such a context, people have interesting needs that deserve our help—needs like food, clothing, and housing.

But in an affluent, consumerist, capitalist culture, attempting to "help people" becomes extremely problematic among the relatively well off. Many of us, having solved so many basic human problems like food, clothing, and housing, now move on to less interesting infatuations. We live in a polity, ruled over by the Constitution, that tells us that we are born with certain inalienable "rights." The Constitution created a definition of a human being as a bundle of rights. The purpose of government is to give us the maximum amount of space to assert and to fulfill our rights. Government enables me to express my rights, without ever making a judgment upon the goodness of these rights.

A major difficulty with this arrangement is that, in this culture, desire becomes elevated to the level of need, and need becomes further elevated to the level of rights. And because we tend to be a pit of bottomless desire, there is no end to our need. Our list of rights seems constantly to expand, driven as it is, not by some public discussion about which rights are worth having, but rather by our relentless desire. Our culture tends to be a vast supermarket of desire. Anyone who goes out to meet my needs is going to be working full time!

I believe this is one reason many pastors are so fatigued. They are expending their lives, running about in such busyness, attempting to service the needs of essentially selfish, self-centered consumers, without critique or limit of those needs.[5] Flannery

O'Connor mocked a clergyman of her acquaintance whom she called "one part minister and three parts masseuse."[6]

The Peculiarity of Pastoral Care

The gospel is not simply about meeting people's needs. The gospel is also a critique of our needs, an attempt to give us needs worth having. The Bible appears to have little interest in so many of the needs and desires that consume present-day North Americans. Therefore, Christian pastoral care will be about much more than meeting people's needs. It will also be about indoctrination, inculturation, which is also—from the peculiar viewpoint of the gospel—care. Our care must form people into the sort of people who have had their needs rearranged in the light of Christ.[7]

The call of Paul the apostle was his experience of finding himself living in a whole new world that had been inaugurated when Christ gave death the slip at Easter. Paul changed because of his realization that, in the resurrection of Jesus Christ, the world had changed, therefore he had to change or appear bafflingly out of step with reality (2 Cor. 5:17-18). That many ministers base their ministry on models of leadership uncritically borrowed from the latest fads in business leadership or therapeutic practices is yet another testimony to our failure to believe that God raised Jesus Christ from the dead, thus radically changing the world. In other words, our care cannot be detached from our politics. Our conviction about who is in charge cannot be disjoined from the call to conversion, the church's challenge to live in the light of Easter.

Sometimes one hears those in authority in the church tell pastors, "The most important thing is for you to love your people. Just be with your people in love, and everything else will work out."

discuss

Not necessarily. More difficult even than loving one's people can be the love of Christ, a truthful love that is the source of, and judgment upon, all our loves. We must be linked to something more significant than a vague notion of loving our people if ministry is to be service to the resurrected Christ rather than servility to the praise or blame of our people. After telling the church at Corinth to regard him and his fellow workers as "servants of Christ and stewards of the mysteries of God" (note he does not say "servants of the people and stewards of congregational finances"), Paul attacks the

Corinthians, telling them, "But with me it is a very small thing that I should be judged by you or by any human court. I do not even judge myself. I am not aware of anything against myself, but I am not thereby acquitted. It is the Lord who judges me" (1 Cor. 4:3-4). We care for others under the judgments of Christ. Perhaps that is why pastors are also prophets. There is some sort of pastoral significance that the New Testament word for "compassion" (*splanchna*—Mark 1:41—from whence we get our word "spleen") is the same word for "guts." There is no way to be a truly compassionate pastor without being a truthful, gutsy prophet.

Throughout 1 Corinthians, Paul keeps calling the church at Corinth back to the authority of the gospel (11:16, 23; 15:3). Paul serves his congregation by being utterly submissive, not to them, but to the apostolic tradition. So should we.

Thus the great nineteenth-century preacher C. H. Spurgeon wrote:

is this a good goal?

> I have striven, with all my might, to attain the position of complete independence of all men. I have found, at times, if I have been much praised, and if my heart has given way a little, and I have taken notice of it, and felt pleased, that the next time I was censured and abused I felt the censure and abuse very keenly, for the very fact that I accepted the commendation, rendered me more sensitive to the censure. So that I have tried, especially of late, to take no more notice of man's praise than of his blame, but to rest simply upon this truth—I know that I have a pure motive in what I attempt to do, I am conscious that I endeavor to serve God with a single eye to His glory, and therefore, it is not for me to take either praise or censure from man, but to stand independently upon the rock of right doing.[8]

true

A pastorate too susceptible to the praise or the blame of the congregation is a betrayal of the larger claims of our vocation. Clergy were the first professionals, not because we had received some high level of specialized knowledge that was unavailable to others, but because we had a body of doctrine to profess. We were those who had our lives yoked to some profession of faith. Without that linkage, our pastoral work too easily degenerates into unfocused, breathless busyness. Consider the dilemma of modern medicine, a predicament that ought to be interesting to us pastors since so much of contemporary pastoral care has been informed by the practice of modern medicine. Medicine, having failed to nurture its attachment to the principles of care, becomes attached to the unrealistic goals of cure. Resisting the clutches of the federal government, medical care in America has fallen into the grip of big business. We now pay the medical industry a fortune to administer our collective fantasies about the possibility of immortality and a risk-free, pain-free human existence. Clinical pastoral education, where most seminarians receive their clinical and experiential training in "pastoral care," is often practiced in institutional hospital settings. Therefore, we clergy have sometimes been guilty of taking our cues in pastoral care from medicine, a profession that is in big trouble today when it forgets what it ought to profess. The term *doctor* comes from the Greek *doceo*, meaning "teacher." The first physicians were teachers, those who taught the nature of illness, the truth about the body.[9]

Jerome, in his Letter 52, urges pastors to take the Hippocratic physician as their model of care, always conducting themselves among their people in the demeanor that befits their vocation:

> It is your duty to visit the sick, to know the homes and children of those who are married, and to guard the secrets of the noble. Make it your object, therefore, to keep your tongue chaste as well as your eyes. Never discuss a woman's figure nor let one house know what is going on in another. Hippocrates, before he will teach his pupils, makes them take an oath and compels them to swear fealty to him. He binds them over to silence, and prescribes for them their language, their gait, their dress, their manners. How much more reason have we to whom the medicine of the soul has been committed to love the houses of all Christians as our own homes. Let them know us as comforters in sorrow rather than as guests in time of mirth. That clergyperson soon becomes an object of contempt who being often asked out to dinner never refuses to go.[10]

But today the model of medicine is problematic in a culture that believes it is important to avoid pain at all costs, where physical deterioration has become the most interesting thing that can happen to us, where the normal aging process is perceived as an injustice, where we have little to do with our dying, and where our lives are owned by nothing more significant than our desires.

Early in my ministry I arrived at a hospital room where a woman in my church had just given birth. I had been told that "there were problems with the birth." A couple sat in the hospital room waiting for the doctor. The doctor appeared shortly after I arrived, and said to the new parents, "You have a new baby boy. But there are some problems. Your child has been born with Down Syndrome. Your baby also has a rather minor and correctable respiratory condition. My recommendation is for you to consider just letting nature take its course, and then in a few days there shouldn't be a problem."

The couple seemed confused by what the doctor told them.

"If the condition can be corrected, then we want it corrected," said the husband. His wife immediately nodded in agreement.

"You must understand that studies show that parents who keep these children have a high incidence of marital distress and separation. Is it fair for you to bring this sort of suffering upon your other two children?" said the doctor.

At the mention of the word "suffering" it was as if the doctor finally began speaking the woman's language. She said, "Our children have had every advantage in the world. They have really never known suffering, never had the opportunity to know it. I don't know if God's hand is in this or not, but I could certainly see why it would make sense for a child like this to be born into a family like ours. Our children will do just fine. When you think about it, this is really a great opportunity."

The doctor looked confused. He abruptly departed, with me following him out into the hall. "Reverend, I hope that you can talk some reason into them," said the doctor.

The couple was already using reason, but it was reasoning that was foreign to that of the doctor. For me, it was a vivid depiction of the way in which the church, at its best, is in the business of teaching a different language from that of the world. The church, through its stories, worship, and life together, teaches a different language whereby words like "suffering," words that are unredeemably negative in our society, change their substance. Here was a couple that had listened to a peculiar story, namely the life and death of Jesus Christ, in which suffering could be reasonably redemptive.

Pastoral care involves not simply caring for people where they are, but working with God in order that they may be moved to a new location. Our care is linked by the Christian faith to moral transformation. We are moved to a new location, a new world, a new politics through the inculcation of language that enables us to name a new citizenship. All worlds begin with words.

For instance, in my own denomination there has been a debate raging for sometime between two groups over something called "abortion." Who gave us this word? It was the same people who gave us words such as "appendectomy," thus turning what might be described as a moral matter into a merely surgical procedure. One group argues that there is a "right to life." Another group argues that we must do nothing that would deny "freedom of choice."

Undeniably, these are positive, socially approved terms within our culture. We live in a culture of "rights." A human being is defined as a bundle of rights, and the best society is that which gives me the maximum amount of space to exercise my rights. In such a society, even life itself becomes a "right."

Likewise, we live in a society where freedom of choice is a supreme virtue. After the European Enlightenment, a human being is defined by choices. A human being without choices is less than a human being. The best human being has the maximum number of choices and the maximum amount of freedom to choose in this great supermarket of desire we call Western culture; so Bill Moyers's PBS series on the end of life is called *On Our Own Terms*.

Unfortunately, both of these terms—"right to life" and "freedom of choice"—are at some odds with the language of Scripture. Where in the Bible do we find a "right to life"? In Scripture, life is not a right. Life is a gift. God gives life and God commandeers life and God takes life. Only the giver of life can be the taker of life. Our lives are not our own, rather they are accountable to the God who gave us life.

Furthermore, it is difficult to find scriptural support for "freedom of choice." Mary, Paul, Peter, Sarah—what was their "freedom of choice"? The story is concerned more with the free and sovereign choices of God, rather than the autonomous choices of people. The goal of the gospel story is not to make us free, to be those who live and die on our own terms, but rather to have our lives linked to something and someone worth living and dying for. If Christ makes us free, we will be free indeed.

One of the most influential books on a generation of pastors in mid-twentieth-century North America was Seward Hiltner's *Preface to Pastoral Theology*, a book in which the older discipline of pastoral theology became pastoral care.[11] Hiltner based his theology of the pastoral ministry mostly upon a sociological/psychological model. The pastoral arts of care became reduced to a set of skills to be applied by the "shepherd," Hiltner's primary pastoral image.[12] Pastors were thereby moved from a theological mode into the therapeutic mode in Hiltner's stress upon mostly inductive care. He urged pastors to attempt a nonjudgmental, "client-centered" approach to care of troubled souls. Taking his cues from Carl Rogers and his Rogerian "nondirective counseling," Hiltner told pastors that through empathetic reflection, the pastor was to "educe" or bring out from troubled persons their own solutions and initiatives to address what troubled them.[13]

Hiltner underestimated the complexity of both people's needs—which sometimes demand a firm, directive, judgmental hand upon their tortured lives—the depth of human sin, and the peculiarity of pastoral care. Pastoral care, worthy of the name, is care that places our lives and our care alongside the peculiar account of what is going on in the world, which we call Scripture. In our care, we are to lay over our people's lives a counternarrative to the officially sanctioned ones. We are to give them a lens whereby they refocus their lives. Through this scriptural lens (the image is that of John Calvin)[14] certain things in our lives come into focus that we would have missed without the lens. Certain things that the world tells us to value are put out of focus. Our cares are rearranged. The words through which we describe ourselves are changed and thus our world is changed.

Don Browning in *The Moral Context of Pastoral Care* notes that many people in our society are troubled, not because of some exclusively psychic reason, but rather because they are in moral confusion.[15] Browning asserts that there is a place for moral confrontation in pastoral care and counseling. In a counseling session, the pastor has a responsibility to establish and to name the peculiar ecclesial context for our caring. There are times when ethical judgments need to be "bracketed" out of the conversation between pastor and parishioner, says Browning, suspending judgment so that the pastor and the counselee can be free to examine the various dynamics of a situation in a relatively nondefensive way. But unlike Hiltner, Browning maintains that this must be a momentary and tactical suspension of pastoral judgment that must not be overgeneralized to apply to every person in every pastoral care situation.

> The minister has a clear duty to counsel the ill and dying, but he should first have helped create a community with a religiocultural view of the meaning of illness and death. Certainly the minister should counsel persons with marriage problems, sexual problems, and divorce problems, but he should first have helped to create among his people a positive vision of the normative meaning of marriage, sexuality, and even divorce. The difficulty with much of pastoral counseling today is that more time is spent discussing the tools of counseling than in the more challenging process of developing the structure of meanings that should constitute the context for counseling.[16]

intop
leadership

In pastoral counseling, we are engaging in the development of Browning's "structure of meanings." Thus Aquinas, in speaking of the work of a pastor in caring for people, lists the first duty as *instruction* in order "to relieve a deficiency on the part of the intellect."[17] All our care must be, in some sense, educational, if it is to be specifically Christian.

The Congregational Context of Our Care

Wayne Meeks, a historian of the social context of early Christianity, notes that when the Romans looked at Christians, what they saw was a way of being religious that was peculiarly communal and therefore countercultural. Early Christians impressed pagan Romans as being

> essentially communal. Even those practices that are urged upon individuals in the privacy of their homes . . . are extensions of the community's practice—indeed they are means of reminding individuals even when alone that they are not merely devotees of the Christians' God, they are members of Christ's body, the people of God. That was how the Christian movement differed most visibly

from the other cults. . . . The Christians' practices were not confined to sacred occasions and sacred locations—shrines, sacrifices, processions—but were integral to the formation of communities with a distinctive self-awareness.[18]

Pastoral care is more than an opportunity for the pastor to be with troubled individuals within the congregation. Pastoral care is an extension of the pastor's communal edification. One of the greatest gifts we have to offer persons who struggle through life is the Body of Christ, that people whom Jesus has formed as his presence in the world.

"I am so glad, since beginning my residency here, that I am a Missouri Synod Lutheran, the graduate student said to me. He was a student in our university's M.D./Ph.D. program.

"Why would you be glad of that?" I asked.

"I don't know if you know much about us," he continued, "But we Missouri Synod Lutherans are very big on sin. We believe that one is always a sinner. Even after you become a Christian, you are still a sinner. In fact, we believe that Christians are among the greatest sinners."

"Why would that be a help to you?" I asked.

"Well, each morning as I enter the hospital I stop for a moment and look at this huge medical apparatus laid out before me. I think to myself that a lot of good will be done here today, but a lot of bad will be done as well. And the sad thing is, we usually won't know the difference until much later, until we can't do anything about it. For nearly every astounding medical advance, there is a corresponding medical tragedy. I had never been with a group of people who always thought they were right, who indeed *must* be right. When something goes wrong in there, say when a patient dies, you wouldn't believe the defensiveness. They keep reassuring themselves that 'we did everything right,' that 'we followed proper procedures,' that 'nothing can be blamed on us.' Then I say, 'Well, the patient did die. Surely something went wrong.' You just can't imagine what a great gift it is to begin something as morally ambiguous as modern medicine with the assumption that you are a sinner—a forgiven one—but still a sinner."

I marveled at the conceptual apparatus given this young man through which he was able to reframe his life situation, indeed, to rename the world through the metaphors, the images, the story that is called Scripture. He seemed to me therefore not only a product of good pastoral care, but also a reminder to us pastors of the power available to those who have learned to read the world truthfully through the lens of the gospel.

One of the duties of pastors in their preaching is to renarrate our lives in the light of the story of Jesus. Thereby ordinary people have their lives rescripted, caught up in a great drama that is called salvation. People have become the victims of narratives that are inadequate to enable the truthful living of our lives, narratives that are derived from psychology, economics, sociology, and other secular (i.e., godless) means of naming our selves and what happens to us. Thus Eugene Peterson praises pastoral visitation over pastoral counseling because it forces a pastor to encounter parishioners in their own setting, in the sheer ordinariness of their lives. Here, in the middle of what Henry James called "the enormous lap of the actual," a pastor is forced to face the forlorn, trapped, caught, dreariness that constitutes so many of our people's lives. Here, over coffee in the kitchen at home, beside the sickbed, across a crowded desk at the place of work, in the pastor's listening and responding, in the pastoral visit, through words we enable our people to fit their lives into the plot of God's story.

There is no substitute for the pastor who counsels to also be the one who visits, who knows parishioners in the actual setting of their lives.[19] Thus Richard Baxter wrote:

> When we are familiar with them, they will be encouraged to open their doubts to us. But when a minister knows not his people . . . it must be a great hindrance to his doing any good among them. By means of it, we shall come to be better acquainted with *each person's spiritual state,* and so the better know how to watch over them. We shall the better know how to preach to them when we know their temper, and their chief objections. . . . We shall the better know how to lament for them, and to rejoice with them, and to pray for them.[20]

One great difference between a pastor and other givers of care in our society is that a pastor can take initiative and intrude into the troubled lives of his or her people. It is part of a pastor's role not simply to wait until hurting people reach out for help, but also to seek out and save the lost. Thus Jeremy Taylor, Anglican bishop of the seventeenth century, advises his pastors:

> A minister must not stay till he be sent for; but, of his own accord and care, go to them, to examine them, to exhort them to perfect their repentance, to strengthen their faith, to encourage their patience, to persuade them to resignation, to the renewing of their holy vows, to the love of God, to be reconciled to their neighbours, to make restitution and amends.[21]

In seminary, many of us pastors when we took courses in "pastoral care" basically took courses in various forms of psychological counseling. Our image therefore became the one-to-one conversation. The equation of pastoral care with pastoral counseling is unfortunate. Although much has been gained in the past century by urging pastors to attend carefully to the individual, the "living human documents" (so called by Anton Boisen, one of the founders of the modern pastoral care movement) who are our parishioners, something has been lost as well. Mainly what has been lost is a sense of the church, the gathered congregation, as the context of our care.

We pastors do not work alone. We work with a God whose nature it is to care. Much of our care is subsequent to, or prelude for, the intrusions of God among us.[22] As we have stressed, we work out of the common heritage of the church, the accumulated wisdom that is the witness of the saints. We also work in concert with the whole congregation. It is clear when Paul writes to his churches that he is writing as "we," writing on behalf of his "yoke-fellows" in Christ (Phil. 4:3). It is also clear that Paul is writing to those fellow workers whom he has left in charge of the congregations. Being a pastor in charge of the care of the souls within the congregation is more like being a coach, or the manager of a baseball team, rather than the star player.

I therefore believe that we pastors would do well to spend more of our time as encouragers and coordinators of care, rather than thinking of ourselves as the sole caregiver.[23] Many pastors are deeply burdened by having to bear too many secrets within the congregation. It can be a risky situation for the pastor to be the only one in the congregation who is burdened with all of the troubles of struggling people. True, there are many secrets that only the pastor ought to bear. But we must learn to take more of our people's cares and concerns pastorally rather than personally, in concert with the rest of the congregation rather than on behalf of them. An example of such congregational care is the Stephen's Ministries program whereby laypersons are trained to work with the pastor in intensive care for persons in need within the church.[24] The *Disciple Bible Study* program of the United Methodists has trained thousands of laypersons to be skilled Bible teachers of hundreds of thousands of laity. The burgeoning small group movement within the churches is another resource for making our care congregational.[25] As with the pastor's care of the flock, the care of members by other members must constantly be examined to ensure that our care is truly, peculiarly, distinctively Christian care.

> For just as the body is one and has many members, and all the members of the body, though many, are one body, so it is with Christ. For in the one Spirit we were all baptized into one body— Jews or Greeks, slaves or free—and all were made to drink of one Spirit. . . . Now you are the body of Christ and individually members of it. (1 Cor. 12:12-13, 27)

An important pastoral role is helping pain go public, encouraging the public processing of pain. We do this in our leadership of worship when we urge the congregation to engage in public confession and forgiveness; when we receive the monetary offering; when we, through various acts of worship, urge people to lay their lives upon the altar of God to be blessed, broken, and given to the world as the Body of Christ. We also urge them to go public with their pain through our counseling and pastoral care. Alone, as isolated individuals, they are cut off from the communal, congregational resources for healing. Ministry to alcoholics ought to be a matter for those within the congregation who are recovering alcoholics. People who have been through the pain of marital separation often have been given experiences and resources to help others with the same problem—resources that are unavailable to the pastor, resources that ought to be claimed as part of their baptism-ordained ministry. The pastor as giver of care ought not to rob the laity of their call to care.

We live in a society that zealously guards a "right to privacy." Our culture tends to divide up the world into segments, the public and the private, the personal and the social. This is an inheritance from the European Enlightenment, which tended to withdraw religion away from the public sphere, leaving the public arena to politics and economics, and relegating religion to the private sphere where it could not be touched by public concerns.[26]

Christianity tends to see most things that the world regards as private, as intensely public. For us, sex is not a private matter. Sex is a public responsibility, intertwined with politics, something to be engaged in for the common good, not merely for individual satisfaction. We do not believe in sex apart from the public promises and social commitments that make sex interesting. Let us not forget how curious it is for the church to take an act so carnal as coitus and insist that before a couple become "one flesh," they have a wedding in order to talk about it in front of God and the whole church.

For example, in the middle of advice concerning congregational squabbles in the first church of Corinth, Paul wades into the intimacies of marriage. "For the wife does not have authority over her own body, but the husband does" (1 Cor. 7:4) is just the sort of thing one would expect from a first-century male. Then Paul adds, "likewise the husband does not have authority over his own body, but the wife does," something we would not expect to hear. Then Paul gets quite specific about what husbands and wives ought to expect from one another for sex in marriage, no matter that this epistle will be read in front of the whole church.

Paul then tells wives and husbands not to separate, for this is an irrevocable and undeniable command straight from the Lord. Curiously, Paul quickly adds that if marital separation occurs, remain unmarried or be reconciled. We have a pastor here who is struggling to uphold the difficult demands of Jesus (Jesus, it appears, had a prejudice toward marital cohesion), and at the same time to uphold those in the congregation caught in real-life dilemmas that complicate those commands.

All of Paul's instructions for the behavior of individual Christians take place against the background of his assumption of the church. Christians are not expected to worship this God on Sunday, or to live this faith on Monday, in isolation. In the church, we are not to isolate persons in pain, telling them, "you have a problem." We are to place their pain in the context of the struggling congregation, that fellowship of suffering that enables even pain to be a means of redemption because our heartache is placed in the context of the story of God's people. Pastors help the stories of struggling individuals become subsumed in the larger story called the outbreak of the kingdom of God. There is no sin that we confront in our care that we are not at the same time able to confess in the congregation. People do not have to be whole to be saved.

As Paul said to one of his churches, "I hold you in my heart" (Phil. 1:7 RSV). In his heart Paul had lodged the Philippian jailer and his family, Euodia and Syntyche, who could not get along with one another, his yokefellow Epaphroditus, and all the others. Paul's letters ought to provide special guidance and encouragement for us pastors because therein the apostle reveals himself as pastor, as someone caught in the tug and pull of the daily cares of the church, someone focusing upon the real needs of real people, a coordinator of care rather than the sole giver of care. Thus Paul is able to hold fast to Jesus' teachings against remarriage after divorce, but still provide care for Christians caught in conflicting commitments. He can chastise the Galatians for being "stupid," and still in the same letter have sympathy with their plight. As pastors, we ought to take Paul's pastoral letters as our model in the manner in which Paul is able, amid a congregational quarrel, to insert some of his grandest theological affirmations—the way that Paul, even while correcting the church, is able to break forth in sweeping doxology. One of the great challenges of our pastoral care is to be present with people in their need and not be overwhelmed by their need, to be available to our people as their pastor without being captured exclusively by them, to take their pain seriously and at the same time to take seriously our task to proclaim Jesus Christ and him crucified and resurrected. Paul points the way.

Forgive Paul's paternalism/maternalism as he speaks tenderly of the sort of pastoral wisdom he needed when dealing with the congregations in Thessalonica:

> We were gentle among you, like a mother caring for her little children. We loved you so much that we were delighted to share with you not only the gospel of God but our lives as well, because you had become so dear to us. Surely you remember, brothers [and sisters], our toil and hardship; we worked night and day in

order not to be a burden to anyone while we preached the gospel of God to you.

You are witnesses, and so is God. (1 Thess. 2:7-10 NIV)

Pastors are persons who, like Paul, care for God's people by sharing not only the gospel, but our very lives with God's people. Thus, in so many places in Paul's letters, when he is encouraging his congregations, one gets the impression that Paul is also engaging in self-encouragement. In a number of places, the Paul of Acts engages in this ministry of encouragement (Acts 16:5; 18:23; 20:2). To comfort our people (literally, *with strength*), we offer them the reassurance that we ourselves so desperately need, and in giving, we receive. The pastor does much giving, but as Paul notes, this way is more blessed than the other (Acts 20:35).

There would be no way for a pastor to be exposed to the great pain that accompanies so many people's lives, no way for a pastor to know the deep, ugly secrets that are imbedded in so many people's stories, were it not that the pastor's care occurs within the context of the congregation at worship. There, on Sunday, we are able to confess and to be forgiven, to lay our lives upon the altar, to give to God those aspects of ourselves that we are not able to handle by ourselves. The pastor, in leading worship, keeps overhearing the same gospel that the pastor proclaims—our hope is not in ourselves, but in the Lord. We care by pointing people toward the God who cares for them, in whose life is our light. We care by laying our people's cares upon the altar, lifting up to God in prayer the life of God's people.

CHAPTER FIVE

The Pastor as Interpreter of Scripture: A People Created by the Word

When I was in seminary, I got the impression that my toughest task as a preacher was to somehow relate the ancient, primitive world of the Bible to the modern, progressive new world in which we lived—the old "the preacher stands with the Bible in one hand and today's newspaper in the other." Not too long into ministry, I learned that my task, as congregational interpreter of the Word, was considerably more complex.

"What is the strangest thing about Sunday morning worship from your point of view?" I asked a group of students. I had been invited to say something about Christian worship, and I was desperate to pique their interest.

"It's when they bring in that great big book," one student replied.

"The Bible?"

"Yeah, that. In the opening parade of people."

"The procession?" I asked.

"Yeah, that."

And I thought to myself—that we, a group of early-twenty-first-century folk, gathering for about an hour, and submitting ourselves to this ancient, disordered conglomeration of texts, produced by a people so different from ourselves, at a time and place quite different from our own—this, as the students seemed to know, is strange.

Modernity has conditioned us to think that we are privileged to live at the very summit of human development, from which we look down with condescension upon everyone who arrived here before us. The Christian reading of Scripture is thus countercultural, provocative, strange. Christians, along with Jews and Muslims, may be the last close readers left in this culture.[1] A major task of pastors is to assist congregations in reading carefully in order to align ourselves to a text, in order to submit and bend ourselves to the complex redescription of reality that is Scripture.[2]

The Westminster Confession states the centrality of Scripture succinctly:

> Although the light of nature, and the works of creation and providence, do so far manifest the goodness, wisdom, and power of God . . . It pleased the Lord, at sundry times, and in divers manners, to reveal himself, and to declare that his will unto his Church; and afterwards, for the better preserving and propagating of the truth, and for the more sure establishment and comfort of the Church against the corruption of the flesh, and . . . to commit the same wholly unto writing; which maketh the holy Scripture to be most necessary; those former ways of God's revealing his will unto his people being now ceased.[3]

A People Subservient to the Word

In our role as interpreters of Scripture, we are heirs to Ezra. Sometime during the mid–fifth century B.C., Israel returned from exile. Their beloved Jerusalem lay in ruins. A decision was made to rebuild the walls, a first step toward reclaiming Israel's identity as a people. During the reconstruction, a scroll was found, "the book of the law of Moses, which the LORD had given to Israel" (Neh. 8:1). Before the Water Gate, from morning until midday, in the presence of all the people, the priest, Ezra, read and "all the people were attentive to the book of the law" (8:3). Ezra stood upon a wooden platform and read. Ezra's fellow priests "gave the sense" of the words being read, "so that the people understood the reading" (8:8).

The people wept when they heard the words read and interpreted. They wept for joy at finally having recovered words lost to them in exile. They wept for sadness at how far they had strayed from God's appointed way. Ezra told them not to weep. He proclaimed the day a great holiday, a holy day, telling them to go and have a great party, "for the joy of the LORD is your strength" (8:10). They celebrated greatly because "they had understood the words that were declared to them" (8:12).

Here is a portrait of Israel at its best. The Word is read and interpreted in worship, the people weep and then celebrate and align their lives accordingly. Israel is constituted, corrected, resurrected, redeemed by words. As Walter Brueggemann says, in his commentary on Nehemiah 8, "This peculiar community is not self-generated, but understands itself in terms of a special authorization in a script available for steady and regular, attentive reiteration."[4] Christian clergy stand, as public readers and interpreters of Scripture, in that place once occupied by Ezra. Like Israel, the church is gathered— but not as the world is gathered, on the basis of race, gender, nation, or class. These words of Scripture are not spoken merely in order to elicit agreement or noble feelings among the hearers, but rather to form, reform, the hearers. It is the nature of Scripture to be "political," that is, formative. It is the nature of Scripture to want power over our lives. David H. Kelsey says that we come to the Bible not merely with the question, What does the Bible say? but also with, What is God using the Bible to do to us?[5] In reading the Bible, God is not merely revealed to us, but is allowed to have God's way with us.

It is our peculiar service to the church, as its lead biblical interpreters, to lay the story of Israel and the church, as recorded in Scripture, alongside our present modes of church. Ezra did that at the Water Gate. Jesus did it in his hometown synagogue in Luke 4. In exilic conditions, the Word gathers a people. This is Israel in diaspora: the people listen, aligning themselves to the word, singing the songs of Zion, naming the name, telling the story, and thus surviving as God's people.

> By the rivers of Babylon—
> there we sat down
> and there we wept
> when we remembered Zion. . . .
> For there our captors asked us for songs,
> and our tormentors asked for mirth, saying,
> "Sing us one of the songs of Zion!"
> How could we sing the LORD's song
> in a foreign land?
> If I forget you, O Jerusalem,
> let my right hand wither! (Ps. 137:1-5)

I believe that *exile* is not too strong a term with which to characterize the current social location of the North American church. Stanley Hauerwas and I suggested this in our *Resident Aliens: Life in the Christian Colony,* where we said that the church has been given the task of being "an alternative *polis,* a countercultural social structure called church . . . something the world is not and can never be."[6]

The theme of exile has been extensively developed in the work of Walter Brueggemann, who reminds us that most of Israel's Scripture was written by a community either in exile or coming out of exile, Scripture like that found in Nehemiah. Only exilic literature could adequately express the pain and the loss felt by disestablished, relinquished Israel in the catastrophe of exile. Yet some of Israel's most assertive, visionary, hopeful, pushy poetry and prose was also written in exile—testimony to Israel's great faith in the reign of a resourceful God who is determined to have a people.[7] To understand how a defeated, displaced people could still express evangelical *chutzpah* in the face of Babylonian imperialism, one would have to know a God who tends toward the oppressed. Think of all of our biblical interpretation and study as our attempt to "sing the Lord's song in a strange land."

When John the Baptizer is challenged by authorities, John tells them that God is able to raise up a people out of the stones in the Jordan, if need be, if God's people will not turn, repent, and return. God is determined to have a family. God's way of making a people is through the Word, through preaching like that of John, through promises (Luke 3:1-21).

The church is gathered by the Word. In just a few centuries the church defeated Rome on the basis of nothing more than this rather disordered collection of writings called Scripture. By water and the Word, God constitutes a family—the church. And pastors have the function of helping the church in exile read, reflect, and embody the Word of God. Our God is loquacious, creating the world with nothing more than words. Every time God's Word is uttered, new worlds come into being that would be otherwise unavailable without the gift of the Word.

> By faith we understand that the world was created by the word of God, so that what is seen was made out of things which do not appear. (Heb. 11:3 RSV)

Scripture reading and interpretation is a challenging pastoral activity. Of course, any Christian may, and should, read and interpret Scripture. Yet when the pastor reads, he or she does so as priest, as the one who listens to the text for the whole church, who interprets Scripture in light of the reading of the whole church down through the ages. The pastor's reading reminds the church that the Bible is produced by the community of faith and must be interpreted within that community under the inspiration of the Holy Spirit. Since the Reformation, the Bible has been abused *discuss* through individual readings, readings that are attempted outside of the context of the church, which corrects and contextualizes our reading of Scripture. Reading in community implies the time-honored practice of interpreting Scripture with Scripture, reading in context of the whole canon, allowing individual texts to be in dialogue with other texts.[8] The Bible is meant to be read in community as the church's book—the text that both creates and critiques the church.

Making Sense of the Bible in Modernity

Reading Scripture in the context of modernity has proved to be particularly challenging for us pastors. The Bible is old; the newest parts of it were written about nineteen hundred years ago. Because modernity believes in the notion of progress, it tends to be arrogant, taking a superior position toward all things that preceded modernity. Here we stand in sovereign judgment on everyone and everything that got here before us. Our entertainment culture renders all of us into "neophiles," lovers of the new. Martin Luther, in presenting his reform of the Mass condemned, "the fickle and fastidious spirits who rush in like unclean swine . . . who delight only in novelty and tire of it as quickly, when it has worn off."[9] Still, it is difficult for people like us not to believe that what is new is progressively better than what is old.

In the nineteenth century, particularly in Germany and England, much intellectual energy was expended upon problems related to the gap between the Bible being old and antiquated and our world being new and modern. The Bible portrayed the miraculous and the supernatural; the modern world was rendering the world into the completely explained and the exclusively natural. The Bible depicted a God who acts, who intervenes in history. The modern world became a closed, cause-and-effect system that worked without reference to supernatural intrusion. Once we allowed the likes of Immanuel Kant to divide the world into the phenomenal and the noumenal, the natural and the supernatural, the Bible was on its way to becoming incomprehensible. The Bible had been pushed out of the world and into some ethereal realm where nothing could be declared or proved with any conviction. The events of the Bible became supernatural, miraculous, episodic intrusions into the fixed laws of nature.

Jews and Christians ought not to believe in "nature." We know the world as Creation—gift and possession of a Creator. In a sense, after Genesis 1 and 2, it is all miracle as far as we are concerned, all miraculous creation of a God who continues to be involved in the world and refuses to be relegated to "supernatural," ahistorical irrelevancy. Any God who would create a world out of formless void is just the sort of God who would enter a virgin's womb or raise the dead.

Modern biblical interpretation tended to pick through the literature of the Bible, hoping to find some unassailable, unquestionable, historical datum that could be immune from doubt, that is, "what really happened." Historical criticism tended to be a method that attempted to peel away the pious exaggerations and accretions that burdened Scripture's historical testimony and thus uncovered the historical kernel that could be reliably believed as true.[10]

History, being one of the few humanities that could presume to be "scientific," that is, to follow some scientific, objective method for uncovering the truth—what "actually occurred historically" to history—was given the task of interpreting Scripture. Biblical interpreters became biblical historians. History was asserted as that scientific method that gets us to the truth of things—what really happened. Through the methodology of history, we attempted to get back "behind the text" to its original meaning. Modernity tended to assume that most of its problems were historical. We live in a time of great human advancement, therefore anything that is not of our time is suspect.

In the Acts of the Apostles, most of the narration is in the third person singular and plural, a third-person's account of the activities of the early church. Suddenly, in the middle of chapter 20 of Acts, the narration switches into the first person:

> We went ahead to the ship and set sail for Assos, intending to take
> Paul on board there. . . . When he met us in Assos, we took him on
> board. (Acts 20:13)

What is happening here? Some historical critics suspect some sort
of crude editing, in which an account from one era or place has
been awkwardly joined to a version from another. Perhaps there
was an "early Luke" who wrote one part of Acts and another "late
Luke" who wrote the rest. In other words, our interpretation is
dependent on some sort of historical reconstruction and retrieval
that leaves the Scriptures as a sort of puzzle to be solved, or a
makeshift quilt that falls apart in our hands.

But what if the challenge here is more literary than historical?
What happens in a switch from the third person (they, he, she) to the
first person (we, I)? The writing suddenly becomes more direct, personal, having the feel of an eyewitness account. Something happens
to the reader because of this change of voice, this switch of perspective. Perhaps Luke, the author of Acts, wanted to bring us more
closely into the action of the narrative. Scripture does not just report;
Scripture wants to change the reader. Transformation of humanity
rather than mere inculcation of information is its goal. The world "in
front of the text"—the prejudices and limitations that we bring to our
biblical interpretation, as well as the transformation that is occurring
in us as a result of our reading—ought to be as interesting to us as
the world "behind the text." Scripture does not just want to recreate
some world of the past, but rather wants to form a new world in the
present, to recreate us. Because of the liveliness of the biblical text,
enlivened by the Holy Spirit, much is going on in front of the text.[11]

The attempt to "get behind the text" acts as if the text is something
to be shattered in order to get through the obfuscation of the text to
what the text "really says." This is the preacher who announces,
"Now what Jesus was trying to say in the parable of the prodigal son
is . . ." No. What Jesus was trying to say *is* the parable. If one
removes the form of the text, attempts to abstract some generalized
concept or principle from behind the narrative, the result is something less than the narrative. The literary form has a function, a
meaning that is irreplaceable by some other more abstract meaning.

Scripture is not some primitive, crude means of communication,
but rather a sophisticated, resourceful means of transformation
through words. When James Joyce, in *Ulysses,* has Molly Bloom

lying in bed, thinking about men, thinking about her husband Leopold—and then inserts a section from that day's Dublin newspaper, then has us watch as Leopold enters the room, then takes us back inside Molly's head—we are not reading a botched editorial job. We are reading an author's attempt at portraying some of the complexity of human consciousness. In the human mind, voices compete with other voices, a number of things go on at one time, images tussle with other images, and there is a surplus of sensation and meaning—far too much for any single interpretive grasp.[12] Well, something very much like that may be happening in the twentieth chapter of Acts.

Modernity tends toward reductionism; the Bible revels in thick, multilayered readings. Modernity, that mode of thinking whose ultimate goal is complete certainty and an unimpeded grasp of the facts, fostered a way of reading that moved toward the "point" of the text. I have argued here for a break with modernity, an admission of our inability to come to a clear, sure certitude about everything—including God's Word.[13]

Modern methods of interpretation are frustrated by Scripture's delight in a cacophony of voices. The Bible tends not to speak in a unified, univocal way. Rather, the Bible presents a whole range of stories, often providing a variety of commentaries on those stories, sometimes reading them in quite different ways within the Bible itself. One can see this going on with the various interpretations of Jesus within the Gospels. Jesus is said to be the Messiah, God's anointed one. Yet he frustrates those expectations. He seems intent on rearranging, reinterpreting the very expectations he says he is fulfilling.

Pastoral interpretation of Scripture then involves a willingness to engage in an ongoing argument with the text, as well as to endure the text's ongoing argument with us. Richard Lischer says that it will involve a series of respectful questions asked of the text in order to better understand the text, so as to enable the text to penetrate our incomprehension and speak to us. In calling these "respectful questions," we admit that we are questioning the text out of our own very real moral, historical, and cultural limitations. We are respectful in our questions, knowing that sin takes many forms, one of them being arrogant biblical interpretation as embodied in our questions.[14] As Robert McAfee Brown puts it:

> Christians make the initially bizarre gamble that "the strange new world within the Bible" is a more accurate view of the world than our own and that we have to modify our views as a result. This means engaging in dialogue with the Bible—bringing our questions to it, hearing its questions to us, examining our answers in its light, and taking its answers very seriously, particularly when they conflict with our own, which will be most of the time.[15]

The literary critic Erich Auerbach noted that "Scripture is more difficult than it ought to be."[16] Here is the Bible, telling us that it wants to make God's Word available to us, then seeming to frustrate our attempts to hear that Word. Scripture beckons us toward a world where there is mystery, a world thick with meaning and wonder, where something is afoot that cannot be contained within our systems of knowledge. Here is a literature whose intention is to render an external agent (the God of Israel and church) so that there is bound to be some space between the text and our grasp of it, sure to be considerable slippage between our systems of explanation and making sense and what the Bible says.

Scripture delights in a surplus of meaning; it revels in eluding our interpretive grasp. Even after we have applied our very best and most reliable methods of interpretation, there is still more to be said about a given text, still more meaning to be spoken, still something left over to be revealed to us upon later reading, still one more sermon to be preached on "the real meaning of Christmas," thank God. Thus Scripture engenders interpretive humility, particularly among modern people who enjoy grasping and comprehending everything. Indeed, the very elusiveness of some Scripture is itself an encouragement, a catalyst to human imagination, teasing us toward itself, beckoning us to use our God-given abilities to decipher and to understand. Thus Karl Barth compared the style of Genesis to the vast, too rich, uncontainable novels of Fyodor Dostoyevsky.[17]

Scripture requires the activity of the Holy Spirit to speak. Words become the Word by the empowering presence and activity of the Holy Spirit. Modernity taught that most rational human beings, regardless of background, training, or character, were perfectly capable of unaided understanding, perfectly able to grasp and comprehend everything in the world simply by the use of reason. Scripture frustrates such limited knowing. Scripture opens itself up

to us through the work of the Holy Spirit, whom we cannot ratio-
nalize or control, and modernity is high on control and rationaliza-
tion. Thus, interpretation of Scripture is a communal, pneumatic
affair—a work of grace—requiring considerably more than the
lone, reasoning reader.

The Truth of Scripture

When we say that the Bible is "true," we mean that the Bible's
way of narrating the world is truthful. The Bible's means of making meaning is trustworthy. Its way of understanding and con-
structing the world is faithful to things as they are, and in God's
good time, shall be.[18]

The truth of any statement depends upon what it means, as well
as the way it means what it means. Different literary genres have
different ways of making meaning. If I say, "What's in a name?
That which we call a rose by any other name would smell as
sweet," is this statement true? It's truthfulness depends on the sort
of literature employed and the way it means what it means. The
statement is a quotation from *Romeo and Juliet.* If it were a theory
being proposed by a biologist, or a press release from a government official, that would make a difference.

If, through historical research, it could be shown that *Romeo and
Juliet* is not historically accurate, that the Capulets were not as bel-
ligerent as they are portrayed in Shakespeare's play, who cares?
Different genres of literature play by different rules. If I were to say,
"There was once this traveling salesman, see? And he came upon
this farmhouse and . . ." You are hearing a clue, a code. You are
probably about to hear a tasteless joke. You would apply different
rules for interpretation than if I were to begin in the jargon of con-
tractual law by saying, "Whereas the party of the first part, in consideration for the sum of fifty dollars from the party of the second
part. . . ."

One of the challenges of biblical interpretation is that the Bible
contains a wide array of genre. We contemporary preachers of the
Word marvel at the resourcefulness of these early communicators
of the faith. They use poetry, myth, parable, genealogy, invective,
hyperbole, and a host of other literary devices and conventions to
communicate the truth about God. We do them a disservice when

we apply inappropriate standards of interpretation to the literature that they employ.

Theologian William Placher once noted that when we read the story of the good Samaritan in Luke, no one needs to check a police blotter from the Jerusalem to Jericho highway patrol to understand the story. If we find the story difficult to understand, it will not be because there is some historical problem with the story.[19] Jesus tells this story to initiate a theological transformation, so the challenge to our understanding will be theological rather than historical.[20] As it has been noted, Genesis may not be scientifically true. It is eternally true. It is making a claim not so much about *how* the world came to be, but about *who* enabled the world to be.

Fortunately, biblical texts often provide clues that enable us to identify their genre and thus aid in their interpretation. If the rabbi says, "The kingdom of God is like . . ." we are going to hear a simile, something is going to be compared to something else. "In those days there went out a decree from Caesar Augustus. . . ." It sounds like we are going to read history, because a historical figure is being named. The Bible enjoys often employing a history-like genre in which historical people and places are mentioned in order to give a sense of time and place to the story, in order to give the narrative more location than the merely "once upon a time."

When we read apocalyptic literature in Daniel or Revelation, we are reading a specific genre that has its own conventions and rules for reading. "Apocalyptic" comes from the Greek, meaning "to uncover" or "to reveal." In these strange, gripping images, we are meant to see something that we could not see without the aid of the images. We cannot peel away the layers of metaphor and get the literature down to some abstract theological statement without doing damage to the intent of the literature. There can be no "demythologizing" (Bultmann) that does not end up with something considerably less than the "myth" intends.

We tend to delude ourselves into thinking that we have difficulty with biblical literature, such as apocalyptic, because we are sophisticated and modern, whereas apocalyptic is primitive. But as modern people we are caught in a constricting social location that limits our ability to understand. Apocalyptic is often difficult to understand, not because the literature is communicating in some primitive secret code, but rather because the literature of apocalyptic is attempting to get us to look at something that it is difficult for us to see. This is, namely, that God, not nations, rules the world; that the end of the world is in God's hands, not ours; and that God shall bring all things to fulfillment in accordance with God's purposes. In other words, many of our interpretive problems are more political than linguistic in origin. We say that Jesus' healing miracles are a problem for sophisticated, scientific people like us. What we may mean is that we no longer look to God for our healing. We believe in medicine rather than miracle. Medicine is our major means of achieving immortality, healing, and a life free of pain. So when we make a judgment about what can and what cannot be, what is possible and impossible, our judgments are also testimonials to the sort of world in which we think we live, the sort of gods whom we serve.

We are not taking apocalyptic more seriously when we attempt to apply this literature to our own day, attempting a one-to-one correlation between the supposed events described there and specific politics of our own day. When we fail to take biblical literature on its own terms, we abuse the Bible and fail to respect its own distinctive voices and the rich, resourceful array of genres that biblical writers use in order to communicate the truth. The result is spiritual starvation.

To return to the illustration with which we began, to say, "What's in a name? That which we call a rose by any other name would smell as sweet" is to make a demand upon the listener's imagination. If the imagination is truncated, as I fear the mind's eye of modern folk tends to be, then we will be inclined to ask inappropriate questions of the statement. We may fail to appreciate how the words are creatively attempting to engage a greater range of our interpretive powers than if Romeo had simply asked, "Why is it so important that Juliet has a last name different from mine?"

Peter Gomes calls the Bible, "a book of the imagination."[21] Here is literature meant to stoke, to fuel, even to enflame the imagination. If this is so, then think of the church and its dealings with Scripture as encouragement in the exercise of the imagination.[22] One reason many of our people fail to "get" the Bible is not that the Bible is too old, but rather that our minds are too small.

The Distance Between Us and the Bible

Although issues of history are important, they should not be the primary issues in a pastor's biblical interpretation. Nothing is more frustrating than telling a perfectly good joke only to have someone ask the dumb question, "Now, did that really happen?"

Well, what really happened? There is an undeniable distance between the time of the Bible and our own. Although we should not make too much of that gap between our time and the time of the Bible, we should not deny its existence and the challenges this gap in time and culture pose for our contemporary interpretation. Such gaps are a problem only for the limited modern mind that refuses to learn from any time or culture other than its own. For instance, the biblical writers were not exact about dates and numbers. I have always appreciated this, since I have never been too good at numbers myself. In the Bible, numbers are often of mystical, deeper significance than just the numerals themselves—such as the twelve disciples of Jesus echoing back to the twelve tribes of Israel, perhaps signifying a reconfiguration of Israel in the disciples of Jesus. The number seven and the number three are perfect, holy numbers in the Bible. "Forty days and forty nights" or the thousand years of Revelation mean "a very long time." We must love the way that in the Bible more is going on in most places than meets the eye. The Fathers of the church had a marvelous time with the 153 fish of John 21:11. Why else would the exact number of fish be so carefully and lovingly recalled, they reason, if not for us and our salvation?

For us, a number is just a number—a fact, a solitary piece of data. In the Bible, numbers mean more, whereas in modernity, they tend to mean less. Flannery O'Connor complained that one reason it was so difficult to be a writer in the twentieth century was that modern people had ceased to expect to be surprised by the world, thinking that reality was fairly much whatever they happened to see at the moment.[23]

We read of slavery in Scripture. Although any form of slavery is an evil institution, Hebrew slavery was not simply analogous to African American slavery. Hebrew slavery never had any racial connotations. Making your captives slaves was surely more humane than slaughtering them at the end of battle. Hebrew slavery was more like lifetime indentured servitude and was more a fact of the culture than a prescription for all time.

We know little about the practice of homosexuality in ancient Israel. Homosexual sacred prostitution seems to have been practiced in connection with Baal worship as part of the fertility rites of that religion. When this practice is condemned, is it not safe to assume that the Old Testament's main concern is with idolatrous behavior rather than sexual sin? (Though admittedly, in Leviticus, sexual sin and idolatry tend to go together, as they may in our own day.) When Leviticus 18:22 and 20:13 say, "You shall not lie with a male as with a woman; it is an abomination," the Hebrew *toevah* (abomination) is used to refer to acts that make one ritually unclean—such as eating pork, or engaging in sexual intercourse during menstruation. How ought this apply to two consenting Christian adults today? Any simple correlation, without regard to differences of time and culture, would be an abuse, rather than an honoring of Scripture.

Is Paul's condemnation of the *malakoi* and the *aresenokoitai* referring (as in the *Apology of Aristides*) to the "obsessive corrupter of young boys"? Is this what we mean today when we say "homosexual"? Respect for Scripture urges some care in our application of difficult texts today, as well as even greater care in our dismissal of such texts.

The gap between the cultures of the Bible and our own does make some, but not all, scriptural applications difficult. Sometimes there is a tendency to focus on those passages that are questionable and difficult, and ignore those that are all too clear in their directives. Jesus appears to have been relatively straightforward in his condemnation of marriage after divorce, though it is also clear that early Christian interpreters struggled with his condemnation, and so do we. We struggle to interpret some difficult passages, not simply because we want to weasel out of the Bible's plain demands, but also because we know that sometimes Scripture corrects Scripture. Within the canon is an ongoing argument with itself over certain subjects. In Matthew's Gospel, Jesus often pronounces, "You have heard it said [in Scripture], but I say to you . . ." Most scholars see the book of Job as an extended argument of the smug equation of good works equaling easy lives that occurs in some of the Wisdom Literature. Scripture interprets Scripture.

From Scripture, the church is given more than directives, rules, codes for contemporary Christian behavior. The main gift of Scripture is a world, a culture, a reality constructed (as all worlds, cultures, and reality are fabricated) through words. Words make the world. In the beginning, God created the world through the Word. The world belongs to those who name reality truthfully. Christians are those who, through Scripture, are taught to name the world, not merely as "nature," but rather as "Creation." We learn to name our lives not as under the grip of fate, or luck, but as guided and cared for by providence. We do not make "mistakes." We sin. We do not want to be improved. We hope for salvation.

The Bible has a privileged place in our communication. We are not free, as the church, to rummage about among other authorities, sources of inspiration, and revelation until we have first been encountered by Scripture.[24] To be a Christian means to be someone who learns to lay one's life alongside the biblical text, allowing the text to serve as canon or rule ("canon" means literally "ruler," or "yardstick") for how one gets on in the world. In that primal, originating act—that which we read of in Nehemiah or Luke 4, where the text is set against us in order that we might more faithfully read ourselves into the text, where the Word is read and interpreted and the people respond—is the origin and the sustenance of the people of God who become that way by being the people of the Book.

We believe that the institution of the synagogue arose during Israel's exile. What do a people do who are sojourners in a strange land far from home? You gather together (Greek: *sunagogue*), you sing the songs of Zion (Ps. 137), you tell the story, you name the Name that is above every other name. Thus in our own day the church gathers around the words of Scripture with the expectation that these words will become for us the Word of God Incarnate, that the Word will dwell richly among us, and that we shall be sustained in exile in a foreign land.

Trusting the Bible

The church is never-ending training in learning to trust the Bible, learning to take ourselves a little less seriously and the Bible a bit more so.[25] We gather on Sunday, the Scriptures are opened to the church, we say, "Let's all believe that this ancient book—written in a time and a language quite different from our own, by a people in many ways different from us—knows more than we." Then we attend to Scripture. Bending our lives toward the text that reaches out to us through a wide array of literary devices, thus the church is forever formed, reformed into the church of Christ.

We trust the Bible in much the same way that we learn to trust another person. William Placher notes that when you trust someone, you know them and allow them to know you. You spend time with that person, some of it with serious intent, some of it simply to be with that person. When you converse together, because you have learned to know and to trust one another, you know that person's jokes as jokes, their tall tales as tall tales, their admonitions as words addressed to you out of love. Although we may not understand everything about that person, may not be able to connect everything that is said to us by our friend, we learn to trust that person as having our best interests at heart. We trust that we will not be led astray. We take some delight that our friend, even when we may have known her for many years, is still able to shock, surprise, and confuse us, because such shock and surprise remind us of the delightful, mysterious, not fully comprehensible otherness of our friend.

We trust the Bible because it keeps making sense of, as well as disrupting, the world in which we live. The Bible does not just "make sense" in the sense that the Bible is congruent with our present experiences of and definitions of reality. We must read the Bible in a way that is more careful and respectful than simply going to the Bible, rummaging about, picking and choosing on the basis of what we consider to be possible and permissible within our present context. To do so is not to align our lives with the witness of the saints, but rather to, in Barth's words, "adorn ourselves with their feathers."[26] The temptation is to discard that which makes us uncomfortable or that which does not easily fit into our present conceptual scheme of things. Therefore, an appropriate hermeneutical question is not simply, What does this text mean? but rather, How is this text asking me to change?

Part of the joy of being a biblical preacher is that we get a front-row seat on the spectacle of the creation of a new world. The Bible wants to give us new experiences, to create a new reality that would have been unavailable to us without the Bible. The Bible does not simply want to speak to the modern world. The Bible wants to change the world, to create for us a world, through words, that would have been inaccessible to us without our submission to the text called Scripture. This is not some imaginary world. This is the real world, a world more real than today's newspaper headlines or government press releases.

I read in the newspaper of a woman—I think she lived in Louisiana—who had raised about a dozen foster children despite her meager income as a domestic worker. Why did she do it? She replied, "I saw a new world a comin'."

A major challenge for the biblical preacher is that biblical speech is not easily translated into the prevalent speech of the world. As George Lindbeck put it, when we preachers teach and preach Scripture, we engage in a complex redescription of reality in which we place present, officially sanctioned, received "reality within the scriptural framework rather than translating Scripture into extrascriptural categories. It is the text, so to speak, which absorbs the world, rather than the world the text."[27] My colleague Richard Lischer notes that in most of our seminary preparation we preachers are taught to step back from the text, to attempt to assume a detached, cool, objective, and dispassionate disposition toward the text—Scripture as a cadaver to be dissected. In the African American church, says Lischer, the pastor attempts to step into the text, to try on the text, walk around in it, assume some of the roles that are depicted in the text.[28] The pastor, in preaching, leads the church in stepping into the text, trying on the text, assuming a world in which the text's description of reality is more real than that which we typically privilege as "real."

It is not only "reality" in the sense of the world truthfully described. (During the sex scandal in the Clinton White House, the lectionary directed that we read the story of David's adultery with Bathsheba.) It is also reality in the sense of the world as it is meant to be, a world where Jesus Christ is Lord, rather than Caesar. The reading of Scripture has transferred our citizenship to a world where we are residents of the kingdom of God rather than the kingdoms of this world.[29]

John Calvin compares the reading of Scripture to the donning of eyeglasses that enable us to see things that, without the glasses, we would not have seen.[30] It is of the nature of Scripture to be imperialistic, to impose a world upon its readers and hearers. Erich Auerbach spoke of Scripture as "tyrannical":

> The world of the Scripture stories is not satisfied with claiming to be a historically true reality—it insists that it is the only real world, is destined for autocracy. All other scenes, issues, and ordinances have no right to appear independently of it, and it is promised that all of them, the history of all mankind, will be given their due place within its frame, will be subordinated to it. The Scripture stories do not, like Homer's, court our favor, they do not flatter us that they may please us and enchant us—they seek to subject us, and if we refuse to be subjected we are rebels.[31]

Jesus begins a sermon saying, "Blessed are you who are poor. . . . O how fortunate are those of you who are hungry. . . . How lucky are those of you with a terminal illness. . . . How blessed are those of you who are unemployed. . . . Curse you who are rich. . . . Damn you who are content and satisfied. . . . Pity those of you who are successful."

The congregation does a double take. What is this? In the real world the poor are doomed to lives of grinding poverty with no exit. In the American Way if you are unemployed you must have some sort of social disease. If you had played by the rules, you would not be in this fix.

The preacher clarifies, "I was not talking about your kingdoms. I am rendering the kingdom of God. This is the way God is—lover of the poor, protector of the downtrodden, savior of the lowly. Now you ought to get in step with God's way or else be stupidly out of step with reality now that the Son of God is taking over the world."

We keep trusting the Bible because we keep meeting God in the Bible. In the words of Scripture, we are encountered by the Incarnate Word. We call the Bible "inspired" because the Bible keeps reaching out to us, keeps striking us with its strange truth, keeps truthfully depicting God. God keeps truthfully speaking to us through Scripture as in no other medium. We trust the Bible because on enough Sundays we discover that God's Word has the power to produce the readers that it requires. In the reading of Scripture, the Creator is at work, something is made out of nothing, the church takes form around the words of the Word.

To read Scripture is to risk transformation, conversion, an exchange of masters. You might think of Sunday morning as a struggle over the question, Who tells the story of what is going on in the world? Scripture reading can be uncomfortable, as we are made by the Bible to see things we would have just as soon ignored, as we hear a word we have been trying to avoid. Reading is not only a formative activity but also a potentially disruptive means of exiting our culture, of defamiliarizing and making the normal seem strange and the strange seem normal, of having a delightful respite from conventional, culturally sanctioned accounts of "the way things are." Therefore, the primary interpretive question is not, "Do I understand this passage?" but rather, "How is this text attempting to convert me to Christ?" Behind all Scripture is not simply the question, "Will you agree?" but rather the more political, "Will you join up?"

John Wesley made Jesus' words in his Sermon on the Mount, in Matthew—that we should "be perfect as your Father in heaven is perfect"—a central text in his life. Wesley was stunned by these words, wondering to what sort of church these words might be addressed. It would not be the church as he knew it, a church all too imperfect with worldly accommodation. It must be a church that knew how to organize its life together in such a way as to hear and to live such demanding words. It must be a church that knew how to forgive, because a church attempting to be perfect would have much sin to absolve.

Wesley, borrowing from German Pietists, created a movement based upon small groups—face-to-face accountability groups where ordinary eighteenth-century English people met together, challenged one another, prayed for and forgave one another. Thus was created the Wesleyan revival in England.

Note that Wesley did not consider his role as a biblical interpreter that of modifying the text in order to suit the limitations of the church. Rather, he attempted to change the church to suit the demands of the text. He hoped to produce a church worthy to read and interpret Scripture, rather than explain Scripture in such a way that it might be easily accessible to and easily dismissed by a compromised and adulterated church. When the authority of the Bible is challenged with, "Is the Bible true?" we are not to trot out our little arguments, but rather our little lives. The truthfulness of Scripture is in the lives it is able to produce.

Obedient Playfulness

Pastors, in their counseling, preaching, and teaching, cultivate the virtues of humble, obedient listening to Scripture. We must discipline ourselves not to take a superior attitude toward the text. We ought to nurture, in the words of Walter Brueggemann, an "obedient playfulness"[32] with the text—submitting to Scripture, being willing to be judged and changed by the text, and at the same time playfully delighting in the wonder, the weirdness, the sheer otherness of the text.

I vividly recall the Sunday when the lectionary assigned me Ephesians 5:1-33. Any text that includes, "Wives, be subject to your husbands as you are to the Lord" (5:22) is going to have rough going in my congregation! I know preachers who would simply refuse to even read such a text in the congregation. It seems, at first glance, patriarchal conservatism at its worst. Yet in obedience to the text, I stuck with the text, and with the help of a commentary was made to note that the passage begins not with verse 22, but with verse 21, "Be subject to one another out of reverence for Christ." This is the verse that sets the tone for the whole passage. If subjection is being urged, it is *mutual* subjection, in the manner of Christ, not women's subjugation to men in marriage. Besides, as we read on in the passage, we find that it does not end with this talk on marriage, but rather with the writer stating clearly, "This [i.e., Christian marriage] is a great mystery, and I am applying it to Christ and the church" (5:32). Is it not curious that I immediately wanted to read this passage as concerning what women ought to do in marriage, rather than what all of us are enjoined to be in the church? Why are we more concerned with marriage than with the church? Why did I note the call for the subjection of women without noting the call (5:21) for all of us to be "subject to one another out of reverence for Christ"? I was on my way to a sermon that was derived from the text's playfulness with me, along with my attempt to be obedient to the text. Every sermon ought to be the pastor's demonstration of playful obedience to the text.

We come to a biblical text, raising questions about its relevance to our present daily lives, only to find that the text questions us about *our* relevance to the way of Christ. Sometimes the way that Scripture makes our conventional lives look weird, unmasks our normality as abnormal, is also funny. Although the dour Jerome says that the purpose of preaching is "to set in motion the groan,"[33] humor is a great gift for those who would take Scripture more seriously and themselves less so.

As Barth once said to us preachers:

> We can and must act as those who know. But we must not claim to be those who know. . . . Those who really know will always find and confess that they do not know. The attitude of those who know in this power [of God's self-revelation to us] can only be one of the greatest humility. . . . It is just because they can have no doubt as to the liberation which is quite outside their own control that those who are really free to know this matter can never lose a sense of humor in relation to themselves.[34]

We must live in the text, keeping it constantly before us. This is not so difficult for pastors who must preach on the text each week. However we must read Scripture as more than a source for sermons, something to be explained and delivered to the congregation. We must read, allowing Scripture to have its way with us, to change us, to remake us, call us, embarrass us. Regular, prayerful, playfully meditative reading of Scripture is perhaps the most important pastoral spiritual discipline.[35] Jean Leclercq wonderfully depicts the monk as one whose reading is daily ingestion, chewing in order that Scripture might have the maximum effect upon mind and body. *Lectio*, reading, must be for the interpreter of Scripture always a form of *meditatio*—prayerful, risky contemplation.[36]

In one of the most memorable gyrations of patristic exegesis, Jerome, in his Letter 52, recalls how King David, in his old age, insisted that the young Abishag the Shunammite (1 Kings 1:1-4) sleep with him to keep his old, cold body warm. "A chilly old man is wrapped up in blankets, and only grows warm in a girl's embrace." Who was this warm-bodied young woman? asks Jerome. She cannot possibly be just a warm young woman, for Bathsheba was yet David's wife, and how could the author of the Psalms be in bed with a young woman, be she warm or cold, who was not his spouse? Jerome recalls how Solomon spoke of Wisdom in the feminine, urging us to let Wisdom "embrace" us in order that she not forsake us in our "old age" (Prov. 4:5-9). Jerome makes the happy discovery that the one called Abishag is in reality Lady Wisdom. Thus Jerome urges all pastors to snuggle up close to Wisdom, make her our only comfort during the cold nights of our advanced years, and we shall be eternally warm and comforted. Take that as a counsel constantly to keep close to Scripture![37]

I have been told that the great Old Testament scholar Gerhard von Rad attended a small church in his native Germany—a small church with a young pastor who was not noted for his skill or his preaching. When asked why he kept returning to the church, Von Rad responded that, despite the pastor's inadequacies, he had one great strength. When he read the Bible on Sunday, he always approached Scripture "as if he were opening a package that contained a ticking bomb."

> The voice of the LORD is powerful;
> the voice of the LORD is full of majesty.
> The voice of the LORD breaks the cedars;
> the LORD breaks the cedars of Lebanon. . . .
> The voice of the LORD causes the oaks to whirl,
> and strips the forest bare;
> and in his temple all say, "Glory!"
> May the LORD bless his people with peace!
> (Ps. 29:4-5, 9, 11)

The pastor's interpretive duty can be a resource for pastoral audacity. To be forced through our daily reading and interpretation of Scripture to see ourselves not primarily as servants of the congregation, but of the Word, can be true pastoral freedom.[38] As I heard Walter Brueggemann say, "If you are a coward by nature, [And who among us is not?] then you can get down behind the text. You can peek out from behind it and say to the congregation, 'this is not necessarily what I would say to you, but I do think this is what the text is saying to you.'"

I love that image of the pastor hunkered down behind the text, pushing the text out toward the people. To love the text and its voice more than our own, or even that of our people, is the beginning of wisdom. Toward that end, we pastors do well to cultivate in our reading the practice of *Lectio Divina,* literally the "sacred reading" of Scripture, in which we meditate and ruminate and chew upon Scripture, not merely as a source for sermons, but as a means of regeneration of our souls and adoration of the God who has called us into ministry.[39] We take such care with Scripture in our efforts to obey the voice at the Transfiguration, "This is my Son, the Beloved; with him I am well pleased; listen to him!" (Matt. 17:5).

> O taste and see that the LORD is good. (Ps. 34:8)

It is our conviction, as Jews and Christians, that what we receive in Scripture is more than stories, words, ideas. What we are given is God. Barbara Brown Taylor says that she often asked the people in her Episcopal congregation what sort of Christian education classes they desired. They always responded, "We want more Bible." But when she organized these classes, they were often poorly attended. "Finally," she says, "I got the message. 'Bible' was a code word for 'God.' People were not hungry for information about the Bible; they were hungry for an experience of God."[40]

Time and again in ministry when our well of inspiration appears to be running dry, when we come to question the point of it all, come to doubt our call, Scripture is that which keeps us going. The text reaches out to us in our need. We receive encouragement not of our own devising. We rediscover the wonder of being servants of the Word rather than slaves to the status quo. We are given insight that demands to be shared with the congregation, and the Word of Christ dwells richly in us—or at least we are handed a bomb that blows us to bits.

> Thy word is a lamp to my feet and a light to my path. (Ps. 119:105 RSV)

INTERLUDE
The Wonderful Thickness of the Text[41]

good stuff - if this leave some of for preaching class

Have you ever noticed that when publishers wish to create a comprehensive guide to a particular subject, they like to employ the term *Bible* in the title? *The Quilting Bible, The Backpacker's Bible,* even *The Jeep Owner's Bible* promise clear, practical, down-to-earth guidance on everything and anything related to their particular subject. If you want to know what to do, how to do it, and when to do it, these are the books for you.

I wonder, however, if the authors and publishers of these books ever opened the real Bible. The Bible, you see, is anything but a "how to" kind of book. Move from one of these know-it-all handbooks to, say, the Gospel of Luke, and you'll find it hard to imagine why these authors and publishers ever thought they were producing something that can be called a "Bible." Luke is "thick," the literature is polyvalent, predominantly narrative, almost never propositional, open to multiple interpretations, defying reductionistic reading. If you were to read one or two of these other "Bibles," and then switch to Luke, you would be apt to feel that the biblical texts are almost intentionally obscure, more difficult and strange than they need to be.[42] The thick, impenetrable nature of these texts may be by conscious design. A difficult to understand text catches our attention, begs for attention, and engages our natural inclination to figure things out. On the oher hand, the texts may be difficult, obscure, and distant simply because they are talking about what is true, whereas most of what we live is false. A living, righteous, prickly God tends to produce difficult Scripture.

G. K. Chesterson delighted in the creed, despite its strange complexity, because it demonstrated by its compexity a faith that was "rich in discoveries": "When once one believes in a creed, one is proud of its complexity, as scientists are proud of the complexity of science. It shows how rich it is in discoveries. If it is right at all, it is a compliment to say that it's elaborately right."[43]

For example, one Easter the lectionary demands that my congregation struggle with John 20. John first does the story of Easter as a footrace between the disciples in which they came and then they "saw and believed" (John 20:8). Believed what? John says, "as yet they did not understand the scripture, that he must rise from the dead" (20:9). Presumably they believed that the body had been stolen. Or maybe they believed something else, such as the return of the robin in the spring, or the emergence of the butterfly from the cocoon. Whatever they believed was not quite resurrection yet. Easter ends with everyone going back home (20:10), and that was that. At least the men go home. Mary stays behind to weep. She is confronted by the risen Christ, whom she regards as either the gardener or a body snatcher, or perhaps both (20:15).

Then, just to keep things interesting, John 20:19 begins Easter all over again with the story of Thomas and his doubts. It is Easter evening. Defying resolution or simple understanding, the risen Christ appears again in John 21 in a complex, utterly enigmatic appearance in the dark of evening rather than the first light of morning—an appearance that becomes quite convoluted with details of fish, fishing nets, Peter, and feeding sheep.

We have a problem with this literature. Our problem is not, as we sometimes flatter ourselves into believing, that we are modern, critical, and skeptical, whereas the text is naive, primitive, and credulous. That was historical criticism's reading of our interpretive dilemma in which the readers of the text always take a superior position to the text.[44]

I have come to believe that our problem is that we have become tone-deaf to a text so thick, so opaque, and so rich as John 20–21. We are ill equipped to hear the Easter text. After all, we are modern Western folk who have taught ourselves to be content with a flat, well-defined, and utterly accessible world. Our world has become "user-friendly," for we can imagine no world worth having that is not subject to our utility. Our ways of knowing are positivistic, historicist, and inherently reductionistic.[45] The goal of our thinking, as we sometimes say, is to "grasp" a subject—to know, to seize, and to make certain.

In modernity, we like our readings "thin." Thick readings frustrate us. We want a center, a sequence. When a text works with reality on a number of levels—exploring the complexities of human consciousness, the mystery of time, the polyvalence of words, as so many biblical texts do—we find it difficult to know what to do with them, or to know what they want to do to us.[46]

William C. Placher makes the evocative suggestion that the very messiness of the biblical texts—the way they parallel one another, conflict, repeat, fail to connect—is an embodiment of the God whom they try to bring to speech: "The narratives of this God who eschews brute force were not edited with the brute force necessary to impose a single, clear framework." [47] Just as this God, according to a number of the parables of Jesus, is willing to live with wasted seed, a net full of good and bad fish, and a garden where the weeds mix with the wheat, eschewing violent, coercive purification and harmonizing, so the willingness of the biblical writers and canonizers to live with the messiness of the texts is a testimonial to their faith in a God who chooses to suffer, to embrace human messiness, and to love us in our inconsistency rather than to force us to make sense.

I recently said to a friend who is an expert on Russia, "Things have really become messy over there since the demise of the Soviet Union, what with the breakaway republics, the rebellions, and the difficulties."

He replied, "No. Things were always messy, interesting, and conflicted there, though for a time Soviet tanks made it seem unified and coherent."

The modern lust for unity, for a center, for coherence and cohesiveness, produced not only perhaps the most violent century the world has ever known, but also some of the most dreary centralized governments and collective schemes, to say nothing of some of the ugliest architecture that the world has ever seen.

How do we know what we know? A friend of mine says that there are at least two ways of knowing. One way is that of mathematics and similar endeavors, such as when you are working with a tough mathematical problem, struggling, and then at last you say, "I got it!" That is one way of thinking.

Another way is, say, when you have been to see a great movie, one that makes you a different person in the seeing. You emerge from the theater. You do not say, "I got it." No. What you say is, if you are able to say anything at all, *"It got me."*

The interpretive skills that many of us learned in seminary invariably took a superior stance toward the text; modernity is inherently arrogant. We arrogantly believe that everything lies within the range of our interpretive grasp. All knowing is tied to some scheme of power, and in a capitalistic, democratic culture all knowing begins and ends with the sovereign consumer. So we ask, "What does this text mean to me?" or more precisely, "What can I do with this text?" before simply sitting quietly and letting the text have its way with us.

We cut apart the text, split it up into its smallest units, sever it from the community that produced it, lop off that which offends our modern sensibilities—my verbs are intentional. We are doing the same violence to the text that we do to any culture or people who are strange to us, who do not fit into the categories that we received from the Enlightenment, who refuse to produce the commodities we value.[48]

Much of our violence begins with our modern lust for the one "right" interpretation, the one official reading.[49] All interpretation, including historical criticism (especially historical criticism), serves some configuration of power, some social arrangement. I once thought it shameful that "uninformed" laypersons were busy interpreting biblical texts in all sorts of ways, without the benefit of academic training. I now honor such diversity of readings—particularly when they occur among folk who are not only seeking to understand the text, but to embody and perform the text—as ecclesial resistance against the powers that be who serve the academy rather than the church.

What we need is an interpretive approach to Scripture that is true to the form of the Scripture itself. The Bible, by its very form, renders certain kinds of readers, so the Bible, by its form, is more congenial to certain interpretive strategies than to others.

The text itself encourages, provokes uncentering, dislocation, and dislodgment. The very thickness of the text may be part of the text's strategic assault upon our received world. Literary critic Frank Kermode focuses on the strange moment in Mark 14:51-52 where, as Jesus is being arrested, a "young man" flees naked into the darkness, leaving his cloak in an astonished soldier's hands. Mark does not tell us who the young man is or why he is there at this dramatic moment. The incident seems to intrude, to break the coherence of this important episode in the life of Jesus. No interpretive explanation works to ease the cognitive tension that the reader feels at the mention of this young man streaking into the darkness. Kermode says that the intrusion is much like life itself—at times rough and disordered, not susceptible to simple explanation. In any given moment, more is going on than we know. Perhaps this inexplicable, rough, intrusive character of the episode is intrinsic to Mark's presentation of the Gospel.[50] Thus Mark loves words such as "astonish" and "amaze," for that is the effect that the Incarnation has upon our settled stories.

We pastors need to condition our people to expect interpretive difficulty on Sunday morning, to relish the multiplicity of messages, to love the thickness of the text, to come to church expecting to have their present reality subverted by the demanding text. Too many of us preachers say, after reading a troublesome text, "Give me twenty minutes and I will explain this for you." Even to read a troublesome text and then to say, in a well-modulated voice, "Now I have three things I want to say about this," begins to defuse the text, make it make sense without allowing the text time to make us make sense. To be baptized is to be willing to let the text stand in a superior interpretive position to us, not the other way around. Rather than treating the text like a cadaver to be dissected, we ought to pray with the psalmist, "O LORD, you have searched me and known me."[51]

Easter is true because the text says it is true, because what the text says is true to the church's continuing engagement by the living Christ. It requires, not certitude, the sure fixing of truth, but rather trust, a playful willingness to let the strangeness of the text have its way with us.[52] The text has subsumed us into itself, rendered unto us a world that would have been unavailable to us without the world having been constructed (as most worlds are) by the text. Yet that does not mean that the world rendered thereby exists only in the imagination of the text. Every time the church gathers, breaks the bread, and drinks the wine, we proclaim to any who dare listen that what the text says is true. The text, we believe, has the power to evoke that which it describes. After all, look at us. If Easter is not true, then how do you explain the existence of the church?

We have the text, we believe, as a gracious gift of a God determined not to leave us to our own devices. What happened on Easter, namely, Jesus coming back to us, refusing to leave us alone, intruding among us, is what happens each Sunday in the reading and preaching of the text. Scripture, read and preached, is Easter all over again. And, thank God, we never exhaust the significance of it, despite our most thorough interpretive efforts, for the text and world it renders is thick. There is always a surplus of meaning, even after the longest of our sermons.[53]

Thus John ends his account (at least one of his accounts) of Easter by preaching:

Now Jesus did many other signs in the presence of his disciples, which are not written in this book. But these are written so that you may come to believe that Jesus is the Messiah, the Son of God, and that through believing you may have life in his name. (John 20:30-31)

CHAPTER SIX

The Pastor as Preacher:
Servant of the Word

A person emerged from our church a few Sundays ago, saying to me at the door as she left, "I know that you would not intentionally hurt anyone with what you say from the pulpit, but I was hurt by what you said today in your sermon."

And I thought, "Where you would have gotten the notion that I would not want to hurt you? I'm a preacher. Some infliction of pain comes with the job!" Luther compared the Word of God to a surgeon's scalpel.[1]

Luke 4:16-30 stands as constant warning to us preachers, and to our congregations. Preaching has to do, not simply with our words, but with the Word of God, a Word intruding into our settled arrangements, a Word not of our own concoction. To be the recipient of that Word is sometimes to be in pain because of it. As Luther said, here is a Word that first kills in order to make alive, that damns in order to bless. Preaching is something akin to surgery.

Kierkegaard noted that many people have become famous and prosperous by making modern people's lives easier, inventing labor-saving devices, enabling people to live more comfortably. He said that he felt called to make people's lives more difficult and painful. Therefore, he felt called to be a preacher, a servant of the truth.[2]

One of the major goals of the Continental Reformation was a sweeping reform of the clergy by making them primarily preachers.[3] The Reformation rediscovered the reading and preaching of Scripture. Luther, Calvin, and Zwingli all stressed preaching as a chief pastoral act. Luther spoke of the church as a "mouth house," stressing, as Paul says, that faith comes "by hearing."

The Lutheran *Augsburg Confession* (1530) defines the church as "the congregation of the saints in which the gospel is rightly preached and the sacraments are rightly administered." Note the stress upon the church as "congregation"—a recovery of the sense that all the people of God, gathered about the Word of God, are the "saints"—and the stress upon preaching.

Later Calvin wrote that "where the Word is heard with reverence and the sacraments are not neglected, there we discover the appearance of the church."[4]

For the Reformers, the Word precedes and forms the church. Salvation is rooted in the Word and in faith, not in the good works of the individual or in the offices of the church.

Luther wrote:

> Three great abuses have befallen the service of God. First, God's word is not proclaimed: there is only reading and singing in the Churches. Second, because God's word has been suppressed, many unchristian inventions and lies have sneaked into the services of reading, singing and preaching and they are horrible to see. Third, such service of God is being undertaken as a good work by which one hopes to obtain God's grace and salvation. Thus faith has perished and everyone wishes to endow churches or to become a priest, monk or nun.[5]

This led to new conception of the pastoral ministry. The pastor is now primarily preacher, a *minister verbi divini,* a servant of the Word of God.

Preaching as a Gift of God

When Luke sought to edify Theophilus, he did so through *kerygma,* proclamation of something that has happened (Acts 1:1-5). Preaching is prior to the New Testament, the Scriptures themselves being modes of proclamation in literary form. Through preaching, the Word of God keeps growing, multiplying, leaping over all boundaries (Song of Sol. 2:8; Acts 19:20). Our contemporary proclamation is not a lecture about the Word of God, rather, the church has testified on the basis of its own experience that to encounter preaching is to encounter God, *Praedicatio verbi dei est verbum dei.*[6] God graciously allows the words of us poor preachers to be, in the action of the Holy Spirit, the very Word of God. Nothing, not kings and armies, not even the infidelity of disciples, can defeat the indomitable Word. "The body they may kill; God's truth abideth still," sings Luther's great hymn "A Mighty Fortress Is Our God."

An illuminating episode occurs in Acts 17. Luke has taken Paul to a variety of situations where he has spoken eloquently to the power of the gospel. But can the gospel hold its own in a sophisticated university town? Luke brings Paul to Athens, the cradle of classical civilization, the city of the art of Polyclitus and Phidias. Frankly, Paul is unimpressed. Good Jew that he is, he sees Athens as a wasteland "full of idols" (17:16). So he does a very Jewish thing. "He argued in the synagogue with the Jews . . . and also in the marketplace every day. . . . Also some Epicurean and Stoic philosophers debated with him" (17:17-18). Many mock what Paul has to say, but some, the more open-minded among them, ask him to speak in their Areopagus because they mistakenly believe that he is presenting a "new teaching" (17:19)—even though Paul has been testifying rather laboriously throughout his previous speeches in Acts that the gospel is not an innovation, but rather the fulfillment of God's historic promises to Israel.

This gives Luke the opportunity to depict Paul as a great classical speaker, putting on his lips one of the most perfectly formed of classical orations, conforming perfectly to Aristotle's concepts of a good speech. In earlier sermons, Paul has cited much Scripture. But this sermon is to a group of pagans, so he uncharacteristically begins by basing his argument on a sort of natural theology, adapting his presentation to the limits of his pagan audience.

Aristotle advised winning the trust of one's audience early in the speech. Is that what Paul does when he begins, "Athenians, I see how extremely religious you are in every way. For as I went through the city and looked carefully at the objects of your worship, I found among them an altar with the inscription, 'To an unknown god' " (17:22-23a)? Or is Paul, good Jew that he is, saying something to the effect of, "I see how extremely religious and spiritual you are [not necessarily a Jewish compliment]. I've seen some idolatry in my time, but I think you have more idols in this place than anywhere I've visited. I noticed that you even have an altar to a god whom you don't know. You are ready to worship that god before you even know its name. You've never seen a idol you couldn't bow before."

Whether Paul is praising their groping after the divine (17:27), or criticizing their credulous idolatry, I do not know. He does cite "some of your own poets" (17:28) and our common humanity

(17:26). But then Paul moves to a claim for which there is no natural evidence in nature, no commonsensical access. Paul speaks of one who shall judge the world in righteousness (17:31), one who was vindicated by being raised from the dead. Having lowered their guard by implying that they have access to the divine through their present experience, Paul then inserts that for which there is no prior human experience—judgment and resurrection. These eschatological realities determine the limits of a Christian appeal to human experience, for they reveal a content of Christian proclamation that can only be had as a gift of God, not by our experientially based efforts.

Reaction of the crowd is reminiscent of the responses of some to Peter's speech at Pentecost in Acts 2. "When they heard of the resurrection of the dead, some scoffed," says Luke (17:32). At that point, church is out. Only a couple are converted—Dionysius and a woman named Damaris (17:34). These are rather modest results for one of the most perfectly formed speeches—one of the only classically rhetorical speeches—in the New Testament.

The meager response is proof that Christian communicators such as Paul have a problem. They may try to build upon people's common experiences of the world and nature. They may establish linkages with their culture. Yet at some point the faithful Christian communicator must cite revelation, must put forth that knowledge that does not arise from human experience but rather as a gift. Apostles are defined in Acts as "witnesses to the resurrection" (Acts 1:21-22). When the Resurrection is preached, apostles risk rejection and communicative dissonance. Ultimately, Christian communication, like preaching, is not based upon human experience or upon skillful oral presentation. Preaching is a gift of a God who is graciously self-revealing. Preaching "works" because this God intends to speak, to make contact with a beloved, still being redeemed creation. "[The one] who hears you hears me" (Luke 10:16 RSV). Many a failure of preaching is due not to the poor talents of the preacher, but to the difficulty of the gospel, the strangeness of hearing tell of a world upheld by the one in whom we live and move and have our being, a one quite different from the art and imagination of humanity.

Because preaching is a gift of God, it is prone to failure, as the paltry results of Paul's sermon at Athens prove. We are sinful creatures whose hearing, like our other capacities, is perverted. Pastors are sometimes frustrated by the lack of congregational response to their sermons. Yet, as Paul noted in one of his congregations, we plant the seed and nurture the soil, but it is up to God to give the harvest. Faithful preaching is always more than a respectful conversation between the gospel and the world as we have received it. Though it is that, preaching is also confrontation, assault, announcement, and collision with the received world—all of which can be painful.

The New Testament speaks of "preaching" with a variety of words—the act of proclamation *(keryssein)*, the announcement of good news *(euangelizesthai)*, conversing *(homilien)*, witnessing *(martyrein)*, teaching *(didaskein)*, prophesying *(propheteuein)*, and exhorting *(parakalein)*. All have their roots in the peculiar speech of the synagogue, in the confrontation that occurred there between God's people and God's Word (Acts 13:16-41). Whereas classical rhetoric fashioned public speeches in conformity to the rhetoric of the empire, Christian speaking arose out of the peculiar and manifold intentions of the biblical text. Whereas classical rhetoricians such as Aristotle spent much of their energies concerned with the limitations and desires of the listeners, urging speakers to take care to tailor their speeches to the disposition of their listeners, Christian speaking is first concerned with the disposition of the biblical text and its power to evoke the hearers it deserves before it troubles itself about the desires and deficiencies of those who hear or refuse to hear. The biblical preacher proclaims as the text proclaims, confident that the text is still quite capable of evoking a good hearing despite the limits of either the preacher or the listeners. Or as Acts sometimes says it, even through our pitiful efforts, by the grace of God, "The word of the Lord grew and prevailed mightily" (Acts 19:20 RSV). "The word of God increased; and the number of the disciples multiplied greatly" (Acts 6:7 RSV).

Acts portrays the first days of the early church as a veritable explosion of the Word into all the world. There are some twenty-eight speeches in Acts, mostly preached by Peter and Paul, that account for nearly a third of the entire text. Time and again, often after some episode of fierce resistance to the preaching of the gospel, Acts notes parenthetically, "But the word of God grew and multiplied" (Acts 12:24 RSV). Christ made some extravagant claims for us poor preachers. "[The one] who hears you hears me, and [the one] who rejects you rejects me" (Luke 10:16 RSV). The Holy Spirit is God's creative power that brings things to speech, that prophetically speaks truth to power, that enables the Word of God to overleap all boundaries and overcome every obstacle. The last word in the Acts of the Apostles is a significant "unhindered" (28:31). Nothing, we find in Acts—not the power of Rome, not resistance from God's own people, not the infidelity of the church and its leaders—will hinder the advance of God's Word.

Preaching as Biblical

Acts also presents early Christian preaching as yoked to the Scriptures. Most of the speeches in Acts are tireless, and at times tedious, retellings of the history of salvation, citing events from the history of Israel that in the minds of early Christian preachers show the truth of who Jesus is as the long-awaited Christ. Preaching therefore becomes *Christian* preaching through its subservience to and its conversation with biblical texts. We go to Scripture in the confidence that there we have not only a truthful rendering of God, but also the church's primary means of encountering God. The Bible is the major means of God's speech. In preaching, we pray that our people will not just meet the Bible, but will also be met by God.

Tom Long gives a helpful description of the pastor's task in preaching. Long says that the biblical preacher goes to the biblical text, in service to the congregation, hoping to make a discovery. Then the preacher announces the discovery to the congregation.[7]

Long highlights the key aspects of homiletics. Preaching begins in encounter with the biblical text. As preachers, we do not rummage about in other texts until we have done business with this text, until we have prayerfully, playfully, obediently attempted to listen to the text. This interpretive work is done on behalf of the congregation. The preacher is the one who is ordained by the church to engage in what Leander Keck has called "priestly listening"—listening to the text on behalf of the church, listening to the church so that the preacher might listen with them to the text.[8] Preachers are sometimes characterized as great talkers. But if we are effective and faithful, we are actually great listeners. Bonhoeffer speaks of listening as a holy act:

> Christians, especially ministers, so often think that they must always contribute something when they are in the company of others, that this is the one service they have to render. They forget that listening can be a greater service than speaking.
>
> Many people are looking for an ear that will listen. They do not find it among Christians, because these Christians are talking where they should be listening. But [the one] who can no longer listen to his brother [or sister] will soon be no longer listening to God either. . . . This is the beginning of the death of the spiritual life, and in the end there is nothing left but spiritual chatter and clerical condescension arrayed in pious words.[9]

Think of all of our skills of biblical interpretation as skills in service of faithful listening to the text. It is enough for other Christians to encounter the Bible in order that they grow in their personal relationship with Christ. The pastor bears the burden of listening on behalf of the whole church.

In order to cultivate priestly listening, preachers find themselves grubbing about in other preachers' sermons, perusing novels, attending the theater and movies, scanning the artifacts of their culture in order to better understand and to speak to the inhabitants of that culture. Having learned to expect God's revelation in say, the book of Job, they are not surprised to find Christ lurking, darting in the background from tree to tree (as Flannery O'Connor once put it), present, but not seen except by the eyes of faith. One of the challenges of preaching, for those of us who are called (in Augustine's words) to be "peddlers of words," is to be attentive to words, to be curious about those who make their living through words—such as novelists, comedians, and dramatists—to value those who have the gift of saying things well. Wordsmiths, we are. If preachers are to be good talkers, we must first be good listeners and voracious readers.

I particularly like Long's emphasis on the role of discovery in biblical interpretation. The conventional, the expected, and the already known are uninteresting. Although the Bible is old—very old—the Holy Spirit enables the old to become radically new. Jesus, after reciting a string of parables, told his disciples, "Therefore every scribe who has been trained for the kingdom of heaven is like the master of a household who brings out of his treasure what is new and what is old" (Matt. 13:52). Every "scribe"—that is, faithful, careful reader of Scripture—is also engaged on a voyage of discovery, not simply because congregations love to hear what is new and surprising, but because the gospel of Christ, penetrating our lives of slavery to sin, tends to be, when it is heard, full of shock and surprise. Discovery, that moment when revelation is received, is the beginning of an interesting sermon. Once the preacher, in being engaged by the biblical text, has made a discovery, the preacher will find a way to share it. That is the nature of discoveries; they demand to be shared. In order to share the discovery, the preacher simply recapitulates the process that occurred within the preacher's study of the text. Thus Calvin speaks of sermons as being "twice born"—once in the study, then again in the pulpit. In the sermon, the preacher attempts to recapitulate before the congregation the process of discovery, the surprise and delight of revelation, which the preacher experienced in the study.

The preacher wants to take the congregation along on the same journey with the text that the preacher experienced. A sermon is not an object that sits there, awaiting delivery to a passive congregation. A sermon is a journey through time,[10] a dynamic encounter with the living Christ. Kierkegaard once complained that the preaching in his day was like reading a cookbook to someone who was starving.

Melville famously portrayed the pulpit itself as the prow of a great ship that ventures into uncharted waters:

> The pulpit is ever this earth's foremost part; all the rest comes in its rear; the pulpit leads the world. From thence it is that the storm of God's quick wrath is first descried, and the bow must bear the earliest brunt. From thence it is that the God of breezes fair or foul is first invoked for favorable winds. Yes, the world's a ship on its passage out, and not a voyage complete; and the pulpit is its prow.[11]

For this momentous journey to begin, the form of most sermons is determined by a pattern of biblical discovery. One Sunday I am confronted by the assigned gospel for the day, Luke 13:18-20. Jesus offers two pithy parables, one comparing the kingdom of God to the germination of a tiny mustard seed (Luke 13:18-19), the other to a woman who hides some yeast in three measures of flour (Luke 13:20-21). Seeds are small, so are grains of yeast, yet they result in spectacular growth. The kingdom of God is like that. From the small comes something great. Do not be discouraged by the smallness of the origins of the kingdom of God—just twelve disciples to help Jesus take over the world. By God's grace there will be grand growth.

However, on my way to a sermon on small to great, I consult a biblical commentary that tells me that it is doubtful this could be the main meaning of the parable of the woman and the yeast. It is probable that it is the meaning of the parable of the seed, but not the yeast. Yeast, the commentary tells me, is never used as a positive image in the Bible. Yeast was that putrid, smelly stuff mixed into dough to leaven bread. Leaven was thus a symbol of decay, corruption, and infection. What does it mean for Jesus to say that the kingdom of God comes through that which we regard as decadent, corrupt, and infecting?

This is the only parable in this section of Luke's Gospel that involves a woman, a person on the margins of society, someone outside the usual paths of power. Furthermore, Jesus does not say that she mixed the yeast into the dough. He says that she "hides" it there, as a thief hiding the loot. It is a strange word to find in the kitchen.

I make, with the help of a commentary, a discovery. The kingdom of God sometimes comes from the margins, through people whom we regard as those of little account, in strange, unexpected, hidden, even illicit ways.

I thus begin my sermon asking, "Have any of you ever known God's kingdom to come among you through the wrong person, in the wrong way?" With that, I am on my way to a sermon that recapitulates the discovery I made in my study. I was given, by God's grace and my study, something fresh and engaging to say to the congregation, something derived from the peculiarity and truthfulness of the Scriptures.

In a previous discussion, we have characterized the move from the biblical text to the sermon as "a series of respectful questions of the text." We tend to ask questions of the Bible, such as, What is of relevance here for today's Christians? How can I help my people hear this text on its own terms? What is the most pressing message of this text?

Yet my questions ought to be respectful. As the preacher, I am not in a superior position to the text. As Elizabeth Achtemeier once said, our role as preachers is to preach the Bible, not apologize for it.[12] In regard to the Bible, I am Scripture's advocate rather than its judge. One of the chief responsibilities of baptized Christians is to submit to Scripture, to let Scripture judge our discipleship rather than for us to judge the possibility and permissibility of Scripture's demands. Preaching is a major means of helping us fulfill that responsibility.

It may be more accurate to think of the Bible questioning us, rather than us questioning the Bible. "Lord, you have searched me and known me," says the psalmist. We must read the Bible in such a way that the Bible is allowed to read us, to interpret our world in the light of the reign of God in Jesus Christ. "Adam, where are you?" the Lord asked our first ancestor in the Garden of Eden. So our primary question may not be, Is this biblical material relevant to me? But rather, How can we better align our lives to the demands of Scripture? It is not, Does this passage address my needs as a twentieth-century person who uses a fax machine? But rather, How does this passage rearrange and judge our notions of our needs? The burden of Scripture is also a blessing that relieves us of the pointless burdens that this society places upon our backs.

Among the "respectful questions" that we might ask of a biblical text on our way to the sermon, I think of these:

1. *What is there about the text that is unusual, challenging, strange, or engaging?* We have been conditioned to search for the familiar, the useful, and the compatible in the text, assuming a basic congruence between our questions and the answers of the text. Yet I am pleading for a fresh recognition of the great difference between our ways and God's ways—Kierkegaard's "infinite qualitative distinction" between us and God. We come to the text expecting to be challenged, shocked, jolted by the text. Therefore, we preachers must ask questions such as, Where is the trouble within the text? What about this text is weird? Where, in the words of James Forbes, does lightning strike? At what point does the text appear to be an assault upon our worldview? We pray that God will give us the sort of bold, imaginative receptivity whereby our reading of Scripture will

be a catalyst toward proclamation of Scripture. My job as a preacher is not to smooth out all the rough edges of Scripture, to repackage the gospel in such a way that it makes sense on the basis of our conventional ways of making sense. My job is to enjoy the distance between us and God, working that space for all it is worth. Preachers learn to exploit the unusual, challenging, and strange aspects of Scripture, to see such incongruities and points of incomprehensibility as doors into the text, as revelatory of ways in which the gospel wants to transform us. We are hoping to make a discovery, to hear something that we would not have heard without an encounter with this text.

This is not really exegesis as some of us learned it in seminary—the laborious picking apart of a biblical passage into its smallest parts, its allegedly earliest strata. Such questions can be revealing about the text, but the preacher desires more than information from the text. The preacher is looking for a message that moves, an announcement that is crying out to be shared, a summons that makes a claim upon us, that which the church calls "the Word of God." A sense of playfulness before the text, and a willingness to be surprised by the text, can be helpful qualities for the biblical interpreter who interprets the text for preaching. Our series of respectful questions is our attempt to be engaged by the text. Whereas the joy in much Scripture is the joy of hearing again that which is already known and loved, there is much joy in the strange and the unknown. First impressions are important during this phase. I have sometimes told students, "If you can find nothing in your study of a biblical text that excites you, then don't preach on it. There is no way for you to engage a congregation in a biblical passage that has not engaged you." I can say this out of the conviction that, with nearly any biblical text, careful, creative study of the text will yield excited engagement with the text.[13]

2. *How shall I develop my sermon on this text?* Now the journey is recapitulated. This is a series of moves whereby the preacher attempts to recapitulate for the congregation that same process whereby the preacher made a discovery in the text. How did you get from where you are to where the text is? For instance, on Pentecost, the interpreter makes a discovery that Acts 2 depicts strange, ecstatic acts—quite a contrast to most mainline American religions. The story ends with the crowd mocking the church,

calling us drunk, even though it is only 9 A.M.! That contrast, that rather humorous event, is recapitulated for the congregation. The gap between our buttoned-down, respectable, overly rationalized, moderate discipleship is noted and exploited. The congregation is given permission for a more exciting, even drunken experience of the Holy Spirit. Many dull sermons begin by having nothing interesting to say in the first place. If we have something interesting to say about a biblical text, we shall find the means to say it. In fact, the text itself is often our chief clue to how to say what the text says.

3. *How shall I design my sermon on this text?* Now is when we make judgments about the sermon's form. Will I deal with the text early in my sermon, or will I wait until later to bring out my text? Which illustrations and metaphors will I use, and when will I use them? How will the sermon *do* to the congregation something analogous to what I believe this text *did* to its original hearers? The Bible not only means to speak to us; the Bible means to do something to us. Stories unfold over time. Narratives take us from one place to another. Save your central idea until the end of your sermon. Take your congregation on the journey. Do not announce the destination of that journey at the beginning. Let them discover the destination for themselves. The form of a sermon ought to be congruent with our encounter with the biblical text. If the text is narrative, then the sermon ought to have a narrative feel about it. If the text is inconclusive, without a stated conclusion or "point," then the sermon can mirror some of that inconclusiveness. We do not arrive at the end of the story until we have been carefully prepared for it, teased. Sermons ought to be events that unfold over time. If we announce the end too early, if there is no conflict to be resolved, no dilemma to be worked out through the course of the sermon, the sermon is dull and uninteresting. In preaching, form is an indispensable aspect of content. The arguments we make in oral communication cannot be separated from the form we use to make those arguments. Form is not a passive, neutral container for what is expressed. Attentiveness to the movement, structure, and form of the biblical text can be a great help toward composing a sermonic form that does what the text does.

4. *How shall I say this sermon?* This is what we sometimes call "delivery." It is one of the most important of preaching steps, though an often neglected one in our sermon preparation. Issues of

style, voice, pacing, inflection come here. You want to get the sermon off the printed page and into an oral form. Some preachers are prejudiced against concerning themselves greatly with delivery. Their theology of preaching tells them that the truth of God is self-evident, needing no fancy frills or rhetorical presentation. This attitude overlooks the considerable range and skill of biblical communicators who, in the Scriptures, utilize remarkable literary creativity and diversity in their presentation of God. In preaching, style is substance, the way the truth is presented is part of the truth. Just as we cannot boil a parable of Jesus down to one abstract idea without losing much of the force of the parable, so we cannot simply list a series of good ideas and have a proclamation of the gospel. Sometimes preachers spend so much energy in their exegesis and initial study and preparation of what they are going to say in a sermon that they have no time or energy left for struggling with *how* they are to say a sermon. In most studies of lay reaction to preaching, issues of style and delivery are foremost in the listeners' minds, perhaps because our listeners instinctively know that style and delivery are integrally related to substance and content. When they say, after a sermon, "That was a good enough talk, but it just wasn't a sermon," what they usually mean is they have been subjected to an artless, cold presentation rather than an announcement of good news. The preacher stands up to speak as the herald who bears news that stays news because it is the good news that is essential for our salvation.

Preaching as an Art

To be sure, preaching is one of the most demanding and difficult of pastoral tasks. Good preaching requires so wide a range of gifts and skills. It is no wonder that some have asked if it can be taught at all. "Preachers are born, not made." Although the natural gifts of the preacher count for much, good preaching is an art, not magic. It must be learned. As with any art, preaching is an alloy of gifts and training, natural inclination and cultivated dispositions. Because preaching is an art, the best methods of homiletical education tend to be modes of apprenticeship—a novice looking over the shoulder of an experienced master of the art in order to get the insights, moves, and gestures required to practice that art. For this reason, homiletics is often the most difficult practice to teach at a seminary, and often the most poorly learned. Preachers are made through intense engagement between a master and a novice—the master being willing to take the time to get to know the novice, the novice being willing to submit to the moves, habits, and insights of the master. Preaching cannot be learned, as it is often attempted to be taught, with a group of twenty passive seminarians sitting through lectures in a homiletics class, handing in a few written "sermons" during the course of the semester.

John Chrysostom says that a preacher needs two basic attributes: "contempt of praise" and "force of eloquence." I find it fascinating that he links these two particular qualities. If the preacher lacks eloquence, then the preacher "will be despised by the people and get no advantage from his sublimity." On the other hand, if the preacher "is a slave to the sound of applause," the preacher will speak more "for the praise than the profit" of the congregation.[14] Thus, the great Chrysostom does not shrink from calling for artful eloquence in preaching, yet always for art in service to gospel truth.

There has always been a certain uneasiness among Christian preachers in admitting that preaching is an art, a craft with certain techniques and skills that can be learned and refined in the practice of preaching. If preaching is a gift of God, an act of revelation, does it not seem disingenuous of a preacher to prepare, plan, craft, and practice the delivery of a speech that ought to come straight from God? Paul shows this tension when he tells the church at Corinth:

> When I came to you, brethren, I did not come proclaiming to you the testimony of God in lofty words or wisdom. For I decided to know nothing among you except Jesus Christ and him crucified. And I was with you in weakness and in much fear and trembling; and my speech and my message were not in plausible words of wisdom, but in demonstration of the Spirit and of power, that your faith might not rest in the wisdom of men but in the power of God. (1 Cor. 2:1-5 RSV)

It is noteworthy that Paul says that he "decided," that is, planned and contrived, to speak in a certain way to the Corinthians. He self-consciously constructed his appeal to them in order that it not appear self-consciously constructed, so that the Corinthians might not be impressed by Paul's oratory, but rather by the "power of

God." In other words, there is no way around the necessity of rhetoric—consciously or subconsciously contrived ways of speaking that aim to persuade listeners. Paul is a great model for us preachers as we marvel at the wide array of creative rhetorical devices that he employs in order to communicate his beloved gospel.

Homiletical Disciplines

It is essential that pastors nurture a life of study and reflection to undergird their preaching ministry. "When your head droops at night, let a page of Scripture pillow it," advises Jerome.[15] The work of communicating the gospel with the congregation on a weekly basis is too intellectually and spiritually demanding to attempt to do it without regular contact with the wellsprings of inspiration that keep us alive as preachers. Thus most good preachers find it essential to *schedule certain times during the week when they engage in that difficult, solitary task of study.* The intense, public roles of pastors at times compete with, and sometimes overwhelm, the pastor's ability to make time to prepare for preaching. The result is all those congregations who lament the demise of vibrant proclamation in today's church.

Experience tends to be a great teacher of preachers, if preachers *develop a pattern of self-criticism and reflection.* Long ago Aristotle noted that friendship takes time, hours of conversation, sitting quietly with the friend, observing the friend in a variety of contexts and situations. Perhaps, therefore, we ought to think of biblical study for preaching as a lifelong attempt to make friends with Scripture, letting God be God, allowing Scripture to speak on its terms rather than ours.

It takes most of us preachers a number of years before we feel that we have found our "voice" in the pulpit, before we have confidence in ourselves and in our own way of speaking that enables us to claim our gifts as preachers. Constant involvement with the biblical text and the congregational context becomes the catalyst whereby the gospel strikes fire in our hearts, whereby we receive a message that needs to be given, and thereby we find the means to deliver the message. When a message grips the heart and mind of the messenger, that messenger will find the means to speak it.

As we have noted, Augustine referred to himself as a "word merchant." Even amid the tug and pull of a busy, often fiercely controversial episcopate, Augustine found time to preach almost daily. Let us preachers take him as a guide. When it comes down to it, all we have are words to do our work. No one has given us an army, or a set of laws, or great wealth—the way the world gets done much of its work. Therefore, *we must read everything, and talk to everybody, and listen too, noting how people speak and how they hear. And go to movies.* I find it helpful always to have with me a little notebook (some of those new computer notepads also ought to be useful) where I jot down interesting phrases, stories, and insights.

While on my way down the sidewalk to preach at the Episcopal Cathedral in Buffalo, I was forced to walk around a fiercely arguing couple. She yelled, "Man, you don't tell me nuttin'." To which he replied, "Woman, I done told you, now I tells you, and before I'm done, I'll retell you. Don't tell me what you won't be told!" Such sidewalk poetics demanded to be noted by someone who makes his living doing a great deal of telling and retelling.

John Wesley took pride at being "a man of one book"—the Bible. But it is clear that Wesley read widely among the pagan authors, citing contemporary plays and secular writings, "plundering the Egyptians," as he called it. I heard Fred Craddock say how much he had been inspired by Gustave Flaubert at that point in *Madam Bovary* where he makes the aside, "Of all the winds that blow on love, the request for money is the coldest." In such moments we preachers feel a kinship with a fellow worker with words, even though the writer may not share our faith commitments.[16]

Eugene Peterson, in expressing his debt as a preacher to the novels of Dostoyevsky, says that he loved the Russian because he was "God-intoxicated and word-drunk."[17] What a wonderful friend for a preacher.

Oddly enough, *imitation can be an aid in the task of at last finding our own voice.*

Classical rhetoricians made their students memorize the speeches of others for years before they allowed them to construct speeches of their own. John Wesley told his preachers to preach all of his sermons before they attempted to preach their own. Through audio and video tapes, developing preachers have the opportunity for critical reflection upon the preaching of others. Most preachers inculcate the timing, the gestures, and some set pieces from the sermons of other preachers, eventually making them theirs, integrating them into a repertoire of sermonic style to be drawn upon as needed.

Richard Lischer shows how Martin Luther King Jr. was heavily indebted to the master preachers under whom King served as homiletical apprentice. As a student at Morehouse College, King carefully studied, and systematically imitated, the stylistic devices of Morehouse's dynamic president, Benjamin E. Mays. Then, at Crozer Seminary, King spent many a Sunday afternoon at "Barbour University," the name that African American students gave to the parsonage of the most learned and influential black-church preacher in the area, J. Pius Barbour. The developing preachers would memorize the sermons of distinguished homileticians of the day and deliver these sermons to one another in afternoon preaching marathons in Barbour's living room. "He made the gospel live for me," said King of Barbour's tutelage.[18]

Style, though often neglected in seminary homiletics classes, is probably the last aspect of preaching to develop in a pastor. Elements like sermon design, arrangement of material, logic, and substance are easier to teach and can be learned earlier. Style has to do with congruence between the form and movement of the biblical text, the expectations within the congregational context, and the personality of the preacher. Aristotle said that we make our appeal to our hearers through *logos (reason, logic, and rational argument)*, pathos (emotion, appeals to sentiment and feeling), and *ethos* (the character of the speaker and the audience's respect for the speaker). The most important element, according to Aristotle, was *ethos*. Listeners respond first to who we are, our credibility with our audience, before they hear what we say. The Latin orator, Quintilian, stressed the importance of the speaker's character even more, defining the good speech as *vir bonus dicendi peritus* ("a good person speaking well"). Probably the most popular definition of preaching in the modern era was that of Phillips Brooks, "preaching is the bringing of truth through personality."[19] When I coedited the *Concise Encyclopedia of Preaching*, I noted that this was the most frequently cited definition of preaching in the articles submitted. Although I think it is important to lay the stress more upon "truth" than upon "personality," Brooks's definition strikes experienced preachers as essentially right. *It is the nature of preaching to demand embodiment by the preacher, performance, and incarnation,* in order that it evoke response, embodiment, and enactment among the hearers.

In the middle of a sermon, Augustine wonders at the ability of his spoken words in the sermon to become the Word made flesh in the lives of his congregation:

> The word in my mind exists before it is put into language. I search for the right sound to carry it abroad. I need a way for it to reach you without leaving me. And even now you are hearing what I have in my heart, and it is in yours. It is in both of us, and you are now possessing it without my losing it. And just as my word had to take on sound in order to be heard, so God's word took on flesh in order to be seen. (Sermon 225.3)[20]

Thus the Benedictine scholar Jean Leclercq depicts our role as interpreters of Scripture as one of total involvement of all our capacities:

> To meditate is to read a text and to learn it "by heart" in the fullest sense of this expression, that is, with one's whole being: with the body, since the mouth pronounced it, with the memory which fixes it, with the intelligence which understands its meaning and with the will which desires to put it into practice.[21]

All of this stress upon the quality of a preacher's life as essential to good preaching undoubtedly makes many of us preachers nervous. Did we not begin this book (chapter 1) by noting the church's condemnation of the Donatists for their emphasis upon the character of the pastor as determinative of the effectiveness of the pastor's ministry? The Donatists may have been wrong as far as an orthodox theology of the sacraments is concerned, but they seem to have been right when it comes to preaching. Congregations need to believe that we preachers either do or do not believe our own witness and are attempting, as best we can, to embody that of which we speak. Who preaches seems to be very important for congregational receptivity to what is preached. Because of the nature of Scripture—words that demand performance and discipleship—congregations are right to want a preacher who not only talks to them, but also walks the faith with them.

Congregations have an excellent vantage point from which to observe the congruence between the pastor's exhortation and the ethics of the pastor's own life. Preaching is ethically demanding. Because the gospel tends to be more powerful when it is performed and embodied within the lives of a specific congregation, and because the gospel is an intensely communal activity, the congregation is the native habitat for, and the best place to practice, Christian preaching. It is precisely this attempt at congregational embodiment of the words of the Bible that, in David Kelsey's words, makes a text "Christian Scripture." To call a text "Scripture" means "that it functions to shape persons' identities so decisively as to transform them . . . when it is used in the context of the common life of Christian community."[22] In the words of P. T. Forsyth, "The one great preacher in history . . . is the Church. And the first business of the individual preacher is to enable the Church to preach."[23]

In the book of Job, rising up from his ash heap, in great misery for many, many chapters, Job cries out to the Lord. He attempts to understand God, to ask questions of God, to explain God. His friends come to him and they also speak, without much beneficial effect upon Job's plight. Finally, God appears. God speaks from out of a terrifying whirlwind, raving, shouting, mocking, "Where were you when . . . ? Who are you to . . . ?" Job then must have wondered why he was so insistent to hear the voice of God!

The presence of God, the discernment of God's speech, is not always easy or pleasant. Sometimes that voice—that voice that is not ours, but God's—makes our lives more difficult and painful. Yet in that voice is our life, and that abundantly. It is the preacher's awesome task to be an instrument of that voice within the life of the congregation.

A master wordsmith gives masterful encouragement to contemporary servants of the word:

WORDS WE TREMBLE TO SAY OUTLOUD[24]
Barbara Brown Taylor

From the beginning of time the speaking of God's word has been an act of great power. God said, "Let there be light," and there was light. Moses delivered the Law to Israel, and Torah became the covenant of their life together. John the Baptist cried in the wilderness, "Prepare the way of the Lord" and the way was prepared, his very words paving the desert where Jesus would walk.

Sometimes the power of the Word is not so evident. Jeremiah was a laughing stock; Hosea, a cuckold; and Ezekiel, an exile—which may be God's way of telling us that no one can judge the power of God's word by its results. God is in charge of the results. It is enough for us to proclaim the word and to believe that in doing so we change the world whether the world knows it or not, whether we know it or not, simply by standing and speaking the words we have been given to say, words of love and challenge, words of judgment and grace, words of such truth and terrible clarity that sometimes we tremble to say them out loud. You don't need a grand pulpit to utter them from; any old housetop will do. Take the sun room at the nursing home, where you stand by the piano surrounded by wheelchairs full of old people, some of them dozing, some of them whimpering to go back to their rooms, less than half of them even aware that you are there. Say "resurrection" in their presence. Say "life everlasting." Say "remember." Just let those words loose in the room, just utter them in the light and trust them to do their work. Or speak to a support group for people with AIDS. Worship with them if you can, lay hands on their heads and pray for their healing. Say "mercy" to them. Say "hope." Say "beloved children of God." Set those words free in their hearing and trust in their power to make people whole. Or let something you care about land you on the steps of city hall, where you stand staring into television cameras wondering what in the world you have gotten yourself into. Say "justice." Say "peace." Say "the righteousness of God," and never mind what other people say. Never mind that they walk past you without reading your sign or put you in the back of a paddy wagon and take you away. God is in charge of the results.

Wherever you are and whatever happens to you, just speak the word that has been given you to say, whatever it may be. Never forget that the very act of speaking sets God's word into motion, that your own willingness to utter it out loud is the best proof that it is an active word, as true and lively now as it was when it separated light from darkness and filled the earth with living things. Dare to create a new world with God's words. Give the people who listen to you new images of a new earth full of new people. And be careful of the power you have been given. Treat it as carefully as a stick of dynamite and use it with as much respect. Learn all that you can about the word you proclaim: study it, argue with it, fear it, love it, live it. Then let it go. Set it free.

INTERLUDE
Preaching in Acts[25]

In Luke's Acts of the Apostles, when the Pentecost crowd out in the street divides itself between those who ask, "What does this mean?" and those who explain the outpouring of Spirit as mere drunkenness (Acts 2:12-13), Peter preaches. This is the same Peter who only a short time before had nothing to say when confronted by the maid (Luke 22:54-62) at midnight. That the one previously so frightened should now be the one so bold, that outsiders' curiosity and scoffing should be countered with pure proclamation, is preview to the centrality and power of the Word in Acts. In Acts, there is just about nothing that the Word cannot do.

Today, many pastors wonder if preaching does much good. When the sermon is finished and the preacher has done his or her work, what becomes of our preaching? On the one hand, the TV church is gripped by razzle-dazzle, slick techniques for evangelistic entertainment—God's Word is too boring in itself. On the other hand, liberationists praise praxis and political action against injustice as more faithful than the empty religious words of a bourgeois-ensnared church.

Added to these options is yet another: Preachers must be more creative, they must learn to tell stories, to create drama, to be poets. Urged to be television showmen, revolutionary warriors, twenty-minute novelists, no wonder that preachers often seem tired and depressed. Where can preaching be renewed?

Something to Preach

The need for renewal is not new. In his double preface (Luke 1:1-14; Acts 1:1, 2), Luke states why he wrote for Theophilus: "That you may know the truth" (Luke 1:4). The name "Theophilus" means literally "lover of God." Acts is written to this early lover of the God that he may know the truth, the *asphaleia* that has occurred in Jesus Christ. Among the possible meanings of the noun *asphaleia* as Luke uses it (Luke 1:4; Acts 2:36; 5:23; 21:34; 25:26) are those that denote reassurance with regard to one's faith. We wonder what predicaments affected Theophilus and his church, how his faith was being tested, in what areas of belief and practice he needed to be strengthened and reassured. We can only infer the specific issues that Luke is addressing, for he is too good a storyteller to turn aside from his narrative to explain to us. What is certain is that Luke— the most subtle and self-consciously "artistic" of New Testament communicators—uses every literary device in his homiletical bag of tricks to minister to Theophilus and his church. Any servant of the Word must marvel at Luke's communicative abilities, must realize that in confronting Luke-Acts we are in the presence of a master preacher.

How sad, therefore, if the preacher goes to Acts looking for a sermon and comes away only with history ("Is this Paul's second or third journey?") or moralism ("If we could only be more like First Church Jerusalem!"). Although history is important to Luke as he writes his allegedly "orderly account" (Luke 1:3), history here is the vehicle of kerygmatic art; not art in its modern expression—the chic pastime of a jaded bourgeoisie—but art in service of the conversion and sanctification of the church. We preachers would do well to preach Acts as we preach Luke's Gospel, interpreting Acts as a novel rather than church history. (Ezra Pound once defined a novel as "news that stays news.")

But let preachers be warned about the peculiar way in which Acts is art. There is currently much interest in inductive and narrative preaching, "new homiletic" and storytelling. Luke appears to be the New Testament example par excellence of these trends. He can tell a good story, and he likes nothing better than to slip up on us from behind and surprise us with the truth.

Yet unlike some contemporary practitioners of narrative preaching and homiletical storytelling, Luke's artistic abilities are subservient to his theological assertions. Acts never claims to be a very entertaining story. It is a very *true* story, not some soothingly subjective expression of *my* story, but rather an embodiment of *the* story. Through instruction, correction, and catechesis, Luke wants Theophilus to know *asphaleia* not only as assurance and security of faith, but also as faithful rendering of the testimony of "those who from the beginning were eyewitnesses and ministers of the word" (Luke 1:2 RSV). Make no mistake about it, says Luke; something has really happened here. We must attend to this "accurate and orderly account" of eyewitnesses in a time when there is hermeneutical suspicion about anything that is past. Diverse Gnostic theologies of this or that attempt to enlist an imaginatively reconstructed Jesus to back up their ideologies. The "Jesus Seminar" reads the New Testament and devises a Jesus that looks suspiciously like a West-coast professor, a Spirit-intoxicated peasant, a wandering cynic, a social revolutionary, or some other Jesus more congenial to our sensibilities than the prickly Jesus whom the Gospels give us.

Luke would have us listen to his "eyewitnesses," allowing them to judge contemporary interpretations, not vice versa. The "Word of God" (Acts 4:29, 31; 6:2, 7; 11:1; 12:24; 17:13), when uttered faithfully, unleashes the power of God to accomplish God's purposes.

For Luke, the preacher has significance only as faithful bearer of this Word. For instance, if I, like Peter and John, had had a close and potentially disastrous brush with the authorities (Acts 4:23-31), my prayer would be for divine protection. But the disciples' prayer is "grant to thy servants to speak thy word with all boldness" (4:29). It is God's business to work signs and wonders in the name of Jesus (4:30). It is the community's business to speak the Word with boldness. For Luke, "eyewitnesses" are those who have witnessed the power of Christ's presence and its effects. In stressing eyewitnesses to the Word, Luke maintains the "objectivity" of the Word, the Word as divine gift and fact of God's self-disclosure. As Peter said, "This Jesus God raised up, and of that we all are witnesses" (2:32). Faithful preaching rests not upon the personality of the preacher, the preacher's homiletical ability to work up a crowd, or the artistic excellence of the sermon, but upon the facts as delivered, a faithful assertion of what has happened in the Christ. Success—response—is not our worry.

Luke's address to Theophilus suggests that Acts is preaching as a catechetical proclamation to strengthen those who already know, rather than an evangelical appeal to those who do not. Chief among his various intentions was Luke's effort to reinforce Theophilus's trust in the power of the Word to deliver him and his church from whatever trials beset them. In confronting the powers of this world, be they Caesar's legions, or adversaries within the community or without, some power other than our own is needed. That power comes through the Word.

By the end of the story, Theophilus shall be strengthened in belief, although not through his assent to certain doctrines of the church, or by his subjective resonance with what he feels personally to be true for him. Rather, Theophilus will have encountered an independent, self-disclosing power set loose in the world. Like a thief in the night, the birth of a child to a virgin, a flash of light, the rush of a mighty wind, it shall come upon him, stealing in as a word from without, changing him while he thought he was just reading history. Behind Luke-Acts is the confidence that Christian life and proclamation become significant for the world when Christians are grasped by something significant to say. When the message grips the messenger, the renewed messenger will find the means to speak, even as Peter finds his tongue at Pentecost to tell the crowd in the street that something indeed has happened "to you and to your children and to all that are far off, every one whom the Lord our God calls to him" (Acts 2:39 RSV).

As noted in the previous chapter, though the Word is powerful, even when it is preached by one so able as Paul (Acts 17), the preached Word is not utterly omnipotent, though Isaiah 6:9-10 is about the New Testament's most quoted text. Room is left for rejection of the Word. Not only are the preacher and the congregation sinners whose ears are stopped, but preaching is of God. We have no means, no technique for controlling preaching's power, of ensuring a hearing. Only the Holy Spirit does that. The results of Paul's preaching in Athens are mixed. Some believe; others scoff, just as they did at Pentecost when Peter preached. There are modern commentators who charge Luke with triumphalism. Gabriel tells Mary, "With God nothing will be impossible" (Luke 1:37 RSV). We read about the heroic Paul in Acts, and virtually nothing of the historical Paul's theology of the cross. Acts is replete with stories of the power of the gospel to break all barriers and to surmount all hurdles, of the "many wonders and signs" accomplished by the apostles (Acts 2:43; 5:12). These suggest that Theophilus and his church needed encouragement for Christian proclamation in a time of discouragement. Luke ministered to their discouragement with all these accounts of how, despite constant resistance, "the word of

God grew and multiplied" (Acts 12:24 RSV). The conscientious interpreter may become more than a little uneasy after the twentieth account in Acts of some miraculous effect of the Word of God. Might such homiletical triumphalism boomerang against Theophilus? If where the Word is rightly preached, all barriers are overcome, the church unites, every sermon ends in converts, and demons are put to rout, then how is Theophilus to explain his discouragement? The attempt of the television evangelist to minister to his listeners' despair by accounts of divine intervention, miraculous healings, and material blessings can lead to even greater despair when life fails to deliver the promised goods.

At nearly every turn, Luke qualifies his stories of gospel-inspired success with honest admission of gospel-related rejection. The first sermon in Acts, that of Peter on Pentecost, ends with the audience split between those who wanted baptism and those who thought the preacher was drunk. After the martyrdom of Stephen, "a great persecution arose against the church in Jerusalem" (Acts 8:1 RSV). Jesus' first sermon in Nazareth ended with the congregation trying to kill him rather than shaking his hand at the door (Luke 4:16-30). Acts says that the followers of Jesus get to preach like Jesus and get to die like Jesus. Stephen's sermon ends in his death and the church's persecution. Not only preachers, but the whole church, pays for good gospel preaching.

Paul's masterful sermon in the Areopagus yielded mocking, curiosity, and the conversion of Dionysius and Damaris plus a few others (Acts 17:32-34). One could hardly call the sermon a great success. If this is Luke's "triumphalism," it is a curious kind that mixes sporadic triumph with much pain. Nothing within the power of the Word protects bearers of the Word from rejection. Was not Paul's own conversion accompanied by the divine promise (not that he would go on to be healthy, wealthy, and wise) that Paul would be shown "how much he must suffer for the sake of my name" (9:16 RSV)?

Yet no power within the world protects it from the ultimate triumph of the Word. Luke does not state it so prosaically as I. For instance, Luke's account of the great persecution after the stoning of Stephen ends not with, "But Saul was ravaging the church" (Acts 8:3 RSV), but with, "Now those who were scattered went about preaching the word" (8:4 RSV). The Word of God is like a wildfire; stamp on it in one place only to have it blaze forth else-where. No obstacle, not even bloody persecution by one so resourceful as Saul, ultimately silences the Word. The risen Christ told his people they would "be my witnesses in Jerusalem and in all Judea and Samaria" (1:8 RSV). Who could have predicted that the vehicle for the evangelistic thrust into Samaria would be perse-cution? Preachers who are driven out of Jerusalem reappear in Samaria healing (8:7-8), rebuking local gurus (8:9-24), and "preach-ing the gospel to many villages of the Samaritans" (8:25 RSV). Quite abruptly, we are out in the desert with Philip (and in the mid-dle of the day!) where we encounter, of all people, a dried-up Ethiopian (8:26-40) who hears and wants to be baptized. Philip resists. Water is needed for baptism. Amazingly, the Ethiopian spots a stream of water in the desert. Nothing hinders the realiza-tion of the Word. Such preaching produces fruit. With this power unleashed, who knows where good news may happen next?

In reading Acts, by the very mode of Luke's proclamation, we are moved beyond a simple "What does the Bible say?" to a more dynamic "What is God using the Bible to do to us?" As Stanley Hauerwas notes, the church exists as a "story-formed commu-nity."[26] The church is at the center of the new world that results from acts of imagination that we call stories. Something happens to us in listening to stories of converted Ethiopians and Roman cen-turions. We come to view and review our world as infinitely more open and unfinished than we first imagined, because the world is an arena where God is busy making good on divine promises.

With Theophilus, we contemporary preachers may read these stories and take heart. The Word of God, thank God, has a power of its own (Acts 3:12; 4:7, 33; 6:8; 19:11). The good news for preach-ers is not that our preaching of the good news will always yield painless and positive results. The good news is that the good news is not limited by the abilities, or lack thereof, of its preachers. Philip did not know what he was doing out in the middle of Gaza at noon, or why he had been summoned there. Peter, who at first thought that his dream was of unclean food rather than unclean people, had to be led by the hand to the house of Cornelius. Repeatedly, Acts goes to great lengths to assure us that if the preacher is out on the boundaries preaching good news to some-one strange, it is not due to the preacher's own inclinations, but rather to the prodding power of the Spirit. No sociologically derived programs for church growth, no theories of effective communication or techniques of church building can account for what is happening in Acts. Here is Luther's *verbum externum* in motion. The preacher has significance only as he or she is obedient to the movements of this external word that is neither self-derived nor self-controlled by the preacher.

Acts in Preaching

Among the challenges that face the contemporary minister of the Word who desires to preach not only in the mode but also with the substance of Acts are the following:

The Common Lectionary does not deal generously with Acts. Portions of twelve chapters, at Pentecost or during Easter, provide the sole representation of Acts during the lectionary's three-year cycle. The traditional choice of Easter as a time for reading Acts is well founded. Here are the concrete, political, ecclesial results of Easter. Yet it is unfortunate that nothing of Acts appears in the season after Pentecost—so much of Acts is of potential value for church order, community life, doctrine, teaching, and a rediscovery of the church as the gift of the Holy Spirit. The neglect of Acts is another good reason to note that the Common Lectionary is not meant to be a homiletical straitjacket. The preacher is free to read the lectionary-appointed lessons that are appointed for the day, then go elsewhere for a text. We ought to more often go to Acts.

There is widespread skepticism about the value of the church. Luke's preoccupation with the communal embodiment of the gospel led some early German historical commentators to accuse him of "early Catholicism." The epithet betrays the odd idea that when one has become greatly concerned about church formation—the one holy, apostolic, and catholic church—one has become less concerned with the pure, unadulterated kerygma of Jesus. Acts is an eloquent rebuke to attempts to disembody Christ or to sever this Messiah from his messianic community. In Acts, the risen Christ is so closely linked to his church that he can say to Saul, "Why do you persecute *me?*" when Saul persecutes the church (9:4-5; 22:8; 26:15). Those who accuse Luke of an "absentee Christology" should be reminded of Luke's assertion that the church (for better or worse!) is the presence that Christ has chosen to take in the world.

Perhaps the principal reason Acts's accounts of the dilemmas of church formation, growth, and fidelity may sound parochial or institutionally preoccupied to our ears is that many of us live in a church that no longer quarrels with Caesar's definitions of peace and justice, a church enabled by its culturally accommodated preachers to bridge the gap between the gospel and the status quo. A church that presents the gospel as personal fulfillment or a sort of primitive effort to be politically useful in making a better America has little need to worry about ecclesial matters. In such a climate, Theophilus will be told stories of people who overcame personal anxiety or boredom and went on to liberation or self-discovery, rather than people who were converted and detoxified by a countercultural phenomenon called "The Way."

Acts preaching has as one of its goals change of mind and life. Scoffers become repentant believers (2:14-41), a person from the exotic ends of the earth is baptized (8:26-40), a raging enemy becomes a brother (9:1-31), a Gentile soldier is adopted (10:1–11:18), and the Spirit is poured out on all flesh. Accounts of conversion are lovingly retold by the church as confirmation of the continuing power of God to create the Christian community *ex nihilo* in each generation by the power of the Spirit. The future is not left up to us nor is the community of faith solely of our creation.

Whereas church life in my part of Christendom is mostly a matter of maintaining and subsidizing what we already have, conversions in Acts are *stories about beginnings*—the beginning of a new chapter in the life of the church; the initiation of a new mission, as well as the beginning of a new life for the individual; the beginning of the Christian journey, not its final destination. Moreover, conversions in Acts are *stories about vocation*—conversion is not for the smug, individual possession of the convert, but rather for the ongoing thrust of the gospel. Finally, conversions in Acts are *stories about the gifts of God*—God is the chief actor in all Lukan accounts of conversion. Even the smallest details are attributed to the work of God. Conversion is not the result of skillful leadership by the community, or even of persuasive preaching or biblical interpretation. In many accounts, such as those of Philip's work with the Ethiopian, the mysterious hand of God must direct everything. In other stories, such as the story of Peter and Cornelius, the church must be dragged kicking and screaming into the movements of God. Too much of mainline Protestantism is focused not upon conversion, but upon accommodation, adjustment, and the gospel reduced to the utterly conventional. Acts reminds the preacher that change, turning, allowing oneself to be jerked about by the Spirit, is at the heart of the Christian message.

Preaching from Acts has a peculiar kind of political pushiness. In Acts, disciples are constantly running afoul of the authorities, both secular and religious. They make their testimony before people like Felix and Agrippa. At first glance, it may appear that Luke is attempting to help the church strike some sort of balance between the claims of Caesar and those of Christ. In the last century, some commentators thought of Acts as an early apology for the Christian church to the Roman Empire—leave the church alone because it is not too troubling to the empire, can even be a friend of Caesar—a rather strange reading that could only come from biblical commentators who could not imagine any other defense of the church than that it was helpful to the nation.

My own reading of Acts suggests that, in Acts, Luke helps Christians put the government in its place. The church must tell true stories, stories that are counter to the claims of Caesar. If Paul can use Caesar's protection in order to live to preach another day, fine, but preachers have no stake in whether or not Caesar understands or permits the proclamation of the gospel. In general, Roman governmental officials are depicted in Acts as incomprehending of the church's message, as passing along Paul as a political pariah they cannot figure out and want to dismiss. When, in Acts 10, the first Gentile convert is, of all people, Cornelius, a member of the Roman occupation forces, we see that the church has every intention of mounting a full challenge to Caesar's claims of omnipotence. The first Gentile to get the point is one of Caesar's finest. Of course, a church that feels that Christ has no quarrel with Caesar as long as he is democratically elected, a church that reduces everything it says to the world to the conventionally political, may have trouble understanding the subversiveness of stories like the conversion of Cornelius, or the seditious humor of Paul's baiting of the tribune in Acts 22. Acts is full of politics—politics that begins with the assertion that the crucified Christ is risen and ascended, and that he will tolerate no rivals to his sovereignty.

Had not Mary warned in her Magnificat that the proud shall be humbled (Luke 1:52-53) and the mighty cast down from their thrones? Jesus was the occasion for the falling and rising of many. Through Luke's ministry, we become eyewitnesses that God, not kings, has the last word.

> The grass withers, the flower fades, when the breath of the LORD blows upon it . . . but the word of our God will stand forever. (Isa. 40:7-8)

Such an extravagant, exuberant boast, made by the nascent church in the face of widespread persecution, is great comfort to those of us who work weekly with the Word. How dare the church utter some of its most sweeping claims for the power of the Word precisely at a time when it is fighting for its very life? These Christians must really be living in a different world. They must know something that the world does not. And thus reading Acts, we later-day Theophili take heart.

CHAPTER SEVEN

The Pastor as Counselor: Care That Is Christian

The Historic Functions of Pastoral Care

Chaucer's prologue to *The Canterbury Tales* presents a snapshot of a medieval pastor going about his duties among the congregation:

> Wide was his parish, houses far asunder,
> But never did he fail, for rain or thunder,
> In sickness, or in sin, or any state
> To visit to the farthest, small and great,
> Going afoot, and in his hand, a stave.
> This fine example to his flock he gave,
> That first he wrought and afterwards he taught . . .
> There is nowhere a better priest, I trow.
> He had no thirst for pomp or reverence.
> But Christ's own lore, and his apostles twelve,
> He taught, but first he followed himself.

Though Chaucer had a bundle of anticlerical sentiments, it is pleasing to see this positive picture of an early pastor's care. Indeed, in conversations with laity in my own denomination concerning what qualities they desire in a pastor, I hear them ask for someone who embodies, in our day, those qualities so praised by Chaucer in his parson. They want someone to care for them, to visit, to show concern, "In sickness or in mischief to visite," in general, to care as a shepherd for the sheep.

Yet as we noted in chapter 4, simply to care for other people is not our chief pastoral goal. To *care in the manner of Christ* is pastoral care's great challenge. Fortunately, the history of pastoral care has for us both encouragement and some warning.[1] In their survey of the history of pastoral care, Charles Jaeckle and William Clebsch delineated four historic functions of pastoral care: healing, sustaining, guiding, and reconciling.[2]

171

Clebsch and Jaeckle note that although all these forms of care are present in the church throughout all ages, during changing circumstances the church tended to emphasize some forms more than others. For instance, during the church's first two centuries, pastoral care stressed the sustaining of souls through the vicissitudes of life in an often hostile world. Sustaining and supportive acts such as the Eucharist and unction provided the community with the sustenance it needed to live during difficult times.

For the next hundred years, as persecution of Christians by the state accelerated, many Christians, under pressure of persecution, fell away or lapsed from the faith. After this period, reconciliation of lapsed souls into the life of the church through acts of penance and contrition became a central focus of the care of souls. Another important shift in pastoral care occurred after the establishment of Christianity as a state religion by Constantine in the fourth century. Now the church was faced with the immense task of assimilating various groups into the ethos of the empire and the church. The catechetical lectures of Cyril of Jerusalem, explaining the "holy mysteries" of the church in a step-by-step fashion to new converts after their baptism, and Benedict's rules for monastic spirituality, are examples of the kind of guidance and discipline that went on during this time. In the medieval period, healing became an important function of the *cura animarum* ("cure of souls") mediated by the church's well-defined sacramental system that offered healing of maladies that beset any segment of the common life.

Reconciliation to God was a prominent theme during the Renaissance and the Reformation. In his *Babylonian Captivity of the Church*, Luther frequently extolled the virtues of baptism as the Christian's greatest comfort in life and death. Luther's question, "Where can I find a gracious God?" had consequences for Lutheran theology and pastoral care. Later the Enlightenment brought new pressures on the church to sustain souls as they passed through what the church considered to be an often treacherous and wicked modern world, and acts of personal devotion, including small groups, were designed to sustain the faithful.

The "post–Christendom era" of post–Enlightenment Christianity has presented pastoral care with a number of serious challenges, many of which have their roots in the developments of society and the church in the last three centuries. The Enlightenment called the efficacy of the church's rites and sacraments into question. Healing, once the exclusive domain of the church (as were education, social work, art, and so on), gradually separated itself from its ecclesiastical roots and emerged as an independent, secular activity. Newfound "reason" questioned the church's old formulas of individual well-being. Many souls began going elsewhere for healing, sustaining, guiding, and reconciling, and many priests and pastors felt a loss of authority in their care of their people. The revolutions of the late eighteenth and early nineteenth centuries brought with them the pluralism and voluntarism that sought guidance that was educed from the values and norms of personal convictions rather than from the older, traditioned guidance the church had previously offered. Sunday school was invented during this period, an innovation in Christian formation led by the laity.

Likewise, the Protestant Reformation created a crisis in the care of souls. The source of the pastor's authority shifted from the nature of the church to the authority of the Bible or the leading of the Spirit. The identity of the pastor shifted from the conveyor of the sacraments and their healing grace to the one who is trained and called to preach the Word. The beliefs and practices of the first generation of Reformers to the contrary, the sacraments in particular and public worship in general lost their place as chief loci of pastoral care in the churches that emerged from the Reformation.

The Protestant emphasis on the centrality of the Word, its concern with education, inner authority, and individualism eventually made the Reformation, in part, complementary to the developments within the Enlightenment. On the other hand, Protestant Pietism's stress on subjective feelings and personal, experiential validation of one's religion tended to go against the excessive rationalism of the Age of Reason. Curiously, nineteenth-century Revivalism, which was particularly influential in American Protestantism, managed to blend many Enlightenment and Pietistic (and therefore Puritan) themes. The liberal theological stance for the modern age was set for Protestants by Friedrich Schleiermacher, who declared in 1799, "The mission of a priest in the world is a private business, and the temple should also be a private chamber where he lifts up his voice to give utterance to religion."[3] Religion became viewed as a private, subjective, personal affair—what we do with our subjectivity.

The results of the confluence of these movements are apparent when one looks at the dilemma of Protestant pastoral care. Clebsch and Jaeckle note that "the Reformation's great upheaval in doctrine and in ecclesiology never generated a corollary revolution in the cure of souls."[4] (I wonder if Wesley might disagree.) The Reformation destroyed the Roman synthesis between speculative theology and practical guidance, between penitential piety and visible means of grace. It attacked the old calculus of sin and penance, stressing the radical nature of human sinfulness, the impossibility of salvation by works, and the sovereignty of God's grace. But the Reformation inevitably produced its own brand of legalism, basing many of its norms for personal behavior (as Max Weber showed us) on the demands of emerging economic systems. Salvation became a commodity experienced by many outside the church, the sacraments, the community, and the tradition. The naked, solitary individual was left to make his peace with an often wrathful God.

Preaching, far from conveying a sense of Luther's gracious God, became synonymous in many people's minds with judgmental, paternalistic scolding. Pastoral care gradually became relegated to one-to-one dealings between the pastor and individual members of the flock. Protestant skepticism over the more exaggerated claims of late-medieval Roman piety led to a deep distrust of any outward, priestly, ritualistic means of grace. The pastoral functions of sustaining, guiding, and reconciling ceased to be, as they had been in earlier periods, acts and signs done by the pastor for and with the community of faith, and became almost exclusively thoughts, words, and feelings conveyed by the pastor to individuals. Many Protestants assumed that Luther's "priesthood of believers" (albeit in misunderstood, misinterpreted form) called into question any priestly acts on the part of pastors. "Pastor" became antithetical to "priest," and the pastoral aspects of so-called priestly functions were overlooked.

The same could be said of the Reformation's effect on the practice of public worship. Liturgiologists have documented how the movement that set out to reform the liturgy—to transfer worship from the exclusive domain of the clergy and restore it to the people, thereby to return Christian worship to its participatory, biblical, corporate, acted character—ended in virtually dissolving the sacraments. The corporate worship of the church became fragmented into private devotions. Sunday morning worship degenerated into a preacher-choir performance heavy with verbosity, didacticism, and moralistic scolding.

In an earlier time, a pastor caring for the flock, engaging in the activities related to the cure of souls, meant, in great part, leading them in worship. There is much truth to the Jesuit liturgical scholar Jungmann's sweeping statement that "for centuries, the liturgy, actively celebrated, has been the most important form for pastoral care."[5] Healing meant anointing with oil, or unction, prayers to the saints and to the relics of the saints, and various forms of exorcism. Reconciling, pastoral care for the reestablishment of broken relationships among people and between people and God, traditionally meant those ritualized acts of forgiveness, confession, penance, and absolution. Sustaining meant administration of the Eucharist, confirmation and other visible, concrete acts of communal support and divine grace.

A major difference between the pastoral care of previous ages of the church and that of our modern era is the switch from care that utilized mostly corporate, priestly, liturgical actions to care that has increasingly limited itself to individualistic, psychologically oriented techniques heavily influenced by prevailing secular therapies.

Admittedly, earlier pastoral care was not exclusively a corporate, liturgically oriented activity, and may have been more individualistic than the existing documents show. John Chrysostom's touching "Letter to a Young Widow" and the *ars moriendi* ("the art of dying") literature of the Middle Ages come to mind as examples of personal, one-to-one acts of pastoral care. But in works such as Richard Baxter's *The Reformed Pastor*, an undeniable change of emphasis is evident. Discipline and strict pastoral guidance of individual souls are the principal activities of the Protestant pastor. Baxter defines the two major concerns of the pastor in caring for the parishioners: "to turn the stream of their cogitations and affections, and bring them to a due contempt of this world" and "the evil of all sin must be manifested, and the danger that it hath brought us into, and the hurt it hath already done us, must be discovered."[6] Jonathan Edwards, the most creative of the early American theologians, first developed what was to be a Protestant concern for the next two hundred years: the investigation of personal religious experience and "affections." A century later, when

William James's influential *Varieties of Religious Experience* was published, James continued a theme that Edwards had taken up before him: the delineation and validation of the great variety of individual religious experiences, though with little of the theological commitments of Edwards. James pioneered the psychological study of religious phenomena and as a pragmatic philosopher emphasized the therapeutic value of religious practice. Faith is good for you. James's Varieties set the direction for the individualistic, pragmatic, utilitarian, psychologically oriented nature of modern pastoral care that has continued to have difficulty finding a theological rationale for its work.

A final touchstone in the development of modern American Protestant pastoral care was the adoption, during the 1920s, of the medical model by pastoral care and the close methodological relationship between pastoral care and psychology. A key figure in this period was Anton Boisen, who during his own hospitalization for mental illness became convinced that the best method for training seminarians in the art of pastoral care was to expose them to people in crisis, the "living human documents," as Boisen called them. Freudian psychoanalytic theory was all the rage at this time (although Boisen was not a pure Freudian), and, at a time when American theology was in somewhat of a stupor due to the demise of the old fundamentalism and the declining interest in the Social Gospel, Boisen's experientially based, "nonacademic" approach to theological training was well received.[7] Clinical Pastoral Education (C.P.E.), as Boisen's training program came to be called, was a major part of the seminary curriculum in nearly every Protestant seminary by the 1950s, and continues to be a significant component in the training of clergy. Though now utilizing some parish-based settings, C.P.E. primarily used medical institutions such as hospitals and nursing homes as the setting for its work with seminarians, and relied heavily on medical, psychiatric, and psychotherapeutic techniques in its training for pastoral care. Generations of seminarians vividly remember their hours on duty as student chaplains in a hospital emergency room, their often painful periods of personal reflection in a C.P.E. peer group, or their first encounter with sick, dying, confused, disturbed patients in the course of their clinical training. Clinical Pastoral Education training has been of immense help as a means of enabling pastors and seminarians to better understand themselves and others. However, C.P.E. may have left its trainees with a very limited concept of "pastoral care."

Pastoral Counseling

In his survey of patristic writings on pastoral counsel, Thomas C. Oden notes five recurring themes that describe the effective therapeutic relationship:[8]

1. Accurate empathic listening
2. Congruent, open awareness of one's own experiencing process and trust of one's own experiences[9]
3. Unconditional and accepting love[10]
4. Rigorous self-knowledge[11]
5. Narrative comic insight[12]

Martin Luther complained that marital problems within his churches consumed his pastoral attention. "Nowadays one has more to do with marriage relations than with all other matters. Because of them we can hardly read, preach, or study."[13] For many pastors, one of the great burdens of ministry is the continual, unrelenting exposure to the intensity of human pain through their counseling of troubled souls within the congregation. Yet this is historically one of the essential acts of Christian ministry. One of the most important ways that pastors differ from mental health professionals is that pastors have the freedom, indeed the obligation, to intervene in the lives of troubled souls within their congregations. Much of counseling in the secular realm is a matter of passively sitting back, waiting for people to take the initiative and seek help. One of the reasons why people are in trouble is that they cannot take that first long step toward admitting that they need help. Pastors do not have to wait for a person to come forward. It is the pastor's responsibility to care for the flock.[14]

The pastor not only gives in counseling, but also receives. In counseling, the pastor is exposed to the raw edges of human pain. Human need is given a face, a specificity that is intense and absolutely essential for the pastor's accurate knowledge of a congregation. In counseling, the people experience their pastor as one who cares, and cares deeply, one who is willing to enter that dark risky place where human pain resides. Perhaps most important of all, pastoral counseling is a place where both the pastor as counselor and the parishioner as counselee have the opportunity to explore how the Christian faith relates to real people caught in real human binds. Here is where the gospel and human need meet.

Richard Baxter notes that the one who preaches must first be the one who is able to listen; the one who teaches must be the one who is taught:

> When a minister knows not his people, or is as strange to them as if he did not know them, it must be a great hindrance to his doing any good among them. . . . By means of [our pastoral knowledge of our people] we shall come to be better acquainted with *each person's spiritual state*, and so the better know how to watch over them. We shall the better know how to preach to them, when we know their temper, and their chief objections, and so what they have most need to hear.[15]

What is required is a recovery of our pastoral counseling as a means of spiritual direction, a theologically grounded endeavor to equip the saints for the work of ministry, a form of catechesis for Christian growth. A major pastoral responsibility in counseling is to lay our need alongside the story of the good news of Jesus Christ in such a way that both the gospel and our need are illuminated.

Much of our best counseling is a complex act of pastoral imagination, taking troubled sisters and brothers in Christ and laying their troubles next to the gospel, seeing what new connections, relationships, and alternatives might be present that could not have been imagined without the light of the gospel.[16] Our first imaginative act is to identify with those who suffer. Ambrose advises clergy to "show compassion for those who are bound by chains, as if you yourself were bound with them. . . . Suffer with those who are in trouble, as if being in trouble with them."[17] Then we are to imagine with them alternatives to their current suffering. John Patton underscores this empathetic, innovative, imaginative work of counseling when he defines the chief purpose of pastoral counseling as offering "something new . . . so that the persons within it will experience some freedom to change, to consider some new alternatives about their lives."[18]

Few pastors have the time or the training to engage in more in-depth counseling, that is, counseling beyond more than a half-dozen sessions. As a good rule of the thumb, most of us pastors should never engage in long-term counseling. A major skill of pastoral counseling is the knowledge and the willingness to refer deeply troubled persons for longer-term psychotherapy and psychiatric care. Major depression, addiction, and psychoses are examples of human difficulties that require skilled psychotherapeutic and psychiatric care. Often the pastor's support and referral are crucial factors in enabling a troubled person to seek and to receive skilled therapy from a person other than the pastor. Without knowing when to refer, we pastors are in danger of hurting in our misguided attempts at helping. We attempt to do more than we are equipped to do, wasting valuable time, and robbing other pastoral activity of needed focus and energy.[19] Yet referral does not mean abandonment of our most troubled parishioners. Referral enables us to work in concert with other givers of care who know more than we do about severe psychological distress.

Our counseling is a means of the historic pastoral work of spiritual direction, not an attempt to do psychotherapy. Most of our counseling ought to be short term, with clear goals in mind. Modification of behavior, better understanding of a situation, accurate information about the persons who are in a crisis, decision about intervention, formation of short-term strategies are more appropriate goals for short-term counseling than major changes in personality.

During the first session, the pastor engages in open, attentive, inquiring conversation with the troubled person, seeking to determine the nature of the complaint. This can be the most difficult aspect of pastoral counseling and may require more than one session. During this early stage of care, the pastor needs to determine if this person is bringing a problem to the pastor that is within the pastor's range of expertise and fitting to the pastoral role. A fair question to ask is, "Why have you sought me out for help with this problem?" Also, the pastor must assess if this person is able to benefit from pastoral counseling. Is the person able to articulate the problem—even if he or she is not presently able to fully understand it—in a way that enables the counselor to hear the problem? Is this person desiring to grow in this process, or is the counselee content merely with the voicing of the symptoms of the problem?

Gregory Nazianzen stressed that pastoral care must be keyed to the particular temperament of each person. The meek ought to be treated with meekness "in order to encourage them to a better hope. Others seem to require that we combat and conquer them and never yield an inch."[20] Therefore, the pastor must practice self-discipline in the first counseling sessions to ensure that persons in need are not thoughtlessly pigeonholed, generalized, and categorized.

After these first sessions, the pastor and counselee ought to be able to articulate the goal of future sessions, such as, "To help you come to a decision of whether or not you ought to marry John," or, "To come to an understanding of whether or not you will be able to continue to live with a wife who is an alcoholic." Both counselor and counselee then become allies in dealing with a particular problem.[21]

Among the skills and the tasks of pastoral counseling are these:[22] active and critical listening; a willingness to enter into the world of the counselee; careful attention to what is being said, and more important, to what may not be being said; constant attentiveness to the affective, emotional content of the issues that are being discussed; honest and truthful feedback; continual refocusing upon the issues at hand, particularly the painful ones; frequent self-examination on the part of the pastor, carefully asking oneself, "What is happening to me within this counseling session? What is at stake here in my own feelings? How is this story that we are telling related to the story that is the gospel of Jesus Christ?"

In counseling sessions, the pastor will want to watch for *resistance* on the part of the counselee in dealing with the problem, point out this resistance, and ponder with the person possible sources of the resistance. The person who is asked, "Tell me, how is your relationship with your father involved in this issue?" only to avoid, deny, or evade the question in conversation, ought to be invited, by the counselor, to focus on the meaning of that avoidance, denial, and evasion.

The pastor must set limits on the time for the counseling. It is better to establish, at the beginning of a session, exactly when the session will terminate. The pastor must guard against taking inappropriate responsibility for the person's problem. Troubled persons often attempt to transfer responsibility for their problems onto other people who are attempting to be helpful. Above all, pastors must be aware of the possibility, even the inevitability, of *transference,* the displacement of reactions to and the need for another person in one's past toward a person in the present, what John Patton calls "an error in time."[23] Transference takes place when an adult gives over to another person (such as the counselor) the childhood need for parental love, protection, blame, praise, and punishment.

A lonely, emotionally needy person comes to her pastor expressing unhappiness in her marriage. In the process of counseling, she transfers her desire for love and companionship to the pastor, thus misplacing her affection to the caregiver. Counselors ought to resist a counselee's tendency to transfer, to place inappropriate responsibility for the problem on the back of the counselor rather than let the counselor help him or her assign and accept appropriate responsibility.

Patton gives three ways a pastoral counselor can keep transference from destroying the proper pastoral counseling relationship:[24]

1. Set clear limits for yourself, for what you will and will not do in a counseling relationship. Limits on time and on physical contact are essential. If a counselee is late for a session, note the tardiness and ask if it may be evidence of resistance to the insights being provided by the counseling. Keep remembering that you are the pastor, not the husband, best friend, mother, and so forth.

2. Expect intense feelings to emerge in counseling sessions. Pastors are often quite uncomfortable with persons who have great anger. Be curious about the feelings that are being expressed by the counselee, and those that you suspect are being suppressed.

3. Think of yourself as a patient, listening teacher. You must care for another person by helping that person separate reality and fantasy in a situation. When transference emerges, discuss it openly with the counselee, firmly separating yourself from the counselee's projected image of you.[25]

Pastors should also be aware of the possibility of another psychic phenomenon, *countertransference.* The one who seeks counseling is not the only one with needs, feelings, and psychological issues. The counselor also has personal needs and desires. Sometimes the counselor unintentionally cooperates with the counselee's transference. The counselee wants an all-powerful parent to fix what is wrong in the counselee's life. The pastor wants to be an effective and helpful counselor. So, out of the pastor's need to be an all-powerful savior in this situation, the pastor becomes the messiah, the person who takes inappropriate and unrealistic responsibility for the counselee's problem. Pastoral psychologists speak of the need for "abstinence," in which the counselor makes an intentional, self-conscious effort not to use the counselee to gratify the counselor's emotional needs. We pastors are servants of the Savior, not saviors ourselves.

When pastors have little self-awareness or an inadequate theological self-understanding of their work, they are vulnerable to unwitting participation in the phenomenon of countertransference in counseling. Any pastor who goes into the intimate and emotion-laden pastoral counseling session simply wanting to "help people," without regard to adequate definition of role, boundary, limits, and with inadequate self-knowledge of his or her own limits, fantasies, and needs, is in dangerous territory.

I find it important to admit that not all of my pastoral care is offered because I love God and my people. I also love myself, and my love of my people is at times a means of using my people to love myself even more! I therefore need to keep learning suspicion of my motives when I say something like, "I'm telling you this for your own good," or "I am not going to confront her for her behavior because I am so sensitive and caring." Although I am meeting the needs of my people, I am also getting my needs met as well. Christians claim that the confession and forgiveness offered in the gospel enables us to be honest. Let us pastors prove that in our own lives and work. In a discussion among pastors of these challenges, a pastor confessed: "I have had to admit that I love to be loved and need to be needed. I'm not sure I was ever certain that my parents loved me. Maybe that's one of the reasons why I was attracted to the ministry. I therefore am particularly vulnerable in those situations where there is a person in my church who comes to me needing to give and receive love, or full of need. Just knowing who I am and in what situations I ought to be cautious, is an important attribute for my pastoral care."

One of the most important tasks for pastoral care is to find and to own an appropriate metaphor for our work as pastors engaged in the care of persons within the congregation. One of the weaknesses of the Clinical Pastoral Education that many of us received in seminary is that it laid over our care, at a formative stage, a medical model for our care. In most of the pastor's counseling, the goal of "cure" is unrealistic or even undesirable. We are called to offer pastoral care—not cure. Care enables us to go on, even when we are not fully healed of our afflictions. Care places us in a safe holding environment wherein there is a possibility of cure of our ailments, but also the assurance that we do not have to be completely whole in order to be loved and sustained by Christ and his church. Christ appears to have loved and blessed more of the sick and the hurting than he healed.

Perhaps our overarching goal in our pastoral counseling ought to be contributing to our people's maturity in Christ, rather than to their health. A teacher helps people grow in new knowledge, and in the ownership and embodiment of their newly gained knowledge. Virginia Satir, in her *Conjoint Family Therapy*, defines maturity as "congruence," that state in which a person takes responsibility for her life, is in possession of a fairly accurate assessment of herself and others, and accepts responsibility for the choices and decisions she has made.[26] Christians believe that we are at our best when there is congruence between who we are and how we live *in Christ*, between what we know about ourselves and how we utilize that knowledge in our relationships with others *through Christ*. We know no "congruence" that is not a more faithful alignment of ourselves to those persons whom God has created us to be.

Many pastors have found the family systems therapy of Edwin Friedman to be helpful in their care of both the congregation as a family system and the families of the congregation. Friedman's systems approach to human need helps free us from our captivity to individualistic conceptions of human need and pastoral care in order to reclaim the systemic, political, corporate dimensions of care.[27] What is needed, in our peculiar language, is for our care to be systemic, corporate, communal—that is, *ecclesial*. The church is the context of our care and that makes our care unique.

The Pastor as Guide

In order to reclaim the explicitly ecclesial, theological basis of our care, I agree with Rebekah Miles in her assertion that we need to refurbish the image of the pastor as guide.[28] As we have seen, guidance is a historic pastoral function.[29] Yet too many pastors in mainline Protestantism forsook this historic role in favor of allegedly nonjudgmental, empathetic listening that failed to honor the formative, pedagogical, guiding functions of specifically pastoral care and the moral context of our care. Seward Hiltner feared "moralism" as the greatest danger in pastoral care. Others have urged pastors to "offer pastoral care unconditioned by judgment."[30] Aside from the question of whether or not it is even possible to care in a way that is devoid of certain moral and theological commitments (Hiltner tended to have some quite judgmental things to say about those who failed to be nonjudgmental in their care!), the pastor cannot forsake the role of bearer of the witness and tradition of the church.

A guide is one who knows something—perhaps not everything—but something. As a guide, the guide is expected to lead and to advise. The guide has no power to force those who seek guidance to accept the guide's leading and advice, but the guide has a responsibility to guide. Luther noted that even the preaching of the pure Word of God seems impotent to transform alcohol abuse once alcohol "has got too firmly the upper hand."[31] The guide is free to speak but not to coerce.

Yet Miles says that a guide must speak. "A guide who refuses to advise and share knowledge is no guide at all."[32] The good guide is the one who not only has traveled the route before, but one who also has an ability to know the strengths and weaknesses of those under his or her guidance. The Christian faith offers a wealth of resources for our care of our people, a more than two-thousand-year story of those who have attempted to walk the narrow way of the cross before us. More than a helpful "resource," the Christian faith, as practiced in the congregation, also offers us the necessary means to live better lives, faithfully to follow, and in the following, to be better people than we would have been had we been left to our own devices.

The pastor not only counsels and controls the troubled, but also confronts the complacent. I recall hearing the great preacher George Buttrick say that almost any pastor can visit a parishioner who has just received news that she has a terminal illness, or has just lost his job, or whose child has just flunked out of school. People in such distress are happy to hear from anyone, even their preacher, said Buttrick.

It takes a very special pastor to visit that person who has just been promoted at the bank, or the person whose child has just been accepted at Harvard University, contended Buttrick. The skillful pastor knows the spiritual peril that lies in what the world considers good news, or health, or success.[33] Thus pastoral counsel is more than merely tending the wounded, lifting up the brokenhearted. It is also a matter of teaching, guiding, and admonishing the well and the well fixed, the satisfied and the content. The Christian faith is both comfort for the afflicted and an affliction to the comfortable, and it is the pastor's vocation to be one of the church's agents of that good news.

Listen as Martin Luther places the story of a man who is sick, Elector Frederick of Saxony, next to the gospel story. A suffering man is, through Luther's counsel, placed in the context of the sufferings of Christ. A skilled pastor is able to see Christ within the life of a pained parishioner. Luther offers pastoral care to Frederick through a letter:

> When, therefore, I learned, most illustrious prince, that Your Lordship has been afflicted with a grave illness and that Christ has at the same time become ill in you, I counted it my duty to visit Your Lordship with a little writing of mine. I cannot pretend that I do not hear the voice of Christ crying out to me from Your Lordship's body and flesh and saying: "Behold, I am sick." This is so because such evils as illness and the like are not borne by us who are Christians but by Christ himself, our Lord and Saviour, in whom we live.[34]

The caring pastor places the sufferings of this present time next to the sufferings of Christ, allows the compassion of Christ to shine through our acts of care, helps troubled souls see the trials and tribulations of this life as preparation for and participation in life eternal in Christ, puts our present troubles in an eternal context, and dares to assert that even in our pain and difficulty Christ calls us to lives of holiness and hope. This is care worthy of the name *pastoral*.

INTERLUDE
Augustine's *Confessions* as a Word-made World

I worry about the preceding chapter on pastoral counseling. Despite my intent, the chapter reads as if our care and counsel are mostly matters of skillful technique. Counseling is in service to the modern fiction that our lives are what we do and decide, the result of our humane technique, a story that we are telling ourselves.

No. Christians are those who discover that their lives are also a story told by God. We are not the authors of our lives. God speaks in such a way that, eventually, by God's grace, our lives become a word to be spoken to the world. It is our faith that nothing will silence or hinder the creation of that world.

In Acts 8, after the brutal martyrdom of Stephen, "a severe persecution began against the church" (8:1). As a result of the persecution, "the apostles were scattered throughout the countryside of Judea and Samaria." With persecutor Saul ravaging the fledgling church, "dragging off both men and women" (8:3), the church was greatly imperiled.

Then Luke laconically adds, "Now those who were scattered went from place to place, proclaiming the word" (8:4). Thus began the mission to Samaria in a veritable explosion of the Word. Earlier in Acts, we are told that "you will be my witnesses in Jerusalem, in all Judea and Samaria, and to the ends of the earth" (1:8). Witnesses are those who simply tell what they have seen and heard. The gospel spreads through witnesses who are willing to be used by the intrusive, effusive Word. One might have thought that under threat of persecution the fragile church would keep silent. But in Acts, the Word spreads like wildfire. Stamp upon it here, in Judea, and it will break out in Samaria. Acts is, in great part, a history of the invincibility of the Word, an account of the ability of the Word to leap over all boundaries and sweep away all obstacles in its path.

Vocation tends to be a function of the Word's invincibility. Ministry is God's idea before it is ours. Ministry begins in the heart of God, in God's determination to have a people, a family. Ministry is an aspect of God's relentless determination to get back the world by the outbreak of the Word. God is determined to have the last Word.

Through Words to the Word

Paradigmatic in any account of Christian vocation is Augustine's account of his call in his *Confessions*. The story told there is an account of his call to be a Christian, rather than a call to be clergy. True, only eight years after his baptism, Augustine was made a bishop (ca. 395), four years after he had been made a priest. It is significant that Augustine wrote *Confessions* when he was a bishop, struggling with church conflicts, needing to justify his own episcopal authority. Augustine defends himself, explaining who he is, by recounting how he was called. Augustine's *Confessions* reminds me that the story of how I came to be called "pastor" rests upon the story of how I came to be called "Christian." As Augustine later said to one of his congregations, "For you I am a bishop. With you I am a Christian."

The *Confessions* can be read as Augustine's story of a lifelong struggle with, and wonder at, words.[35] The first book of the *Confessions* begins with his early childhood fascination with, and frustration over, words.

> Little by little I began to be aware where I was and wanted to manifest my wishes to those who could fulfil them as I could not. For my desires were internal; adults were external to me [could be translated: my wishes were inside me, while other people were outside] *(intus eras et ego foris)*. . . . So I threw my limbs about and uttered sounds, signs resembling my wishes. (1.vi [8], p. 7)

As an infant, without the means of communication, Augustine is totally isolated from the human community. One reason Augustine makes for such good reading in this century is that he had a lifelong fear that we might be alone in the world. Our age is widely noted as a time of widespread alienation and loneliness. Fear of isolation, of loneliness, permeates much of Augustine's account of his life. Are we here by ourselves? Is there anyone else out there or in here, or are we left to our own devices? "Was I anywhere? Was I anybody?" he asks. Without the means to make connection with others, we are others even unto ourselves. C. S. Lewis says, "We read to know that we are not alone."[36]

Reaching into his infantile past, Augustine discovers that words are the mechanism whereby he is enabled to make connections. Words enable his interior to be made exterior as he gradually learns that by making certain sounds, he is able to reveal his wants and needs to adults around him. Making these words enables him to move out into the world and he celebrates that he is "now a boy with power to talk. . . . I communicated the signs of my wishes to those around me, and entered more deeply into the stormy society of human life" (1.viii [13], pp. 10-11). Words are the means toward community, communion.

Augustine's life begins, not with birth, but with learning to speak. His first words are baby steps toward the world. As we shall learn before the story ends, these words were also the tether by which Augustine was drawn by the Word. I believe this to be a major purpose of the *Confessions;* to chronicle Augustine's movement from words to the Word. As he matures, we see a man gradually accumulate enough words that eventually he is able to hear the Word. He moves in his conversation from monologue to dialogue. The *Confessions* begins with "I, I," and ends with "You, You." All of our little words gesture toward the Word.

> What has anyone achieved in words when he speaks about you? Yet woe to those who are silent about you because, though loquacious with verbosity, they have nothing to say. (1.iv [4], p. 5)

Augustine's book is about this movement through words to the Word, a movement Augustine teaches us to name as salvation. Augustine lures the reader in with the expectation that we are going to read an autobiography. But we have not read long before we realize that we are not merely reading an autobiography, an account of events in a person's life. We are witnessing a healing from the first frustration of the infant who is in the world but knows not the world (nor is he known by the world), and the frustration that accompanies the pain of not having the words rightly to be in the world, toward that rest in God that is the culmination of Sabbath rest in the Word.

We are also witnessing the creation of the Christian sense of the self. Augustine marvels that people gaze upon the high mountains, and examine the oceans, and wonder at the stars in their courses, but pay no attention to themselves, the greatest of the world's mysteries (10.vi [10], p. 184). And yet, Augustine's is not the modern self. It is a self-conscious self, but it is a self that is constantly being impinged upon by God. Augustine manages to have a self because he discovers that he is a being who is addressed by God. (Karl Barth commented that our relationship to God rests upon our being addressed: "Adam, where are you?") In fact, as one reads the *Confessions*, it is sometimes difficult to know if one is reading a story about the life of Augustine, or a story about the life of God. Augustine uses "I" in a way that sounds like the birth of the modern sense of the ego. Yet at key points in the narrative of his life, Augustine discovers that what he had been taught to regard as his own agency at work was really "You," God intruding, pushing in, enticing him.

Toward the end of *Confessions* he says, "I tell my story for love of your love" (11.i [1], p. 221). *Confessions* is perhaps best read as a love story of one who went out to love only to discover that he was already the beloved.

I find Augustine's *Confessions* far more engaging than his theological works, such as *The City of God* or *On the Trinity*. God, in Augustine's theological books, seems a force, something like gravity, a series of interacting philosophical principles. But in the *Confessions*, God is always personal—a character, an agent, an author. It is not simply that the *Confessions* are in narrative form, which makes them congruent with the way the Scripture presents God. It is that, like the Bible, the *Confessions* are busy rendering an agent, a person, a personality. We take them up and think that they are rendering the personality of Augustine only to find by the end that they are rendering a personality—God. They depict an author of a story—not Augustine, but the God of Abraham, Isaac, and Jacob. The *Confessions* are an extended love story, not only of Augustine's awakening love for God, but of God's prevenient love for Augustine. "You, O God, were leading me on," he says.

Thus Augustine learns to name his life, not in the conventional modern way as a story about the inner yearnings and the development of the ego, but rather as a story about God's dealings with him. Augustine was blessed with what he describes as a "restless heart" *(cor inquietum)* that threw him off balance and staggering toward what he needed, though he did not know yet how to desire what he needed. We read about his restlessness, his action, his yearning and striving toward that One in whom we move and live and have our being, but we are also reading a story about the yearning and striving of God toward Augustine. Once, in the middle of a sermon, Augustine said to his congregation, "As far as I can, I'm turning myself inside out for you" (Sermon 120.2).[37]

He is writing circa A.D. 400. The battle of Hadrianople has already been fought in which the Goths have defeated the Romans. That defeat is the first death knell for the empire. In a mere ten years, Rome will be invaded. As the Roman Empire crumbles, Augustine writes about the dawning of the new world. Augustine's own life becomes a kind of metaphor for the world around him. In his life, as an old world is decaying, the classical conception of the self is loosening its grip over the imagination of Western people. Augustine is forsaking the heroic self of the empire, that active, assertive self sung into being by Homer and praised by Pericles, and taking on a new self that is fabricated more by the love of God than by human self-assertion. Rome is dying, and Jerusalem is being born, subsumed in a text called Scripture, and Augustine's own life becomes the microcosm for that new birth.

There are thirteen books in the *Confessions*. Thirteen is not a perfect number. Perhaps Augustine means to indicate a sense of incompleteness in his story. In this sense, the *Confessions* is similar to the Gospel of Mark, which has no conclusive ending, so perhaps Augustine means us to see that the story he tells is more than the story of his life. Having no satisfying conclusion, the story is not completed; it goes on in our stories of God's dealings with us.

Later in his life, Augustine reread his *Confessions* and noted that the first ten books were about him, and the last three books were about the Bible. I take this oddity, the oddness of the last three books of the *Confessions*, the way autobiography ends in biblical exegesis, to be a key to the interpretation of the *Confessions*. I suspect that the whole thing is about God. When one first reads the *Confessions*, the last three books strike one as being tacked on. Why end an autobiography with a discourse on the interpretation of the first chapters of Genesis?

These last three books are thought by some to be a kind of appendix. Perhaps Augustine had intentions of writing a commentary on Genesis and simply affixed these books as an afterthought. And yet I wonder if this may be the whole point, the very culmination of his life. Augustine begins with yearning for communion with the world around him, including communion with the Divine. He longs to know God, to find a path back to God. In its ending, the *Confessions* becomes an account of God's finding a path toward Augustine.

His life in Christ really begins by being confronted by the Word, "Take up and read" *(tolle, lege)*. His life ends by resting in the Word, in a trinity of three books on the first book of the Bible where we are introduced to God. His is a journey through words to the Word. His life is therefore depicted as ascent from words about himself to words about God. His life culminates in, of all endeavors, biblical exegesis.

The goal of life is the interpretation and performance of Scripture. All of our words are meant to find rest in the Word.

Augustine's Testimony

We run ahead of ourselves. As we noted, Augustine begins his life by remembering his early fascination with words. All of life is a struggle to communicate. Rather than begin with some theory about what life ought to be, the way Plato might have begun, Augustine begins with an intense, empirical examination of his own life, arising out of his own experience, particularly his experience with language.

The story of his infantile discovery of words is followed with Augustine's first discourse on sin (2.ii [2], p. 24). Actually, back in book 1, Augustine ascribed great sinfulness to himself as an infant, saying that the only reason babies do not commit great sin is that they lack the power, though not the inclination (1.vi [8], p. 7). Even as he begins school as a young boy, he realizes that he is using education not as a path toward wisdom, but rather as the means of learning "many useful words" to be used on the path toward power and wealth (1.xv [24], p. 18).

Augustine is notoriously convinced of his own great sinfulness. Adolescence is presented as a time when "the single desire that dominated my search for delight was simply to love and to be loved" (2.ii [2], p. 24). All that he and his friends got for their great classical education at this stage was "how to speak as effectively as possible and carry conviction by [their] oratory" (2.ii [4], p. 26). During this time, when he was learning so many big and fancy new words in order to win the world, there was little room for God to speak. "You said nothing." Without some external word from God, life is little more than a cauldron of restless, relentless desire.

With his mistress he fathered a child out of wedlock. Interestingly, his sexual behavior is not his chief illustration of his depravity. That illustration consists of an adolescent episode with pears (2.iv [4], p. 29). The theft of pears by a group of boys may not seem to us like a great sin, but it becomes for Augustine a revelation of the way in which his problem is not simply the sins that he commits, but his inclination toward sin. He finds that the human being is fascinated with some actions simply because the actions are illicit and prohibited.

He and some friends steal a few pears from a neighbor's pear tree not because they are hungry or need to steal the pears, but from *eo liberet quo non liceret*, "that which is not permitted allured us," which is to say, just for the hell of it. The important thing is not the transgression, for perhaps Augustine intends for the transgression to be pointedly of minor moral significance. Rather the problem is the inclination, the desire.

In the previous book, Augustine noted how, as a boy, his studies in rhetoric taught him many lovely words, but all that meant was that he could describe his moral filth with greater confidence as a result of learning the words. Words are ambiguous. They provide us lovely verbal rationale for the evils we commit. "I bring no charge against the words which are like exquisite and precious vessels [that contain] the wine of error" (1.xvi [26], p. 19). Above all, Augustine noted how much sinful pleasure he took in his verbal dexterity, and for this he was called "a boy of high promise." There is thus a connection between verbal dexterity and sin.

At sixteen, Augustine discovers sex and is "seized hold of [by his] youthful weakness" (2.ii [2], p. 24). As for his family, who should have been concerned about his state, "the only concern was that I should learn how to speak as effectively as possible and carry conviction by my oratory" (2.ii [4], p. 26). He loved memorizing speeches: "The speaker who received highest praise was the one who . . . most effectively expressed feelings of anger and sorrow, and who clothed these thoughts in appropriate language" (1.xvii [27], p. 19). He was a smart young thing who used his intellect to argue against the Christians. "I acquired the armoury of being skilled with words," he ruefully says of himself (1.xx [31], p. 22). As for God, during this tempestuous period of youthful lust, Augustine says that it was as if "you were silent then."

Of course, there was not much room for God's words with bright young Augustine learning so many new and fancy words. "Words actually encourage the more confident committing of a disgraceful action," he notes (1.xvi [26], p. 19). This all makes Augustine wonder, How can the Pelagians be right in their belief that we have the power to turn our lives toward God, when we are full of such misguided inclination? If we will pervert a gift as gracious as language, what might we do with sex and friendship (he stole those pears with friends) and everything else? What could give us different intentions? It must be something from the outside—a gift, grace. The *Confessions* could then be read as an account of the gaining of a new source and object of desire.

Curiously, book 2, which contains the episode about the pears, and Augustine's confession of his distance from God, contains almost nothing about language, which is perhaps indicative of Augustine's feeling that sin is life without the right words. At this stage, Augustine's senses were speaking to him more loudly than God. Language was not his primary concern then because he was sixteen and had surrendered himself entirely to lust (2.ii [2], p. 24).

Augustine depicts his life as a journey, as movement, transition, and transformation. His precedent for this is, if not Homer's *Odyssey*, surely the Gospels themselves, which depict Jesus always on the road. Mark, in inventing the written Gospel form, thus established a great tradition, carried on in Augustine, and continued in works such as John Bunyan's *Pilgrim's Progress* or Anne Lamott's *Traveling Mercies*.[38] Sometimes Christians miss the significance of having our relationship to Christ portrayed not as destination, as a status achieved, but as a journey, an unfolding adventure. The literary critic William Beardslee writes, "A particular literary style is not only appropriate to, but generative of, a life style."[39] The lifestyle generated by a work like the *Confessions* is a life that is on the move, subject to the enticements and allurements and incursions of God who is, though often unknown to us, the very destination of all our journeys. Thus we speak of a biblical "passage." A passage to where? A door opening to what? Reading is a primary means of passing over, of moving, with the aid of another, into a place we would not have known had we not been invited by the text. Thus the *Confessions* establishes Augustine as the archetypal Christian reader, the one who reads with a willingness to be transported by the text to another world that would be unavailable without the invitation of the text. "Where was I when I was seeking for you? You were there before me, but I had departed from my self. I could not even find myself, much less you" (5.ii [2], p. 73).

The *Confessions* contains a series of important encounters with books. One of the first occurs when Augustine is eighteen. Through his studies in rhetoric, Augustine became immersed in Cicero. (At eighteen, I was reading Cicero's essays under the tutelage, and terror, of Miss Amber Boggs at Greenville High. Alas, Cicero had not the same effect on me as on Augustine.)

Cicero was the standard Roman path toward wisdom for a patrician young man, or for young men wanting to be patrician. The common form of education for well-to-do young men in the classical world, the major path toward power, was through the study of rhetoric. All of ancient political life required eloquence, the power of persuasion through speech. So they read and memorized Cicero's orations as well as his rules for eloquence.

In his old age, Cicero wrote not only about rhetoric, but also about philosophy. One of these books was the *Hortensius,* a book that has been lost to us. In this dialogue, Cicero urged (thus the title) people to study philosophy. The *Hortensius* was an exhortation to seek wisdom, to love wisdom, for that is what philosophy means.

Augustine wrote of his reading of this book, in book 3 of *Confessions.* For the first time he was devouring a book for a purpose other than as a whetstone "for the sharpening of my style" (3.iv [7], p. 39). The *Hortensius* inflamed him. "The book changed my feelings. It altered my prayers, Lord, to be towards you yourself. I longed for the immortality of wisdom" (3.iv [7], p. 39). He was "stimulated, kindled, inflamed to seek wisdom." (The Latin words are all extremely sensual. Thank you, Miss Boggs.) Augustine's is quite a claim for a book. Perhaps this ought to be criterion for the greatest of books—they are not only able to inflame, but also to change our desires.

Cicero, as a pagan, knew nothing about Christ. And yet this pagan book set Augustine aflame in desire to seek pure wisdom, the pure wisdom that he eventually found in Christ. From this point forward, the *Confessions* becomes Augustine's account of how he gradually learned to read Scripture. He knew he was making progress when, at twenty-nine, he met a Manichaean bishop, Faustus, who, though he had a charming manner of speech, impressed Augustine as being full of hot air. Augustine was pleased that, "I came to discern [between mere eloquence and] the truth of matters. . . . I was interested not in the decoration of the vessel in which the discourse was served" (5.iii [3], p. 73). At the end of book 5, Augustine moves out of his native North African hinterland to cosmopolitan Milan, where he providentially meets Bishop Ambrose. ("I was led to him by you" [5.xiii [23], p. 87].)

Ambrose, one of the leading theologians of the time, taught Augustine how to read Scripture and thus how to read the world.[40] Augustine was first fascinated by the way Ambrose read Scripture silently and thoughtfully, in contrast to the typical Roman way of reading aloud. Ambrose eventually introduced Augustine to the symbolic or allegorical interpretation of Scripture (which Ambrose had learned from the writings of Origen) as a necessary prelude to his conversion.

Augustine, in his search, had turned toward the Bible. But when he attempted to read the Bible, he found a very poorly written, pedestrian book, not at all eloquent and powerful as the words of Cicero (3.v [9], p. 40). He says, looking back, that he was too proud, at this point, to submit to such poorly written literature.

Augustine had been raised in the classical tradition with its stress on simple, straightforward reading. So when Augustine read Scripture, it sounded to him like inferior literature, like straw, because he was intent on the literal meaning of words. Ambrose introduced Augustine to the notion of a thicker, richer reading of Scripture (6.iii [3], [4]; pp. 92-93). It was Ambrose who pointed out to Augustine that in the Bible bread is not merely bread, fish are not merely fish, but are doors that give us access into a much richer description of reality than the merely literal—something approaching the vividly sacramental.

After this instruction in reading, Augustine finds the Bible to be a mysteriously inexhaustible source of revelation:

> I now began to believe that you would never have conferred such preeminent authority on the scripture, now diffused through all lands, unless you had willed that it would be a means of coming to faith in you and a means of seeking to know you. Already the absurdity which used to offend me in those books, after I had heard many passages being given persuasive expositions, I understood to be significant of the profundity of their mysteries. The authority of the Bible seemed the more to be venerated and more worthy of a holy faith on the ground that it was open to everyone to read, while keeping the dignity of its secret meaning for a profounder interpretation. The Bible offered itself to all in very accessible words and the most humble style of diction, while also exercising the concentration of those who are not "light of heart" (Ecclus. 19:4). It welcomes all people to its generous embrace, and also brings a few to you through narrow openings (cf. Matt. 7:13-14). Though the latter are few, they are much more numerous than would be the case if the Bible did not stand by its high authority and if it had not drawn crowds to the bosom of its holy humility. (6.v [8], p. 96)

Oddly, by the time we are in book 7, Augustine has struggled with Manichaeism, has read Scripture extensively, and conversed with no less a Christian mind than Ambrose, but he still does not consider himself a Christian. He has been a catechumen for nearly a decade. It is one thing to be intellectually convinced, quite another to be converted. How is it possible fundamentally to change? What power can transform the intentions? Augustine's experience with his own limited control over his desires have made him extremely suspicious of claims for the freedom of the will.

He is in huge distress. He has discovered that the change that needs to be worked in him is a change of intention, of thinking and willing, but where can one summon up this sort of will? At this point he has been a catechumen, someone preparing for baptism, for a decade; still he has found no peace. Some of his friends have been reading Athanasius's *Life of Antony,* and its account of the monastic life of total devotion and rigorous discipline appeal to him. But attraction is not conversion.

His conversion shall come, we are not surprised by this time to learn, through a book. He is sitting in a garden under a tree. Earlier, a tree had become a scene for his undoing, in the theft of the pears, just as a tree had been the cause for the undoing of Adam and Even in the first garden. On Calvary's hill, a "tree" shall be the source of our salvation. Is there some sort of connection to be made here between sin and salvation and these trees? That we are even noticing the possible symbolism is a sign that Augustine's text is having its way with us.

In great agitation and torment, he hears a child singing a little song, "Take up and read, take up and read" *(tolle, lege; tolle, lege).* The child's voice sounds like an angel's. Was it an angel, a divine messenger, or only a child? Augustine is drawing us toward a richer, thicker description of, and expectation for, the world in which a voice can be ambiguous and attributed to a number of sources, and trees may not be just trees.

His imagination might seem to us overwrought. However, our modern encounters with Scripture tend to be efforts to suppress the imagination, trained as we are in methods of biblical interpretation that attempt to pare down the text to its plain sense or simplest meaning. Augustine tended to think more exuberantly, tended to expect, to enjoy, a plentitude of meaning in a thing. So, hearing a voice, he is willing to obey, willing to explore its significance and to enjoy the adventure. My own impression is that we suffer from a paucity of imagination rather than a surplus in our interpretation of Scripture.

At the words, "Take up and read," Augustine picks up the handiest book available, which at this point in his life is the Bible. He opens to a random passage. The moment is a miracle. The passage is from Paul's Letter to the Romans, chapter 13, verses 13 and 14: "Not in reveling and drunkenness, not in debauchery and licentiousness . . ." Why these verses with their rather uninspiring lists of prohibitions? Why not a more interesting verse with more specific relevance to his search? The ways of God with Scripture and with us are inscrutable. If God can change a life with these meager verses, God can do about anything.

For Augustine, it is quite enough. In tears, he finds his life named, caught up by the text. It is like Paul's conversion on the road to Damascus. Having been perhaps the longest catechumen on record, Augustine is finally baptized by Ambrose in Easter of 387. "He was immediately 'converted to you'" (8.xii [29], p. 153). Scales fall from his eyes. He sees. How? Through the power of the Word.

Transformation of Desire

Before his conversion, he had prayed, "O Lord make me chaste and continent, but not yet." He lacked the means, the desire. Now, through the Word, he has what he needs to be the self he had only hoped to be. Or is it more accurate to say that, through the Word, God has him. He had thought that he was so full of desire only to find out that God's desire for him was greater. Now it is as if all that passion, once turned toward women, friends, and the world's wisdom, expends itself upon God:

> Late have I loved you, beauty so old and so new: late have I loved you. And see, you were within and I was in the external world and sought you there, and in my unlovely state I plunged into those lovely created things which you made. You were with me, and I was not with you. The lovely things kept me far from you, though if they did not have their existence in you, they had no existence at all. You called and cried out loud and shattered my deafness. You were radiant and resplendent, you put to flight my blindness. You were fragrant, and I drew in my breath and now pant after you. I tasted you, and I feel but hunger and thirst for you. You touched me, and I am set on fire to attain the peace which is yours. (10.xxvii [38], p. 201)

His conversion happens in book 8. But it is interesting that his conversion is not the end of the story. When he is ordained at Hippo in 391, the first thing he does is write his bishop, Valerius, asking him for time off to give himself completely to the study of Scripture. Thus his conversion in the garden leads to his formation by the Word, completing the process of Augustine becoming a person other than who he was before, a man who reads the world differently. In the subsequent books to the *Confessions*, it is as if Augustine's mind explodes into a great burst of intellectual energy as he muses on the meaning of memory, time, eternity—the inspiration of Scripture. In the five million surviving words of his work, we see Augustine pushing language and intellect to their limits in an attempt to rethink the world from the standpoint of his newfound friendship with God. This becomes the intellectual program of the rest of Augustine's life—a theological reading of the world. At points he despairs that the questions he now asks are so large, and the answers so difficult to come by. "The poverty of human intelligence has plenty to say, for inquiry employs more words than the discovery of the solution" (12.i [1], p. 246), he admits.

After his conversion in book 8, his mother Monica is overjoyed. That for which this woman had prayed had at last been given. Then, in book 9, Monica dies. Monica had been one of history's most long-suffering of mothers. All of her life she had prayed for his conversion. She had spent her life trying to bring her wayward and wanton son into the fold. She dies with her prayers answered. As his mother dies, Augustine is preparing to assume leadership of the church. His mind begins its work in service of the church, thinking about the Trinity, eternity, scriptural interpretation, and other matters that need new thought. Thus, as his mother dies, Augustine is acquiring a new mother, "Mother Church."

Surely this helps explain why the *Confessions* ends with the beginning of the Bible, with the first book of the Bible, with the first chapter of that book, Genesis 1. The *Confessions* ends in what seems at first an anticlimax—in books 11–13 with biblical exegesis, exegesis of that portion of the Bible that speaks of the beginning of a world: "In the beginning, when God created the heavens and the earth . . . God said . . ." As a developing adolescent, Augustine felt shame at his nakedness in the bath, even as his father expressed delight in the impressive physique of his growing son. So physically attractive a young man would surely produce fine heirs, the Roman way to immortality. Thus, he was naked, and though his father took delight in his nakedness, he was ashamed (Gen. 3:1-11). Later, as a young adult, Augustine spoke of being "swept away" in a flood of desire. And his great "fall" occurred, as Adam and Eve's, beneath a tree where he committed sin because of simple delight with the forbidden fruit. These and other parallels with Genesis echo the beginning of the world, the start of the story, the first days of a new Word-created world. Augustine had a lifelong preoccupation with Genesis.[41] *Confessions* illustrates that, for Augustine, conversion means the beginning of a world—genesis. A new world has been constructed on the basis of the Word, constituted by a peculiar way of rendering the world, namely, *Scripture*.

At the beginning of the *Confessions* Augustine asks, "Can anyone become the cause of his own making?" (1.vi [10], p. 8). He has answered his question with a resounding No! Our fabrication, the constitution of a human being, comes only as a gift of God's determination to be in conversation with us. Augustine, after such an arduous and stormy journey, has come to rest in Scripture, resting at last secure in a rendition of a new world not of his devising. The world is a result of grace. Conversion is the joyful willingness to be in constant conversation with a loquacious God. It is the assumption of a new world, the glad reception of a gracious gift. Creation. It is more radical than modernity's "coming to a new self-understanding." It is an awakening to a new location, a place constructed by words that emanate from the Word. The *Confessions* shows a man moving from monologue into dialogue, a man making a discovery that his life was not his fabrication, that "you, Lord my God, are the giver of life" (1.vii [12], p. 10). The whole book is addressed, not to the reader, but to God. Augustine's is autobiography as prayer.

Calling this work *Confessions* makes it sound like Augustine's revelation of some dark secret. The Latin *confessio* is better rendered as acknowledgment, or testimony.[42] What young Augustine presupposed to be his swelling outreach into the world, his lust for life, turns out to be God's reaching to embrace him. The book is best read as Augustine's acknowledgment of a God who creates all things new. In writing this account of his life, Augustine has become a witness (Acts 1:7) taking his place among all those who have been created, recreated, empowered, called, sent forth by the power of the irrepressible Word.

By the end, Augustine is at last at rest, having nothing better to do than to spend the rest of is life writing dozens of books in praise of the Trinity, having urged us, through his story, to make this story our own. He had ridiculed his earlier rhetorical occupation as a "salesman of words" (*venditor verborum*, 9.v [13], p. 163). Now he shall use words as a means of loving response to the Word. Augustine's testimony is an invitation to risk vocation, to go on the journey he has made, to venture forth with the expectation of discovering (or being discovered by) a new world, of learning to read as a primary way to God.[43] "Only you can be asked, only you can be begged, only on your door can we knock (Matt. 7:7-8). Yes, indeed, that is how it is received, how it is found, how the door is opened" (13.xxxviii [53], p. 305).

He died in August of 430. At the end, he asked his fellow monks to leave him alone in his cell. The man who so enjoyed and required the company of others was alone at the last. He had requested that the walls of his cell be affixed with the penitential psalms, lettered large so that he could read them. He read them over and over, weeping for his sins. Thus he died, as he had been born and reborn, surrounded by words, moving toward that eternal rest promised by the Word made flesh.

CHAPTER EIGHT

The Pastor as Teacher:
Christian Formation

*Teach me to seek You, and reveal Yourself to me as I seek; for
unless You instruct me I cannot seek You, and unless You reveal
Yourself I cannot find You. Let me seek You in desiring You; let
me desire You in seeking You. Let me find You in loving You; let
me love You in finding You.*

Anselm of Canterbury[1]

*discuss: where is he
going with this*

In their *Habits of the Heart*, Robert Bellah and his colleagues introduced us to Sheila Larson, who described her faith by saying, "I
believe in God. I'm not a religious fanatic. I can't remember the last
time I went to church. My faith has carried me a long way. It's
Sheilaism. Just my own little voice."[2] This gave rise to the widespread use of "Sheilaism" as the real American religion of our
time—"just my own little voice," as the only authoritative word to
our lives. In a study of 1,150 Californians and North Carolinians,
Jackson W. Carroll and Wade Clark Roof found that about 66 percent of them agreed that a person should arrive at his or her religious beliefs independently of any church or religious group (73
percent of those aged eighteen to thirty-four agreed).[3] Quite a difference from Augustine, obsessed with the voice of God. Now, it's
"just my own little voice." This is the climate in which the pastor
leads Christian education. We are all Sheila now.

At the end of Matthew's Gospel, Jesus tells his disciples, "Go
therefore and make disciples of all nations, baptizing them in the
name of the Father and of the Son and of the Holy Spirit, and
teaching them to obey everything that I have commanded you.
And remember, I am with you always, to the end of the age"
(Matt. 28:19-20). I have sometimes wondered whether his "I am
with you always" was meant to be construed as a promise or a
threat. "I, having harassed and prodded you for just three years

while with you, will now, as your resurrected Lord, continue to do so, forever!"

But that does not concern us here. What concerns us is Jesus' rather surprising command to "make disciples."[4] Disciples, as Tertullian noted, are made, not born. Jesus did not tell us to go into the world and discover disciples or evoke disciples. Disciples are made, not born. When Paul speaks of the church as God's building (1 Cor. 5:9), he refers to himself as an *architecton* rather than as one might expect, as a *tekton*. A *tekton* is a carpenter, a builder, whereas an *architecton* is a craftsperson, an architect or engineer. A distinctive pastoral role for Paul is that of designer, of artist with Christ, of the church. Like a skilled artist, a pastor works with Christ to form the church.

Even after so wonderful an outburst of Holy Spirit as is reported in Acts 2, the first post-Pentecost episode is for the church to devote "themselves to the apostles' teaching" (Acts 2:42). Discipleship does not come naturally, is not in accord with our innate inclinations. Being a disciple of Jesus is not contiguous with being a sensitive, caring person. Nor is it enough to say, "I have been born in North America, which is at least vestigially Christian, so I become Christian by drinking the water and breathing the air, therefore I have no need to be made a Christian." The good news of Jesus Christ is at odds with the world's news, stands at some distance from the world's officially sanctioned means of salvation. Christians must be made, not born. Disciples are those who have been formed by the good news of Jesus Christ into certain sorts of people who live in the world in certain sorts of ways that are often counter to the world's ways.

"On the sabbath he began to teach in the synagogue, and many who heard him were astounded. They said, 'Where did this man get all this?' . . . And they took offense at him" (Mark 6:2-3). Mark's Gospel presents Jesus as a teacher, and a rather offensive teacher at that. The primary designation for Jesus in Mark is "rabbi," teacher. "Then he went among the villages teaching" (Mark 6:6). In Matthew's Gospel, where Jesus is frequently depicted as a teacher, Jesus is clear that his teaching is challenging. Often he teaches, not to bring peace, but a sword (Matt. 10:34).

One day, when the apostles reported to Jesus "all that they had done and taught" (Mark 6:30), Jesus suggested that they get away and "rest a while" (6:31). They go to the desert, but by the time they get to where they are going it is anything but deserted. A "great crowd" gathers and Jesus "had compassion for them, because they were like sheep without a shepherd; and he began to teach them many things" (6:34). In a short time we find out that this great crowd is hungry. Jesus will respond to their hunger with a miraculous outpouring of food. Yet is it not interesting that the first thing Jesus does for them, sensing that they are "like sheep without a shepherd," is not feed them, but teach?[5]

Pastors are the chief teachers within the congregation, thus it has ever been. As we have noted, when pastoral leaders are admonished in the Pastoral Epistles, the predominant admonition is that they teach sound doctrine. There are certain aspects of the present moment of the church that suggest that the role of teacher, always prominent for pastors, has become even more important in the context in which the church finds itself today.

Isaiah 5 speaks of the sadness of God's people going into exile "without knowledge." We have those who are forced, by the nature of American society, to live in circumstances of exile without the conceptual means to resist. An African American preacher friend of mine put it more bluntly, lamenting the loss of youth and young adults from many predominantly African American churches. "I fear," he says, "that we have the first generation of African American youth who are growing up ill equipped by the church for the rigors of slavery."

In the previous chapter we focused on the pastor as counselor, as advocate of those in pain. There are many in our society who are in pain, but not because of some psychological malady or because of something bad that happened to them when they were five. They are hurting because they are wandering like lost sheep in a desert. They are confused. It is not that they are sick; rather, they are ignorant. They simply have not taken the trouble, or not had the opportunity, to think through the faith. They confront the complexity of life with bits and pieces of insight cobbled together from here or there. Or they try to live in an adult world with the faith that they received as a ten-year-old or rejected as a fourteen-year-old. In Mark 6 we find that there is a hunger for bread, but also a more substantial hunger for "every word that comes from the mouth of God" (Matt. 4:4). Odd, when we hear the names of Paul,

Athanasius, or Augustine, we tend to think of them as theologians, and they were. Yet these great thinkers spent most of their time being pastors, and most of their theology was thought in response to specific issues of pastoral care.

At the beginning of my ministry, sociologist Peter Berger described us Christians as a "cognitive minority." Christian modes of thought deviate from the officially sanctioned, socially enforced systems of knowledge. The world's "plausibility structures," by which it knows what is possible and permissible, tell the world that the Christian faith is implausible. "It is, of course, possible to go against the social consensus that surrounds us," says Berger, "but there are powerful pressures (which manifest themselves as psychological pressures within our own consciousness) to conform to the views and beliefs of our fellow men."[6] There is a subtle yet powerful policing that keeps certain Christian convictions from being uttered and affirmed within conventional society. Christian education is one of the ways that the church enables us to avoid being conformed to this world, yet be transformed by the renewal of our minds (Rom. 12:1-2).[7]

Invitation to a New World

Loren Mead enabled many of us pastors to reconceive of our work in his succinct book *The Once and Future Church*, a book whose subtitle is its main thesis, *Reinventing the Congregation for a New Mission Frontier.*[8] Mead announced that for the first centuries, the church was molded upon the "Apostolic Paradigm" in which the church understood well the distance between itself and the world. The church had a mission: to evangelize the world, to embody the gospel of Christ before the world. The missionary church lived as an enclave of one culture in the middle of another.

When Emperor Constantine adopted the church and all but obliterated the tensive relationship between the church and the world, this led, says Mead, to the "Christendom Paradigm." Christianity became a state religion and attempted to make the culture Christian. Church and culture worked together to produce a new civilization. In this new arrangement, the church civilized the culture, and the culture served as a prop for the church.

Mead announces the death of Christendom. Though Christianity has not been fully disestablished in our culture, it is rapidly losing its once privileged place. Therefore, we pastors are forced to develop a new paradigm for our work. The most appropriate paradigm, says Mead, has its roots within the apostolic church—the paradigm we see embodied in the Acts of the Apostles where the church is moving into the world, constantly interacting with the world, but always with a consciousness of its radical distinction from the world. In Acts, the church is clearly moving west, toward Rome. But it moves toward Rome with a massive educational effort. Rather than educating Christians to adapt to the world, the church sought to adapt the world to the church, to convert the world rather than to be subverted by the world. Mead says that this is the age in which we now live.

Lesslie Newbigin returned from his time with the church in India, and labeled Western civilization as the newest and perhaps most difficult, "mission field" of the church.[9] He noted that the "plausibility structure" of the West is the scientific worldview that tends to be reductionistic, positivistic, closed to data that does not arise from within its own system of thought, and is based upon the Cartesian "fact-value dichotomy." Newbigin called for the church to confront this limited modern plausibility structure with that of the more expanded consciousness of the Bible.

In my own ministry, a little book by theologian George Lindbeck helped me truthfully name what I had been experiencing within my congregations. In 1984, I found Lindbeck's *Nature of Doctrine*.[10] Lindbeck said that most of us, because we live in a society indebted to the thought of philosophical liberalism, consider religion as a matter of "experiential/expressivism." That is, we think of religion as an institutional means of expressing our personal, inner, innate religious experiences. Religion is merely an expression of a universal human tendency toward the divine. Though there are different religions, these are merely the outward, human-conditioned responses to the inner, innate, universal experience. This is the person who says something such as, "I'm a Christian, you're a Buddhist, but the main thing is that we both believe in God, right?"

We live in a culture, that of liberalism, in which human experience is thought of as the supreme source of most reality, in which religion is seen as a mere accident of birth, a primitive means of expressing a human experience that could be as well expressed through some other medium. All religions are thus only different, culturally conditioned means of saying the same thing.

When religion is viewed in an experiential/expressivist manner, then religious education is mostly a matter of evocation, drawing out (*educare,* to lead out) an innate human experience. Christianity is defended as a provocative, if primitive, account of the human condition—one means of naming those thoughts and aspirations that lie within us. Plato taught that we once knew the good, the true, and the beautiful, but we have temporarily forgotten them. Education merely reminds us, thereby drawing out what we already know. Plato was not a Christian.

Lindbeck argues that although the experiential/expressive manner of construing religion is a popular way of conceiving of religion in our society, it falsifies the way religion actually works among believers. Is it true that religion is merely an expression of an experience that is prior to the religion? Or is it more accurate to say that religion is a way of engendering and forming our experience? Becoming an adherent to a religion is much like learning to speak a language, says Lindbeck. Thus he proposes what he calls the "cultural/linguistic" way of conceiving of religion.

To be religious is to be a participant in a culture—a melange of habits, words, rituals, practices, tradition, and stories that move the participant into a different world than that person would live in without the imposition of the images, practices, and words of a religion. Although liberalism attempts to depict our involvement in religion as something that we choose in order to express our innermost feelings about God, this is not how religion actually works. Although the experiential/expressive mode of conceiving faith depicts us as people who feel certain religious inclinations and then go and shop about for a religion that expresses those inclinations, Lindbeck stresses the cultural/linguistic way that the community of faith forms our inclinations. In this conception of religion, to be converted into a faith is not to discover something within us, but rather to be subsumed into a new culture, to take up a new language that changes what is within us.

Lindbeck says religion is more than a projection out of us; it is an imposition that shapes us. Our religion is more than an expression of certain innate inclinations, rather, gradually, over time, *religion forms our inclinations.* We are enculturated into a system of signs, signals, and symbols, the inculcation of which engenders certain experiences in us, experiences we would never have had without the religion. Becoming a Christian is therefore somewhat analogous to learning French. Just as it is impossible to learn French by reading a French novel in an English translation, so it is also impossible, as Lindbeck notes, truly to learn Christianity by encountering it through the translation of existentialism, or feminism, or the language of self-esteem. One must learn the vocabulary, inculcate the moves and gestures of this faith, in order to know the faith.[11]

Is it true, for instance, that all human beings are born with a natural inclination toward gratitude? After having two children, I think not. One must be taught to be grateful. "Say 'thank you' to the nice person for the candy, or you'll be punished." That's how gratitude comes. Language precedes experience. Theory does not simply arise out of our experiences, but more often shapes, evokes, experience. Perhaps that is why Paul speaks of faith coming through hearing (Rom. 10:17). One must be told the story of Jesus Christ before one can know Jesus. One must learn the habits and gestures whereby Christians encounter Jesus.[12]

In my own congregation, as people are coming forward for the Lord's Supper, we have them hold their hands out in order to receive the elements of communion. I find this simple gesture to be deeply significant. We live in a culture in which we are trained to grab, seize, hold on tight. In the church, we are taught the open-handed gesture that is necessary to confess emptiness, hunger, the need for a gift. We call it grace.

Thus Lindbeck's categories remind us that *Christianity is a culture.* My penchant for speaking of the church as a "counterculture" does not mean that I believe that the church stands aloof from human culture, pointing a critical finger toward the predominate secular world. Rather, the church itself forms a culture that is counter to the world's ways of doing things. The church does not simply reach out to and speak to the dominant culture; it seeks to disrupt that culture by rescuing some from it, then to inculcate people into a new culture called the church.

Christian education is therefore best described, not as a drawing out of something that is already there (in the Latin, *educare*, "to draw out"), rather, Christian education is more traditionally "catechesis," our description of all the ways in which we form people into this culture called the church. There is no other means to catch Christianity than to be caught by the church. Faith for us is not some universal human attribute, but rather it is a matter of having one's life bent toward Jesus Christ through the ministrations of the church.

Jerome, in his Letter 52, advised the pastoral educators of his day:

> When teaching in church seek to call forth not plaudits but groans. Let the tears of your hearers be your glory. A presbyter's words ought to be seasoned by the reading of scripture. Be not a declaimer or a ranter, one who gabbles without rhyme or reason; but show yourself skilled in the deep things and versed in the mysteries of God. To mouth your words and by your quickness of utterance astonish the unlettered crowd is a mark of ignorance.[13]

Because the dominant culture in which we live is that of liberal, expressive individualism, Christianity often strikes hard against conventional wisdom. The sense that we make, when Christians make sense, is not common sense. We live among people who like to think that they have created their own reality, that they "think for themselves," and "follow their hearts." In reality, their declarations of freedom and self-creation are testimonial to how well they have been captured by the officially sanctioned ideology. In such a constricted intellectual climate, dominated by a social consensus that affirms such creeds as "I may be a god," or "I am the sole center of meaning," or "I sit in sovereign judgment upon everything that is outside the range of my personal experience," or "We stand at the summit of human development," or "Religion is inherently oppressive," the teaching ministry of the church becomes one of the church's most prophetic acts. It is not that Christians have been formed by a limited way of thinking, whereas those who think of themselves as secular, liberated, autonomous people are free of any external determination and formation. Rather, it is that all of us have been formed by some socially imposed external determination. Some socially imposed, external determinations are so sanctioned by this economy that they stop seeming socially constructed and imposed. All modes of thought are subservient to some political order, some account of what is going on in the world, some definition of the good and the true.

So, when an early twenty-first-century North American says, "What the church says may be OK for some people, but I think it is important to think for myself," that person thinks that he or she is thinking for himself or herself. No. He is only espousing that self-centered, limited way of knowing that has been imposed upon him by his culture. One could almost say that, because this is North America, because of the United States Constitution's rendering of religion into a private matter, sealed off from everything important like economics, politics, and public matters, that person is not free to think anything more interesting than "I think it is important to think for myself." As Stanley Hauerwas has told us repeatedly, for a contemporary North American to say, "I think for myself," is solid evidence of cultural formation, externally imposed social determination, since she did not think up the credo "I think for myself" all by herself.

Thus the Christian faith ought to admit that it does not simply want to speak to the world. This faith wants to change the world. Or, more accurately, this faith *is* a world. That is, being a Christian means to be someone who has been inculcated into a distinctive culture which, like any culture, has its own series of beliefs, words, myths, practices, rituals, and habits through which it demarcates itself from other worlds. More than that, it is our claim that this world, this culture—the church—is God's way with the world, the appointed means by which Christ is bringing all things unto himself. One reason your church is often so tense on Sundays is that Sunday morning is a struggle over the basic question, Who names the world? The world belongs to those who name it. So when Christians debate which words to use to describe certain events, which stories ought to be given prominence over other stories, what ought to be said and what ought not to be said, it is all part of that linguistic phenomenon called creation of culture, the naming, and therefore making, of a world.

Sometimes Christians are urged to speak to the "wider world," to engage in "public theology." But into which world would Christians go if they wanted to be "wider" and more "public"? The United States? The United Nations? These entities prattle on about "national sovereignty" and "self-determination" while defending

interpretive leadership

their constricted borders with murderous intensity. Why must the church submit itself to such limited worlds? Every "world" is just that; only a world—a system of symbols, language, and rituals through which a culture is constructed. A small world is called the "United States of America." A wider world is called the "Catholic Church." Why ought the world of secular, national imperialism be privileged over the world called *church?*

Christians are often being told by the world to "be realistic." But such demands beg the prior question of, Who gets to define reality? Certain "realities" seem more real, appear to be facts to which we ought to adjust, not because they are more real than other accounts of reality, but rather because they receive the support of a capitalist economy and a national polity that privileges certain accounts of reality and suppresses others.

Acts begins with the question, "Lord, will you at this time restore the kingdom to Israel?" (Acts 1:6 RSV; cf. Luke 9:11). It is an inquiry into a kingdom, a new world, a counterpolitical reality. Christians form a "world" in the ways that any world is formed—through words, rituals, habits, practices, images, metaphors, myths, and beliefs. That the world of the church does not appear to be the dominant mode of construing reality does not mean that the church's mode of thought is "primitive," or "unrealistic," or "spiritual," or those other epithets by which the world seeks to silence alternative, rebellious accounts of the world. It means that Christian modes of knowing and thinking are truthful, whereas many of the world's privileged accounts are not.

Someone asks, "Do you think that we ought to convert people to Christianity? Ought we try to convert everyone else?" Aside from the fact that we have been, by our Lord, commanded to go into all the world and evangelize in the name of a triune God, if we do not evangelize, what is the alternative? The question, Should we try to convert people to Christ? often assumes that there are innocent, unformed, culturally untouched people out there, and then there are these pushy Christians trying to convert them into their limited way of thinking. No. Everyone has been formed by some culture, some external determination; or, in our peculiar way of speaking, everyone has been converted into some point of view that is not innate. The question then is not, Shall my life be formed by some external point of view? but rather, Which externally imposed cultural formation will have its way with me?

From this point of view, all education is transformation, conversion, formation, catechesis. In the middle of a sermon, I noted, "If you take a very young child into a toy store, you will not need to instruct the child on how to behave—greed comes quite naturally in this culture—after all, this is America. But if you take that same child into St. John's on the expressway at eleven on Sunday morning, the child will be disoriented, unsteady, will need instruction."

Then I caught the error of my statement and said, "That's not quite fair to this culture. Nothing, even greed, is 'natural.' Except for an inclination to sin, it is all education. I am overlooking the years of skillful indoctrination and inculcation that has taken place in the life of that child. That child has received some of the best education in the world to convince her or him, 'The highest purpose of your life is consumption. You have no other purpose than to produce and to consume.' Almost nothing is natural."

Because we are the victims of a host of competing stories and countermeans of formation, many of which are sanctioned by this culture and its economy, there will be of necessity a repetitive quality to Christian education. Our intent is not to illuminate what people already know, but rather to form them into a way of life they could not have known without Christian formation.[14] It must be done over and over again, out of habit, retained through repetition.[15] Rather than construe the Christian faith as a set of interesting ideas to be affirmed, I think it is wise to present this faith as a set of practices to be inculcated, a set of habits to be assumed. Rather than lecture people on something vague such as "the Christian view of money," just try to get them to promise to give 10 percent of all that they have to the church. The set of disciplines and understandings required for that will lead them eventually to more faithful understanding, but often, in the Christian faith, one cannot receive the understanding until one gets the right moves.

The primary setting for such inculcation and formation will be the corporate worship of the church.[16] Although 38 percent of North Americans attend a service of worship on a Sunday morning, less than 22 percent of them participate in any other setting for Christian education.[17] If we are going to expose the majority of our people to the signs, symbols, and stories of Jesus, it will be during corporate worship or not at all. A major question for us pastors is therefore, Does the Sunday worship of my church have sufficient substance in order to help my people make it through the week as disciples?

Today, many congregations are engaged in what some have called the "worship wars"—ought we to have traditional or contemporary music, acoustical or electronic, pipe organs or electric guitars? Usually, we debate from the standpoint of taste, personal preference, age, and so forth. We ought to see the traditional versus contemporary worship issue as the formative theological question, What sort of disciples are being formed by singing these songs?

The primary Christian educator is the pastor who, in the multiple acts of ministry, must model what it means for Christians constantly to be growing in their faith. Even as a primary designation of Jesus was "rabbi," "teacher," so the pastor bears the responsibility of leading in the formation and inculcation of Christians.[18] To the pastor is given primary responsibility for worrying about the theological content of our life together, for measuring how well our current practices of the faith match the faith of the saints, for considering the biblical fidelity of our prayer and praise. To the pastor is given the lead role in making disciples, in not only preserving but also passing on the faith to a new generation.

Whether a pastor gives priority to the teaching ministry of the church will depend, to a great extent, on a pastor's political assessment of our situation. If you believe that we work in a basically Christian culture where the faith comes naturally to just about everyone, then there is no need for Christian education. Renewal and refreshment will be the pastor's leadership goals more than reformation or regeneration.

Thus Rodney Clapp stresses the church as a "new and unique culture," which includes, in Clapp's words:

- A particular way of eating, learned in and through the Eucharist.
- A particular way of handling conflict, the peculiar politics called "forgiveness" and learned through the example and practice of Jesus and his cross.
- A particular way of perpetuating itself, through evangelism rather than biological propagation.[19]

Because this faith is countercultural, those who would walk this way need not be surprised that they must assume new practices. Any revolution requires disciplined revolutionaries. The joyful adventure that is called *discipleship* requires the formation of people who are able to resist the powers and principalities in all the tempting guises by which they present themselves. Through the words and practices of the church, such as tithing, worship, forgiveness, prayer, devotional reading, and self-denying service, the church deconstructs the socialization and spiritually stultifying conditioning of the world, and gives people a new means of living in the world.[20] For all these reasons, a primary pastoral task must be teaching. "Keep these words that I am commanding you today in your heart. Recite them to your children and talk about them when you are at home and when you are away, when you lie down and when you rise" (Deut. 6:6-7).

Christian education, in order to form a counterculture, will involve a great deal of repetition, ritual, and reiteration in order that the alternative account of reality—otherwise known in Israel as "Torah," known among Christians as "gospel"—may have its way with us. The community is formed, Christians are made Christian by listening to this story, by keeping it ever before us, by allowing waves of Scripture to sweep over us. Thus is formed a new people, a counterconfiguration that is a political alternative to the world's way of gathering people. Walter Brueggemann says:

> Israel's narrative is a partisan, polemical narrative. It is concerned to build a countercommunity—counter to the oppression of Egypt, counter to the seduction of Canaan, counter to every cultural alternative and every imperial pretense. There is nothing in this narrative that will appeal to outsiders who belong to another consensus, or who share a different ethos and participate in another epistemology. To such persons, Israel's narratives are silly, narrow, scandalous, and obscurantist.... Torah intends to nurture insiders who are willing to risk a specific universe of discourse and cast their lot there.... Shall we risk these stories? Shall we take our stand on them?... The answer is known only when we decide if we want to subvert the imperial consciousness and offer a genuine alternative to the dominant forms of power, value, and knowledge.[21]

Cf. Josh 24

As for me & my house

When a mob attacked some of the believers in Thessalonica, the rabble screamed, "These people who have been turning the world upside down have come here also" (Acts 17:6). What they should have charged is not simply that Christians turn the world upside down and inside out, but rather that they are attempting to live in a whole new world.

The Teaching Moment

At a meeting of pastors, a noted church observer was asked, "What about the length of sermons?"

The observer responded, "From what I observe, sermons are getting both longer and shorter. It's the tasteful eighteen-minute sermon that seems to be disappearing. In postmodernity, the middle disappears. I think the main factor is the median age of your congregation."

Then he added an observation that surprised us. "And the younger your congregation, the longer the sermon." What? We thought the under-thirty, MTV crowd had an attention span reduced to the length of time between television commercials.

He went on to say that those under thirty are unformed, uninformed, and malformed in the Christian faith, and many of them know it. They therefore long for formation, regeneration, so sermons to them will need to take more time to tell the story, to name the name, to go over the basics of the faith.[22]

We could wring our hands and lament the decline of biblical literacy, or we could ask God to inspire us with more creative ways to open up the riches of Scripture to those who have not yet been introduced to the text. We could rediscover the joy of encountering Scripture as if for the first time, seeing the gospel through the eyes of those for whom it is new. We could reawaken to the ways that the symbols of the faith are teaching; forming faith in those who encounter them in Sunday worship. We might recover a sense of the pastor as rabbi, the pastor as teacher, as a peculiarly appropriate metaphor for the pastor in our post-Christendom age.

Years ago, Dean Kelley gave us our first look at the evangelical resurgence in America with his *Why Conservative Churches Are Growing*.[23] Kelley said that those churches that we label "conservative" grow, as opposed to those churches we label "liberal," because these growing churches keep close to the basic intellectual task of the Christian faith. Religion provides people with a plausibility structure, a plausible alternative to the world's ways of making sense. Religion is in the meaning-making business. If religion is only a limp imitation of the dominant modes of understanding within the secular culture, said Kelley, it is going to dwindle. Why bother if church is little more than a sanctified form of Rotary?

We live in an age in which we have the opportunity to recover a sense of the peculiarity of the Christian mode of making sense of the world in distinction from the world's ways of making sense. Christian education is therefore considerably more engaging and controversial than mere transferal of information. In learning the stories and the moves of this faith, we are transformed into something we would not have been had we not been exposed, formed, habituated into this faith. Christian education is considerably more than what is done in Sunday school or in an intentional study group. In all the rites, rituals, habits, signs, symbols, and conversations of the whole congregation, Christians are being formed (or malformed) as disciples.[24]

In our *Liturgy and Learning Through the Life Cycle,* John Westerhoff and I tried to note some of the many ways that Christians are formed and reformed through their participation in the worship of the church, and how pastors are being teachers, and when pastors are being priests.[25] There is not one rite of the church that is not an educational, formative act. Every time we celebrate a wedding, the church is proclaiming to itself and the world what it believes about marriage. When we gather for a funeral, the church is not only caring for those who are going through the acute crisis of grief, but also preparing the rest of us who will one day walk that sad path.

When Ronald Heifetz speaks of transformative leadership in his *Leadership Without Easy Answers,* he says that *all transformative leadership is teaching.* The main thing leaders do, in order to transform organizations, is teach. A leader, according to Heifetz, is the coordinator of education in order that there be transformation:

> The task of leadership consists of choreographing and directing learning processes in an organization or community. Progress often demands new ideas and innovation. As well, it often demands changes in people's attitudes and behaviors. Adaptive work consists of the process of discovering and making those

changes. Leadership, with or without authority, requires an educative strategy.[26]

A few years ago, three sociologists, noting the huge decline in memberships being suffered by the mainline (now fast becoming the old-line or sidelined) denominations, described what they termed "the emergence of lay liberalism" within these churches.[27] After surveying five hundred of the churches' baby boomers, they found that 92 percent described themselves as "religious," but only 62 percent claimed to be church members, and just 47 percent worshiped at least twice a month. Among them, church membership was optional in their practice of faith. Most surprising, *the same position was held among those who went to church.* "Eighty percent of active Presbyterians and seventy-two percent of other mainline participants agree. Even among the fundamentalists this position is held by forty-five percent of the Boomers."[28] Even those who attend church see their church activity as thoroughly tangential to their faith.

Furthermore, the boomers seem to agree that, if they are Christian, it is a mere

accident of birth. . . Many Boomers go so far as to say that they would be content if their children adopted non-Western religions "as long as they are happy" and as long as they are moral citizens. . . . They give little credence to the pronouncements of the institutional church or to religious tradition. Moreover, in the wake of nineteenth-century challenges to biblical literalism, the Reformation's allegiance to *sola scriptura* holds little sway. . . . The basis for religious authority narrows to personal experience, which becomes the touchstone of their religious and moral affirmations.[29]

This phenomenon of a generation trapped within the confines of its own radically individualized personal experience, with no sense of external authority or truth beyond what has personally happened to them, makes "lay liberalism"

very shifting sand on which to build a religious community. It has no inherent loyalty factor upon which institutions can depend for sustained support. Rather, it promotes an ethos in which church involvement is strictly optional, and the option is to be exercised solely at the discretion of the individual. As a result lay liberals become religious consumers, seeking the religious services that meet their personal wants.[30]

Catechesis that addresses these "lay liberals" cannot avoid being confrontational. It will unmask the cultural captivity of their alleged "freedom," the conformist nature of their vaunted "individualism." It will see itself as rescuing these spiritual consumers from the bondage of the self, and liberating them from their notion that reality is nothing more than a personal contrivance. It will tell a counter story to the world's stories of who we are. It will teach us the words and the moves in order to see ourselves as members of the adventurous journey known as discipleship.

The good news is that this is a great season for teaching the good news, which is Jesus Christ. In a debate among students about something called "homosexuality" (not a word that occurs in the Bible), where the group seemed almost evenly divided between those who had been labeled "straight" and those who answered to the name "gay," it occurred to me that my difficulty in speaking to them was not because the Bible and church tradition was negative about homosexuality, but rather because the Bible had a very different notion of a person than that which was operating within the room.

Here were young people who had been told in countless movies and novels that they have no greater purpose in life than orgasm, that their sexuality is the most significant aspect of their humanity, and that labels such as "straight" or "gay" have ontological significance and are deeply determinative of who they are. A consumer economy has found that sex is very effective in selling its goods—there being such a nice fit between sexual consumption and all other forms of acquisitiveness. Is it any wonder that to hear the church say, "We do not like the way you have sex," they hear a vicious attack upon their humanity?

I had the joyful task of proclaiming to them that the Bible has very little to say about their sexuality, and Jesus has nothing to say about sex as a detached, independently significant aspect of human life. For us, sex is interesting only as a way of living out our vocation to be disciples, only within the context of commitments to God and to one another. Through promises, the church makes sex significant as a means of witness, prophetic critique, and discipleship.

I disagree!

Sex should not be nearly so interesting to Christians as promises, commitment, and fidelity.

For me it was a small instance of the way in which Christian thought is a collision with the world's epistemologies, a challenge to worldly ways of making sense. Once we have said something such as, "Jesus Christ is Lord," or "The church is God's answer to what is wrong with the world," or "The Bible is truthful in a way that, say, the United States Constitution is not," then we must go back and rethink much that we have taken for granted. This is the task of all teaching that is Christian.

And the good news is that this is a marvelous time for such teaching. I was speaking at a conference on Christianity and the family. I had the challenge of trying to think about the family in the manner that Jesus seemed to think. I noted that Jesus had minimal interaction with his own family and, when he did go home or encounter his mother, things usually went badly. He made disciples by rescuing people from their families. His, "Follow me!" appears to have meant, "Leave your family." Then there is Paul, and most of us know how negative he was on marriage and family. Indeed, one of pagan Rome's most trenchant criticisms against early Christians was that they tore families apart, teaching children to be disrespectful of their parents, and wives not to submit to their husbands, and nothing was more dear to pagan Romans than their families.[31] Jesus was clear that he had come to turn father against son and mother against daughter (Mark 3). The gospel was a sword that severed families and broke the hearts of many parents (Matt. 10:34-39).

So when Christians say "family," what we mean is "church"— that gathering based not upon natural birth, or social class, or race, or the world's other ways of locating people. We are trying to be members of that family formed by the waters of baptism. Our family consists of those who have been made disciples by being baptized and taught. That is our idea of family.

Most of the older persons present found my remarks on the family to be bizarre, despite my quotes from Jesus. To my surprise, it was the younger members of the group who heard me gladly. One teenager told the group how much the church had meant to him since the divorce of his parents. Another young adult told how a little congregation had taken her in after she had run away from her abusive father and found herself all alone in a big city. "It's great to hear that God has other plans for us besides our families," said one young person. "I didn't know there was any other way."

Sometimes the difference between good news and bad news is where one happens to be when one gets the news. The good news for us pastors who are teachers is that we live in a time of moral chaos, social breakdown, and inhumane institutions, that is, a marvelous time to teach the world that God has another way. When people give up hope for the present order, when people have achieved all that the world has to offer and it is still not enough, what a marvelous moment to offer them Christ.

Christian formation is the work of the whole church, not just in the classroom, but in all the activity of the church. Therefore, pastoral leadership is inherently educational in nature. As we have noted, Ron Heifetz believes that all leadership is "adaptive work" in which the leader is always a teacher. "Because making progress on adaptive problems requires learning, the task of leadership consists of choreographing and directing learning processes."[32] Artistic director, choreographer—these are good images for the work that must be done by the pastor as chief Christian educator.[33]

In Mark 6, Jesus and his disciples have gone out to the desert to be alone. With so much human need and pain pressing in upon them, they need a respite from the work of ministry. And so he begins to teach (Mark 6:34), as Jesus so often does in this Gospel where he is usually the teacher and his disciples are learners.[34] Later he will miraculously offer them food. He will heal. But first he will teach. He will teach them words of life that will enable them to know the secret of what is afoot in the world, enable them to lay hold of their lives so they will cease to be jerked around by the principalities and powers of the present age. His good news finds them in their lostness. He becomes their shepherd in teaching them. So do we.

Although the purpose of Sunday worship is the glorification of God, it is also the major location for the sanctification of the faithful. Here is the major means of encountering the symbols, stories, rituals, and practices of the faith. We must take care that our Sunday service has sufficient substance to sustain our people in the rigors of discipleship. We must also ensure that the whole congregation is present when the congregation gathers—including children.

In my last congregation, we decided that a major purpose of our Christian education was to prepare our young for full participation in worship. Therefore, we set an educational goal: "By the time a child in our congregation is six years old, that child will know by heart the Apostles' Creed, the Lord's Prayer, the Gloria Patri, and the Doxology." Children do not have to know the full meaning of these acts of corporate worship (who does?), but they ought to know the joy of full participation when the congregation gathers to enact its faith. Rather than "dumb down" the liturgy of the church to accommodate our unformed, uninformed sensibilities, the church's time is better spent giving us the insights, habits, and language we need more fully to participate in the church's praise and prayer.

When I was beginning my pastoral ministry, older pastors told me, "The laity say they want Bible study, then when you organize a Bible study, they remember why they dropped out of the last one."

In my own denomination, *Disciple Bible Study* was created. Now nearly three million laity have been through the *Disciple* program, which requires more than thirty weeks of intense, thorough study, with a lot of homework.[35] The program was so successful that the church created *Christian Believer,* a thirty-three-week study of Christian doctrine. From all accounts, the laity are flocking to this demanding study of doctrine. Thus we pastors have lost one of our favorite alibis for not teaching our congregations!

A few years ago I visited a number of allegedly "fundamentalist" churches. All of these congregations were growing, and all of them had, by my estimate, a high percentage of young people. What impressed me was the "intellectual" quality of their Sunday services. Most of the worshipers carried a Bible and a notebook into the service. The sermons were all at least forty minutes long—lectures really—more than my idea of sermons. One of the preachers engaged in rather complex Greek word study during the sermon while the congregation carefully took notes. That congregation seemed to be mostly blue-collar working people. I was quite moved by the scene. Here were people, I supposed, who were having a wide range of experiences in life, but had little conceptual help in dealing with those experiences. The church took their need seriously, giving them the theoretical, theological framework they needed to make sense out of their lives in a Christian way.

The African American preacher and teacher Samuel D. Proctor, pastor of Abyssinian Baptist Church in New York City, my colleague at Duke Divinity School, and great teacher of preachers, wrote a book in which he joined with Gardner C. Taylor to give advice to fellow pastors. Proctor expended a large part of the book on "the pastor as teacher":

> Theology never comes alive in abstract debate. It is best understood when it is lived. A good pastor will take the time to show the people how life should be lived, given such a great God as we are privileged to know, and given how marvelously we are made. From this wonderful knowledge comes an awareness that our purpose is to cultivate our gifts in God's honor and to God's glory, and to live all our days in loving obedience to God. It means finding joy in pausing to praise God and to find fellowship with others. . . . It means lifting up the life stories of others who have done so well in walking with the Lord, learning and hearing the music and the poetry that edify our lives in obedience and joy. It means finding our highest fulfillment in following Christ in service to others. Celebrating the lives of victorious Christians is a great opening for good teaching.[36]

I predict that in our age we shall rediscover the role of the pastor as the chief Christian educator within the congregation, the one who fosters and critiques the practices of the church in order for the church to be the church.[37] I expect that more of a pastor's time will be spent making disciples where Christians are made, not born.

CHAPTER NINE

The Pastor as Evangelist:
Christ Means Change[1]

Now as he was going along and approaching Damascus, suddenly a light from heaven flashed around him. He fell to the ground and heard a voice. (Acts 9:3-4)

Luke begins his first volume, his Gospel (Luke 1:1-4), assuring Theophilus that he intends to present him with an "orderly account" of the Christian movement. Yet when we get to Luke's second volume, the Acts of the Apostles, we soon realize that this faith is anything but orderly. A mob of scoffers is transformed into repentant believers (2:14-41), a person from the remote ends of the earth is transmuted into the baptized (8:26-40), a murderous enemy is transmogrified into "brother Saul" (9:1-31), and a despised Gentile soldier is adopted by the church (10:1–11:18). Whatever the Gospel is, it is about major alteration.[2] Luke's good news of Jesus Christ is inherently disruptive. The creator God, who made a world out of next to nothing in Genesis 1, loves to keep creating, to wrench life out of death. God delights in making a family where once there had been no people (1 Pet. 2:10).

Although this faith may not come as dramatically to all as it came to Paul in Acts 9 (the New Testament has a wide array of accounts of conversion), the Christian life comes neither naturally nor normally. Little within us prepares us for the shock of moral regeneration that is occasioned by the work of Christ among us. What God in Christ wants to do in us is nothing less than radical new creation, movement from death to life.[3] This means that ministry among the baptized tends to be more radical, disruptive, and antagonistic than we pastors admit. We are awfully accommodated, well situated, at ease in Zion—or at least disgustingly content with present arrangements. We reassure ourselves with the comforting bromides of a lethargic church: everyone in mainline Protestantism is in decline, everyone has become geriatric, even the

225

Baptists are losing members, people can't change, you can't teach old dogs new tricks. Sociological determinism has got us. What is to be done?

Despite our settled arrangements with death, as an African American preacher friend of mine puts it, the gospel means, "God is going to get back what God owns." C. S. Lewis spoke of his life before his conversion as "before God closed in on me."[4] Conversion—being born again, transformed, regenerated, detoxified—is God's means of closing in on us, of getting God's way with the world, despite what that reclamation may cost God or us.

Deep in my Wesleyan once-warmed heart is a story of how a priggish little Oxford don got changed at Aldersgate and thereafter. John Wesley's life was well formed, well fixed by a host of positive Christian influences upon him, before the evening on Aldersgate Street. Yet what happened afterward has led us Wesleyans to see his heart "strangely warmed" as nothing less than dramatic ending and beginning, death and birth, a whole new world.[5]

Such a story, fixed deep in our souls, challenges a church that has become accommodated to things as they are, the cultural status quo. It stands as a rebuke to a church that has settled comfortably into a characterization of the Christian life as pleasantly continuous and basically synonymous with being a good person.

Scripture enlists a rich array of metaphors to speak of the discontinuous, discordant outbreak of new life named "conversion"; "born from above," or "born anew" (John 3:7; 1 Pet. 1:3, 23); "regeneration" (John 3:5; Titus 3:5); "putting on a new nature" (Eph. 4:24; Col. 3:10); and "new creation" (2 Cor. 5:17). Paul contrasts the old life according to the flesh with "life according to the Spirit" (Rom. 8:1-39). Baptism tries to tell us that the Christian life is at times discordant, dissonant, and disrupting. When one joins Rotary, or the League of Women Voters, they give you a membership card and lapel pin. When one joins the Body of Christ, we throw you under, half drown you, strip you naked and wash you all over, pull you forth sticky and fresh like a newborn. One might think people would get the message. But, as Luther said, the old Adam is a mighty good swimmer.[6] A conversionist faith is very disconcerting, particularly to those for whom the world as it is has been fairly good. Those on top, those who are reasonably well fed, fairly well futured, tend to cling to the world as it is rather than risk the possibility of something new. For all these economic, social, and political reasons we pastors tend toward the maintenance of stability rather than the expectation of conversion.[7]

discuss

New Creation

Paul was stunned by the reality of the resurrection—the way God not only vindicated Jesus by raising him from the dead, but also thereby recreated the whole *kosmos*. In Easter, an old world had been terminated and a new one was being born, so Paul was forced to rethink everything that he had previously thought, including ethics. Much of what Paul says about Christian behavior was formed as his testimony to the Resurrection, an event that he had experienced within the dramatic turnaround in his own life. Whereas Jesus did Easter at the empty tomb, Easter happened to Paul on the Damascus Road.

Yet there was nothing merely subjective in Paul's vocation.[8] The call of Paul the apostle was his experience of finding himself suddenly transferred to a whole new world. He changed because of his realization that, in Jesus Christ, the world had changed. Paul's key testimonial to this recreation is in his Second Letter to the Corinthians:

> So if anyone is in Christ, there is a new creation: everything old has passed away; see, everything has become new! All this is from God, who reconciled us to himself through Christ, and has given us the ministry of reconciliation. (2 Cor. 5:17-18)

Verse 17, in the Greek, lacks both subject and verb, so it is best rendered by the exclamatory, "If anyone is in Christ—new creation!"

Certainly, old habits die hard. There are still, as Paul acknowledges so eloquently in Romans 8, "the sufferings of the present time." It makes a world of difference whether or not one knows the Resurrection. Thus, making doxology to God (Rom. 11:33-36), Paul asks that we present ourselves as "a living sacrifice, holy and acceptable to God" by not being "conformed to this world," but by being "transformed by the renewal of your minds" (Rom. 12:1-2). All of this is Resurrection talk, the sort of tensive situation of those who find their lives still in an old, dying world, yet also now conscious of their citizenship in a new world being born. Our lives are eschatologically stretched between the sneak preview of the new world being born among us in the church, and the old world where the principalities and powers are reluctant to give way. In the meantime, which is the only time the church has ever known, we live as those who know something about the fate of the world that the world does not yet know. And that makes us different.

Conversion as Justification and Sanctification

There are those who might like to have new life, but at their worst do not want to give up anything for it. Something is gained in conversion to Christ, yet something is lost as well and the loss can be painful. Although the church has struggled with how to talk about the transformation that occurs in us through the work of Christ, at our best we have spoken of that new life by holding two terms in tension. Conversion is a twofold process of transformation whereby we are *justified*—made right with God through God's redemptive work among us, and *sanctified*—transformed, enlisted, commandeered, joined to the saints[9]—in a lifelong redemptive journey with Christ. Vatican II spoke of the worship of the church as "the glorification of God and the sanctification of the faithful."[10] While we are praising God in worship, we are being changed; our lives are being transformed by the object of our affections. Among Protestants, Luther tended to stress the power of justification, and Calvin stressed the need for sanctification. It was Wesley's theological vocation to attempt to keep these two movements of conversion in tension with one another, stressing the complementarity of justification and sanctification.

American evangelical Protestantism has been guilty, in its past, of making conversion a momentary, instantaneous phenomenon—come down to the altar, confess your sin, and you are instantaneously "saved." The Protestant Reformers, on the other hand, tended to think of conversion as a process rather than a moment. Thus Calvin said that being "born again" through baptism "does not take place in one moment or one day or one year; but through continual and sometimes even slow advances."[11]

Our culture lives with a fantasy of instantaneous transformation and change without cost. Wade Clark Roof's massive study of contemporary American spirituality depicts a nation where there are many people on a spiritual quest, cobbling together their faith from a patchwork quilt of a little of this and a little of that, a nation full of people who want the benefits of adherence to a religious tradition with none of the limits.[12] This "spiritual marketplace" as Roof aptly titled it, is a world where the consumer is king, where bits and pieces are extracted from a religious tradition and few demands are made for costly ethical transformation. Though Roof did not put the matter like this, I would characterize the new spiritual market as a place where many would like to be converted, justified without cost, and few desire to be sanctified.[13]

Sanctificationists stress the power of new life in Christ to make us more than we would have been if we had been left to our own devices. We must take up our cross *daily*. The Christian faith takes time, a lifetime, to get right. Therefore Calvin speaks of the new life in Christ as "regeneration," understanding new life as a process, as a long-term, lifelong inculcation of a set of practices that do not come naturally. Too much of American evangelical Christianity depicts the Christian life as a momentous, one-time turning—an instantaneous event that occurs in our subjective consciousness. But the Reformers were convinced that sin is so deeply rooted in our thinking and willing that only a lifetime of turnings, of fits and starts, of divine dislodgment and detoxification, can produce what God has in mind for us.[14] Daily we turn. Daily we are to take up the cross and follow. Daily we keep being incorporated into the Body of Christ that makes us more than we could have been if we had been left to our own devices.[15] Thus says Calvin:

> This restoration does not take place in one moment or one day or one year; but through continual and sometimes even slow advances God wipes out in his elect the corruptions of the flesh, cleanses them of guilt, consecrates them to himself as temples renewing all their minds to true purity that they may practice repentance throughout their lives and know that this warfare will end only in death.[16]

Conversion, regeneration, mystical union, *metanoia* are all attempts to speak of this turning of heart, body, and mind toward

God—a turning that is occasioned by God's prior turning toward us in Christ. John Bunyan's *Pilgrim's Progress* depicts new life as a journey, a rendering that was invented by Mark for his Gospel. The appearance of Jesus made necessary a new literary form, unknown before Mark, called *Gospel*, which is a literary embodiment of the transformation that is occasioned by Christ. Robert Wuthnow, after studying the dramatic upsurge of spirituality in America, says that we have moved from a stable "spirituality of dwelling," in which folk sought to find a place to stand, to dwell secure in their faith, toward a "spirituality of journey," in which we celebrate a moving, changing life of the Spirit.[17] If this is true, then the church may need to be ever more discerning in helping people figure out whether or not the journey they are on is with Christ or with some other god. Nevertheless, Christians down through the ages have testified that to be with Jesus is to be following Jesus, as if on a journey. We are not there yet. Discipleship is adventure. We fall behind, then we catch up only to again fall back, but we are moving.

Hans Mol has illuminated steps within typical conversion accounts: detachment from former patterns of identity; a time of meaninglessness and anomie; a dramatic transition from darkness to light, from chaos to meaning; and finally, the acceptance by the community of the initiate into a new life together.[18] The initiate is now in a new existence, a new world, having experienced a dramatic journey named as "conversion."

Yet this journey metaphor has its limits. For instance, the contemporary notion, articulated by James Fowler and others, of the Christian life as a movement, a journey through stages of human development in the normal human life cycle, may be an inadequate metaphor for the new life in Christ.[19] Karl Barth has a wonderful survey of the history of vain Protestant attempts to make the Christian life into a series of ordered developmental moves, onward and upward.[20] Barth correctly saw all such efforts as attempts to "outline the development of the natural man into a Christian, and the Christian into an increasingly perfect Christian, in a way which can be mastered and recounted." In Barth's estimate, "this whole attempt implies an attack on the substance of a genuine understanding of the process of vocation."[21] A "genuine understanding" of new life in Christ surely must include some recognition of the God-initiated, human-responsive, discontinuous, surprising quality of new life. In the previous chapter we considered Christian education as inculcation, indoctrination, inculturation. Yet these metaphors imply that there is something purely gradual, developmental, and predictable about becoming a disciple. The pastor, as Christian educator, merely orchestrates this program of discipleship. But now, in considering the role of pastor as evangelist, is the time for us to be reminded that notions of ordered development—slow, continuous movement through various stages—simply do not do justice to the jolts, bumps, fits, wallops, and starts that *metanoia* inevitably entails.[22] The pastor not only orchestrates the gradual formation of Christians, but also witnesses the dramatic transformation of ordinary folk into disciples of Christ.

Conversion as Destruction and Reconstruction of Worlds

Nothing so exposes the fashionable stoicism of American faith—faith in a vague God who, though generally approving of human projects, neither speaks nor acts—as the notion that our God means to change us. Conversion is a radical assault upon the conventional, officially sanctioned American faith that we are basically OK just as we are, and that this world, for any of its faults, is all there is. Conversion is a statement of faith that this God means to have us—all of us—that this God will have God's sovereign way with us. Whether or not one believes in even the possibility of conversion will relate in great part to one's conviction about what sort of God we have; or, more biblically, what sort of God has us. Conversion is one of God's most gracious, intrusive, demanding, sovereign acts. "*By his great mercy* we have been born anew to a living hope" (1 Pet. 1:3*b* RSV, my italics).

Faith is known by its subject.[23] Faith, the Christian faith, is more than the development of natural, universal human qualities. Human capacities and human development are also in the grip of sin,[24] therefore much of our "development" involves ever more sophisticated means of turning away from God toward our various gods. Very little of what it takes to be a Christian is innate. Radical turning is required—turning that is initiated external to the person being turned. Conversion occurs because God needs a people, a holy nation of priests, not because of what we think we need to be happy. Conversion makes sense because it is an awakening to the fact that the world has changed. Therefore, we must change.

Yet that radical turning must be embodied in a set of practices that enable remarkable transformation. Although American evangelical Christianity has rendered conversion into a subjective change of heart, a purely personal event, sanctificationists, at their best, stress conversion as both a spiritual and an ethical process. Justification and sanctification belong together. What we feel in our hearts must be rooted in our heads and hands, embodied in the assumption of a set of practices, corporately tested and formed so that conversion keeps on happening to us. Richard Heitzenrater, in his *Wesley and the People Called Methodist*, showed how Methodism was an extraordinary effort to preach to the underclasses of England in the eighteenth century and to form those people into small groups called "classes."[25] Those classes arose from the need of the Methodists to collect money for the paying of the debt for building houses where Methodists could gather. It was suggested that everyone in the "society called Methodist" contribute a penny a week (which had already been done at the foundry society in order to assist the poor). When someone protested that not everyone in the society could afford that much, Captain Foy suggested that each Methodist society be divided into groups of twelve, each with a leader who would be responsible for turning in twelve pence a week, making up themselves whatever they could not collect. He volunteered to take as his group the eleven poorest members.[26]

So Methodism began as a disciplined body of people to transform one another and the poor through the means of rather demanding face-to-face small groups. Its theology of sanctification and perfection found its soteriology in these classes, through which Methodists made their lives vulnerable to one another so that they might "move on to perfection," as the Methodists put their way of sanctification. That is why Methodists, and in particular Wesley, always maintained that they were not saying anything different than that for which classical Christianity had always stood. Rather what they sought was the discovery of practices that they could hold in common and thereby be Christians. As my friend Stanley Hauerwas says, the Methodists of the eighteenth century were the

Black Muslims of their day. They covenanted to be disciplined in terms of both their theological language and of the practices commensurate with that language, to be a people who would not be forced into lives of degradation simply because they were poor.

In his codification of the examination process in order to be a member of the Methodist society, Wesley spelled out the rules for membership: "In order to *join* a society, persons were required to demonstrate only one condition: 'a desire to flee from the wrath to come, to be saved from their sins.' Those who desired to *continue* in the societies, however, were expected 'to evidence their desire of salvation, First, By doing no harm . . . Secondly, By doing good . . . Thirdly, By attending upon all the ordinances of God.' "[27] These rules were fleshed out with specific examples that drew on the experiences Wesley had of actually having to exclude people from the societies. Thus, for example, two had been excluded for cursing and swearing, two for habitual Sabbath breaking, seventeen for drunkenness, two for retailing liquor, three for quarreling and brawling, one for beating his wife, three for habitual, willful lying, and railing and evil speaking, one for idleness and laziness, and twenty-nine for lightness and carelessness.

Transformation in Christ was the clear goal of these small groups, a goal that sets them at some distance from much of the small group movement in the contemporary church. Robert Wuthnow found that more than 40 percent of Americans say that they are involved in some sort of small group, most of which have a "spiritual" basis. Yet he also found that many of these groups pride themselves on their respect for "diversity," which leads them to a subtle but rigidly enforced ethos that all opinions held within the group are of equal value. Rather than risk confrontation, challenge, and growth, members simply "live and let live" in the group so that, in Wuthnow's estimate, small group spirituality tends to be "personal and subjective":

> Small groups encourage many members to regard biblical wisdom as truth only if it somehow helps them to get along better in their daily lives. Groups generate a do-it-yourself religion, a God who makes life easier, a programmed form of spirituality that robs the sacred of its awe-inspiring mystery and depth. . . . In simplest terms, the sacred comes to be associated with small

insights that seem intuitively correct in the small group rather than wisdom accrued over the centuries.[28]

Jackson Carroll has noted how the new paradigm churches, the (in Carroll's description) "posttraditional churches," and the megachurches appear to be basing a whole ecclesiology on the use of small groups.[29] When asked about the purpose of these groups, these churches often say that they are their major means of "discipling." It remains for these groups to show that they are, in truth, disciplining people in order to walk the way of the cross, rather than merely pooling their collective spiritual yearnings.

Methodism grew in great part because it offered salvation by saving people from the degradation of the general habits of eighteenth-century English society. True, the Methodists reflected as much as reacted against the society in which they found themselves. However, the genius was that people were embedded into God's salvation because they were given a new way of life that saved them from the expectations of their social order.[30]

In Ephesians, the same writer is able to assert the conversionist notion that "God, who is rich in mercy, out of the great love with which [God] loved us . . . made us alive together with Christ . . . and raised us up" (2:4-6 RSV), and also the sanctificationist sentiment that we have been "created in Christ Jesus for good works, which God prepared beforehand, that we should walk in them" (2:10 RSV).[31]

The church exists, not for itself, but rather to save the world by announcing the advent of a new world, to "proclaim the mighty acts of him who called you out of darkness into his marvelous light" (1 Pet. 2:9). That process can be instantaneous and dramatic as well as gradual and growing. Christ is infinitely resourceful in accomplishing his will for our lives. The joy of being a disciple of Christ is the adventure of transformation, of movement from death to life, light to darkness, all as a work of grace in our lives. The joy of being a pastor is being enabled to witness this transformation among our people. In our preparation for baptism, in our preaching, and in our Christian education, images of conversion and detoxification, of relinquishment and regeneration, must replace images of gradual development and measured nurture.[32]

Hans Küng gives us preachers a challenge to preach conversion:

We are to preach *metanoia*. We must entice people away from the world to God. We are not to shut ourselves off from the world in a spirit of asceticism, but to live in the everyday world inspired by the radical obedience that is demanded by the love of God. The church must be reformed again and again, converted again and again each day, in order that it must fulfill its task.[33]

Sanctification is a work of God in us, a movement from heaven, a light not of our devising, something that is due to God's grace rather than self-derived. This insight saves us from speaking of sanctification in a moralistic way. Wesley taught that even for those who have yet to experience the full inbreaking of the love of Christ, if they are able to live to some degree free from the enslavement to sin, their freedom is due to the work of Christ in them, whether they yet know of that work or not. Full redemption means holiness, the reception of both justifying and sanctifying grace, the accomplishment by the gospel of something that the law can never do.

When the church fails to stress the grace and judgments of God as the source of all possibility of new life, the church degenerates into insufferable, sentimental moralism in which the Christian life is depicted as simply another helpful means of making nice people even nicer. Discipleship is not a sanctimonious twelve-step program. A holy person is a testimonial, not to the innate, positive possibilities within people, but rather to the insistent, transforming love of God in Jesus Christ, despite our sin. Rather than attempting to reduce our theology to the lowest common denominator or to render our life together into an inane civic club mentality, we pastors must lead our churches in finding practical, institutional means to reiterate among ourselves that the church has rather extravagant notions of how hearts and lives can be radically regenerated through the love of God in Christ.[34] There is something built into the Christian faith, at least since Augustine, that yearns for transformation, that cultivates that humble receptivity toward the sovereign power of God to kill and to make new.

I heard the historian Gary Wills say that if you are a white male Southerner over fifty (and I am), there is no way to convince you that people cannot change. Having experienced radical transformations of heart and mind within your own family, deep within your own soul, you have an unshakable belief in the possibility of human alteration. As a white male Southerner, I am fascinated by the literature of white Southerners in this past century who have experienced racial conversion and have lived to tell about it.[35] Anne Braden largely grew up in Kentucky, Alabama, and Mississippi. She was an heir to all the racial attitudes of the Old South. Her conversion into an eloquent and courageous spokesperson for racial justice occurred, not like Paul's, "in any blinding flash of light," but rather in a gradual awakening that the preachments of her conservative Alabama Episcopal church were more radical than the church itself knew. When, as a college student, she had dinner with a young African American woman, there at the table she experienced a kind of eucharistic conversion. In language worthy of Augustine (or Acts) she describes her change:

> It was a tremendous revelation. It may sound like a small thing when it is told, but it was a turning point in my life. All the cramping walls of a lifetime seemed to come tumbling down in that moment. Some heavy shackles seemed to have fallen from my feet. For the first time in my nineteen years on this earth, I felt I had room to stretch my arms and legs and lift my head high toward the sky. . . . Here, for a moment, I glimpsed a vision of the world as it should be: where people are people, and spirits have room to grow. I never got over it.[36]

I believe that one appeal of an autobiography like Braden's is that it holds out an invigorating promise—*you can change.* Your life as it is, is not all there is. By the grace of God, you can be better than you are at present. A recent biographer of Billy Graham, in attempting to account for Graham's popularity, says that he has preached one theme consistently throughout his ministry—"the power of the second chance."[37] And of course the great biblical example of the power of the second chance is Paul in Acts 9.

Saul, church enemy number one, bloody ravager of the church, is encountered by a voice and a blinding light on his way to Damascus (Acts 9:1-19). The sudden, disjunctive quality of what happened to Paul that day makes his a paradigmatic story of conversion.[38] The making of a murderer into a missionary is quite a testimonial to the grace of God. Saul's conversion was not the end of the story, but its beginning. As the voice speaks to Ananias, explaining to him that Saul's transformation is also his vocation, "He [Saul] is an instrument whom I have chosen to bring my name before Gentiles and kings and before the people of Israel" (Acts 9:15). The light, the voice from heaven, is sign of a dramatic transformation, a lifelong journey that begins in having a life commandeered, caught up in the loving purposes of God, nothing less than new birth that leads to new lives in Christ, the Light of the World.

INTERLUDE
Evangelism and the Irresistibility of Jesus

> Batter my heart, three-personed God; for You
> As yet but knock, breathe, shine, and seek to mend;
> That I may rise and stand, o'erthrow me, and bend
> Your force to break, blow, burn, and make me new.
> I, like an usurped town, to another due,
> Labor to admit You, but O, to no end;
> Reason, Your viceroy in me, me should defend,
> But is captivated, and proves weak or untrue.
> Yet dearly I love You and would be loved fain,
> But I am betrothed unto Your enemy.
> Divorce me, untie or break that knot again;
> Take me to You, imprison me, for I,
> Except You enthrall me, never shall be free,
> Nor ever chaste, except You ravish me.[39]

Ravish, break, usurp, shine, court, overthrow, John Donne's words are intentionally outrageous when applied to God. Too often the modern church is content with an empathetic but mostly inactive deity, who cares, but not enough to act; who invites, but seldom ravishes, breaks, usurps, or overthrows.

On the face of it, when one considers the rather remarkable resourcefulness, to say nothing of the relentlessness, of Donne's three-personed God, one wonders why faith in this God should be so difficult for so many. Yet then one recalls the remarkable ingenuity of contemporary godlessness, along with the invention of modern atheism, which made the modern world possible. We call it sin. First, we kill the Father (with help from Freud), and then we are free to build the modern, democratic, officially atheistic state with its Promethean sense of control and its propensity for unrestrained violence. When one considers the extraordinary resources given to the effort of shutting us up, all curled up within ourselves, it is quite a credit to God that we are enabled to hear anything other than the sound of our own voices.

I asked a student how he enjoyed majoring in history. "It's OK," he answered, "but also a challenge."

I thought he meant it was a challenge to read so many books and articles in order to major in history. But I thought wrong.

"First, to major in history, you have to become an atheist, then everything else is fairly easy," he explained.

What?

"You quickly learn that the answer to a question such as, 'What was the cause of the French Revolution?' or, 'What was the main motivation for Roosevelt's New Deal?' is never 'God.'"

In history, there can be no causes, no goals, and no sources of historical events other than us. In the contemporary university, all knowledge comes through personal discovery, the application of essentially atheistic methodology. Nothing comes through revelation. There is a sort of epistemological policing in modernity whereby all explanations other than exclusively materialistic and naturalistic ones are not permitted into the discussion.[40] Our world has been rendered into a closed system, a hermetically sealed box where nothing is admitted from the outside. All information and insight must be self-derived. Call it demystification, a propensity for thin explanation, reductionism, or simply a failure of the imagination. We have made it quite difficult for anyone, even the heart-battering, three-personed God, to get to us.

Yet, thank God, it is of the nature of the Trinity to be loquacious, invasive, and persistently gregarious with his Creation. Luther, in explaining how on earth Christ might become present in a loaf of eucharistic bread, speaks of God's "ubiquity." Evangelism, mission, begins in the heart of this sort of God. Any God who would impregnate a poor, unmarried virgin in an out-of-the-way place like Nazareth—well, this sort of God will stoop to anything to get to us, including ravishment, breaking, usurping, and all the other divine resources that we name as "evangelism," divine ubiquity.

I once asked a pastor, who had labored thirty years in an out-of-the-way Missouri crossroads, how on earth he was able to do it. He replied, "God loves these sorts of places. Read Luke 2. We may be off the beaten path, so far as the world is concerned, but at least, by

God, we are not as remote as Bethlehem! I've found that if you are going to be close to God, you need to get yourself to those sorts of places where God hangs out."

There is only one way to describe this sort of incarnating, invasive God: relentless.

The Conversion of the Church   *missional church stuff]*

Pastors must be the sort of people willing to risk conversation with this sort of God. One aspect of our pastoral care is the formation of people who delight in, wait for, and relish the ubiquitous activity of a God named Trinity. Pastors must enjoy cleaning up after the intrusions of this God. As pastors, we do not work alone. Pastoral fatigue is more often than not the result of a theological failure of nerve to enjoy the intrusions of this God, rather than the result of pastoral overwork. In fact, much pastoral overwork is a result of disbelief in the relentlessness of Jesus. Atheism leads to the assumption that it is up to us to save the world or it will not be saved.

A fundamental insight (derived from Karl Barth) was David Bosch's contention that "mission is not primarily an activity of the church, but an attribute of God. God is a missionary God. . . . Mission is thereby seen as a movement from God to the world; the church is viewed as an instrument for that mission. . . . There is a church because there is mission, not vice versa."[41] Church is what we pastors manage after God ravishes the world.

It is the nature of this God to reach out. In the Trinity, God the Father sends the Son, and the Father and the Son send the Holy Spirit, and the Father, Son, and Holy Spirit send the church into the world. This God insists on having the last word. "Jesus came to Galilee, proclaiming the good news of God, and saying, 'The time is fulfilled, and the kingdom of God has come near; repent, and believe in the good news' " (Mark 1:14-15). A chief defining content of this good news of God (1 Thess. 2:1, 8, 9; Rom. 1:1) is this sort of relentless reach. This God has a gregarious determination to draw all things unto God's self (John 12:32). Think of your own ministry, your pastoral vocation, as evidence of this God's compulsion to finish what was begun in Creation, to have what God desires. God is going to get what God wants.

That includes the church. Evangelization is not only of the nature of the church evoked by the work of the Trinity; the church is also the object of this work. The church is to work with God to evangelize the world, but the church is always also being evangelized. The New Testament itself is addressed primarily to believers, to those who believe and hope to be helped in their nonbelief (Mark 9:24). There must be, as Darrell Guder asserts, a "continuing conversion of the church."[42] Saints we may be by the call of God, but yet ambiguous ones. God promises to complete the good work begun in us (Phil. 1:6). The church never becomes so adept at faithfulness, so sure of its vision of God, that it rises above the need to be born, reborn, called, recalled. Contemporary pastors sometimes wring our hands over the poorly formed state of contemporary Christians, their biblical illiteracy, their poor commitment, and so forth. But continuing conversion is always at the center of the church's agenda in any age. Pastors must not simply assume that our people are well fixed in the faith. Much of what we pastors call "Christian education" or "pastoral care" is best thought of as evangelism, the continuing conversion of the church.

The church *is* mission also in the sense that the church exists not for itself, but rather to sign, signal, and embody God's intentions for the whole world. God is going to get back what belongs to God. God's primary means of accomplishing this is through the church. "The community, in its corporate life, is called to embody an alternative order that stands as a sign of God's redemptive purposes in the world," says Richard Hays.[43] If we have, despite our ecclesial failings, no semblance of a sign, no visible foretaste of the kingdom of God in the church, then we have nothing to say. This means that the time spent by the pastor in church administration and other acts of congregational edification, such as teaching, preaching, and pastoral care, are essentially acts of evangelism and mission. Just as we spend hours of solitary study and preparation so that we might publicly proclaim God's Word in a sermon, so also when we show pastoral concern for the building up of the congregation, we are not turning inward, rather we are participating in the public ministry of the church. The mission of the church to embody the good news of Christ to the world is not an activity of the church, but rather *is* the church. This brings us close to the heart of who the church is and therefore at the center of what pastors are for.

As that great missionary, Lesslie Newbigin has said, "The coming of Jesus has introduced into history an event in which the reign of God is made under the form of weakness and foolishness to those to whom God has chosen to make it known, and . . . it is made known to them so it may be proclaimed to all."[44]

The church is not the substance of our witness, but its means.[45] Even as Israel was called by its unique life together to be a light to the nations, so the church is called to be a light to the world. It is not for the church to save the world, but rather God's saving of the world graciously includes the church. Thus, evangelism and mission must of necessity include inclusion into the church. Evangelism is not a matter of the church going out to recruit new members. It is a matter of the church being God's appointed means for our salvation—a means, though not an end. To proclaim Christ is to proclaim his embodiment; to give one's life to Christ is to be joined to his Body. A Christian outside the church is an incomprehensible anomaly. A church that is not constantly converting, calling, incorporating, evangelizing, is not Christ's church.

discuss

In the Acts of the Apostles, the church is under constant threat from foes within and without, hanging on for its very life at the fringes of classical culture. Yet the church in Acts keeps turning outward, insists on intruding into imperial arrangements, keeps conversing with whomever will talk, insists on baptizing anybody "whom the Lord our God calls to him" (Acts 2:39).

Thus the New Testament scholar Gerhard Lohfink shows how the New Testament can be best construed as training in how to be incorporated into the Body of Christ. God's means for salvation is, by its very nature, incarnational, sacramental, corporate. "God has selected a single people out of all the nations of the world in order to make this people a sign of salvation," says Lohfink.[46] The church is thus an embodiment of the mystery of election. Just as one people, Israel, can be elected by God to serve as a light to the whole world, so one people, the church, can be elected by God to save the world, so one person, Jesus, can be given for the salvation of all persons. Why does God save through election, through designation of one for the service to all? We do not know. Election, the choice of God, is, in Scripture, inscrutable. Throughout Acts, one senses the church's wonderment that God has chosen these "ignorant and unlearned people" to be those who turn the world upside down.

Because of the corporate quality of salvation, evangelism will always, of necessity, have a "political" challenge in it. The call to follow Christ is nothing less than a call to transfer citizenship, to be moved from one polity to another. The challenge is not simply the personal or the intellectual, "Do you agree?" but rather the more political, "Will you join up?"

There is a reason Jesus proclaims "the *kingdom* of God." A kingdom implies boundaries, a difference between what is the world, and what is the church. Evangelism comes from *evangel*, which in the classical world was a public announcement of some noteworthy political event, such as the winning of a battle or a visit of the emperor. Thus Allen Verhey says that when Mark opens his Gospel as "the beginning of the *evangel* of Jesus Christ" (Mark 1:1), he means to use *evangel* as it was used in the emperor cult to announce the birth or the ascension to the throne of an emperor.[47] Rodney Clapp suggests that we ought to translate, the "Gospel According to Mark," as the "Political Tidings According to Mark."

To be a Christian is to exchange allegiance, to answer to the summons of a different emperor, to transfer citizenship to a new world. So Barth says that "we understand by the Christian a [person] whom Jesus Christ has called to attachment to Himself, to His discipleship and to living fellowship with Himself, and whom, as we finally say, He has bound and indeed conjoined with Himself."[48] The call to Christ is for the purpose of attachment to Christ and Christ's Body, the church.

discuss Thus a primary evangelistic event is the corporate worship of the church.[49] Here, as the gospel is read and proclaimed, as the gospel is enacted in bread and wine, the church is gathered. We show forth who we are and who, by God's grace, we hope to be. We pioneer new social arrangements that the world can never know. The world is quite right in judging the gospel on the basis of the quality of life it is able to produce. Therefore we pastors do well to evaluate the worship of our congregations not on the basis of the conventional question, Is it boring? (Though boredom in worship does seem an offense against the infinitely interesting "three-personed God.") Rather we are to worry, Are we praising the Trinity in our worship or some other god? Does our praise proclaim the fullness of Christ, or have we limited ourselves to a more manageable deity?

When contemporary Christian worship worries about communicating with the secular, unformed, and uninformed seeker, or the casual participant, the result is usually to adapt and to change the worship. Such adaptation claims to be based in a concern for evangelism, to reach out to the unchurched. Although a passion for reaching the unchurched is an essential aspect of faithfulness to the gospel, evangelism can have a negative impact upon the fidelity of the church's worship when evangelism becomes the main test of worship. We would do better to concern ourselves that our worship focuses upon God; to worry that our modes of praise arise out of the peculiar quality of the God named Trinity. Rather than change our worship to suit the limitations of contemporary secular people, we would do better to convert contemporary secular people—to fit them for the arduous yet usually quite joyful task of worshiping the God of Israel and the church.

Robert W. Brimlow says that in our evangelistic witness, our problem "is *not* that of finding a way to translate the gospel so that pagans can understand it in their idiom. . . . Rather, our problem as church is to find a way to let the world know that there is another language and another way of viewing and understanding reality that they should want to learn."[50]

I heard a distinguished preacher complain that "when the average Joe hears us preach, he sits there thinking, 'None of this really relates to my world.' " But evangelism is more than some limp attempt to relate to the world of the "average Joe." Evangelism is an assault, a rearrangement, a reconfiguration, a recreation of a world that would not be there had not Jesus commanded us to go into all the world and make disciples.

The way I read church history, some of the greatest theological mistakes made by the church have been made in the interest of evangelism. In so wanting to reach out to speak to the world, sometimes we fall in. We substitute worldly wisdom for gospel foolishness. We offer the world, in the name of the gospel, what the world wants before it is told by the gospel those wants worth wanting. We become but a pale imitation of the world, a mirror reflection, a mode of life that is already available in the world, without bothering with the church. Therefore we must judge our prayer and praise theologically so that we might be confident that the God to whom we testify is the Christ who has given us something to say and to show to the world in the first place.

Christ Making Appeal Through Us

Yet we are mandated, in Christ's name, to reach out. He is making his appeal to the world through us and our worship of him. Our worship must be theologically faithful and substantive, yet to be faithful to Christ it must be hospitable. Darrell Guder uses the example of the worship of the burgeoning African churches. In Africa, it is typical for a church to put up a framework with a roof, and there praise God and hear the gospel. Those in the village who are not yet Christian are welcome to stand around the building. Because there are no walls, they see and hear everything that Christians do when they worship. This enables those wonderful evangelistic moments when the observers move from observation to participation in the church's life.

While praising God as believers, we must look for ways to be hospitable to nonbelievers. Each congregation ought to ask itself, "What do we need to do to make our worship more enticing, inviting, and appealing to nonbelievers, *and* how can we prepare them for full participation in our praise?" In answering that question, our Christian education becomes worship preparation and evangelism. As George Lindbeck has noted, Peter did not learn of Christ through the Socratic method of question and answer, or by reading a book or having a dramatic personal experience. Peter became a Christian by being incorporated into a community, by gradually taking up the ways of a counterculture called the church, by being made into the Body of Christ through practice.[51]

The failure of mainline Protestant congregations to reach out in the name of Jesus is based, I believe, upon a political misconception. We assumed that North American culture was "our world." We had a guaranteed market share, a virtual monopoly on American religious life. If people wanted to worship Jesus, they had to do it when, where, and how we dictated. Therefore, we thought we did not need to overly trouble ourselves about the world because, after all, it was "our" world.[52]

As we have noted, these essentially Constantinian notions of church and world are now under scrutiny. Our congregations must join Jesus in reaching into the world, in speaking up and speaking out for the gospel, or we shall be left behind as relics of an outmoded era in which the church assumed that evangelism had been made irrelevant due to our cozy settlement with the world. Exile requires us intentionally, carefully, yet exuberantly to move into the world in the name of Jesus, telling the world something that it cannot know on its own, namely, that it is God's world.

Christian worship keeps making manifest the peculiarity of the Christian counterculture called the church. In our worship, Christians show the world, and reinforce among ourselves, the oddness of worshiping a God named Trinity. As Walter Brueggemann says, like Israel before us, our liturgy is subversive of the present order. In our worship, "this distinctive community is invited to affirm that *the world constructed in liturgy* is more reliable and more credible than the world 'out there.' The purpose of such liturgy is to nurture imagination and to equip Israel with the nerve to act out of its distinctiveness in the face of formidable, hostile power."[53] Thus, we have a peculiar way of eating called *Eucharist*, a strange way of being in community called *forgiveness*. One of our prominent peculiarities is evangelism itself. Here is a community that is not formed the way the world gathers people—on the basis of race, or class, or natural propagation. The church grows and gathers through baptism, through call and summons, incorporation and indoctrination. Here is a people who have been told to love strangers enough to call them neighbors, to do something that this culture abhors, namely, to care enough to intrude into their lives by listening to them and telling them the story of Jesus.

Service to a Ubiquitous God

Frankly, one great difficulty of being a pastor is working with a community that is answerable to a God whose nature it is to be the Good Shepherd out seeking and saving the lost (Luke 19:10). We pastors would have it easier if the call to ordained leadership were merely a call to manage, to keep house, to reassure and make comfortable the faithful. Rather, we reside at the busy intersection between the world and a Savior who is determined to ravish, break, and usurp until he has us all. This keeps us pastors on our toes, our tiptoes, eager for a glimpse of what God is up to in the world. Something is afoot in the world, and we get a front-row seat at the spectacle. Odd people keep showing up who have had their lives rearranged by the intrusions of a living, active, talkative God. People, strange people whom we would not have of our own accord invited to Christ, are being sought and saved by the incursions of the Holy Spirit. So the church had better be ready to be surprised when they show up, "cut to the heart," asking, "What must we do?" (Acts 2:37). The image I get of the church in Acts is a group of people breathlessly attempting to keep up with the wildfire movements of the Holy Spirit, a church always just a step behind the extravagant outreach of the gospel of God.

In my book *The Intrusive Word*, I introduced the world to Verleen:

> In my last congregation, we decided that we needed to grow. We voted to launch a program of evangelism. Evangelism. You know what that means. It's the, "We-had-better-go-out-and-get-new-members-or-we'll-die" syndrome. Beginning in the sixties, our church had begun a two-decade decline in membership, so we figured that a little church-growth strategy was in order.
>
> We studied a program from our denomination telling us how to get new members. Among other things, the church-growth program advocated a system of door-to-door visitation. So we organized ourselves into groups of two and, on an appointed Sunday afternoon, we set out to visit, to invite people to our church.
>
> The teams went out, armed with packets of pamphlets describing our congregation, pamphlets telling about our denomination, fliers portraying me, the smiling, accessible pastor, inviting people to our church. Each team was given a map with their assigned street.
>
> Helen and Gladys were given a map. They were clearly told to go down Summit Drive and to *turn right*. That's what they were told. I heard the team leader tell them, "You go down Summit Drive and turn right. Do you hear me, Helen, that's down Summit Drive and turn right?"
>
> But Helen and Gladys, both approaching eighty, after lifetimes of teaching elementary school, were better at giving than receiving directions. They turned left, venturing down into the housing

projects to the west of Summit Drive. We told them to turn right; they turned left.

Which meant that Helen and Gladys proceeded to evangelize the wrong neighborhood and thereby ran the risk of evangelizing the wrong people.

Late that afternoon, each team returned to the church to make their report. Helen and Gladys had only one interested person to report to us, a woman named Verleen. Nobody on their spurious route was interested in visiting our church, nobody but Verleen. She lived with her two children in a three-room apartment in the projects, we were told. Although she had never been to a church in her life, Verleen wanted to visit ours.

That is what you get, I said to myself, when you don't follow directions, when you won't do what the pastor tells you to do. This is what you get, a woman from the projects named Verleen.

The next Sunday, Helen and Gladys proudly presented Verleen at the eleven o'clock service, along with her two feral-looking children. Verleen liked the service so much she said that she wanted to attend the Women's Thursday Morning Bible Study. Helen and Gladys said they would pick her up on Thursday.

On Thursday, Verleen appeared, proudly clutching her new Bible, a gift of Helen's circle, the first Bible Verleen had ever seen, much less owned.

I was leading the study that morning, a study on the lection for the coming Sunday, Luke 4, the story of Jesus' temptation in the wilderness. "Have any of you ever been faced with temptation and, with Jesus' help, resisted?" I asked the group after presenting my material. "Have any of you refused some temptation because of your Christian commitment?"

One of the women told about how, just the week before, there was some confusion in the supermarket checkout line, and before she knew it, she was standing in the supermarket parking lot with a loaf of bread that she hadn't paid for.

"At first I thought," she confessed, "why should I pay for it? They have enough money here as it is. But then I thought, 'No, you are a Christian.' So I went back in the store and paid them for that loaf of bread."

I made some approving comment.

It was then that Verleen spoke. "A couple of years ago, I was into cocaine really big. You know what that's like! You know how that stuff makes you crazy. Well, anyway, my boyfriend, not the one I've got now, the one who was the daddy of my first child, that one, well, we knocked over a gas station one night—got two hundred dollars out of it. It was as simple as taking candy from a baby. Well, my boyfriend, he says to me, 'Let's knock off that Seven-eleven down on the corner.' And something in me, it says, 'No, I've held up that gas station with you, but I ain't going to hold up no convenience store.' He beat the hell out of me, but I still said No. It felt great to say No, 'cause that's the only time in my life I ever said No to anything. Made me feel like I was somebody."

Through the stunned silence I managed to mutter, "Well, er, uh, that's resisting temptation. That's sort of what this text is about. And now it's time for our closing prayer."

After I stumbled out of the church parlor and was standing out in the parking lot, helping Helen into her Plymouth, she said to me, "You know, I can't wait to get home and get on the phone and invite people to come next Thursday! Your Bible studies used to be dull. I think I can get a good crowd for this!"[54]   *Why does this story make me cry?*

And the ubiquitous, almost (but never quite) irresistible, three-personed God laughed with delight.

CHAPTER 10

The Pastor as Prophet: Truth Telling in the Name of Jesus

A little tattletale comes running to father Moses, "Daddy, Daddy, Eldad and Medad are prophesying in the camp" (Num. 11:27). Earlier, the Lord, after speaking to Moses, took a notion to spread a little Spirit on some of the elders, a Spirit that the Lord had previously disbursed mainly to Moses. Now, having received the gift of the Spirit, Eldad and Medad get downright loquacious, and begin speaking up for God. Joshua, one of the "chosen men" (11:28) doesn't like this effusive spirit. "My lord Moses, stop them!"

We cannot have uncredentialed, uncertified people prophesying, speaking for God. Today Medad and Eldad (Can these names be real or are they only here for comic relief?), tomorrow my son or daughter. Joshua asks Moses for a prophetic restraining order.

Moses' response: "Would that all the LORD's people were prophets, and that the LORD would put his spirit on them!" (11:29b).

Moses, who had been none too adept at speaking the truth to power himself until God gave him a spirited shove (see Exodus 3–4), is not miserly of spirit. Would to God that all of God's people were prophets! There are never too many spirit-gifted prophets.

The lectionary on Pentecost wisely uses this obscure episode from Numbers 11 as a setup for an even more effusive, more prophetic spiritual breakout in Acts 2. At Pentecost, we were all gathered in one place. Then there was a rush of wind, tongues of fire, Holy Spirit. As in Numbers 11, the Spirit's gift is the gift of speech, prophecy. As in Numbers 11, the Spirit's creation of a multitude of preachers results in communal bewilderment (Acts 2:6). Amazed and astonished, we ask, "What does this mean?"

In reply to the mocking of the mob, Peter speaks. Apparently, Pentecost has enabled Peter to find his tongue. Peter explains the ruckus in the upper room by reference to the prophet Joel. In earlier days, the Spirit was poured out on a few gifted (or at the least, offensive) individuals called prophets. But there will be a day, according to Joel 2:28-32, when God's Spirit shall be poured out on all. *All.* Even among the typically voiceless—old women and old men (pensioners, usually institutionalized, nonproductive, therefore nonvalued), young people out of work, underpaid maids, janitors—God's Spirit shall descend in the later days, bringing things to speech. Those who never appear on the pages of the *New York Times,* those who are never asked to say a few words at the microphone, shall speak.

Later the world would marvel that such "ignorant and unlearned" people like Peter (Acts 4:13) were speaking, each telling in their own words "God's deeds of power" (Acts 2:11). The holy wind at Pentecost is power unto speech. The gift of Acts 2 is the gift of prophecy. That day, surely somebody remembered Moses' swaggering, "Would that *all* of God's people were prophets!" That day is now, those prophets are us.

As a young pastor Reinhold Niebuhr felt tension between the roles of pastor and prophet:

> I am not surprised that most prophets are itinerants. . . . I think the real clue to the tameness of a preacher is the difficulty one finds in telling unpleasant truths to people whom one has learned to love. . . . Once personal contact is established you are very prone to temper your wind to the shorn sheep. It is certainly difficult to be human and honest at the same time. I'm not surprised that most budding prophets are tamed in time to become harmless parish priests.[1]

Niebuhr himself did not remain long in the parish, perhaps because he saw how easy it was for a true "prophet" to be too constrained by the average congregation.

We now know, thanks to the work of scholars like Walter Bruggemann and Joseph Blankinsopp, that Israel's prophets were, in the deepest sense of the word "traditionalists."[2] The prophets called Israel back to its originating event, urged a return to its unique Yahweh-given vocation. Prophetic remembrance had the formation of a peculiar community as its intention, rather than mere free-floating criticism of present social arrangements. Prophets were communitarians in the sense that their concern was the edification, survival, and integrity of Israel, the prophetic community.

Today, there are those who call preachers "prophetic" when they offer a few constructive criticisms to the government for more just use of resources and power. Prophets are those who stand somewhere to the left of the Democratic Party. Yet such "prophetic" calls for "justice" are rarely as critical or as "prophetic" as we claim them to be because our "justice" is usually based on a thoroughly conventional understanding of what is possible within the parameters of present political arrangements. Ironically, far from being an attack on the present order, such "prophecy" becomes a legitimization of it.

I therefore had misgivings about including in this book a chapter devoted specifically to the pastor as prophet, for I do not want to underwrite the misconception that it is possible to be a pastor who is not a prophet. A pastor is not an ex-prophet who has lost his teeth. Because pastors are called to witness, in all that they do and say, to the truth that is Jesus Christ, all pastoral activity must be "prophetic." Furthermore, the goal of the prophetic pastor is the constitution of a prophetic community ("Would that all God's people were prophets."). The courage to be a prophet arises from a wide array of sources—a conviction that there is truth worth telling, the security that the truth is more important than popularity, and the faith that Jesus has made possible the means whereby even ordinary people can be prophetic. The primary source of such prophetic conviction, security, and faith is the church's Sunday worship, where the truth keeps being refurbished by a fund of imaginative images, metaphors, and the judgment and forgiveness whereby we are enabled to live the truth in a world of lies. Embodiment of truth is prophetic worship. We ought to be like Gandhi, who called his life an experiment with the truth.[3] Prophetic ministry occurs when we, in the words of the African American church, do not just "talk the walk, but walk the talk."[4]

Not long ago, a person emerged from my place of preaching quite upset by the sermon. As I stood there, listening to her complaint, I thought, "I don't really care that you were upset by the sermon." Which is amazing considering that I am a coward by nature. (I was elected president of my school class every year from the time I was twelve. One does not get elected by being truthful.) And yet here at the door of a church, I was standing, amazingly impervious to the assaults of an offended church member. Simply by going about the tasks of preaching, teaching, showing up on Sunday, attempting to listen to the Word, trying to bring the truth to speech, I had been made into somewhat of a prophet. That is great testimony to the grace of God in the church.

Of course, in this matter of truth telling, it helps greatly to be preaching at Duke Chapel. There, when I preach, I've got statues of Savonarola, Luther, and Wycliffe looking over my shoulder, encouraging me to be more courageous than I would had not God called me to join them in this business.

While Augustine was preaching in Hippo in the fall of 395, he became aware that the Christians of the city were reveling in the feast of Laetitia, often coming to church in a drunk and disorderly manner. "By the hidden foreordination of the Almighty God," the assigned Gospel was from Matthew 7:6, warning not to cast what is holy to the dogs, or pearls before swine. "I discoursed therefore concerning dogs and swine in such a way as to compel those who clamour with obstinate barking against the divine precepts, and who are given up to the abominations of carnal pleasures, to blush for shame."[5] It was, for Augustine, a good example of the way in which ordinary fidelity to the Word enables us to speak the right word in due season in a prophetic, truthful way. By being more securely attached to the Scriptures, by desiring to honor the saints in our pastoral work, we become the prophetic pastors we are meant to be.

"Would That All the Lord's People Were Prophets"

In *Resident Aliens*,[6] Stanley Hauerwas and I told the story of Gladys, a feisty church member who disrupted a meeting of the Christian Education Committee with her simple prophetic question, "Why is the church in the day-care business?"

Speaking in Kentucky, a woman came up to me and said, "I am Gladys."

"Gladys who?" I asked.

"Gladys in the book," she said. "I'm the one you described in the book. I have to be. Our vestry was meeting and our priest was enthusiastically describing the upcoming youth retreat at Disney World. Something in me made me ask, 'Why are we taking a bunch of overprogrammed, affluent youth to Disney World and calling that ministry?' The priest said something about 'building community.' I said that they could build community just as well by working on our Habitat for Humanity project. The priest got really defensive. Fortunately, the oldest member of the vestry, an eighty-year-old woman, backed me up and said that she didn't see what a trip to Orlando had to do with ministry either. We had quite a meeting that night!"

As we said of Gladys in *Resident Aliens*, "The greatest challenge facing the church in any age is the creation of a living, breathing, witnessing colony of truth, and because of this, we must have pastors and leaders with training and gifts to help form a community that can produce a person like Gladys and people who can hear Gladys speak the truth without hating her for it."[7] Or as Moses put it, "Would that all the LORD's people were prophets, and that the LORD would put his spirit on them!"

The Acts 2, pentecostal test for prophecy is not how outrageous we have managed to be in the pulpit, but rather how many people like Gladys we have produced—people who are able to say No; people who can speak the truth to power; old men and women, janitors and maids with visions and dreams, and who do not mind telling the world about them.

From my reading of Acts 2 and Luke's account of the birth of the church, I derive a few principles for prophecy. To be sure, we do not channel or have a hold on the Holy Spirit, but in my experience of being prodded by the Spirit, I have seen the third person of the Trinity work in these ways:

1. The Spirit has given the world a *prophetic community*, not simply a few outspoken social critics. The goal of the Spirit's descent is the creation of a *polis*, a people who look, speak, and act differently from the world's notions of community. No individual prophets are possible without the existence of a peculiar prophetic community whose life together is vibrant enough to produce a band of prophets who do not mind telling the truth to one another and the world, no matter what. The goal of our pastoral care, preaching, visitation, prayer, and praise is the production of whole gaggle of prophets who will let God use them to get back what God owns.

Charles Williams said of the church, "Her spectacles and her geniuses are marvellous, but her unknown saints are her power."[8]

How true. That ordinary, everyday people like Gladys might be sanctified, made bearers of the holy, witnesses to the truth, is the great glory of God in Christ. Sociologist Rodney Stark dramatically demonstrates how the engine that drove the miraculous movement of church growth in the first three centuries was the witness by the whole church to a new world through the benevolent work of the church. Whereas pagan Romans practiced exposure of infants, abortion, and pederasty, and routinely abandoned their sick and dying, Christians cared not only for the vulnerable among themselves, but for the whole community. As Tertullian testified in his *Apology*, "It is our care of the helpless, our practice of loving kindness that brands us in the eyes of many of our opponents. 'Only look,' they say, 'look how they love one another.' "[9]

Philip Hallie's *Lest Innocent Blood Be Shed* is an account of some extraordinary deeds by some ordinary folk in the Huguenot community of Le Chambon.[10] More than three thousand Jewish refugees were rescued by ordinary women and men who had little to account for their remarkable witness other than their pastor's sermons, week in and week out, that enabled these unheroic people to perform acts of heroism. When, in 1942, the buses arrived to cart away the Jews, and the Vichy French police demanded that Pastor Trocme tell them where the Jews were being hid, Trocme refused. There was a search, and only one Jew could be found. When they put him on the bus for the trip to the prison, the son of the pastor broke through the ring of guards and placed a piece of precious chocolate in his hands. Then the rest of the village began "passing their little gifts through the window until there were gifts all around him—most of them food in those hungry days during the German occupation of France."[11] Perhaps even more impressive, these people considered even the Vichy police their neighbors. They resisted the police, used all the cunning at their disposal to keep them from finding the hidden Jews, and lied repeatedly to the authorities, but they did not attempt to kill these police, their mortal enemies. Why? Because their study of Scripture had convinced them that even the police were their neighbors. They felt that they ought to do all they could to keep the police from becoming victimizers of the victims.[12]

Pastor Trocme had established many small groups of laypersons who studied the Scriptures with his help. When asked by Hallie, their most frequently cited biblical story was, unsurprisingly, the parable of the good Samaritan.[13] This story created a world in which ordinary people were enabled to move beyond mere passive prohibitions against hurting others, to active, positive deeds of love and mercy to both victim and victimizer. In the church's continual act of reading the lives of ordinary people into the story of Jesus, character is formed, saints are made, a new world is offered, and goodness is made possible.

2. The prophetic community is composed of young and old, maids and janitors, sons and daughters, those who have not had much opportunity, in the world's scheme of things, to speak. In other words, *the Holy Spirit produces uppity speech.* When I once asked an African American friend of mine, "Why does African American preaching tend to get loud and raucous?" he replied, "Because my people have been told so often, for so long, that we ought to be seen and not heard, or better, invisible and quiet. We are to stand politely on the margins while the majority culture does its thing. So the church gathers my people and enables them to strut and shout, to find their voice, to stand up and be heard."

Much Christian worship ought to be predicated on the premise that, if we can get a group of people—elderly people, youth, maids, and janitors—to strut their stuff before the throne of God on Sunday, we will be able to do the same before the city council, or the Pentagon, or the administration on Monday. Acts is in great part the story of how a bunch of "ignorant and unlearned people" (Acts 4:13), with the empowerment of the Holy Spirit, got too big for their britches, and by the power of the risen Christ, "turn the world upside down" (Acts 17:6).

Fortunately, when these prophets speak out and speak up, they do not have to come up with something to say on their own. Jesus promises that the Holy Spirit will give them the right words.

> And when they bring you before the synagogues and the rulers and the authorities, do not be anxious how or what you are to answer or what you are to say; for the Holy spirit will teach you in that very hour what you ought to say. (Luke 12:11-12 RSV)

One Sunday in the fall, I check the lectionary, and to my dismay, the first lesson is assigned from the book of Proverbs. Generally, I dislike the book of Proverbs with its lack of theological content, its long lists of platitudinous advice, its "do this" and "don't do that." Pick up your socks. Be nice to salesclerks. It doesn't hurt to be nice. Proverbs is something like being trapped on a long road trip with your mother, or at least with William Bennett. Still, I stuck with the text, Proverbs 22:1, "A good name is to be chosen rather than great riches."

I told the congregation that Proverbs tends to be full of conventional, worldly wisdom, tips for better living, helpful hints for making it through life. Here is literature of the establishment, words that the old pass on to the young to keep the kids on the straight and narrow.

But this particular proverb, 22:1, may challenge that. "A good name is to be chosen rather than great riches." A value judgment is being made. One way is "better" than another. Do we believe it? How many of us are at a university to get a good name? Donald Trump believes the proverb that says, "Go for the gold!" "A GOOD NAME IS TO BE CHOSEN RATHER THAN GREAT RICHES"— put that on a T-shirt and wear it about a university campus for a couple of weeks and let me know how you fare in fraternity rush. We live in a society where there is not much that we are unwilling to sacrifice in order to get the gold—even our reputation.

Since the sermon was from the book of Proverbs—conventional wisdom of the establishment—I was more than surprised when, at the end of the service, a sophomore emerged from the chapel saying, "That was a great sermon. Thanks. I now know that I'm not going to law school and tonight I'm going to call my old man and tell him that he can go to hell."

"Well don't mention where you were this morning at eleven when you call him," I said.

Even seemingly tame timid words of conventional wisdom can, once the Holy Spirit gets hold of them, be dynamite.

3. The consequences of Spirit-filled speech tend to be political, economic, and social, therefore *we must discipline ourselves to read Scripture congregationally, ecclesially, and therefore politically*, rather than therapeutically, subjectively, inductively, or relevantly, as the world defines relevance. Harold Bloom has demonstrated that *the peculiarly American religion is the notion that we and God are tight.*[14] We sense little disjunction between us and God. "God's Word comes only because God sends it. . . . It comes only because

it is sent from heaven. . . . There's a vast difference between the Word that is sent from heaven and that which by my own choice and device I invent," says Luther.[15] The world, when it is in the mood for change, seeks some efficient, significant, usually legislatively coerced means of modifying itself. When Jesus wanted to change the world, he summoned a rather ordinary group of inexperienced, not overly talented folk to be his disciples. This is the typical way Jesus does revolution. Although to the world such means may seem hopelessly ineffective, unrealistic, and impossible, the church is, for better or worse, God's answer to what is wrong in the world. Just let the church begin telling the truth, speaking the truth to power, witnessing to the fact that God, not nations, rules the world, that Jesus Christ really is Lord, and the church will quickly find how easily threatened and inherently unstable are the rulers of this world. If Christians were not being persecuted in China and the Sudan, and being ridiculed in Hollywood and Athens, we might think that the age of prophecy had ended. That thousands still pay for this faith with their lives and their freedom is proof positive that God is still able to raise up a family of prophets. At least give the principalities and powers, as well as the rulers in high places, credit for being able to look at the poor old church and see there a threat to everything upon which their world is built.

> "The kingdom of the world has become the kingdom of our Lord
>   and of his Messiah,
> and he will reign forever and ever." (Rev. 11:15*b*)

One of our recent graduates, now living in California, told me about dragging himself out of bed one Sunday morning and attending the little Episcopal church around the corner. The service went as expected until the priest stood up, at the time of the sermon, and said, "I suppose that some of you expect me to make some statement about the sexual shenanigans of our president. What have we to say to the moral mire in Washington? Well, permit me just a moment to go over this again, if I must. People, we are Christians. We do not have sex with those to whom we are not married! For us, there is no sex outside the promises of marriage! Must we belabor the point? I hope not. Now let us move on to more pressing concerns."

With that, he launched into his sermon on the saints of the church as our models for life. Christians understand that so-called political matters tend ultimately to be worship matters. Behind many political issues is the liturgical question, "Whom do you worship?" The pastor as prophet is the one who keeps reminding the church of how oddly wonderful it is that God has chosen us to help take back the world, that God has chosen "what is foolish in the world to shame the wise; God chose what is weak in the world to shame the strong; God chose what is low and despised in the world, things that are not, to reduce to nothing things that are" (1 Cor. 1:27-28).

This is why Stanley Hauerwas can say, in so many places in his work, that "the church doesn't have a social ethic, the church *is* a social ethic."[16] The gospel not only renders problematic and subservient any relationship other than the relationship of believers to Christ, it also forms a people who know who sits upon the throne. One of the great prophetic gifts that the church gives the world is the church—a political reality that presents, in its speech, in its life together, in its love for the world, an alternative to the world.

4. *The purpose of prophetic preaching is the production and equipment of a community of prophets.* Therefore, our prophetic preaching has as its goal the evocation of prophetic schoolteachers, shopkeepers, nursing home residents, and sixteen-year-olds who can speak the truth to power. The real test of preaching is not the praise of the public, or even its faithfulness to the original Greek of the biblical text, but rather the ability of a sermon to evoke a prophetic people. We preachers therefore are justified in pointing to someone like Gladys with pride, for in her we see the ultimate validation of all of our effort in the pulpit. The Hebrew prophets are often depicted as lonely people. After Acts 2, prophecy is a group thing.

Ephesians 4:15-16 establishes a link between truth telling and community, truth telling and maturity:

> But speaking the truth in love, we must grow up in every way into him who is the head, into Christ, from whom the whole body, joined and knit together by every ligament with which it is equipped, as each part is working properly, promotes the body's growth in building itself up in love.

"Speaking the truth in love" is linked to maturity and growth. Without truthful speech, we are left with immature Christians. In the church, in my experience, we usually opt for love at the expense of truth. Of course, from a gospel point of view, dishonest love is hardly love at all. On the basis of Ephesians 4:15-16, prophetic speech is an aspect of the practice of love, a necessary component of Christian unity among a people for whom there is "one Lord, one faith, one baptism, one God and Father of all" (Eph. 4:5-6). Too often, in too many congregations, unity is purchased by the world's means—suppression of information, deceitful flattery, niceness, and subterfuge—rather than through the Christ-appointed means of speaking the truth in love. In order to have unity or love worthy of the designation "Christian," we need to be more in love with truth than with either unity or love.

A woman accosted me at the front door, at the end of service, after I had preached on forgiveness.

"Do you mean to tell me that Jesus expects me to forgive my abusive husband who made my life hell for ten years until I got the courage to leave him? I'm supposed to forgive him?"

I got nervous. Defensively I said, "Well, we only have twenty minutes for the sermon. I can't properly qualify and nuance everything. But I do feel that, though I am deeply concerned about the problem of spouse abuse, Jesus does tell us to forgive our enemies, and who is a greater enemy than your ex-husband? I do think that Jesus probably did mean for us to . . ."

"Good!" she said. "Just checking!" With that she went forth, going forth, I think, with a burden placed upon her back, a burden not of her own devising, to walk a narrow way quite different from the ways of the world. Who told me as a preacher to attempt to lessen that gap, that life-giving gospel gap, between her and the gospel? Who told me that she was unable to be called by Jesus? Why did I think that she could not be a prophet?

The good news is that in a chaotic and careless society, lost and loveless, just by being a people who worship God, Christians are recognized as prophets. Sometimes we do not have to say anything to be prophetic. In *Where Resident Aliens Live*,[17] Stanley Hauerwas and I told the story of the young man who called me early one Monday morning to tell me that he needed to talk. He was in terrible shape, having wandered about the university campus all night, crying most of the time.

"I had the worst night of my life," he explained. "Last night, after the fraternity meeting, as usual we had a time when we just sit around and talk about what we did over the weekend. This weekend, during a party we had on Saturday, I went upstairs to get something from a brother's room and walked in on a couple who were, well, 'in the act.'

"I immediately closed the door and went back downstairs, saying nothing. Well, when we came to the time for sharing at the end of the meeting, after a couple of the brothers shared what they did over the weekend, one of the group said, 'I understand that Mr. Christian got a real eyeful last night.'

"With that, they all began to laugh. Not a good, friendly laugh; it was cold, cruel, mean laughter. They were all laughing, all saying things like, 'You won't see nothin' like that in church!' and 'Better go confess to the priest,' and stuff like that.

"I tried to recover, tried to say something light, but I couldn't. They hate me! They were serious. I walked out of the meeting and stood outside and wept. I've never been treated like that in my life."

I told him, "That's amazing. You are not the greatest Christian in the world, are you? You don't know the Bible that well. Don't know much theology."

"You know me, I don't know anything," he said.

"And yet, even a Christian like you, in the right environment, can be recognized as a threat, can be persecuted," I said. "You are young. You don't know that much about church history. There was a time when to be a martyr, a witness, you had to be good at preaching, had to be some sort of a saint. These days, even a guy like you can be a witness, in the right hands."

Preaching creates in the congregation prophetic tellers of the truth; prophetic tellers of the truth within the congregation create prophetic preachers. Luther says that God sends the listeners that the Word deserves[18] and, I would say to Luther, through God-sent listeners, preachers are created that the Word deserves. During the war with Iraq, I received a note from a parishioner, a woman in her eighties who, due to her mobility problems, was forced on most Sundays to listen to our service on the radio. In the envelope she had enclosed a newspaper clipping that reported on how American troops had buried about seven hundred Iraqi soldiers in their trenches after a battle, some of them still alive. One American reported that "by the time we got there, there was nothing but arms and hands sticking out of the sand." On pale blue notepaper, with a fragile but beautiful hand, she wrote me, "Have you preached on this in one of your recent sermons? I listen on the radio but have not heard you mention this tragedy. You must mention it. Where is the moral voice of our clergy? What is to become of a people who can commit such cruelty and walk away without even a twinge of conscience?"

That elderly woman may even yet shame me into prophecy. Sometimes laypeople get the preaching they deserve.

Pastors are privileged with an excellent vantage point from which to see the saints at work in the world, the prophets being used by God to shame the wise and to bring down low those things that are exalted (1 Cor. 1:26-31). In great wisdom, God chose those whom the world considers to be foolish and weak to shame and to save the world. Perhaps the real miracle of Pentecost is the miraculous evocation of a prophetic *community*, not just the credentialing of prophetic individuals. The claim that "awe came upon everyone . . . All who believed were together and had all things in common; they would sell their possessions and goods and distribute the proceeds to all, as any had need" (Acts 2:43-44), is a political, economic claim about prophecy in the age of the Spirit. That lection is read, appropriately, on Easter 4 of Year A of the Common Lectionary as a claim about the political and economic effects of the Resurrection. Yet remembered now, after Easter, just before Pentecost, as fulfillment of Moses' desire in Numbers 11, it becomes a lens for all our reading of Scripture, a way of locating the church, of setting the preacher in the right place to preach pentecostally, prophetically.

5. *Prophecy arises from the eschatological conviction that Jesus Christ is Lord.* The truth is that God, not nations, rules the world. Reinhold Niebuhr developed what he called "Christian realism." Stressing the power of human sin, Niebuhr urged Christians, in their political thinking, to be realistic about the limits of fundamental change within the realities of human history.

Niebuhr did mostly skillful anthropology without theology, honest sociology without eschatology. Eschatology, talk of "last things," the *eschaton*, is Christian talk about what is ultimately what, so far as the world is concerned. What is, is that Jesus Christ is Lord. He shall rule, putting all things under his feet (1 Cor. 15:25). Biblical apocalyptic literature tends to attempt precise historical identification of the exact shape of things to come, which has always been a difficult task for limited humans to assume. Eschatology tends to assert the ultimate end of things and the relevance that end has for the present. Both modes of thought are politically charged.

Cyprian, preaching to his flock in Carthage, noted that there is nothing too remarkable in showing love to fellow Christians. What witnesses to a really new world is that Christians should do something more than the heathens; we should overcome evil with good, and practice merciful kindness like that of God; we should love our enemies, not merely love those within the household of faith.[19] Rodney Stark, after noting that there is good evidence to presume that women formed the majority in congregations of the first couple of centuries, notes that a major reason for the phenomenal growth of the church was its appeal to women in the Roman Empire. The church, in its life together, provided a visible alternative to the world's social arrangements. Christians differed from both Romans and Jews in their welcome of women into leadership roles in the church.[20] Christian doctrine stripped ethnicity, gender, and class of its power over the Roman imagination and thus, bit by bit, changed a world. Alas, when the church's new-age, eschatological tension is relaxed, the old world has its way with us, and the church slips back into life as if nothing has changed. Eschatology is thus the very basis of a radically Christian ethic.[21]

In conversation with a Lithuanian pastor, who had suffered terribly under the iron fist of the Communists, I was amazed at his ability to resist, to maintain hope during the bleak seventy years of Communist rule. What had enabled him to do it?

"We tended to take the long view," he explained. "Seventy years is not that long in the mind-set of the church. We knew the Communists would fail. See? It only took God seventy years to bring down a well defended, deeply entrenched political system. That's not bad!"

Taking the long view. That is the eschatological consciousness of the church that enables this prophetic community to keep honesty and hope in tension, that enables us to fight seemingly unbeatable foes, to keep looking for outbreaks of the Kingdom, even when all seems hopeless.

Right after the Acts account of the conversion of Saul, there is an account of a dramatic event at Joppa. There, a woman named Tabitha (Acts 9:32-43) becomes the center of a prophetic moment for the church. Tabitha is the only person in the New Testament to merit the feminine form of the word for "disciple." Her discipleship, indeed her ministry, is caring for the widows. In other words, Tabitha ministers among the most vulnerable of the community.[22] When she abruptly dies, all the hope that these desperate women may have dies with her. They pitifully show the clothes, which she has provided for them, as tangible evidence of their great need now that Tabitha is gone.

Surprise! Death will not have the last word in the ministry of Tabitha among the widows. Peter speaks bold words of resurrection: "Tabitha, get up!" (9:40). And she does. Her name, in Aramaic and in Greek, means "gazelle." Tabitha leaps into life like a gazelle at the word of resurrection.

This is a vignette of the Easter community at its most prophetic. The old, fixed, dead social arrangements under which these women have scraped out an existence are being disrupted. In this new community, no one—neither Tabitha, nor the widows, nor Gladys, nor Peter—touched by the gospel stays fixed in place. Jesus has defeated death; so has the church. God is using those whom the world considers to be powerless and poor to shame the powerful and the rich (1 Cor. 1:26-31). Tabitha's good works among the poor are a sign, a signal of a new world. Her resurrection is only one of the wonders since Easter. A new world is being constructed by the people who tell such eschatological stories.

Like Peter here in Acts, pastors keep naming, refurbishing, and pointing to the now-and-not-yet quality of the kingdom of God that is the Christian eschatological hope. We are not there yet, but we are on the way. We have seen a new world, but that world has not yet fully come to be. Without a continually articulated, lovingly reiterated eschatological vision, prophetic ministry perishes. To all who are trapped in old, dead, fixed arrangements, we keep crying, "Get up!" Surely this is what Paul means when he speaks of a ministry of encouragement, a ministry based upon a conviction in the "God of steadfastness and encouragement" (Rom. 15:5) whereby we are enabled to "encourage one another and build up each other" (1 Thess. 5:11). The world and its wiles, the principalities and powers, are too great for mere humanistic altruism. What we need, if we would engage the powers in all of their tenacity and complexity, is some vision beyond today. Eschatology is not an escape from prophetic ministry ("Pie in the sky by and by"), an evasion of concern about justice issues in the present through dreams of some ethereal heavenly future. Eschatology is the very basis of prophetic action. We are able to act with courage and conviction because we know the last chapter of the story.

Walter Brueggemann links our prophetic ministry with the nurture of an eschatological, alternative perception of reality: "The task of prophetic ministry is to nurture, nourish and evoke a consciousness and perception alternative to the consciousness and perception of the dominant culture around us."[23] Prophetic ministry consists in offering an alternative perception of reality and in letting people see their own history in the light of God's freedom and his will for justice.

Christians whom we meet in places like Acts were convinced that they were privileged to live in a new age that was configured on the basis of something they knew about the end of the age. They began their thought about the world not with the "realistic" judgments about the limits of the present order, but rather with their assertion of how the life, death, resurrection, and ascension of Jesus had created a new reality. Thus Acts begins with the ascension of Christ, with a dramatic claim about who now sits on the throne, who rules. That the one who rules is also the one who was crucified makes all the difference for the nature of that rule (i.e., this God gains victories not in the violent ways of the old age, but through the way of love), which in turn makes all the difference for how then we ought to live (i.e., by forgiving, suffering love that trusts in the power of God rather than ourselves to make history turn out right). Christians are every bit as "realistic" as anyone else. We simply have a fundamental quarrel with the world's conventional definitions of what is real.[24]

What is real is the rule of the Lamb, the crucified Lamb who now, according to the end of the story, sits upon the throne (Rev. 7:9-17).

> Christ Jesus,
> who, though he was in the form of God,
>   did not regard equality with God
>   as something to be exploited,
> but emptied himself,
>   taking the form of a slave,
>   being born in human likeness. . . .
> Therefore God also highly exalted him
>   and gave him the name,
>   that is above every name,
> so that at the name of Jesus
>   every knee should bend,
>   in heaven and on earth and under the earth,
> and every tongue should confess
>   that Jesus Christ is Lord,
>   to the glory of God the Father.
>
> (Phil. 2:6-11)

Our prophetic testimony is not, therefore, so much our judgment upon the world, for judgment is up to God, not us. Rather it is our joyful announcement, in word and deed, that God is bringing all things unto himself in Christ Jesus.

INTERLUDE
Sin in Christian Ministry

A number of years ago I gave a series of lectures at a pastor's school on the West Coast. My subject: sin and its consequences. My remarks were not universally well received. A number in my audience—mostly men, middle-aged mainline Protestants—seemed rather baffled by my presentations, hurt even. After all, they seemed to say, we are educated, enlightened, socially progressive folk living in the Pacific Northwest who have overcome gloomy matters like sin that once were so overstressed by orthodox Christianity. Onward and upward, better and better everyday in every way, that's our motto.

Among those who heard me gladly was a group of clergywomen. At first this surprised me. A number of feminist theologians back then were quite critical of Augustinian preoccupation with sin, particularly the sin of pride, saying that such concern was oppressive to the full self-expression of women.

But in talking with these clergywomen about their experiences in the pastoral ministry, I realized a cold truth: if one is on top, well fixed, secure, then one can afford to be sanguine about sin. We people in power always think of ourselves as basically good people living in a well-ordered world. Why not? It is *our* world. To such folk, "prophetic ministry" means mostly minor tinkering with the present political structures, the passage of new legislation, helpful advice to Congress. Our world, while needing certain modifications, is basically good because it is *our* world.

But if one is on the bottom, at times a victim of other people's cruelty and disregard, then one tends to have a different view of the world. As one of these clergywomen put it, "There is no way to explain how such nice people, the sort of people I have in my congregation, could be so mean—except that they are sinners." These women, having been called to ministry, were finding the church to be a risky place. The traditional Christian sense of sin made new sense to them. As Kierkegaard noted, "sin presupposes itself" into human endeavor, even (especially) endeavor that is ecclesiastical.[25]

In his *People of the Lie*, M. Scott Peck says that if one is looking for genuine evil, then one ought to look first within the synagogue and church.[26] It is of the nature of evil to "hide among the good." Satan masquerades as an angel of light. Lucifer is his name, after all. Leaders of the church beware, not only because we work among the godly, but also because we ourselves, called to speak to and for God to God's people, are in a morally vulnerable position where sin is always lurking about the door (Gen. 4:7).

A friend of mine, an economist, was asked to serve on the board of a church charitable organization that helps needy children. His first days on the board were a sort of religious conversion experience, so inspired was he by the work of the organization, so impressed was he by the tremendous amount of need. But then he learned of the salaries, the *real* salaries of some of the clergy staff. He uncovered accounting irregularities. After prayerful consideration, he brought it to the attention of the directors, and he was dismissed from the board.[27]

He told me, "I think clergy, because they tell themselves that they are doing the work of the Lord, are particularly susceptible to self-deceit. If you're feeding hungry children, none of the moral rules apply to you that apply to other mere mortals." If you are visiting the sick, preaching the truth, offering up the Body and Blood of Christ, who is there within the congregation or even among your clergy peers to judge you? If pastors are prophets who speak the truth, then there is great possibility for us to lie. If we are called to handle the powerful Word of God, then there is great potential for an abuse of that power.

For all these reasons, clergy must cultivate a robust doctrine of sin—their own and the church's—or clergy are dangerous. Although sin appears to be a neglected aspect of much contemporary theology,[28] the practice of ministry requires a healthy appreciation for the ubiquity of sin in the church and its leaders. As C. S. Lewis noted, "It is the policy of the Devil to persuade us there is no Devil."[29] It is a sure sign of a compromised church—a church that has retired from the battle with the principalities and powers, a church without prophets—when one finds a church that has stopped dealing with sin.[30]

Clergy who attempt to be faithful preachers of the Word, prophets to the community of prophets, bearers of the Body and Blood of Christ, tellers of the truth, will have ample opportunity to learn the truth, that "the inclination of the human heart is evil from youth" (Gen. 8:21). How do we integrate that somber insight into the work of ministry? That is the pastor's challenge as chief of sinners in ministry to sinners.

Will Campbell

Will Campbell grew up poor in Mississippi. Baptized at age seven, he preached his first sermon at sixteen, holding in his hand a large Bible that had been given to the East Fork Baptist Church by the Ku Klux Klan and bearing the Klan's insignia. He left his native Mississippi for service in the army, and on an Island in the Pacific read a book, *Freedom Road*, by Howard Fast. For Will, it was Augustine and the book and the garden all over again. His eyes were opened by Fast to the connection between Southern racism and the oppression of poor Southern whites. Campbell said that, when he put down that book, "I knew that the tragedy of the South would occupy the remainder of my days. It was a conversion experience comparable to none I had ever had, and I knew it would have to find expression."[31] When Campbell finished Yale Divinity School, he returned to the South. He described himself as "a missioner to the Confederacy, bridge between white and black, challenging the recalcitrant, exposing the gothic politics of the degenerate southland; prophet with a Bible in one hand and a well worn copy of W. J. Cash in the other."[32]

His experience of bitter poverty as a boy, as well as his encounters with racial hatred as a young campus pastor at Ole Miss, instilled in Will Campbell a twofold conviction (in his biographer's words) in the "inherently evil nature of man"[33] combined with the famous Campbell credo, "We are all bastards, but God loves us anyway."[34]

In the early 1960s, after Campbell had been fired from his campus ministry post at the University of Mississippi for his civil rights agitation and was working for the National Council of Churches, his father urged him not to visit back in his hometown because, "He had learned from a neighbor that a local racist group had said if I came home that summer I would leave in a box."[35] At about this time, Campbell stated that Christians ought to view American racism as "a symptom of man's estrangement from God and a symbol of the brokenness of the body of Christ." He called the then current Civil Rights movement evidence of both "the redemptive purpose of Jesus Christ" and the "judgment of God upon his people."[36] This twofold conviction of the grace of God and the sinfulness of humanity characterized Campbell's ministry. It enabled him to see the morally self-serving hypocrisy in the involvement of many white liberals in the Civil Rights struggle,[37] as well as the mixed motives of some African Americans in the days when the movement was in decline.[38]

As a young campus minister at the University of Mississippi in the mid-1950s, Campbell—who had grown up with the racism of poor, uneducated whites—had his first experience of the racism of the Harvard-educated lawyers and urbane university administrators. This preacher found that sin abounds among the high and the low of society, outside of the church and within. In his novels and other books, Campbell tends to be as tough on the subtle class and economic sin of the urbane, liberal, high-minded social activist as he is on the openly racist, backward, uneducated member of the Klan. Moreover, in Campbell's writing, he does not spend much effort making distinctions between personal and corporate sin, between individual and systemic evil. Our sin is all mixed up with our oppressive systems of class and race and our crooked little hearts as well.

So we are made to pray on Sundays, as individuals and as the church, a prayer of corporate confession:

> Almighty and most merciful Father;
> We have erred, and strayed from thy ways like lost sheep.
> We have followed too much the devices and desires of our own hearts.
> We have offended against thy holy laws.
> We have left undone those things which we ought to have done;
> And we have done those things which we ought not to have done.[39]

That his sense of the utter frailty of humanity did not paralyze Campbell's courageous and creative witness is testimonial to the importance of a sense of sin in ministry. Karl Marx accused the Christian doctrine of original sin of being a means of enslaving the masses within present economic systems—why work for change if, after the revolution, we are all still corrupt and sinful? But to believe that we live in a fallen world is also to believe that the structures of this world are not divinely ordained and stand in need of correction. We are called to conversion. To be a Christian is thus to be called to share in Christ's redemptive work in the world. When asked to explain his own commitment to racial justice, or his later ministry to poor whites in the Ku Klux Klan, Campbell usually replied that Christians have what seems to the world a simple response—we are obligated to help those in need.[40] Yet in simply helping those in need, a healthy sense of human sin preserves us caregivers from assertions of moral superiority through honest admission that even our very best motives are invariably mixed, a conglomeration of altruism and self-love. It also preserves us from needing some idealized image of those in need—that they are not only poor, but also basically good, and therefore deserving—before we can reach out to their need.

Somehow we must hold cross and resurrection together as we think about these matters, as we go about the work of ministry. To be a Christian preacher is to lay the story of Jesus' cross—what we sinners did to God's only Son—next to the story of what God did to us in the cross and resurrection. Jesus was constantly criticized for the company he kept—eating and drinking with sinners. He kept noting their sin, then kept forgiving them, even as he hung dying on a cross forgiving. He even forgave the sinners who happened to be his own disciples, coming back to them after they had fled and forsaken him, giving them the ministry of forgiveness of sin (John 20:19-23).

The Peculiarity of Christian Sin

Part of the prophetic ministry of the church is to teach people that we are sinners. Think of church as lifelong learning in how to be a sinner. For Christians, sin is not so much inherent in the human condition, though it is that; rather sin is the problem we have between us and God. The gospel story is that we are forgiven, being redeemed sinners is the means whereby we are able to be honest about our sin. Many sensitive and thoughtful people are aware of a general disease and disorder in human existence. This generalized awareness has little to do with the Christian notion of sin. Sin is more than taboo, dread, or shame. The Septuagint's translation of "sin" by *hamartia* or "missing the mark" only compounds the confusion. Sin is more than simply not quite living up to our human potential; stumbling, making mistakes. When Christians say "sin," we are saying more than the universal cultural phenomenon that human beings live as they ought not.

Reinhold Niebuhr, citing Herbert Butterfield, is well known for his remark that the doctrine of original sin is the only empirically verifiable Christian doctrine. Even those who do not know that Jesus Christ is Lord, know sin. Niebuhr was wrong. Christian sin results not from our unhappiness with the limits of human existence and our inappropriate response to our discontented finitude (Niebuhr).[41] Rather, Christian sin is derivative of and dependent upon what Christians know about God as revealed in Jesus Christ.

As a young pastor, Karl Barth had been trained in the standard liberal theology of nineteenth-century German theological education. Human beings were making progress, at least in German culture, and the church was there to help celebrate an essentially optimistic account of human betterment. Then came World War I. Barth picked up the morning paper on 4 October 1914, and was shocked to learn that some of his most admired theology professors had signed a declaration of support for the war effort. Even in the face of the German bombing of innocent civilians and the destruction of the library at Louvain, the young pastor "found to my horror the names of nearly all my theological teachers whom up to then I had religiously honored. Disillusioned by their conduct, I perceived that I would not be able to accept their ethics and dogmatics, their biblical exegesis, their interpretation of history."[42] Barth saw how their theology was but another means of their subservience to German *Kultur*. Their compromised, accommodated theology was in a moment unmasked for the young pastor out in the hinterland in what he later referred to as the "dark day" of his pastoral history.[43] Thus began Barth's attempt to reconstruct Christian theology, not on the basis of the older overly optimistic belief in philosophical inquiry, but rather on the basis of the Bible.

Now one might have expected Barth to begin with Genesis and a review of the doctrine of original sin, as classical Christian theology had begun, at least since Augustine. But that is not what Barth did. In all of his massive *Church Dogmatics*, Barth did not get around to original sin until the very end. The traditional path had been to begin with the problem, our sin, and then move to doctrines of redemption and atonement, God's answer for our sin. Barth refused to take this path because if human beings are as sinful as Christian theology claims us to be, then even our attempts to admit to our sin will be deceitful, sentimental, and self-serving. The "sins" of non-Christians are puny. We can only speak about sin after telling the story of our redemption.

As Barth says, "*Only* Christians sin."[44] That is, only Christians have inculcated the insights and the sets of practices that make sin comprehensible. Christians learn to sin, not by beginning with allegedly universal observations about the "human condition," but rather by beginning with a story of redemption. Only later are we able to move to an account of sin. The joyful story of our forgiveness precedes any honest telling of our sin. The doctrine of original sin, at its best, is not a generalized account of universal human waywardness and inescapable degradation, however accurate that account of us may be. The doctrine of our sin is an attempt to indicate just how amazing is the grace that we have received in Christ.

The church's notion of sin, like that of Israel's before it, is peculiar. It is derived not from speculation about the universal or general state of humanity, but rather from a peculiar, quite specific account of what God is up to in the world. What God is up to is named as Covenant, Torah—or for Christians, Jesus. If we attempt to begin in Genesis, with Adam and Eve and their alleged "fall," we will be mistaken, as Niebuhr was, into thinking of sin as some innate, indelible glitch in human nature. We must start with Exodus rather than Genesis, with Sinai rather than the Garden of Eden, with Calvary. Only by getting the story straight—God's story of redemption—are we able to understand our sin with appropriate seriousness and without despair, because only then will we know of a God who manages to be both gracious and truthful. Our human situation is not that we are all dressed up with a will to power and transcendence with nowhere to go but finitude and failure. Our situation is that we view our lives through a set of lies about ourselves, false stories of who we are and are meant to be, never getting an accurate picture of ourselves. Through the lens of the story of Jesus, we are able to see ourselves truthfully and call things by their proper names. Only through the story of the cross of Christ do we see the utter depth and seriousness of our sin. Only through this story do we see the utter resourcefulness and love of a God who is determined to save sinners (Rom. 3:21-25). Thus Barth could claim that "there is no knowledge of sin except in the light of Christ's cross."[45]

I therefore agree with James McClendon when he says that in order to reform the church's received doctrine of sin:

> It will be necessary to make a starting point, not in Adam's (or Eve's!) alleged act of sin on behalf of innocent babes and faithful believers born an aeon later, but rather in the full faithfulness of Jesus of Nazareth, who resisted the temptation that confronted him all the way to his cross, who overcame the principalities and the powers of his day even at the price of his life, and who, risen from the dead, summoned followers to abandon every sin and to follow in good faith the pioneer of their salvation.
>
> A doctrine of sin linked to this central narrative . . . [will not

only show] the dark shadow sin casts . . . [but it will also] hold up this divine faithfulness as the measure of every life, and it must confess that whatever falls short of, denies, or contradicts Christ's faithfulness is sin.[46]

How is it possible for the pastor to be prophetically truthful, courageous, loving, and bold despite the pastor's sin and that of the congregation? How is it possible in our ministry to keep both honesty and hope together? It is an impossible vocation for sinners such as we, were it not that our ministry is reflexive, responsive to the ministry of Christ among us. Easter, and its succeeding Sundays, provides us with proof that Jesus keeps coming back to seek and to save the lost. He eats and drink with sinners—some of whom live as the homeless, scraping out a living at the bottom of garbage cans and ash heaps; some of whom live as the church, politely feeding one another from casserole dishes and paper plates in the fellowship hall—only sinners.

To witness to that peculiar story is to keep asking for forgiveness for the sin that we know and that which we do not know. It is to beg, Sunday upon Sunday, for absolution from the sin that is the result of our insidious evil intent, and the sin that is the result simply of our being humans who sometimes screw up. It is to take care to be the pastor who leads the congregation in both the confession of sin and the pronouncement of forgiveness. It is to keep living with our people in the faith that Jesus really does intend finally to have the world through the inept ministrations of a bunch of sinners like us.[47] It is to sit lightly on our ministerial triumphs, knowing that they are tinged with more than a touch of sin, at the same time to be gentle with our ministerial failures, not expecting too much from people like us. It is to have a sense of humor that is born out of our amazement that Jesus Christ died, not for national glory, or for a two-car garage, or for a fat pension (all those ideals to which we give our lives), but to save sinners. We pastors are able, even in our sin, to have faith, hope, and love, because even in our sin we are able to believe that "we are more than conquerors through him who loved us" (Rom. 8:37). Or, as preacher Will Campbell puts it, "We are all bastards, but God loves us anyway."

Thus we ought to pray with particular conviction, the prayer that we lead on Ash Wednesday:

O God,
maker of every thing and judge of all that you have made,
from the dust of the earth you have formed us
    and from the dust of death you would raise us up.
By the redemptive power of the cross,
    create in us clean hearts
    and put within us a new spirit,
that we may repent of our sins
    and lead lives worthy of your calling;
through Jesus Christ our Lord. Amen.[48]

CHAPTER ELEVEN

The Pastor as Leader: The Peculiarity of Christian Leadership

It is called "The Acts of the Apostles," but the church could have just as easily called it "Christian Leadership 101," for that is what Acts is. Acts narrates the history of the earliest churches by telling of the trials, tribulations, and triumphs of the church's first leaders.

> But a man named Ananias, with the consent of his wife Sapphira, sold a piece of property; with his wife's knowledge, he kept back some of the proceeds, and brought only a part and laid it at the apostles' feet. "Ananias," Peter asked, "why has Satan filled your heart to lie to the Holy Spirit and to keep back part of the proceeds of the land? While it remained unsold, did it not remain your own? And after it was sold, were not the proceeds at your disposal? How is it that you have contrived this deed in your heart? You did not lie to us but to God!" Now when Ananias heard these words, he fell down and died. And great fear seized all who heard of it. (Acts 5:1-5)

To our ears, this is a peculiar and funny story. Let us attempt to read it as an account of early Christian congregational leadership. Too many of our church meetings are dull and uninteresting; not those when Peter was presiding! At first glance, it appears that two prominent church members, with the wonderfully odd names of Ananias and Sapphira, have let their greed get away with them. However, upon closer inspection, we find that Peter accuses them, not of greed, but of lying to the Holy Spirit (5:3). Furthermore, Peter tells them, "You did not lie to us but to God!" (5:4). In Acts, the Christian community is so close to God that to lie to the church is to lie to God. And at that, poor Ananias drops dead.

By the end of the meeting, two preeminent church members are untimely deceased (5:7-10). What sort of pastor would provoke such an ending? In seminary pastoral care courses I was trained to note that, despite their wealth, Ananias and Sapphira are also poor struggling sinners who deserve our sympathy rather than our rebuke. I am a more sensitive, caring pastor than Peter.

Truth to tell, I am less wedded to the truth, less willing to confront and to call to account, particularly if the recipients of such pastoral care are a pair of my more prominent laity. These two were willing to give up about two thirds of their property. In my church, where even the tithers are few, we call that sort of stewardship spectacular Christian commitment. Besides, I practice that mode of pastoral leadership that is often more protective of individuals than concerned about the communal edification of the community.

Peter, on the other hand, appears to consider the ministry of truth telling superior to that of my protective paternalism. What is more, Peter is committed to the nurturance of a people of the truth. Truth telling is more Peter's concern than even my allegedly empathetic care. As we say, sometimes the truth hurts. Here, it kills. But lies are the death of community—at least a community that hopes to be a prophetic community of truthfulness in service to the Lord who is the Way, the Life, and the Truth. The Epistle of James (1:9-11; 2:1-7) suggests that many early congregations were destroyed by the failure of Christians to keep wealth in its place.

And great fear seized the whole church (Acts 5:11). I'll say. It is a fearful thing to fall into the hands of the living God, to be the instruments of God's creation of a countercultural community of truth telling and unrestrained generosity. Perhaps that is why Acts uses the word *church* for the very first time here.

I recount the story of Peter and Ananias and Sapphira in order to underscore the peculiar nature of leadership in the name of Christ. Christian leadership tends to be abrasive because it is service to the Body of Christ rather than to popularity, efficiency, productivity, and celebrity—goals that have tended to corrupt and demean leadership within some communities. Great care must be exercised in correlating the nature of the church with any other institution or community in the world. As Karl Barth contended, "the Christian community . . . is an alien colony for the nature and existence of which there are no analogies in the world around, and therefore no categories in which to understand it, and therefore no real use."[1] Only rarely, and then very carefully, can the church's ordained leaders take their cues from secular models of leadership, because our leading is to be congruent with the leadership of Christ himself.

Pastors as Transformative Leaders

Most of a pastor's time is given to matters of congregational leadership. And this is as it should be. The formation of a living, breathing, visible, corporate sign of the presence of Christ and the advent of the kingdom of God is why we need pastors in the first place. Biblical scholar Gerhard Lohfink says that Jesus means community. The church, like Israel before it, is called to be present, embodied, formed in God's miraculous messianic production of a *"sign of salvation,* when God's salvation transforms his people recognizably, tangibly, even visibly."[2] Thus leadership, administration, is best thought of as an aspect of evangelism and mission since the church itself is prophet, evangelist, missionary to and for the world.

As Hauerwas puts it, the gospel itself is training in how to be incorporated in the Body of Christ.

> To be a disciple is to be part of a new community, a new polity, which is formed on Jesus' obedience to the cross. The constitutions of this new polity are the Gospels. The Gospels are not just the depiction of a man, but they are manuals for the training necessary to be part of the new community. To be a disciple means to share Christ's story, to participate in the reality of Christ's rule.[3]

It is my impression that seminaries receive a high percentage of women and men who are introspective personalities. The genesis of their religious pilgrimage is usually a "Campus Crusade" dormitory prayer group. They are in love with God and enjoy quiet reflection on mystical matters. Alas, the ordained ministry is not primarily about that. Pastors are ordained by the church to lead the church—to be, as we have said earlier, "community persons" whose lives are expended in essentially community, group, and ecclesial concerns. Good pastors keep building up the Christian community, keep wondering what it takes for this conglomeration of individuals to become the Body of Christ.

One of the greatest weaknesses in many of my moves from the biblical text to the preached sermon is that I neglect the communal, corporate intentions of Scripture. I turn a text that addresses itself to the whole congregation and its concerns into an existential, subjective matter. Yet Scripture tends to be communally concerned before it is individually so. I wonder why I generally preach so seldom from the Letters of Paul. The Epistles are concerned with essentially in-house, parochial, congregational concerns—urging the rich and the poor to share with one another in the church, pressing Euodia and Syntyche to lay aside their differences and quit their squabbles, attempting to advise young Timothy to utilize his God-given authority, despite his immaturity. In short, Paul's Letters are occupied with just the sort of problems that vex us pastors—communal, corporeal concerns. It may be enough for most Christians to tend their own spiritual gardens, without much thought for the needs of their fellow Christians, but it is not enough for the pastor.

Some of the literature of leadership in the past took the "great man approach" to the subject, implying that leaders are "born, not made," focusing on those personality traits that make people leaders. The "great man" theory of leadership tended to foster delusion and irresponsibility in the lone leader, as well as implying that, when it comes to leadership, one either has it or does not. Then leadership theorists began to note that good leadership tends to be contextual, that different situations require different styles of leadership. Whereas one group may require a democratic type of leader, others respond better to the benevolent autocrat.[4] Recently, the best research and theory on leadership has stressed the transactional nature of leadership. True, leaders have certain traits of personality and character that enhance their leadership. But leaders are also in a reciprocal relationship with their followers. Leadership is a shared process; leaders not only influence their constituency but are under its influence as well. This aspect of leadership is very true of pastors in congregations, leaders whose leadership is, in great part, a gift of the congregation. Leaders are servants of organizations, providing the best sort of leadership for the organization that is appropriate at that time and place.[5] Particularly in the church, where the pastor often leads by convening and empowering lay congregational leaders, leadership is something that is done in concert with others, rather than as expression of the traits of the lone leader.

Leadership is, to a great degree, a learned activity. It is an activity in service to a group of people who want to do something. Leadership is needed only if an organization wants to accomplish something. Real movement and change in an organization requires more than simply having a leader who will "get people to do what I want them to do." Organizational change requires changing people, transforming them into different sorts of people than they would have been without the service of the leader. Yet specifically Christian leaders are convinced that deep transformation is something that God does. So one of the challenges of church leadership is to be the sort of leader whom God uses to change people.

A number of years ago, James MacGregor Burns wrote a classic book on leadership in which he contrasted two types of leaders, the "transactional leader" and the "transformative leader."[6] The *transactional leader* discerns the needs of followers, and performs leadership as a set of expectations to be met, a series of jobs to be done. Leadership is thus a transaction between the expectations of the followers and the meeting of those expectations by the leader.

Transformative leadership seeks more than merely managing the felt needs of the followers. The transformative leader elevates followers to a higher level, refusing to be either trapped or driven by the conventional expectations of followers, calling followers to a larger purpose—a higher moral commitment—thus transforming the organization and its members. Social progress requires that there be a leader who is willing to risk disapproval and even rejection in the interest of transformation.[7] In a Christian context, I would say that being a transformative leader means believing that God is always making all things new, even us, and that conversion, change, transformation is a typical, expected gift of this faith.

Thus I advise young seminarians, "Be reluctant to change anything until you have been at a parish for at least a year." But I always add, "On the other hand, be sure to change anything that you can get away with."

When Mark Twain was learning how to be a pilot on the Mississippi, his tough, experienced teacher told him that he must master "the shape of the river," the river that is constantly changing, the river that looks so different in the daylight than in the dark.

Twain wrote, "Two things seemed pretty apparent to me. One was, that in order to be a pilot a man had got to learn more than any one man ought to be allowed to know; and the other was, that he must learn it all over again in a different way every twenty-four hours."[8]

Ronald A. Heifetz might confirm Twain's vision of leadership when Heifetz calls leadership a matter of "adaptive work."[9] Good leadership requires a leader who is willing to learn the specifics of the leadership context, who is willing to address the conflicts between the values people say they hold and the reality they face. Then the adaptive leader must be courageous enough to orchestrate conflict so that people might learn new ways of thinking and acting. Curiosity as well as the willingness to learn, to grow, to be surprised, and to adapt are therefore essential attributes for effective leaders. This suggests that pastors who received one image of pastoral leadership from their seminary education a decade ago must be prepared to adapt to the new leadership needs of the church today. A style of leadership that worked well in one congregational context may not work well in another. Then the leader must work to recapitulate among followers some of the same adaptive moves that were made in the leader's own life, in order to mobilize the entire congregation for adaptive work.

Acts 15:1-35 shows a dispute within the early church over the status of Gentile Christians, where there is "no small dissension and debate." Peter urges an openness to the Gentiles, citing his own experience (in Acts 10:1–11:18) of the way in which God "makes no distinction" between Jew and Gentile (15:9). James, on the other hand, quotes scriptural precedent in Amos 9:11-12. Finally, after much debate, a sort of compromise is reached and the church officially moves to a new, transformed situation once James's proposal meets with the approval of "the apostles and the elders, with the whole church" (Acts 15:22 RSV). I take this "Jerusalem Conference" as an example of biblical adaptive and transformative leadership, even though it served later as a proof text for fossilized conciliarism in the church.

Adaptation means movement, transformation, change; and, from my observation, far too many pastors are too willing to settle into present arrangements, too willing to manage the church as it is, rather than stretch themselves and risk envisioning the church as God intends it to be. The prophetic critique of the temple priesthood in the Old Testament was based on the prophets' belief that the priests were merely content to keep house, to manage the status quo, rather than to be open and receptive to the movements of a living God. Because church leadership is leadership in service to a dynamic, synergistic God named Trinity, leadership in the name of Christ is called to risk being at the center of transformation.[10]

The countercultural quality of the gospel requires leadership that is willing to be a means of constant conversion, constantly willing to stand in that tension between the end of an old world and the beginning of a new, always reformed and reforming. And, as the story of Ananias and Sapphira reminds us, such leadership is nothing less than a life and death matter for the church. Thus Heifetz distinguishes between leadership that means merely manipulating "the community to follow the leaders' vision" and leadership that means "influencing the community to face its problems."[11]

Challenges for the Church and Its Leaders

We can specify the peculiar nature of some of the transformation that is needed in the church of the future with the help of veteran church observer Loren B. Mead. In his influential book *Five Challenges for the Once and Future Church,* Mead says that we pastors must orchestrate the *transference of the ownership of the church to the laity.*[12] Church history shows not that we clergy have always been grabbing power for ourselves, but that the laity have been only too willing to shirk their responsibility and then give it to us. Every great reformation of the church has been a restoration of the legitimate baptismal ministry of the laity. At every step along the way of our ministry, we must find ways to authorize the laity to live up to the promises of their baptism.

I therefore think it a good idea for us preachers to view ourselves as the managers of a potentially winning baseball team rather than the team's star players. In every sermon, we ought to include some story or illustration that narrates some exemplary way some person (other than the preacher) has embodied the gospel. Such exemplification leads to identification and empowerment. Or perhaps we are the coach, rather than the manager, actively developing the talents and vocations of our laity. In studies of the rapidly growing "new paradigm churches," sociologist Donald Miller notes the rather remarkable way in which their pastors keep giving away ministry to the laity; keep trying to sit loose on the organizational reins of the church in order to foster as much lay initiative and empowerment as possible.[13]

Next, Mead notes the challenge of *lack of trust within our denominations as shown by our complex democratic structures.* Some years ago, another great church observer, Lyle Schaller, noted that in my own denomination we began by saying, "You can't trust the laity," and structured the church accordingly with overly articulated structure, heavy doses of procedure, and rigidly interlocked systems of accountability. Later, Schaller says, we moved from the premise that the laity could not be trusted to acting as if the clergy could not be trusted either!

When outsiders look at the church, they are often dismayed by our nonproductive, impervious denominational structures. Many people who now have power in our denominations were young people in the 1960s. My own theory is that they therefore have great faith in legislation, organizational mandates, and structure. They love to go to meetings and think that any good that is worth accomplishing is worth effecting by the inclusion of some rule. Therefore they are big on writing and administering rules.

The rule-driven approach to church structure has proved to be uniquely unsuitable for a new generation. Alas, too many church leaders, who were put in positions of power through this structure, have proved unwilling to modify the organizational structures by which they got power. In church life, "the Spirit blows where it will," empowering first one and then another surprising person with the ability to lead. An openness to the leading of the Holy Spirit requires a structure that is flexible, adaptable, lean, and trusting in the surprising intrusions of the Spirit among us. The church is not meant for the mere maintenance of internal organizational machinery.[14] The church is meant for proclamation and enactment of the gospel.

We preachers are big on structure when it comes to preaching. An unstructured sermon is an incomprehensible sermon. Yet we preachers also know that when all of our sermon design and construction is over, we are still utterly dependent upon the gift of the Holy Sprit for preaching to "work." We need to take some of that sense of dependency upon the Spirit into our administration of the church. Sometimes I fear that elaborate church structures are either a defense against the incursions of the Holy Spirit or sure evidence that the Holy Spirit has left us, but we are determined to keep the whole thing cranking along anyhow![15] James Dittes calls administration the great pastoral scapegoat, that which we pastors do in order to keep from doing the more threatening tasks of ministry.[16] It is easier to keep the machinery oiled than to be open to the promptings of the Holy Spirit.

Mead then moves to affirm that perhaps our greatest challenge is *to develop a passionate spirituality.* Though both passion and spirituality are virtues that God gives rather than we "develop," I believe Mead means to link this challenge to the previous ones. We have forsaken charismatic images of the church for bureaucratic ones. The basic purpose of the church is to develop a dimension of life that is too often excluded from other aspects of our lives. In modernity, there is a powerful policing at work to make sure that spiritual matters are kept compartmentalized, safely excluded from the real challenges of life. The church is a countercultural protest against all of this modern positivistic flatness. Mead says we must recover that stress in all aspects of our life together. We must rise above being a program-driven church to being a faith-forming community.

Mead's final emphasis is not surprising, if one is familiar with his previous work on church renewal. Mead stresses the importance of *each church member being engaged in mission.* The time has passed when there was a generation who enjoyed simply keeping the machinery going, coming to church, going through the motions. A new generation of activists, when they think of mission, do not think of sending their money to someone in New York or Nashville to do mission, but rather want face-to-face, self-involved service to others. People want to have their lives caught up in something greater than themselves.

Mission begins with commissioning. Therefore, preaching is an essential part of mission. I suppose that we preachers ought to strive, in every sermon, to have some illustration or example whereby ordinary Christian people could sense God's vocation. Mission begins in the heart of God, in God's determination to love the world, to have a people. Mission involves individual Christians hearing their names called to be part of that mission.

One of the greatest hindrances for mission is lack of imagination. Too many people in the church think of mission as something exotic, something that goes on somewhere else, something that cannot work here. In preaching, particularly when stories of mission activity and success are narrated, people are disarmed, they let down their defenses, they come to see themselves as part of God's gracious activity in the world. Thus, mission and preaching are powerfully related. I know of no congregation where there is active, bold, engaging mission where there is not also vibrant preaching. People are in mission because in preaching they have heard a commission by the pastor, who is the chief missionary of the missional congregation.[17]

Rules of Transformative Leadership

Pastor Anthony Robinson helpfully lists ten "rules of leadership" that are particularly applicable for pastors who serve congregations where people are resistant to change.[18] They are a good list of working principles for pastors who want to be transformative leaders within the congregation.

Give responsibility back. When a layperson says, "Somebody ought to be doing this," Robinson says he learned, as a pastor, to say, "That sounds like just the thing God may be calling you to do." We must, in our pastoral leadership, help the laity reclaim that baptismally bestowed ministry.

Expect trouble. Too many pastors see themselves exclusively as peacemakers, reconcilers. Most of us pastors like to be liked; we enjoy pleasing people. But conversion is inherently part of the Christian faith. The call for relinquishment of one belief and the embrace of another can produce conflict. People do not give up power easily. Sometimes, the congregation is dependent upon the pastor to ignite needed changes within the congregation. I vividly recall the morning after an unusually stormy board meeting. I sat in my study wondering what went wrong. Had I pushed too soon? Should I have been more patient? Ought I to have been more careful in my advocacy of a controversial position? Then I turned to the work at hand, preparation for next Sunday's sermon from the Gospel of Mark. As is typical of Mark, the text was a story of conflict. Jesus preached. The congregation reacted in anger and rejection. It was as if a light went on in my brain, as if a voice from the text asked, "Now what about your situation do you find surprising? Jesus encountered trouble. Are you a better preacher than Jesus?" Trouble comes with the territory when the truth is involved.

Value small steps. It is a virtue to have a long-range vision, but it is essential for the pastor to realize that one gets there by a series of many small steps. There appears to be something inherent within the nature of the gospel that values small things—the widow's coin, the pearl of great price, the few seed that fell upon good soil small things that the world regards of low account. Robinson urges us to remember—as we have the one-to-one conversation, as we teach the only two children who showed up for Sunday school, or visit the one sick person—that the exodus from slavery began with one step toward the promised land.

Plan. If you do not know where you are going, almost any road will take you there. Laity complain about the wasted time and dissipated energy that result from having no long-range vision for the congregation, no means of holding ourselves accountable, no way to know when we have actually accomplished something and ought to celebrate. Planning helps keep a church on course, enables a pastor to prioritize pastoral time and focus energies in a commonly conceived direction.

Identify the vital few. Who are those who like to get things done? Who in the congregation can be counted on to make things happen? You may not be able to rely on the officially elected leaders in order to initiate transformation. Sometimes the traditional leadership structure has too much at stake in preserving the status quo. Do not tackle too many things at once; stick with the few things that are essential and possible. Give the congregation a few victories to celebrate rather than risk constantly being overwhelmed with many defeats.

Do not overvalue consensus. Pastors tend to want to bring everyone along with all congregational moves. But intransigent individuals should be given the dignity of not being expected to approve of and not having to participate in every ministry of the church. Not everything needs to be put to a vote. Sometimes we need to ask members who have grave reservations about some course of action to trust those who want to move. Things can be evaluated later. If we wait until everyone is on board, we disempower those who are ready to take risks, and risk takers are usually in short supply in most churches. There may even be rare, difficult times when a pastor must be willing to split a congregation, be willing to let dissident, obdurate members disaffiliate with the congregation. Pastors are called to a ministry of reconciliation and peacemaking, yes. But we are also called to ministries of transformation, rebirth, and renewal. In order for something to be transformed, its old form must give way to the new, and that can be painful—but the pain must be endured, expected, even welcomed, if there is to be new life.

Count the yes votes. We sometimes worry more about those who are not yet ready to move, or may never be ready to move, than we worry about those who are bored, frustrated, and disheartened when too little takes too long to happen in the church. I confess that I tend, as a preacher, to hear the voices of the two sermon critics long after I have forgotten the praise of the dozen who like my sermon. Sometimes we need to let the enthusiastic lay leaders go ahead, counting the yes votes. Rarely will a majority support a new ministry from the first, particularly if the new ministry requires risk. One caveat: never launch into a church building program if the vote is 52-48!

Create a new working group for a new job. Established structures tend to protect the status quo. Established boards love to say no. If there is a new ministry to be done, you probably ought to create a new committee, composed of those who feel called to this work, to do the job. Ask the established boards not to stand in the way of new movements within the congregation, promising them an opportunity to help with a later evaluation of the initiative.

Change by addition, not subtraction. It is easier to get approval to begin a project than to kill an established ministry. Why mobilize the supporters of the established program against you by declaring it dead and ready for burial? Go ahead with new initiatives. If the new program succeeds, people will gradually rally around it. People are more likely to let go of the old if they have something new to embrace.

Be persistent. Change, no matter how obviously needed, inevitably provokes resistance. Resistance, particularly where the matter is our devotion to and service of God, can be deep and unrelenting. Constancy is one of the essential virtues for Christian ministry, as we shall underscore in this book's last chapter. Robinson advises, "Don't give up too soon." Studies indicate that it takes about five years before a pastor has gained the trust of a congregation to make significant, threatening change. For many women pastors, it seems to take even longer. Count on a couple of more years before you see significant fruit. In a mobile society, where transiency is the norm, pastors must be in for the long haul if they are to be truly transformative leaders. Those of us (United Methodists) who cherish a proud tradition of pastoral itinerancy may need to admit that a long pastorate has become a countercultural witness in a culture where everyone is on the move.

In visits to countless congregations, and in my own pastoral experience, I have come to the rather frightening conclusion that pastors are a decisive element in the vitality and mission of the church. To be sure, as we have said repeatedly, the pastor is not to assume all ministry in the church. The baptized are the chief ministers in the name of Christ. Pastors are to lead through service rather than dominate. The Holy Spirit is the source of all ministry. But having said all that, we still must say that the pastor is decisive. The pastor's mood and attitude sets the tone for the congregation, conveys hope and energy to the people, hurts and heals, binds and releases. Sometimes, as a pastor, I wish it were not so, but it is. What Jesus wants for the church must become incarnate in a pastor or, in my experience, it does not happen.

I recall a distinguished church growth consultant who, in a workshop on congregational development, spent more than an hour listing all of the factors that were relevant to the vitality and growth of a congregation. There must have been more than two score of such factors listed. Then he led us in discussion. The first person to speak was a layperson who asked, "But don't you think the pastor is a key factor in all of this?"

The consultant replied, "Oh, certainly. If the pastor's leadership is lacking, you can discount everything that I have listed on the board. All of these factors contribute to growth. But if the pastor is inadequate, none of the factors that I have listed make any difference."

In order to "complete the task that you have received in the Lord" (Col. 4:17), there must be bold, visionary, pastoral leadership. To comprehend why we might speak of Peter's work in Acts 5 as an example of "good" pastoral leadership would require the retelling of a whole host of stories, including an earlier one that occurs in the Gospel of Luke. Jesus inaugurates his ministry. He preaches the Word and resists the temptations of Satan (who had some interesting definitions of leadership of his own—see Luke 4). Then Jesus at last begins his ministry. How? By calling a handful of ordinary, unskilled, woefully inept people like the fisherman Simon (later called Peter), saying, "Do not be afraid; from now on you will be catching people" (Luke 5:10). In other words, Jesus says, "I am going to take back the world, turn everything upside down in dramatic revolution, and reclaim the kingdom of God. And guess who is going to help me?"

Such are the origins of peculiarly Christian leadership.

INTERLUDE
Failure in Ministry

In the Roman Catholic rite of Holy Orders, the soon-to-be priest is made to lay prostrate on the floor of the church, face down, arms outstretched, in the form of a cross. How wise is the church in the ways of the ordained!

Management theorist Peter Drucker says, "When a horse is dead, dismount." I know a great many pastors who are in a perpetual state of at least mild depression, and many who, after riding the church for a period of time, finally declared that the horse had died and they dismounted.

To continue the equestrian metaphor, a fellow seminary professor and I were discussing a certain student, marveling at her ability, her intelligence and gifts; congratulating ourselves for developing her gifts so well in the years she studied with us at the divinity school. Then my friend asked, "But don't you worry that we may be harnessing a prime thoroughbred to a broken down wagon?" Ah, yes, life as leader in the Body of Christ.

Last week I received a letter from a fellow United Methodist pastor in Minnesota. You never met him, nor have I, yet most of us pastors know him quite well:

> I have been a pastor for six years. It has been very hard. I came out of seminary very idealistic. The reality of parish ministry was

shattering. You summed up the many stumbling blocks so well in your book. It's helpful to know others have been where I am. . . . I really believed that when a congregation was loved and presented with a clear presentation of the gospel they would "fall into line," "be saved," and "go forth." How naive! So, if they don't care about their souls, or the souls of their neighbors, why should I? Does the pastor, the church, and the gospel really count in this increasingly secular age? That's where I've struggled the past years.

It doesn't help to have been schooled in the milieu of church growth and phenomenal evangelism. As I see others' "success," I feel overwhelming guilt. Where have I failed? What have I done wrong?

Of course, I know that "being faithful" is what counts and "planting seeds" is all God asks—but that's hard. So I find myself at a crossroads. I'm seriously considering leaving the parish and pursuing an MBA or a degree that will put me in a job where I can "see results" and be a part of bringing things to completion.

But it's hard to think of leaving the pastorate. I still love Christ and his Church. I still believe in the vitality of the gospel and every person's need to know Jesus. I still believe in the essential mission of the church.

However, the thought of a life spent painfully wading along in the mire of mediocrity, poorly defined faith, and churches content to die is too much to imagine.

Well, I told you that you knew him.

There is much failure to be had in the ordained ministry, and periodic despair seems to come with the territory. Toward the end of his career of training persons for the demands of the pastoral ministry, my own teacher of pastoral counseling, James E. Dittes, spoke of "ministry as grief work":

To be a minister is to know the most searing grief and abandonment, daily and profoundly. To be a minister is to take as partners in solemn covenant those who are sure to renege. To be a minister is to commit, unavoidably, energy and passion, self and soul, to a people, to a vision of who they are born to be, to their readiness to share and live into that vision. To be a minister is to make that all-out, prodigal commitment to a people who cannot possibly sustain it. . . . The minister is called by their need, by their fundamental inability to be who they are born to be, hence by their fundamental inability to share and live into that vision in which the minister invests all. To be a minister, then, as God knows, is to be forsaken regularly and utterly, by those on whose partnership one most relies for identity, meaning, and selfhood.[19]

Jesus' own earthly ministry ended upon a cross. As Paul reminds us, God's power in Christ is "made perfect in weakness" (2 Cor. 12:9). From what I have experienced as a pastor, the challenge is not to find some means of sure success, as the world measures these matters, but rather to fail in the right way, for the right reasons.

Gradually to lose heart out of sheer boredom at the triviality of the church is to fail for a wrong reason. To be crushed because we put too much confidence in the approval of people or the praise of the world is failure not worth having. But to have failed in the manner of Jesus on the cross, to lie prostrate on the floor, arms outstretched in cruciform, to have confronted the world with the good news of Christ only to have the world fling it back in our face—this is the cross that is the pastor's crown.

Life Along a Narrow Way

In *The Cost of Discipleship* (1937), Dietrich Bonhoeffer wrote eloquently of the conflict that is to be expected when one's life is caught up in service to the gospel:

> The cross is laid on every Christian. The first Christ-suffering which every man [and woman] must experience is the call to abandon the attachments of this world. . . . Thus it begins; the cross is not the terrible end to an otherwise godfearing and happy life, but it meets us at the beginning of our communion with Christ. When Christ calls a man, he bids him come and die.[20]

Furthermore, says Bonhoeffer, "suffering . . . is an essential part of the specifically Christian life."[21] He calls "cheap grace" the notion that sin can be forgiven without a corresponding conversion and commitment to walk the narrow way of Christ. There is no way to sustain the hope that I can "cling to my bourgeois secular existence, and remain as I was before, but with the added assurance that the grace of God will cover me."[22]

In John 6, there is a curious exchange. After some spiritual banter, Jesus turns (as is so frequent in the Gospel of John) to corporeal, bodily, fleshly concerns. He tells his followers, "For my flesh is food indeed, and my blood is drink indeed. He who eats my flesh and drinks my blood abides in me, and I in him" (6:55-56 RSV).

Of course, many of his disciples, when they heard him speak thus, said, "This is a hard saying; who can listen to it?" (6:60 RSV).

> But Jesus, knowing in himself that his disciples murmured at it, said to them, "Do you take offense at this? Then what if you were to see the Son of man ascending where he was before? It is the spirit that gives life, the flesh is of no avail; the words that I have spoken to you are spirit and life. But there are some of you that do not believe." . . . After this many of his disciples drew back and no longer went about with him. Jesus said to the twelve, "Do you also wish to go away?" Simon Peter answered him, "Lord, to whom shall we go? You have the words of eternal life." (6:61-68 RSV)

Did not the disciples speak for us all: This is a hard saying, who can take it? Hard, like flint. To come up against Jesus is to be involved in a collision. Jesus' sermons, whether on bread and wine, flesh and blood, or money and power, provoked many to say, "This is a hard saying." Many, hearing him, "no longer went about with him." As Raymond Brown translates this passage, "This sort of talk is hard to take. How can anybody pay attention to it?"[23]

No wonder that his benediction was sometimes, "Do you also wish to go away?"

Like the flipping of a magnet, one pole attracts, the other repels in this text. Jesus both attracts and he also drives away. "This is a hard saying!" Then, "Lord, where would we go?" These words, these cannibalistic, weird Johannine words, are the "words of life." There is an abrasiveness, a sort of dissonance built right into the gospel that is unavoidable and irreplaceable. Thus we preachers are taught to be nervous precisely at that point that our words appear to be received and accepted, fearing that we must have done something to distort the discordant words of life. We preachers so want to be heard, so long to have people hear and come to Jesus, and yet, if there is no one to be repelled by our words, we should wonder if our words are synonymous with our Lord's words of life. It is a tough way to make a living.

You hear this same attraction-repulsion in my fellow pastor's letter: "I find myself at a crossroads"; "I'm seriously considering leaving the parish," followed by, "But it's hard to think of leaving the pastorate"; "I still love Christ and his church," then, "However, the thought of a life spent wading along in the mire of mediocrity . . . is too much to imagine."

At my first church, a forlorn little congregation in rural Georgia, we planned a revival. "What is your goal for your revival?" asked my visiting revivalist from South Carolina (who was my father-in-law, the only visiting revivalist we could afford).

"We want you just to lift up Jesus," they said.

"Jesus preached away more than he won," said the visiting preacher.

This is a hard saying! Who can listen to it?

One of the attractions of ministry for me was I liked to be liked, I needed to be needed, I loved to be loved. For most of my life I had good luck at this undertaking—president of my high school class; college fraternity officer. I was liked, accepted. Then I served my first church. Surprise! Despite my charming personality, two families left the church in the first month. "We don't like long hair, we don't like the RSV Bible, and we don't like preachers from Emory," they said on their way out the door.

In my first semester teaching at Duke, by the second class I noted that during the class discussions only the men in the class had spoken up. Why didn't the women speak?

"Perhaps because we do not feel invited," said one. "Invited?"

"Yes, invited. So many times we have spoken up, only to be ignored or rejected. Why should we speak up here?" When one is rejected enough, one naturally stops trying, for there are limits to how much pain we can endure, and rejection is painful.

Shelby Steele speaks of the "myth of the open door" in speaking of the dilemma of many black people in America. For centuries the door of opportunity has been locked for African Americans. Now that once closed door is legally unlocked; but the courage it takes to open that door and walk through it! The risk! Risk of what? Rejection. Better not open the door, better not walk through and risk rejection. Here we are—men, women, black, white—fearing, hoping to avoid rejection. And yet here is Jesus with his hard sayings.

In a field education seminar at the divinity school, people presented their case studies from their summer field work assignments in rural churches in North Carolina. One pastor presented her case, an account of the irate reaction of a parishioner after the pastor's second sermon. We read the case—mostly a short narrative involving, "I said, and then she said, then I said, then she said, I said, then she walked out."

We discussed the case. "Did you think of saying *this* to her?" we asked. "Are you sure that you delivered your remarks in the right tone of voice? Shouldn't you wait to establish the proper pastoral relationship before preaching sermons of this kind? Perhaps your inexperience led you to say too much too soon." We groped for reasons to explain this failure in pastoral care.

Then one student wisely asked, "Has it occurred to any of us that maybe what the pastor did was right? Here is a parishioner who has learned, through this pastor's ministry, that she did not want to be as close to Jesus as she once thought. Is there a possibility that this may be an account of ministerial success rather than failure?"

We had immediately assumed that here we had a problem of improper technique. Surely there was something done wrong here—an inappropriate word, an improper attitude, a lack of experience, something we could "fix" in this young pastor so that this rejection would never happen again. This is the problem with the preceding chapter on pastoral leadership, the implication that "good" pastoral leadership means finding the right technique, the proper procedure that will ensure us from failure.

Rejection? Go over the case study one more time. Let's all discover what she did wrong. Surely there is some means, some technique for ministry, some textbook (like this one!) that will ensure that we will get it right and always win acceptance.[24]

Did it occur to us (Who knows John 6 by heart?) that this pastor had done something right?

How long has it been since we ended a sermon, gave the altar call while the pianist played "Just As I Am," and in unison the congregational response was, "This is a hard saying"?

Origen, in one of his sermons, says that pastors, like physicians, are forced, by the nature of their vocation, to work with sick people. Sometimes those who are ill do not take kindly to the prescriptions offered to them by their would-be healers because sometimes the cure being urged by the doctor can be painful. So it is with pastors who would be prophets. He says of physicians:

> According to the purpose of their profession they view the parts affected and handle repulsive cases. In the sufferings of other people they reap their own troubles, and their life is constantly at the mercy of circumstances. They never live with healthy persons but are continually with the disabled, with those who have spreading sores, with people full of discharges, fevers, various diseases. And if one decides to follow the physician's calling, he will not grumble nor neglect the purpose of the profession he has undertaken, when he finds himself in the situation we have described.[25]

I have made this introduction because in a sense the prophets are physicians of souls and ever spend their time among those who require treatment. For, "they that are whole have no need of a physician, but they that are sick." That which physicians undergo for the sake of patients who have no restraint, prophets and teachers also suffer at the hands of those who decline to be cured. They are disliked because their directions conflict with the preferences of their patients' desires, because they forbid delicacies and indulgences to people who even in illness crave to have what is unsuitable for their state of illness. So patients who are without self-control avoid physicians, frequently even abusing and vilifying them, treating them exactly as one enemy would treat another. These people forget that physicians come to them as friends; as those who look to the troublesome character of their regimen, to the pain caused by the incision of the surgeon's knife, to the result that follows such pain. These patients detest them simply as the authors of suffering, not as of suffering which brings the patient to good health.

Try this case study: Luke 18:18-30. A young man—a rich, successful young man—comes up to Jesus. "Good teacher, what do I need to do to inherit eternal life?"

Jesus, who had a short fuse for these good-looking, successful types, says curtly, off the cuff, even snidely maybe, "Eternal life? Simple! Just obey every single one of the commandments!" perhaps thinking that the sheer immensity of that demand would knock the young man down a notch or two. The young man's response floors Jesus. "Simple! I've done all that since I was a kid, never broke a commandment. Jesus, how about giving me a really tough moral assignment to get right, something a high-achieving, multitalented person like me can really sink his teeth into?"

And in one of the greatest understatements in all of Scripture, Jesus says, "OK. I need you to do just one little thing for me. Go sell everything you've got and give it to the poor. Strip down, sell the Porsche, liquidate your portfolio, let your health club membership lapse, throw it away on the poor. Then, you'll have what I've got."

And with that, Luke says the young man slumped down ("his countenance fell"), he got really depressed, and walked away muttering, "This is a hard saying."

And Jesus said, "It's as tough to get one of these into my kingdom as to shove a camel through the eye of a needle."

To which the disciples said, "God! Who can be saved?" Translated, "This is a hard saying." We pastors have sometimes been taught to sugarcoat it, make it therapeutic, wrap it in an American flag and salute it. But it's not the American Way, it's the Jesus way, and it is narrow. Here are healing words that often hurt before they heal, hard sayings on which some may choke and gag. And yet these words are curiously called *gospel, good news. The words of life.*

He preached his first sermon in Nazareth, and the congregation gave him a cliff rather than a black Buick in appreciation. There were many who, upon hearing him, cried out with that wise and crazy man, "Get out of here Jesus of Nazareth, what have you to do with us?"

Many, like that rich young man, went away sorrowful, because they had many possessions.

And on the night when the soldiers came for him, we *all* forsook him and fled into the night. Surely the most painful of rejections that he experienced was that which he received from his own twelve best friends.

Rejection took many forms in his ministry; it will be the same in ours. Some screamed at him and wanted to kill him. Some, like those disciples that day who had come so far with him, simply turned quietly and went away. Perhaps that sort of rejection was the most difficult of all.

The Possible Impossibility

At my place of preaching, rejection more often takes the form of that at the end of Paul's speech in Athens in Acts 17, the polite, urbane, "Well, that was interesting. Yes, very, very interesting. We'll just have to think about that one. Think about it, yes. (We intend to do nothing about it, but we'll think about it.)" It's enough to make you wish for the good old days when congregations had enough self-esteem to throw an offending preacher over a cliff!

Give these folk in John 6 credit. They know. The gospel is worth rejection. The gospel is something worth walking away from. In our pastoral work, we need to restore the dignity to nonbelief. Our little sermons, our petty pastoral care, has taken the nobility out of disbelief by making the gospel sound so easy as to make rejection of it sound stupid. No; that young man who slinked away from Jesus was not only rich but also smart. He knew a hard saying when he met one.

Graham Greene's *End of the Affair* ends with the protagonist, having been pursued by God, having had life shaken up by divine intrusion, saying not, "Come, Lord Jesus!" but rather, "Leave me alone forever!"

I was before a group of pastors in South Carolina, doing a Bible study of the book of Acts. We got to Acts 5, that nasty little story (which we have discussed in the previous chapter) of that church meeting where, in a squabble over church property, two board members, Mr. Ananias and Ms. Sapphira, two of our more prominent members, dropped dead after the preacher called them liars to their faces.

There was murmuring in the group of pastors. What kind of story is this? Is this a Christian story? What kind of pastoral care is this? Where's the grace? Where's the compassion? Two people dead, at a church meeting!

Off the top of my head, I asked, "Has anyone here had to kill someone in order to have church?" Silence. Then one pastor spoke: "I preached on the race issue. There were rumblings, demands that I stop. I preached. Three families left the church. One joined another church. Two left the church forever and never joined any church. My family said, 'We know it's an important issue. But is it worth driving three families out of the church?' "

Is it worth risking the provoking death, in order to preach new birth?

This is a hard saying. Who can listen to it?

This gospel. This Jesus. These words. This life. Hard.

To be a pastor, a preacher, a disciple, and a prophet is to find one-self stretched between the horns of a dilemma. On the one hand, "This is hard! Who can listen to it?" and in the middle, "Will you also go away?" followed by "Lord, to whom shall we go? You have the words (sometimes hard, words) of eternal life."

C. S. Lewis once said, "All things are possible. It is conceivable that it would be possible to get a camel through the eye of needle. But even though it is possible, it will be very rough on the camel."[26]

The One who was crucified is also the One who was, on Easter, raised. Any Christian consideration of failure takes place against a background of resurrection. Nothing, even our ministerial inepti-tude, can thwart the final triumph of the reign of God. In the end, God will have God's way with the world, and this world shall be transformed into the new world called the kingdom of God. We can confidently face our failures because we believe that we know something about the world that the world does not yet know, namely, that this world belongs to the Lamb and he shall reign. Without Easter, and the new world that it offers, I cannot imagine how we pastors could have the courage to go out and risk ministry in the name of Jesus. Yet we do because, despite all odds against it, Jesus shall reign.

CHAPTER TWELVE

The Pastor as Character: Clergy Ethics[1]

Could have them read any chpt. on practices

The first divine [i.e., priest] was the first rogue who met the first fool. —Voltaire

Pastors as Examples

Baptism makes all Christians more interesting persons than we would have been if we had not been so designated. Pastors are interesting characters on whom hands have been laid, a burden has been bestowed, and communal care is expected. Thus any consideration of the morality of pastors begins in their vocation. We cannot say what pastors ought to do (ethics) until we first know who pastors are and what they are for. Pastors are Christians who are called to the particular service of embodying this faith before the congregation, in word and sacrament. Though pastors may chafe at the burdens inherent in their vocation, there is no way to escape the truth that we are called to be "examples to the flock," as most of the rites of ordination put it, quoting 1 Peter 5:3. The pastorals repeatedly stress the congruity between right teaching and right behavior by the elders, deacons, and widows. Pastors are enjoined to practice what we teach and preach.

"Oh how curiously have I heard some preach; and how carelessly have I seen them live! . . . Those who seemed most impatient of barbarisms, solecisms, and paralogisms in a sermon, seemed to easily tolerate them in their life and conversation. . . . We must study as hard how to live well, as how to preach well," advises Richard Baxter.[2]

Often, when a pastor commits some public sin, there is someone around to trivialize the lapse by saying, "Well, pastors are only human." This is not only a curious abuse of the word *human*, but also a degradation of the ministerial vocation. Pastors are called to be more than human, as are all the baptized. The waters of baptism—the imposition of hands upon the head and the gift of the Holy Spirit—make us even more than human, or more accurately, truly human.

Clergy ethics also rests on the unique peculiarity of Christian ethics. Like Israel before it, the church is called to the unique vocation of being a light to the nations, to show the world a way to be human that cannot be lived except by the grace of God. Walter Brueggemann writes that Israel was keenly aware that its peculiar vocation necessitated a peculiar ethic. Israel practiced *"a distinct, self-conscious theological-ideological perspective.* That perspective . . . championed the practice of distinctiveness that is rooted in distinctive disciplines and expressed in distinctive ethical consequences. . . . [That enabled Israel] to maintain its distinct identity and to protect space for its liberated imagination and, consequently, for its distinctive covenantal ethic."[3]

You shall be holy, for I the LORD your God am holy. (Lev. 19:2)

There are those who worry about the supposedly higher moral standards for clergy than for laity. After David Bartlett discusses the rigor of the pastorals' view of the ministry in places like 1 and 2 Peter, and Timothy, he says: "One must ask about the definition of ordination that presupposes a kind of two-tiered Christianity: the relatively moral lay people and the astonishingly moral clergy. Especially for those for whom the gospel consists centrally in the proclamation of God's choice to justify the ungodly, it becomes odd to define that by the heroic godliness of the preacher."[4]

True, "two-tiered Christianity"—a set of relaxed expectations for the laity, another set of higher moral requirements for the clergy— is evidence of a poor theology of baptism. Yet one cannot read the Fathers such as Cyprian, Basil, Ambrose, Jerome, Leo, and Gregory without being impressed with their constant bewailing of the clergy's persistent, widespread moral failure. Rather redundantly they charge their fellow clergy with ignorance, sexual laxity, and covetousness.[5] Those of us who tend toward despair at the present moral state of the clergy may take some comfort in the moral diatribes of the Fathers.

But these early moralists remind us that embodiment of the gospel is inextricably linked to the Christian life. The gospel is not only about "God's choice to justify the ungodly." It is also about God's peculiar way of blessing the world through a church that is sanctified as "a chosen race, a royal priesthood, a holy nation" (1 Pet. 2:9). This call to holiness applies to all Christians. Thus, when Tertullian launches into one of his moral rants, he applies the language of moral purity to the whole congregation, rather than just to the congregation's leaders. But by the time we get to Cyprian, we find a stress upon the purity of the clergy as ordained to be unique moral exemplars:

> The conduct of a prelate should so far surpass the conduct of the people as the life of a pastor sets him apart from the flock. For one who is so regarded that the people are called his flock must carefully consider how necessary it is for him to maintain a life of rectitude. It is necessary, therefore, that one should be pure in thought, exemplary in conduct, discreet in keeping silence, profitable in speech, in sympathy a near neighbor to everyone, in contemplation exalted above all others, a humble companion to those who lead good lives, erect in zeal for righteousness against the vices of sinners. One must not be remiss in the care for the inner life by preoccupation with the external; nor must one, in solicitude for what is internal, fail to give attention to the external.[6]

Cyprian's moral instruction for clergy is an early example of a troublesome development in which clergy eventually came to be seen as a sort of ethical upper crust lording over the lowly laity. Later, Luther chided Cyprian for placing too much stress upon the character of the clergy and too little upon the truth that "the office is not ours but the Lord Jesus Christ's."[7] Therefore even the ministrations of a scoundrel can have sacramental value because Christ ministers even through his wretched representatives. Despite our criticism of this tendency, we must still come to terms with the truth that the nature of the pastoral vocation necessitates leaders whose character is formed to meet the demands of the calling.[8]

My friend Stanley Hauerwas never tires of quoting Athanasius's stress upon well-formed character as essential for good biblical interpretation:

> For the searching and right understanding of the Scriptures there is a need of a good life and a pure soul, and for Christian virtue

> to guide the mind to grasp, so far as human nature can, the truth concerning God the Word. One cannot possibly understand the teaching of the saints unless one has a pure mind and is trying to imitate their life. . . . Any one who wishes to understand the mind of the sacred writers must first cleanse his own life, and approach the saints by copying their deeds.[9]

That certainly raises the bar on what it takes to read the Bible. Athanasius is speaking to all Christians. But because pastors read Scripture in service to the church, a peculiar set of moral expectations is laid upon us. Augustine advised that while we are looking into "the heart of the Scriptures," we would do well also to look "with an eye to your own hearts."[10] In other words, who one is (character) makes a big difference in how one is able to understand and to interpret Scripture. The same could be said for a whole array of pastoral activity. I have been critical of Phillips Brooks's often quoted definition of preaching ("truth communicated through personality") as lacking theological substance, as playing too easily into the hands of American experientialism that always elevates personal experience over truth. However, Brooks's definition works because it is true that those skills required for preaching are heavily dependent upon who is doing the preaching. As John Henry Newman put it, "Nothing that is anonymous will preach."[11] The congregation is quite right in expecting that we are at least attempting, to a greater or lesser degree, to embody the faith that we proclaim. The Christian gospel is inherently performative, meant to be embodied, enacted in the world. To speak the gospel skillfully without attempting to perform the gospel is a false proclamation of the gospel.

Lacking a sense of the peculiar shape of ministerial character, we become the victims of whatever cultural images of success happen to be in ascendancy at the moment.[12] Hauerwas complains that the main clerical skills today seem to be

> knowing how to get along with people, rather than constant study of Scripture, liturgical leadership, and discernment of challenges currently facing his or her congregation. Given the undefined nature of the ministerial task today, only a person of character will be able to sustain the discipline necessary for the development of such skills, for ministers are often rewarded more

for being personally accommodating than for preaching in an exegetically responsible way.[13]

Certainly, ministers need to be schooled for what they do. Yet the nature of the ministry requires schooling unknown in some other vocations because of the requisite character required to do the job faithfully. That is why pastors often testify that the best theological education they receive tends to be apprenticeship—looking over the shoulders of a master, someone who has mastered the craft of biblical interpretation, or homiletics, or pastoral care, or church history, and perhaps even more so, the art of self-mastery.[14]

Aristotle taught that character was contagious. We become persons of character by submitting to formation by those who have character, both the living and the dead.[15] Thus Athanasius urges imitation of the saints and their deeds. When ministerial education degenerates into the mere acquisition of skills, the inculcation of knowledge, and data and ideas, it is detrimental to the formation of pastors. All ministerial formation worthy of the name consists of various forms of apprenticeship because the goal is the formation of consistent clerical character whose personification of gospel foolishness is strong enough to withstand merely worldly wisdom.

We are not being naively idealistic or demandingly unrealistic when we ask our church's leaders to be exemplary persons and, when they show that they are not, to remove them from positions of leadership. The needs of the Christian community are superior to the personal or career needs of its leaders. Furthermore, the church has the good sense to know that in placing a person in a position of ministerial leadership, that person is exposed to a unique array of temptations.

In pleading with those who sought to enlist him to the priesthood, Chrysostom cited his own lack of qualification for such a demanding vocation. In so doing, he gave us his *Treatise on the Priesthood* (ca. 386), still one of the most eloquent testimonials to the grandeur of the ministry. Chrysostom says that no one would risk an expensive sailing ship by placing it in the hands of a weak, inexperienced, unseasoned captain. For this reason, no one who is ill equipped to withstand the multiple temptations of church leadership ought to be put in charge of a church:

I know my own soul, how feeble and puny it is: I know the mag-
nitude of this ministry, and the great difficulty of the work; for
more stormy billows vex the soul of the priest than the gales
which disturb the sea. And first of all is that most terrible rock of
vainglory, more dangerous than that of the Sirens, of which the
fable-mongers tell such marvellous tales: for many were able to
sail past that and escape unscathed; but this is to me so dangerous that even now, when no necessity of any kind impels me into
that abyss, I am unable to keep clear of the snare: but if any one
were to commit this charge to me, it would be all the same as if he
tied my hands behind my back, and delivered me to the wild
beasts dwelling on that rock to rend me in pieces day by day. Do
you ask what those wild beasts are? They are wrath, desponden-
cy, envy, strife, slanders, accusations, falsehood, hypocrisy,
intrigues, anger against those who have done no harm, pleasure
at the indecorous acts of fellow ministers, sorrow at their pros-
perity, love of praise, desire of honor (which indeed most of all
drives the human soul headlong to perdition), doctrines devised
to please, servile flatteries, ignoble fawning, contempt of the poor,
paying court to the rich, senseless and mischievous honors,
favors attended with danger both to those who offer and those
who accept them, sordid fear suited only to the basest of slaves,
the abolition of plain speaking, a great affectation of humility, but
banishment of truth, the suppression of convictions and reproofs,
or rather the excessive use of them against the poor, while against
those who are invested with power no one dare open his lips.[16]

I agree with Chrysostom's exceedingly high view of the moral
requirements for clergy, not because clergy are fated to be some
upper crust of morally exemplary Christians, but rather because
their vocation, as leaders of a countercultural community, demands
certain morally strenuous attributes. I once knew an elderly man
who had been a Communist in the labor movement of the 1920s.
He told me how he was unceremoniously booted out of the party
because he and a woman who was also a Communist slept together after a meeting. "In the middle of a revolution, we must have
comrades who do not mess up the revolution by their lack of personal discipline," he was told. The church is also in a revolution, or
at least is here to start one. The needs of the church are for those
who are well formed in the Christian virtues and are honest
enough about themselves to lead the congregation in confession,

having received enough of the grace of Christ to be gracious with the sins of others, courageous enough to speak the truth in love, and attached so securely to the Word that they love the truth of Christ even more than their congregation's affections.[17] Rigorous moral demands go with the territory.

Chrysostom stresses the public, inherently political character of the pastorate as one of its most morally demanding characteristics. He notes that an athlete who never competes in public will never be tested, will therefore never be proved as an athlete. But when that same athlete strips naked to compete in a contest, then the whole world sees his strengths and weaknesses. It is an earthy image by which Chrysostom points to the peculiarly public quality of the Christian ministry whereby, when a pastor ascends the pulpit to preach, the pastor's moral flaws become more pronounced, unmasked, exposed for all to see:

> For it is quite impossible for the defects of priests to be concealed, but even trifling ones speedily become manifest. So an athlete, as long as he remains at home, and contends with no one, can dissemble his weakness even if it be very great, but when he strips for the contest he is easily detected. And thus for some who live this private and inactive life, their isolation serves as a veil to hide their defects; but when they have been brought into public they are compelled to divest themselves of this mantle of seclusion, and to lay bare their souls to all through their visible movements.[18]

The nature of the pastoral vocation requires those virtues that enable a pastor to be in the political tug and pull of the congregation, as a public exemplar of the faith. Ambrose contrasts the moral demands placed upon pastors with those placed upon monks:

> Who doubts that in stricter Christian devotion these two qualities are the more excellent: the duties of clerics and the customs of monks? The one is a discipline which trains for courtesy and morality, the other for abstinence and patience; the one as on an open stage, the other in secrecy; the one is observed, the other is hidden from sight. . . . The one life, then, is in the arena, the other in a cave; the one is opposed to the confusion of the world, the other to the desires of the flesh; the one subdues, the other flees

the pleasures of the body; the one more agreeable, the other safer
... the one overcomes enticements, the other flees them.[19]

When Paul makes the rather arrogant-sounding demand of his flock to "imitate me," in places such as 1 Thessalonians 1:6, he does so, not simply out of apostolic arrogance (though I would be the last to say that Paul is free of such a failing), but rather out of the peculiar nature of gospel ethics. He says in Philippians 3:17, "become fellow imitators both of and with me and observe those who walk according to the pattern *(typos)* you have in us" (my translation). What they are to imitate is Paul's attempt to conform his life to the pattern that is the cross of Christ. Paul makes this sort of bold cruciform argument in Philippians 2:1-13 where he urges, "Let the same mind be in you that was in Christ Jesus." The one who "emptied himself" and "took the form of a slave" is the one whom we are to imitate in walking a narrow, cruciform path that few in the world wish to walk. Embodiment, imitation, inculcation is unavoidable for all the baptized, especially the baptized who are called to baptize and to lead the baptized. It is important for us to be able to say, as Paul said to one of his congregations, "You yourselves know how I lived among you the entire time" (Acts 20:18*b*).

Few have been more scathing than Kierkegaard in denouncing and satirizing clergy who thought that ordination somehow excluded them from the demands of exemplary cross bearing. "It is absolutely unethical when one is so busy communicating that he forgets to be what he teaches," said Kierkegaard.[20] The Dane is particularly scornful of those who "talk the talk, but do not walk the walk," as it is sometimes said in the African American church:

> Christianity cannot be proclaimed by talking—but by acting. Nothing is more dangerous than to have a bunch of high-flying feelings and exalted resolutions go off in the direction of merely eloquent speaking. The whole thing then becomes an intoxication, and the deception is that it becomes a glowing mood and that they say, "He is so sincere!"[21]

Kierkegaard even charges that the reason we preachers love to preach before large congregations is that if we were forced to say what we preach in an empty room, we would "become anxious and afraid" upon being forced to listen to what we preach. We would be horrified to learn that the gospel is meant to be applied to ourselves. Then he warns: "It is a risk to preach, for as I stand up . . . I have one listener more than can be seen, an invisible listener, God. . . . This listener pays close attention to whether what I am saying is true, whether it is true in me. . . . He looks to see whether my life expresses what I am saying. . . . Truly it is a risk to preach!"[22]

At least since the thirteenth century, Roman Catholic priests have been urged to "imitate what you handle" (*imitamini quod tractatis*).[23] These holy things, this bread and wine, these ordinary, mundane objects that embody sacramental presence are to be internalized in our manner of life so that we clergy come to incarnate that which we profess. There is no pastoral leadership without some attempt to embody the gospel in our lives. We clergy are to "imitate what you handle."

Pastoral Practice

Because of the demanding nature of pastoral work, it is ethically essential for pastors to develop those habits and practices that enable them to keep focused and formed for the work. Aristotle believed that it was too much to expect ordinary people (that is, most of us) to be good. About the best one could expect of ordinary people are good habits, yet these practices are that which makes us good.[24] Some of us clergy have been neglecting our habits, ethically speaking. Financial malfeasance, sexual impropriety, and simple neglect of pastoral responsibility plague our profession. Henry Lyons, former president of the National Baptist Convention, U.S.A., embarrassed his entire denomination by being convicted of various forms of thievery, while blaming his crimes on the media and white racism. A 1990 poll in my denomination reported that 42 percent of the clergywomen surveyed said that they had been harassed by other clergy, and 17 percent of female laity reported being harassed by their pastors. When indicted, the treasurer of the Episcopal Church blamed her massive thefts from the church on the disempowerment she felt at working with so many men. Allan Boesak, who inspired so many of us with his stirring words of resistance to racial apartheid, was sent to jail for misappropriation of funds that were given to help the poor, claiming that he was a victim of European cultural imperialism.

Yet in my experience these spectacular moral lapses are not the main ethical problem among us clergy. Our infidelities are more mundane, less noteworthy, but no less detrimental to the Body of Christ. They are primarily due, not to a dramatic propensity to sin, but to a weakness of character, the failure to persevere, to keep at the challenges of ministry when things are difficult. A shockingly large number of laity have been deeply damaged by the sexual and financial improprieties of their pastors; but one can scarcely conceive of the millions of laity who have been exposed to the moral ravages of bad sermons, sloppy administration, and careless pastoral care.

The practices that are inherent in the tasks of ministry, such as preaching—weekly bending our schedules to the tasks of study, prayer, reading, reflection, and self-examination—are marvelous resources for keeping us pastors on track. Alasdair MacIntyre defines a "practice" as

> any coherent and complex form of socially established cooperative human activity through which goods internal to that form of activity are realized in the course of trying to achieve those standards of excellence which are appropriate to, and particularly definitive of, that form of activity, with the result that human powers to achieve excellence, and human conception of the ends and goods involved, are systematically extended.[25]

The pastoral ministry fits MacIntyre's dense definition of a practice. Ministry is an intensely *human activity*. The pastor is a "parson"—literally, a "person"—who works with individuals cooperatively in the parish. The pastoral ministry is an *activity*. Pastors visit, speak, study, pray, and preside in activities that require the mastery of a whole range of physical, mental, and emotional skills. Learning to be a pastor is a complex process of learning the "moves" of ministry, bending one's life to the practices, conforming body and mind to the demands of the craft. The pastoral ministry cannot be done alone; it is a *cooperative* human endeavor with an intense amount of human interaction. The pastorate is *socially established*. There are rules and roles that make the pastoral ministry what it is. Ministry is an art that can be learned. It takes place over time, down through the centuries. Therefore, contemporary pastors have much to learn from those who have practiced this craft before us, thus the frequent references in this book to the saints who preceded us. As the wide-ranging chapters within this book show, the pastoral ministry is *coherent and complex*, so it takes time to learn the moves and disciplines of ministry.

Marie Fortune stresses that pastors are always in positions of unequal power with their parishioners. Therefore pastors have a high fiduciary responsibility.[26] Because pastors are in positions of power over people, including many people in great need, it is important for us to develop those practices that enable us never to use our pastoral power for our own sexual gratification. Rebekah Miles helpfully lists some of the "ground rules" for our work, including, "It is never appropriate to have sexual contact with parishioners. It is always the pastor's responsibility to keep the appropriate boundaries. Pastors and other leaders are also responsible for setting up and following procedures to hold pastors accountable."[27] Her rules then become very specific, very physical, when she speaks about how pastors are to move and to carry themselves in their ministerial work with others:

> If you are uncomfortable or sense that the other person is uncomfortable, refrain from touch. In private settings, be particularly cautious. Whatever setting, follow [the other person's] lead on whether to shake hands or hug. When hugging, use a side hug, so that the shoulders touch, instead of frontal hugs where the chests touch.[28]

More important than rules, principles, and guidelines, more importance even than the observance of boundaries, is a well-formed character that is clear about those inculcated practices that are necessary to sustain the craft of the pastoral ministry. It is the nature of pastoral work to cross over many culturally sanctioned "boundaries," to intrude into the personal space of parishioners, to be with them in intimate, one-to-one situations. Therefore, pastors must own their power, must be aware that they are constantly placed in positions where discretion and prudence are required, and must develop skills of self-examination that are worthy to sustain them in morally vulnerable situations.[29] Thus Miles counsels: "Take care of yourself. Find Sabbath time. Pray. Cultivate ways to relax and relieve stress. Find responsible channels for intimacy."[30] Or, as Ambrose put it, "Who seeks a spring in the mud?"[31]

Only a pastor of good character will be good for people wanting to be better.

The pastoral ministry is formed by a number of goods that are internal to this practice—intrinsic goods that make sense only from within the practice itself. Homiletical virtues such as honesty before the text, care of one's body and voice, and copious reading and persistent study are intrinsic to the task of preaching. In my experience, pastors who find value and enjoyment in these intrinsic ministerial tasks continue to find joy and satisfaction in the practice of the Christian ministry. Pastors who are able, over a lifetime, to keep curious about the biblical text—to cultivate constant wonder at the Word—keep finding meaning in ministry, and the energy to meet the demands of being a pastor. Pastors who become distracted by the extrinsic goods of the pastorate—popularity, congregational affection, material security—tend to corrupt the practice that generated these goods in the first place and eventually become notable only for their moral failure to live as they have been called.

The Church as Moral Community

Ministerial ethics tends to be intensely communal, corporate, and congregational in nature, not only because pastors are called to upbuild the Christian community, but also because Christian ethics is by nature communitarian. Christians do not seek to think for themselves, or, when faced with an ethical decision, to do what seems "personally right." We try to think and to live by the saints, and in concert with Christians throughout the church catholic. One sees the communitarian basis of Christian ethics most explicitly in Paul. In most of Paul's Letters, ethics is intrachurch ethics. Time and again his test for the ethical appropriateness of a given practice is, *Does this edify the Body?* The foundational Pauline metaphor for the church is the body, "Now you are the body of Christ and individually members of it" (1 Cor. 12:27). He even evaluates worship practices like the Lord's Supper and speaking in tongues on the basis of how well worship builds up the body.

In the letter in which Paul evokes most strongly the image of the church as the body, he writes twice, " 'All things are lawful,' but not all things are beneficial" (1 Cor. 6:12; 10:23*a*). He adds to the second instance, " 'All things are lawful,' but not all things build up" (1 Cor. 10:23*b*). In the first instance, Paul is concerned with the ethics of the body and the perils of bodily self-indulgence. In the second, Paul addresses the pastoral problem of whether or not it is right to eat food offered to idols. Paul agrees with his Corinthian opponents that Christian freedom is a great virtue. He had written as much to the Galatians. Yet his stress upon the "body," the church, trumps even so noble a virtue as freedom. Too often the freedom of the strong can be detrimental to the weak in the community. The conscience of the weak, in Paul's advice to the Corinthians, restrains even gospel-given freedom. As Walter Brueggemann puts it in his discussion of these passages, "The reality of the community comes before any liberty, and certainly before the liberty of any autonomous individual."[32] This is rather amazing when one considers Paul's high regard for the peculiar freedom of a Christian.

Obviously, there is no room in this communitarian ethic for modern Western concepts of the freedom of the autonomous self, or for the liberal attempt to distinguish between private and personal ethics on the one hand and social or public commitments on the other. It is difficult for Christians to imagine a truly isolated individual who is unattached to some communal, social framework. Even the person who says, "My behavior is my own business and no one else's," is thereby demonstrating his attachment to a community, namely, the community that fosters isolated, unexamined, lonely people whose only purpose is self-aggrandizement. In a capitalistic, subjectivistic culture, the church's goal is to make all ethics "public," that is, communal, a function of what ought to be happening in the church. As we have noted with Chrysostom, ordination makes pastors intensely public figures. It is not fair for us to complain on the one hand about the "fishbowl" that is life within the congregation in which everyone seems to be peering into the pastor's private world, while on the other hand attempting to be true to our vocation to serve as "examples to the flock."

In our preaching, teaching, and church administration, we pastors ought to strive to build up a community of truth, where the truth can be told in love, in order that the body might be built up into Christ. Note the way that Ephesians links truth telling with maturity as the Pauline metaphor of the body is developed in relationship to truthfulness:

> But speaking the truth in love, we must grow up in every way into him who is the head, into Christ, from whom the whole body, joined and knit together by every ligament with which it is equipped, as each part is working properly, promotes the body's growth in building itself up in love. (Eph. 4:15-16)

This passage judges our willingness to endure immature, poorly developed Christians rather than to love the Body of Christ enough to tell the truth and thus grow up. It is odd that Ephesians links love and truth, because in too many church judicatory meetings love is cited as the justification for our collective deceit. "I didn't say anything to him about his behavior because I didn't want to hurt his feelings."

> I want to know Christ and the power of his resurrection and the community of his sufferings by becoming just like him in his death, so that I might be like him in his resurrection. No, I have not already obtained such a state, nor have I already reached that goal; but I press on to make it my own, because Christ Jesus has made me his own. Sisters and brothers, I do not consider that I have already made this my own; but this one thing I do: forgetting what lies behind and straining forward toward what lies ahead, I press on toward the goal, the prize, the upward call of God in Jesus Christ. (Phil. 3:10-14; my translation)

Easter is that which enables us to keep going, even in our moral failures, even when being a servant of the Word is difficult. Those who have kept at the Christian ministry longer than I will confirm the essential virtue of humor. One can be a pastor with only modest intellectual abilities, but one cannot remain a pastor for long without a sense of humor.[33] The ability to laugh at life's incongruities, to take God seriously but not ourselves, to embrace the strangeness of our people instead of strangling them to death with our bare hands—this is great grace. Without humor, a bishop could be an insufferable bore, a district superintendent could be dangerous, and a pastor would be in a perpetual state of depression as a result of the state of the church. Humor is the grace to put our problems in perspective, to sit lightly upon our clerical status, to be reminded that Jesus really did need to save us, seeing as we have so little means to save ourselves. Humor is just a glimpse, on a human scale, of the way God looks upon us from God's unfathomable grace. By the Resurrection, the gospel is enabled to be comedy and not tragedy.

There is a close connection between the disruptive quality of humor and Jesus' primary means of communication, the parable. John Dominic Crossan demonstrated how Jesus' parables assault rather than establish a "world."[34] A parable typically takes the predominant, officially sanctioned view of reality within a given culture, the "world," and then subverts that world. The surprise endings of many parables are close cousins to the endings of jokes. The gospel, in order to make its way in the world, must subvert the received world.

Because pastors, if they are half faithful, must be forever challenging the received world, effective pastors are often masters at irony, satire, and other forms of linguistic subversion. In fact, sometimes pastors are parables themselves, subversive indicators of a style of life unavailable through more prosaic professions. Sometimes our example to the flock is more disruptive than we know. There is a clergy couple who asked a congregation to hire both of them for one salary. They promised to work with the congregation to apportion the pastoral duties between them. Their rationale for this creative solution was that both of them wanted to share equally in the raising of their two children. Although they did so out of commitment to their own values, they were surprised that what they did was a witness to the congregation that there is a more diverse set of possibilities available to us in marriage and family than in the conventional culture. Their example freed up a number of couples within the congregation to consider other means of ordering their marriages. Thus pastoral counselor Charles Gerkin speaks of the pastor as a "parabolic person."[35] Through our lives as pastors, at our best we make the familiar strange, and hint at the possibility of another world beyond the taken-for-granted received world.

Humor is a gift, yet it is a gift that, even if modestly bestowed, can be cultivated. The cultivation of humor is a matter of constant attentiveness to the incongruities between God's will and our own, God's intent for Creation and the world's will for itself. Scripture is a great help. I recommend frequent forays into the Gospel of John. There, the people around Jesus, the beneficiaries of his instruction, hardly ever get the point. Corpses are raised from the dead, and water turns to wine, just by his presence, and nobody gets a handle on Jesus. The one who eluded the grasp of sin and death will not be constrained by us, yet he will, out of love, come to us and eat with us.

Clergy ethics, like Easter ethics, is not primarily a matter of rational weighing of all possible courses of action, considering each alternative, narrowing down our prospects to the one right thing to do. Ethics is also an exercise of the imagination, a disciplined attempt to believe that God really is active in our lives, making a way when we thought there was no way, by forgiveness enabling us to act more courageously than if we had been forced always to do right. Our hope for righteousness is based upon our knowledge that on Easter he came back to his disciples, the very ones who had so disappointed and forsaken him, and called them, of all people, to be salt, light, and subversion to the world. Thus we are free to sin boldly, to dare to represent Christ, to be so presumptuous as to try to hope for sainthood, not because of what we might do, but because of what God in Christ has done and will do for us, through us, despite us.

Thus the church is bold to pray, when on Sunday, little Easter, we gather to make Eucharist:

> Give grace, O heavenly Father, to all bishops and other ministers, that they may, both by their life and doctrine, set forth thy true and lively Word, and rightly and duly administer thy holy Sacraments.[36]

CHAPTER THIRTEEN

The Pastor as Disciplined Christian: Constancy in Ministry

In the sixth century, the typical monk was an itinerant, a wandering holy man always on the move from place to place, living a solitary life, usually in the desert. Then Saint Benedict founded his monastic community, building it upon the vows of poverty, chastity, and obedience. To these three holy and ancient promises Benedict added a fourth, the vow of stability, the vow to remain where God had placed you, to persist in community, even when the community did not please you personally, to develop the disciplines required to remain where God wanted you to be.

Almost any Christian could be a pastor, almost anywhere, for a few years. But to remain a vital servant of God—lively, loving, and life-giving over the long haul—that requires the discipline of constancy. Some church observers believe that the most productive year in a pastorate comes about the sixth year. I agree. It takes awhile for a pastor to gain the trust of his or her people, to communicate a vision that is required for effective ministry. I also might add that it takes about six years for your pastoral chickens to come home to roost, for you to be confronted by your failures, for your program of ministry to require rejuvenation and growth. Long pastorates generally make wonderfully grounded and centered pastors, while a series of short pastorates are often an indication of a pastor who has not had to develop the resources for maturation of ministry.

In the preceding chapters of this book, we note the demands of ordained leadership that require perseverance, tenacity, courage, and persistence. Pastors are subject to the same frustrations and difficulties that afflict any other demanding vocation. However, there are some demands that are unique to the practice of ordained leadership that make this a particularly hazardous form of work.

Why Some Pastors Call It Quits

As Jesus observed, some who put their hand to the plow look back (Luke 9:62). There are many reasons for calling it quits in the pastoral ministry. Emotional and physical problems can afflict pastors as much as anyone else. Family problems, marital separation, and other trails and tribulations may make the burdens of the pastorate just too great to bear. But these are problems that afflict us not because we are pastors, but because we are people. What are those peculiar challenges that are unique to the ministry that make the ministry a uniquely demanding vocation? I will list some of the factors that I think are most important as well as unique to life in the church.[1]

1. *The work of the church is never done.* Most of what pastors do is open-ended. How do we know if last month's Bible study series really changed anyone's mind? Have we done all we could do as a pastor to help Sue Smith's alcoholism? A surgeon may have a demanding job, but no surgeon is always in surgery. Pastors have no "Miller Time," as the beer commercial puts it, no time when we can step back and say, "We really did a great job on that bridge, didn't we?"

I interviewed a man who works with elementary school teachers. "A good teacher must be content to be a sower rather than a reaper," he said. "Teachers must not expect to see immediate, specific, concrete results of their efforts. If they have any effect upon their students, it will show up later in life, long after their students have left them." The same can be said of the pastoral ministry. As Paul noted, he planted, but some other worker watered (1 Cor. 3:6) and was probably there to take credit for the harvest, though God gave the growth.

2. *The church does not give us a clear picture of the expectations and the tasks that we are to fulfill.* Too many pastors feel as if congregational expectations for their performance are so diverse and amorphous, related to what each individual parishioner's vague picture of what a "good pastor" looks like, that the poor pastor never feels that he or she is doing the job. What is the job?

"I have six hundred different bosses," said one pastor, "each one holding a detailed job description for me that no one has had the decency to show me!"

Some of the laziest people I know, as well as the hardest-working people I know, tend to be either clergy or professors. Can the reason be that both the pastoral ministry and academic work are open-ended? The job is never finished. What is the job? There is always someone else to be visited, another book to be read, more time to be spent on next Sunday's sermon.

"When I think of my congregation and my responsibility for them, I sometimes feel as if I'm standing before the ocean, and then the bishop hands me a teacup and says, 'Start dipping and call me when you are done,' " said one pastor. Sometimes the sheer weight of human need is almost overwhelming.

As a pastor, time and again I would end my day by closing the church office and saying to myself, "I think I really accomplished a great deal today." Then, when I was in my car on my way home, I would pass by Jane Jones's house and say to myself, "I really should have visited Jane this week. I haven't seen her since her husband died." Then I would think, "I meant to read that new commentary on Matthew before I started on this week's sermon. But here it is Wednesday and I haven't even begun." By the time I reached home, I was already depressed and defeated, robbed of any sense of completion and accomplishment.

Because of the ill-defined nature of the pastoral ministry, the work demands a high level of internal control. Pastors probably have less peer supervision than any other profession. In most congregations we are on our own so far as basic definition of our ministry is concerned. In conscientious persons this encourages a heightened sense of responsibility and can lead to an oppressive situation if the person is not only conscientious but also perfectionistic as well as unrealistic.

3. Because *the church is a haven and refuge for people in great need*, it can be a place of great difficulty for those who attempt to minister to those needs. As is often said, the church is a hospital for those who are sick. Sick, hurting people are often difficult and demanding. They come to the church empty, confused, needy, and hopeful. Many times, when we are hurting, we are hostile; we even lash out at those who try to help us, sometimes refusing their help, even while we say we want help.[2] Yet if the church does its job, it probably has a higher percentage of hurting, needy people than other institutions.

Both clergy and laity sometimes wonder why there is so much unpleasantness at church meetings, why people cannot seem to get along, why even seemingly small things become a big deal. Many people come to church without great understanding of, or commitment to, the true purposes of the church, but rather out of a desire to receive attention and affirmation. Many of them have not joined a church—they have come to an organization that will wave a magic wand over their marriage, make their children behave, and give them great entertainment on Sunday morning.

When these people join the church and find that the church demands commitment of its members, insists on giving rather than receiving, desires to serve rather than to be served, they become disillusioned and angry. They feel betrayed because they are not receiving the attention and support they expected, and they become difficult.[3]

4. John Sanford notes that persons in ministry must function much of the time in what the psychotherapist Carl Jung called the "persona."[4] The *persona* is the mask that was worn in ancient Greek tragedy. For Jung, the *persona* is that psychological mask that we put over our real inner feelings when we must relate to others. In the church, we appear to be deeply concerned about people's problems, even when we really are not. A pastor has a miserable day, comes home to relax, and about 11 P.M. the telephone rings. James Smith's mother has just died. Even though he does not feel like it, the pastor must put on his coat and tie and go be a minister.

The *persona* is not necessarily an act or a deceitful charade. It helps protect us by keeping parts of ourselves hidden. It is the professional face that we present to the world in order to fulfill our responsibilities. The pastor is not being deceitful when he goes and expresses sympathy and care for James Smith. The pastor is putting his own personal feelings aside in order to accomplish the greater good of offering pastoral care to a grieving person.

And yet, the *persona* can be maladaptive. Too many pastors deny themselves an opportunity to "de-role." They are always pastors. There is no point in the day when they put up their feet and hang up the mask. They go through their entire lives feeling as if they are delicately balancing themselves on a pedestal, desperately attempting to fulfill an impossible ideal. This leads to a life of posturing, suppression of true feelings, and loss of touch with our real selves. Generally, Jung felt that the brighter the *persona*, the darker the shadow underneath. The shadow is that dark, hidden, inner self that the *persona* shields. This perhaps accounts for why many pastors appear to be artificial and fake. It takes a great deal of energy to keep the *persona* polished and clean. When too much energy is expended in keeping up this mask, when there is no chance to move out of the role, take off the mask, and let down our image, there is a fundamental disjunction between who we are and the role that we play.

5. *Pastors may be exhausted by failure.* Years ago, Richard Niebuhr defined the purpose of the church and its ministry as "the increase of the love of God and neighbor." If that is our job description, is it any wonder that life in the church is full of failure? At the end of every year, the congregation looks back and feels defeated, frustrated, and discouraged. Jesus preached away more people than he won. His own disciples disappointed him and eventually forsook him and fled when the going got rough. That same dynamic of disappointment and frustration with the high demands of discipleship and the realities of the human predicament is at the heart of church life. Pastors and laity alike often feel suspended across that great gap between what the church is and what it is called by God to be. This gap—experienced at unpleasant board meetings, in encounters with half-committed members, in moments when the hypocrisy and downright deceit of persons is felt—gnaws away at our sense of commitment. No wonder that one meets many pastors who are cynics, full of cute, cutting remarks about the duplicity of the laity and the clergy. The Body of Christ sometimes seems invisible or at least terribly bruised and broken.

Richard Baxter, busily chiding seventeenth-century English pastors to work harder and be more faithful, confessed his own sense of failure to reach his people in his preaching: "I am daily forced to wonder how lamentably ignorant many of our people are who have seemed diligent hearers of me these ten or twelve years while I spoke as plainly as I was able to speak. . . . Many of our people will be obstinately unwilling to be taught."[5]

I once, half in jest, asked a distinguished neurosurgeon, "Why are all the brain surgeons I know such strange people?"

"What do you expect?" she replied. "About 90 percent of the work we do is either just standing by and watching nature take its course, or else a total failure. There is really very little we can do for serious diseases and injuries to the brain. Some days I do nothing but stand by helplessly and watch people die. That does something to a person."[6]

In the church, we also do a great deal of standing by helplessly as people die, their marriages fail, their cancer does not heal, their enthusiasm lags, their old self-destructive habits reappear. It does something to us. Thus Aquinas caps his list of pastoral virtues with "forbearance for those who are weak."[7]

6. *The church and its ministry are not valued by the surrounding culture.* The American church is gradually realizing that the church is not the culturally significant institution that it once thought itself to be. Many of us, particularly those of us in mainline Protestant denominations, conceived of ourselves as the custodians of the nation's civil religion. We were the culturally dominant form of religious expression for most of this nation's life. Who would argue that this is true today?

We live in a culture that values money and measures the worth of people by their salaries. The brain surgeon has a job that is demanding, tension filled, and difficult—and the surgeon is paid quite well to do it. People may admire what pastors do, but when the pastor looks at his or her paycheck, the pastor realizes where he or she stacks up on the materialistic totem pole. Even the most altruistic pastors find it difficult not to feel that they are valued less because they are paid less.[8]

In the past few decades, mainline liberal churches have gone through a frantic attempt to find some socially acceptable function for themselves. We have built gymnasiums, opened counseling services, become centers of political agitation, and so forth. Some of this is directly related to the mission of the church. But much of it is also an attempt to regain our place as a socially approved, appreciated institution in American culture.

Attempts to win the approval of the surrounding, largely secular (or is it pagan?) culture can be a trap for the church. We may put the theological purpose of the church in jeopardy as we breathlessly attempt to be all things to all people, to receive the praise of those who do not hold the church's vision of truth and reality, rather than steadfastly adhering to our true purpose as defined in Scripture and church tradition.

7. Many of us must serve in situations where there is *institutional decline*. My own denomination has lost a couple of million members in less than two decades. What does it do to a church to see itself in constant decline? The empty pews, vacant church-school rooms, monetary troubles, and leaking roof all take their toll on pastoral and lay morale. Institutional blight leads to despair. Unless things change, the majority of pastors in my denomination will spend most of their ministries in churches in decline.

After an exhaustive study of trends in church membership in their *American Mainline Religion: Its Changing Shape and Future,* two sociologists of religion predict:

> The churches of the Protestant establishment, long in a state of decline, will continue to lose ground both in numbers and in social power and influence. The proportion of the population that is Protestant will continue its gradual decline in the decades to come.[9]

All of us enjoy being part of a "winning" organization. Every time a family leaves a congregation to join a more active and vital congregation, there is grief and feelings of rejection and failure on the part of the congregation that must bid them farewell.

8. *Much of the church and its ministry is a "head trip."* Some people think that the church exclusively deals with spiritual and intellectual matters, not fleshly, carnal matters. We come to church to think or to feel, not to be physically active. Many pastors are notorious neglecters of their bodies. We may believe in and preach an incarnational faith, but when it comes to the care and nurture of our own bodies, we live an utterly disembodied Docetism.

A national study of Catholic priests indicated that some 70 percent of those studied reported poor skills in interpersonal relationships. Their training had been highly cognitive in nature, even though their priestly work required a great variety of practical skills. Their seminaries had prepared them for a "head trip," but their actual work required a body/soul "heart trip."[10]

Denial of our own creatureliness easily leads to spiritual and emotional problems. I once heard a pastoral counselor say that when a couple came to him for counseling, he often told them, "Next weekend, get a sitter for the kids. Get a room at a good motel. Sit by the pool all day. Sleep late in the morning. Go out for a good dinner in the evening. Dance after dinner. Then, if you still have marital problems on Monday morning, give me a call."

Many times our emotional or relational problems have their roots in our neglect of the physical. A host of studies show that physical activity can greatly reduce our levels of stress. Generally speaking, the more cerebral the work, the more we need to nurture our bodies. We are not all brains, not disembodied souls. We are creatures, animals who are psychosomatic in all that we do. We forget our creatureliness to our peril.[11]

9. *Poor time management wears down many in the church.* Church is not the place for the impersonal efficiency of the assembly line. Pastors and laity must be people who take time to care for many people whom the world might consider unworthy of notice. In the church's mind, an hour spent visiting a lonely octogenarian may be a more important use of time than an hour spent at a church board meeting.

Because all of this is true, it is also true that church people, particularly the church's pastors, are poor managers of time. Too many pastors are sinking in a tangled web of trivial, unimportant, poorly organized commitments and activities that rob them of the time they need for more important ministry. Pastors constantly complain that they do not have enough time. Many laity find this complaint incomprehensible. What *does* the pastor do?

If the pastor did what time-management experts say, and made a log of all activities he or she does in the week, along with the time spent doing those activities, the pastor might be surprised at how time is spent: Two hours a day opening mail. An hour a day spent hunting for letters and notes on a cluttered desk. An hour spent going back to the hospital to visit because the pastor failed to check the patient registry when he or she visited someone else earlier in the morning.

Pastors often complain that the laity do not respect their time. Even though the pastor keeps office hours, no one calls during the appointed hours, but instead waits until the evening and calls the pastor at home. Someone makes an appointment with the pastor, and then is an hour late. I feel strongly that pastors must respect their own time before they can expect the laity to respect their time. No layperson can possibly know all that a pastor must do within a given week. The laity cannot be blamed if they do not know how stressful a counseling situation has been earlier in the day. The pastor must take charge of his or her own schedule and let laypersons know what can be done and what cannot be done.

Yet here is the root of the problem. Pastors are reluctant to make choices, to say no, to manage their own ministry. They complain about stress brought on by a lack of control over their time, a feeling of impotency and helplessness. At the same time, the laity complain that their pastor wastes time, seems to have no clear objectives or goals, is consumed by trivial tasks, and neglects important responsibilities. Of course, some things are beyond a pastor's control. A pastor may have devised a well-managed schedule but must be willing to junk the whole schedule when there is an acute crisis in the parish. A pastor cannot plan when people will be seriously ill or in grief.

Too many clergy are passive-aggressive in their use of time. They passively agree to all sorts of unrealistic demands upon them— going out to counsel at all hours of the night, neglecting their families, running at the beck and call of their parishioners in the name of pastoral care or deep dedication to ministry. Then they swallow their anger at their feelings of impotency in the face of congregational demands. Their aggression surfaces in a sermon, or at the board meeting, in ways that are destructive, unprofessional, and have little to do with the real problem—which is the pastor's own inability to say no.

A pastor who refuses to set priorities for his or her ministry will be at the mercy and disposal of the first person who calls to claim his or her time. This is not ministry. Sermons will not be prepared, time for study will dissipate, the sick will not be visited, and the pastor's own personal and family commitments will suffer.

Church meetings where there is no agenda, no leadership or direction, are the bane of the laity's existence. Otherwise well-organized and efficient people sometimes seem to shed their efficiency and wander into a sort of dreamlike state when they enter the church building. In the name of kindness, meetings are allowed to drag on and on, certain saints are permitted to filibuster during discussions, and nothing ever happens. A few evenings of this, and the laity begin to exhibit the same passive-aggressive tendencies as their pastors. A meeting is held and no one is there. Excuses are made for their absence, but the real reason is that the laity have discovered that church—a haven from accountability, direction, and vision—is a waste of time.

Time management is a theological issue. Our schedules are testimonial to that which we think is important. Those pastors who have an inadequate theology of ministry, whose self-direction is ill defined, are destined to be at the beck and call of whatever the most outspoken layperson thinks is real ministry. As I heard the late Henri Nouwen say, "If a pastor does not know what is absolutely essential in ministry, then a pastor will do the merely important."[12] Because so much of what a pastor does is important, lacking a sense of the essential, the ordained ministry becomes a tedious, unworkable burden.

10. *Ministry is often a mess.* A pastoral counselor, who had spent fifteen years listening to the problems of pastors and their spouses, told me that the essential personality requisite for happiness in the pastoral ministry was "a high tolerance for ambiguity."

"Personalities who put a premium on neatness, exactitude, and order are miserable in ministry. Life is messy, people are mysterious, and few people—once one really gets to know them—fit our labels. No one should become a pastor who has been in business as a printer or a photographer!"

Of course, he said this partly in jest. But his prohibition is fascinating. Printers, who must be exact, whose goal is neatness and legibility, will find that parish life is messy. And if your idea of life is limited to what you can see through a small hole, with all the action focused and frozen, a church can drive you crazy.

The new seminarian, when asked, "Why are you attracted to ministry," replies, "I like working with people." Wrong answer.

"Have you ever met any of the people with whom you will be working?" I ask. People, when known in depth, are a mess. Beneath the neat facade of their Sunday best, demons roam. I find myself unconsciously wandering about like Abraham, desperately searching for two or three really good people in my messy Sodom.

Of course, it is because of this ambiguity, this mess, this sin, that Jesus came. Confrontation with the messiness of life is an excellent occasion to witness to the grace of God. Without grace, we are doomed to cynicism, futile attempts to "clean up" people and the church, or mushy affirmations that "down deep, these people mean well and are basically good—all evidence to the contrary."

11. *Pastors and laity must be in general harmony with the denominational value system, theological stance, and priorities.* Of course any of us can disagree with our church's hierarchy, adjudicatory, or polity on certain matters. It is fair to fight within the family. But when one no longer feels that he or she is a part of the family, that is a different matter. Pastors and laity must feel that, while they may quibble with this or that denominational program or leader, they are still part of the denomination and are in sympathy with the denomination's general direction. Change in the denomination's direction or personality, or change in the personality or theology of the pastor or layperson, can lead to a serious break between the individual and the institution.

12. *Many women pastors are the victims of the sexist attitudes of those in the church.* We have learned, in the latter part of the last century, that simply ordaining women, permitting them to respond faithfully to their vocation to be pastors, is not enough to sustain women in the pastorate. Constant engagement with resistance, prejudice, and hostility wears down many of our women pastors.[13]

On the other hand, women pastors' expectation of resistance leads many to intentionally develop the skills of friendship, support, and sabbath that enable them to cope. All pastors would be better off to admit what many women pastors know from the start—expect some hostility and resistance to faithful ministry.

13. *The "principalities and powers" are arrayed against the gospel and its preachers.* Too many of the factors listed above imply that the enemy of ministry is the church itself. No, the gospel has foes that are, according to Scripture, cosmic (Eph. 6:12). The challenge of ordained leadership is not only sociological, but also theological. Satan and friends have a stake in defeating our ministry.

Burnout or Brownout?

I never was happy with the metaphor of "burnout" as a description of why some pastors call it quits. "Burnout" implies that our problem, as pastors, is a lack of energy. One day we wake up and simply have no more fuel to give to the demands of ministry.

From what I observe, our pastoral problem of constancy is more a matter of "blackout" or "brownout," the gradual dissipation of meaning in ministry, a blurring of vision, the inability to keep the theological rationale for ministry that is necessary to enliven our imagination. We wake up one day and no longer have a reason or purpose for doing the things that the church expects us, as pastors, to do. Thus, in this book, we have spent a good deal of effort with, and constantly refer back to, the theological purposes of the church and its ministry. If God does not mean for us to be here—preaching, teaching, visiting, counseling, speaking the truth—then ministry is utter misery.

Burnout, brownout, dissipation of energy and commitment, are matters more of distress than stress, a lack of meaning rather than a lack of energy. The church shares many of the same human tensions and demands as any other human institution. Yet, because of the peculiar nature of the church and its work, the church also presents its leaders with some peculiar dilemmas.

On a warm June evening in 1939, Dietrich Bonhoeffer walked in Times Square in Manhattan, deep in thought. Friends had enabled Bonhoeffer to immigrate from his native Germany, a Germany sinking fast into the Nazi nightmare. Bonhoeffer's theology had brought him into conflict with the government there. Here, in the United States, he was safe.

But on that evening, Bonhoeffer heard a call from God to return to Germany, to stand with the church, to prod the church to faithful witness. Eventually, he became one of the most notable of modern martyrs, hung by the Nazis during the last days of the war, giving his life as a witness to the truth.

The ordained ministry is not a profession, not a path to personal advancement or private contentment. The pastorate is a vocation, a particular adaptation of the vocation of all Christians to ministry, to be sure, but nevertheless a vocation—a call, a summons from God, an assignment to a work that we could not, would not, take up on our own. The pastor's life flows from a call, and continues, during difficult days, by being re-called through the refurbishment of our vocations. To know that we are here, in ministry, because God wills us to be here—this is great grace. As the Quaker Douglas Steere puts it, " 'Who am I?' is a question that is dependent upon the answer to the question, 'Whose am I?' "[14] It is therefore of great importance to constancy in ministry, in so difficult and demanding a vocation as that of the pastor, to cultivate the disciplines of Sabbath observance, refurbishment, re-creation, and remembrance of vocation. In prayer, the one who is so often talking about God becomes the one who sits silently and listens to God. The one who so often gives, is enabled to receive. As we have noted, friendship is essential for pastoral perseverance, and prayer is the principal means that we practice our friendship with the one who called us to this ministry.

I have found it essential, before I begin my ministerial day, to engage in some focusing through prayer and Scripture reading. It is so easy to become distracted. A day begun without focus, without centering, without daily renewed sense of vocation, is a day that is too easily wasted in busyness and distraction. Prayer and study become the principal means whereby we are re-called, re-collected for pastoral work.

The blessed Bonhoeffer describes the difference in the day that is made by morning prayer:

> Morning prayer determines the day. Squandered time of which we are ashamed, temptations to which we succumb, weaknesses and lack of discipline in our thoughts and in our conversation with other [people], all have their origin most often in the neglect of morning prayer. Order and distribution of your time become more firm where they originate in prayer. Temptations which accompany the working day will be conquered on the basis of the morning breakthrough to God. Decisions demanded by work become easier and simpler where they are made not in fear of [people] but only in the sight of God. "Whatever your task, work heartily, as serving the Lord and not [people]" (Colossians 3:23). Even mechanical work is done in a more patient way if it arises from the recognition of God and his command. The powers to work take hold, therefore, at the place where we have prayed to God. He wants to give us today the power which we need for our work.[15]

Earlier I mentioned the stresses on women in ministry. Despite the resistance and the difficulties, many women are finding the strength they need to do well in the parish. That strength appears to be dependent on a woman pastor's sense that God really is present in ministry, working out purposes larger than our present experience. Despite the prejudice and the odds against them, women are triumphing in ministry, having their leadership affirmed by the church. In a hopeful book that contains the testimony of twenty-five women pastors, Rhonda Hanisch tells of how her congregation, even amid severe financial crisis, was determined not to back away from its commitment to mission. Her experience there confirmed that

> God's vision is all encompassing. God pours out the Holy Spirit upon all the baptized. Each is given the gift of the Spirit for mission, for building up the Body of Christ. God's grace is indeed extraordinary, and can be experienced in the ordinary ministry of the baptized. . . . The disciples were by no means experts, and yet the Acts of the Apostles reveals the extraordinary mission in which they were boldly engaged.[16]

Among the monks of Alexandria in the patristic period, there is this touching counsel of patience for the despairing pastor:

> Seamen beginning a voyage set the sails and look for a favorable wind—and later they meet a contrary wind. Just because the wind has turned, they do not throw the cargo overboard or abandon ship: they wait a little and battle against the storm until they can again set a direct course. And when we run into headwinds, let us put up the cross for our sail, and we shall voyage through the world in safety.[17]

Our times of wilderness wandering and drought ought to be seen as invitation to return to the wellsprings of our ministry—prayer, Bible study, conversation with our people[18]—all in the expectation that a gracious God will give us what we need to continue in ministry, to "voyage through the world in safety."[19]

Sabbath

In its narrative of the gift of the Decalogue to Israel, Exodus expends more verses on the command related to the Sabbath than on any other.[20] The Sabbath is first presented there as a matter of our imitation of God. God rested on the seventh day; so ought we. There is a sense in which all the commandments of the Decalogue flow from the third commandment. All of the commandments are liturgical before they are ethical—a means of worship, of praising God with our lives. In Sabbath, we are commanded to take the time that is required for the reflection, remembrance, and rest that is the prerequisite for faithful, responsive action in praise of God.

Sabbath keeping is a publicly enacted sign of our trust that God keeps the world, therefore we do not have to. God welcomes our labors, but our contributions to the world have their limits. If even God trusted creation enough to be confident that the world would continue while God rested, so should we. Unlike the Greek god Atlas, we need not bear the world on our shoulders. Like the God of Israel, we can stay away from the office for a day of rest in the conviction that the church will not go to hell simply because we are not there to run it.

Christians believe that Sabbath has been fulfilled and forever changed through the Resurrection. Jesus was raised on the "eighth day," the day when creation was brought to fulfillment, initiating for us a new world, giving us back time in a way we would not have had without God's raising Jesus from the dead. Just as God entrusted the Sabbath to Israel, so that the world might know God's intentions for creation, so Christians worship on the day of the Resurrection, thereby signaling that God's promise to Israel has gone to all the world. All, including pastors, are created to share the rest, the salvation, that comes from worship of the true God.

It is therefore an ethical challenge that pastors must work on Sunday, the Christian Sabbath. Although we are urging our people to pause, to remember, to reflect, to experience God's recreation of their lives on the eighth day, we clergy are busy speaking, leading, preaching, teaching, and presiding. This means that pastors must find some means of Sabbath, since in our peculiar vocation Sabbath is often denied us because of our offering Sabbath to everyone else on Sunday.[21] It is crucial for pastors to carve out some means of Sabbath as a witness that God, not pastors, preserves the church.

Sunday is the key that explains to the world and to the church why we are the *ecclesia,* those who are called out. In our Sunday worship, Christians serve the world by showing the world that God has not left us alone and that we have good work to do. Our work is worship. Liturgy means in its Greek derivation, "the work of the people." Sabbath is a weekly reminder that we are created for no better purpose than to glorify God and to enjoy God forever.

In simply withdrawing from what the world considers its "important business," in taking time to do nothing but worship in a world at war, in celebrating an "order of worship" in a world of chaos, Christians are making a very "political" statement. It takes courage to take time to worship God in a world where we are constantly told that it is up to us to do right, or right won't be done. Sunday is that holy time when Christians perform one of our most radical, countercultural, peculiarly defining acts—we simply refuse to show up for work. Sabbath is how we put the world in its place. This is how we take over the world's time and help make it God's time. We remind ourselves that we are created, not for ceaseless work, but for worship, rest in God. Rest is eschatological. Extricated from the daily, pressing, relentless cares and concerns of the parish, the pastor is given the opportunity for reflection and recollection, recalling why we are in ministry in the first place, to whom we are ultimately accountable, and where our ministry is meant to be heading. We serve God, but we are not gods. In Acts, no sooner do Paul and Barnabas do a good work of healing than the adoring crowd calls them Zeus and Hermes (Acts 14:11-14). These two ministers said, "We are mortals just like you" (14:15)—something we pastors need to say from time to time, in our sermons and in our days off, as a reminder to our congregations.

An overworked, busy and distracted, family-neglecting pastor is often a pastor with an inadequate theology of the Resurrection. We are free to let go of the church, free to take regular sabbatical, because we rest in the conviction that Christ really is present in the church, that Christ will preserve the church, and that the gates of hell or even our day off will not defeat the church. We have been created, not for ceaseless activity, but for rest, for confident Sabbath. Our God was so serenely confident in his work of Creation that God was able to take a day off; so should we.

Gregory the Great stresses pastoral care as the pastor's care of himself:

> In restoring others to health by healing their wounds, he must not disregard his own health. . . . Let him not, while helping his neighbours, neglect himself, let him not, while lifting up others, fall himself. In many instances, indeed, the greatness of some men's virtues has been an occasion of their perdition, in that they

have felt inordinately secure in the assurance of their strength, and they died suddenly because of their negligence.[22]

Some pastors are charged with being "control freaks" who must be involved in every act of ministry within their congregations. They are thus impossible to work with, unable to delegate any authority to their church staff, unwilling to give credit to the work of others, resistant to allowing the laity to exercise their baptismally given ministry. One of the most revealing tests for whether or not a pastor has an inadequate theology of ministry is when that pastor is forced to work within a multiple staff congregation. Pastors who cannot delegate, who cannot constantly give away ministry and share ministry, suffer from a "messiah complex," feeling that, if ministry is to occur in the church, it must be done by them or it will not be done.[23] This peculiar brand of clericalism betrays an inadequate theology of resurrection evidenced in the inability to observe the Sabbath.[24]

Paul strikes a good balance between the grace of God given to him as being an assignment for him to work at ministry, and that same grace being a reminder that it is not his hard work that validates his ministry but rather the "grace of God that is with me."

> But by the grace of God I am what I am, and his grace toward me has not been in vain. On the contrary, I worked harder than any of them—though it was not I, but the grace of God that is with me. Whether then it was I or they, so we proclaim and so you have come to believe. (1 Cor. 15:10-11)

The Church as a Source of Pastoral Constancy

How can clergy possibly persevere amid the great demands of the church? Paradoxically, one of our major resources for ministerial constancy is the church itself. The same church that demands so much of us in ministry is also the church through which God gives us what we need to keep in ministry. The church that has ordained us, and called us forth to leadership, keeps calling us, keeps authorizing us, keeps empowering us to be better than we would have been if we had been left to our own devices.[25] In expecting us to be truthful, courageous preachers, the church makes us truthful and courageous. In the church's weekly routine of worship, forcing us to worship a real God every seven days whether we feel like it or not, the church keeps us close to the well-springs of the faith even when we have been negligent in availing ourselves of those restorative waters. In demanding that we stand between them and God, our people make us priests, and we are thereby surprised by our own priestly effectiveness, despite ourselves.

> But we have this treasure in clay jars, so that it may be made clear that this extraordinary power belongs to God and does not come from us. We are afflicted in every way, but not crushed; perplexed, but not driven to despair. (2 Cor. 4:7-8)

The Enlightenment invented the notion of the unfettered "man come of age"—humanity without some external authority to which obedience is owed, particularly without reference to the external authority of the church. Descartes, Locke, and Kant all contributed to this elevation of the free and unattached subject who is subject to no one and lord of all. Freud gave such philosophy popular expression with his theory that human maturation requires increasing emancipation from extrinsic communal authority. All communal, social restraints upon the personality are forms of external repression, fetters that must be shed in order for us to stand alone as the heroic human beings we ought to be.

Postmodernity has, as we have noted, discovered that such unfettered freedom is an illusion. There is no person without context and commitment. Modernity's "liberation" only resulted in a host of cruel conformities, few of which acknowledge themselves as conformity. The self is largely a social construction, a composite of a host of influences and attachments. In this sense, all ethics is "communal," that is, externally, socially imposed. None of us is self-made, self-composed. All of our selves are subservient to some one else's account of what the world is and who human beings ought to be. Christians attempt to live by the witness of the saints, to be disciplined by those who have preceded us in this faith. In this book, one of the reasons there has been such copious reference to the testimony of pastors of the past, is my belief that attachment to their witness helps keep us apostolic and faithful.

This book began with an assertion of the church as the source and the purpose of clergy. We are who we are, as clergy, in great part because the church, in its rites of ordination, tells us who we are, names us as leaders of the church, gives purpose and direction to our lives. The ordained ministry is a function of the general ministry of all the baptized. Clergy keep going, even without many tangible results and rewards, because of our faith that God wills for the church ultimately to triumph. For better or worse, the Body of Christ is God's answer for what ails the world.

This explains why, for me, my great source of clerical constancy is the corporate worship of the church. Although I am, on most Sundays, so busy leading the congregation in worship that I have scant opportunity to worship, worship I do. In bending my time all week to the study and exposition of the Scriptures in preparation for preaching, in my leadership in corporate prayer, my service at the table, my work at the baptismal font, I am being formed. I am becoming the person the church promised I would be when hands were laid upon my head. It takes time to worship, at least an hour on Sundays. It takes time to worship—about a lifetime of weekly bending of one's life toward God, of following a way that is against our natural inclination. In taking time for such practices, we literally retake time, observe Sabbath, help sanctify all time as God's. Thus Luther says that the purpose of Sabbath is not merely that we should stop work, but that God is given time to work in us.[26]

The only way to keep at ministry amid all the pastoral challenges is from the conviction that God really is present—in Word and Sacrament, in our work of ministry, as a treasure in earthen vessels—bringing all things unto God, despite us, through us, for us. God with us. Yes, God with *us*.

In his *Four Quartets*, T. S. Eliot confessed to his lifelong difficulty in finding the right words to say what ought to be said. As a preacher, one who is called by the church to speak the gospel of a savior like Christ, I sympathize with the poet. I know, fifty-two Sundays a year, what it is like to mount a "raid on the inarticulate." Yet I have also learned that, thank God, my words are not all that is to be said by or for the Word, the Word made flesh among us. Much of what I fret over in ministry is God's business rather than mine. Therefore, I keep preaching, keep teaching, keep at ministry, caught up in God's business more than my own:

And so each venture
Is a new beginning, a raid on the inarticulate
With shabby equipment always deteriorating
In the general mess of imprecision of feeling,
Undisciplined squads of emotion. And what there is to conquer
By strength and submission, has already been discovered
Once or twice, or several times, by men whom one cannot hope
To emulate—but there is no competition—
There is only the fight to recover what has been lost
And found and lost again and again: and now, under conditions
That seem unpropitious. But perhaps neither gain nor loss.
For us, there is only the trying. The rest is not our business.[27]

Constancy and Vocation

In the end, *contra* Eliot, what keeps us going is the peculiarity of the ordained life itself. It is no great achievement for me to enumerate all the ways that this way of life is a burden. But ordination is also, as is typical of many aspects of the Christian life, a burden that is a blessing. In taking up the yoke and the burden of ministry, we find that it is on most days easy and light, even a joy. It is great joy to be here because we have been put here. Our ultimate defense of our pastoral work is simply that we have been called. Thus we pastors, in the words of Eliot's poem, conquer not by "conquest" but by "submission," by daily learning to take up the cross of ministry until that day when it feels not like a burden at all, but rather a great, good blessing. It is a blessing to do what God wants, and to be who God has meant us to be. Ministry is not a matter only of "the trying." It is a matter of response to a divine summons, of saying yes to work together with God, a work not of our own devising, but of God's.

To have faith that God is present, not only in Word and Sacrament, but also in our teaching, visitation, preaching, and congregational care—this keeps pastors going. We work in some mundane, out-of-the-way places, we pastors, but always under the eschatological conviction that we are essential participants in a great cosmic battle in which God is getting back what belongs to God. Large matters are being worked out through our ministry.

I know that such claims seem absurd to the world, but so does the claim that God saves the world in a modest place like Judea, through a crucified rabbi hanging from a tree. Pastors learn to thrive on, to relish and delight in, what seems absurd to the world.

God has called us. It all rests upon the summons. It is not our job to make the world turn out right or to see the church triumphant or even to make this congregation into an unmistakable outpost of the kingdom of God. Only God can do that. It is not my task to work in such a skillful, informed, and competent way that my ministry will ultimately count for something. Only God can do that. And while God is doing that, it is good for me to keep in mind that this God wins victories through suffering, through love that, from a cross, moves the sun and moon and stars. The suffering that faithful ministry sometimes entails is not a sign of failure, but of fidelity.

It is a great gift to be summoned forth to be part of this ministry. Why, just today, as I was laboriously completing the last of this long book, God let me witness (1) a young woman being called to give her life in service to the needs of others rather than to the needs of General Motors, then (2) God gave me a perfectly outrageous text to prepare to preach on next Sunday. And I took heart, and I thanked God that I had been called to such interesting work. In fact, my ministry at that point felt less like work and more like a hymn. Pure praise.

The calling is worth doing because the Caller is so interesting. To have one's life commandeered by a God named Trinity is great adventure for the called. The ordained life would be too great a burden for anyone, were it not that God calls us to do that which God is already doing. Our ministry is subsequent and derivative of God's. We need not labor and struggle earnestly to overcome all of the factors in ministry that lead to burnout or brownout. It is God's labor, not our own, that sustains us. Back in the garden, Lady Continence asks the earnest, miserable Augustine, "Why do you try and stand by yourself and stand not at all? Let God support you" (*Confessions*, book 8). God calls us to do nothing alone.

Augustine, you recall, was converted at a child's singing of a song. The Bible ends in Revelation, the last book, a book that begins in a great shout, a song, " 'I am the Alpha and the Omega,' says the Lord God, who is and who was and who is to come, the Almighty" (Rev. 1:8). Tony Campolo, preaching in our chapel, shouted, "People, evangelism is recruitment for a choir! Read the book of

Revelation!" Our end, according to Revelation, is participation in a great chorus of all angels, elders, and living creatures, a choir "of myriads and thousands of thousands, singing with full voice":

> "Worthy is the Lamb that was slaughtered
> to receive power and wealth and wisdom and might
> and honor and glory and blessing!"
>
> (Rev. 5:12)

If this is heaven, then evangelism is recruitment for a choir, and our ministry means enabling the whole world to sing the song now, on earth, so that one day we might sing it for eternity.

In our ministry, it is this song that gives significance to the singer. The gospel is truth and light and life and those who serve it, and the congregations summoned forth by it are those who are blessed, despite themselves, with the One who is the way, the truth, and the life. The song we are called to sing is God's. Our hope is to sing that song so well that we shall come to forget that we are trying to sing. We will know the words and the music by heart. God's song will be ours. We will not be working at ministry or trying to remain constant in our calling. We shall, in the words of Wesley's hymn, gloriously be "lost in wonder, love, and praise." We will be doing it all for nothing more than love.

By God's grace, the singer becomes the song, and the song we sing is the service of God, the salvation of the world. Thus a whole new world is sung into being.

> "See, the home of God is among mortals.
> He will dwell with them;
> they will be his peoples,
> and God himself will be with them."
>
> (Rev. 21:3)

Notes

Introduction

1. H. Richard Niebuhr, *The Purpose of the Church and Its Ministry* (New York: Harper and Bros., 1956), p. 58. Two historians of ministry write, "Catholic and Protestant thought on who should be ordained to do what is better called flexible than coherent. There remain problems for the church and the individual when the vocation is plain but the office is not." Philip L. Culbertson and Arthur B. Shippee, eds., *The Pastor: Readings from the Patristic Period* (Minneapolis: Fortress Press, 1990), p. 137.

2. Charles Williams, *The Descent of the Dove: A History of the Holy Spirit in the Church*, with an introduction by W. H. Auden (New York: Meridian, 1959).

3. A 1994 study of students entering twelve United Methodist seminaries found that "experienced a call from God" was listed by most of the new seminarians (88%) as the main reason for attending seminary (followed by "desire to serve others," "opportunity for study and growth," and "desire to make a difference in the life of the church"). *Fact Book on Theological Education for the Academic Year 1995–1996* (Vandalia, Ohio: Association of Theological Schools in the United States and Canada, 1997), p. 27.

4. T. S. Eliot, *Little Gidding* (London: Faber & Faber, 1942), p. 15.

5. Robert Bellah and his colleagues dramatically demonstrated a culture in the grip of "expressive individualism" in their *Habits of the Heart: Individualism and Commitment in American Life* (Berkeley: University of California Press, 1985).

6. In his research into those clergy who involved themselves in controversial issues and social activism back in the 1970s, Harold Quinley concluded that a strong sense of external authorization, a sense that "I am here because I have been authorized and sent here by God and the church," was a significant source of pastoral courage. *The Prophetic Clergy* (New York: John Wiley & Sons, 1974), pp. 276-77.

7. This image of ministry "from the top down," and "from the bottom up" is a major theme in Edward Schillebeeckx, *Ministry: Leadership in the Community of Jesus Christ* (New York: Crossroad, 1981).

8. Karl Barth says that the Christian life is never "anything but the work of beginners. . . . What Christians do becomes a self-contradiction when it takes the form of a trained and mastered routine, of a learned and practiced art. They may and can be masters and even virtuosos in many things, but never in what makes them Christians, God's children." *The Christian Life: Church Dogmatics IV, 4 Lecture Fragments*, trans. Geoffrey W. Bromiley (Grand Rapids: Eerdmans, 1981), p. 79.

9. *The Book of Discipline of The United Methodist Church* (Nashville: The United Methodist Publishing House, 2000), p. 182. The Evangelical Lutheran Church in

America puts this matter more succinctly: "It is by Christ's gift that all baptized persons are called to ministry. Every baptized believer is given gifts and abilities for ministry. Every baptized believer is called to ministry in daily life. Some are given gifts and abilities which equip them to provide leadership as one of the rostered ministries of this church." *Candidacy Manual for the Evangelical Lutheran Church in America* (Chicago: Division for Ministry, 1995), p. 11.

10. Like King, John Calvin confesses that he was "unpolished and bashful," always loving "the shade and retirement," tending toward "some secluded corner where I might be withdrawn from the public view." Alas, when the Reformation became violent and difficult, he was forced to leave his native land and move to Basil, Switzerland, there to publish his *Institutes*. "Preface to Psalms," in *John Calvin: Selections from His Writings*, John Dillenberger, ed. (Missoula, Mont.: Scholars Press, 1975), pp. 26-28.

11. See Richard Lischer, *The Preacher King: Martin Luther King Jr. and the Word That Moved America* (New York: Oxford University Press, 1995), pp. 72-89.

12. William H. Willimon, *Worship as Pastoral Care* (Nashville: Abingdon Press, 1979), chap. 9.

13. My colleague Jackson W. Carroll believes that I am overly critical in my criticism of the pastor as a "professional." Jack believes in the need for a strong stress upon clerical expertise in his image of ministry as "reflective and critical leadership." I first criticized the professional model in my book with Stanley Hauerwas, *Resident Aliens* (Nashville: Abingdon Press, 1989). For Carroll's criticism of the critique of the professional ministerial image, see his book *As One with Authority: Reflective Leadership in Ministry* (Louisville: Westminster John Knox Press, 1991), p. 210. Obviously, I would not write a book of this length, with so demanding an appeal for competent clergy, if I did not believe that clergy need expertise. However, our expertise is that demanded of the clerical vocation. Vocation is primary; expertise is derivative of what the vocation demands.

14. James Gustafson, "Professions as Callings," *The Social Service Review* 56 (1982): 514. Cited by Carroll in *As One with Authority*, p. 202. For a great critique of professionalism in medicine and law, see Burton J. Bledstein, *The Culture of Professionalism* (New York: W. W. Norton, 1976).

15. Jackson W. Carroll struggles with the pastor's bearing of the tradition of the church, while at the same time wanting to say a good word for those younger churches that Carroll calls "posttraditional." *Mainline to the Future: Congregations for the 21st Century* (Louisville: Westminster John Knox, 2000), pp. 8-17, 58-68.

16. In Carroll's praise of the innovative, culturally sensitive ministry of the new "posttraditional" churches and their invigorating sense of "freedom," I do not think that he is critical enough of the way that these churches sometimes merely exchange one master (the historic Christian faith) for another (American consumerism). *Mainline to the Future*, pp. 80-81.

17. As recounted in Rebekah L. Miles, *The Pastor As Moral Guide* (Minneapolis: Fortress Press, 1999), pp. 12-13.

1. Ordination: Why Pastors?

1. See "Ministry in Judaism," chap. 2 of *A Biblical Basis for Ministry*, Earl E. Shelp and Ronald Sunderland, eds. (Philadelphia: Westminster, 1981).

2. Bernard Cooke, *Ministry to Word and Sacraments: History and Theology* (Philadelphia: Fortress Press, 1976).

3. I have been assisted, in my thought on Hippolytus, by the article of my colleague Geoffrey Wainwright, "Some Theological Aspects of Ordination," *Studia Liturgica* 13, nos. 2-4 (1979): 125-52.

4. Gregory Dix, ed., *The Treatise on the Apostolic Tradition of St. Hippolytus of Rome* (London: SPCK, 1968), pp. 2-6.

5. *Lumen Gentium* from Vatican II unfortunately confused this foundational understanding, suggesting that the ministry of the laity is somehow subservient to that of priests:

> An individual layman, by reason of the knowledge, competence, or outstanding ability which he may enjoy, is permitted and sometimes even obliged to express his opinion on things which concern the good of the Church. When occasions arise, let this be done through the agencies set up by the Church for this purpose. Let it always be done in truth, in courage, and in prudence, with reverence and charity toward those who by reason of their sacred office represent the person of Christ.

The sacredness of this "sacred office" is in its function of upbuilding the church, not in its representation of the person of Christ in some special way that is not inherent in the ministry of all Christians by virtue of their baptism. *Lumen Gentium's* talk of the clergy's special ability to "represent the person of Christ" has had, in my opinion, sad consequences in the Vatican's prohibition of women priests. For a good survey of the historical documents related to women and ministry, see Thomas C. Oden, *Becoming a Minister*, Classical Pastoral Care Series, vol. 1 (New York: Crossroad, 1987), pp. 137-47.

From the first, the church has leaders, not because it requires some special group of Christians to "represent Christ," since baptism makes all Christians into Christ's representatives, but rather because the church needs a designated group of leaders to enable all the baptized to represent Christ to the world.

Lumen Gentium, in *The Documents of Vatican II*, Walter M. Abbott, ed. (New York: Association Press, 1966), p. 64.

6. See the discussion of the second-century developments in *The Study of Liturgy*, C. Jones, G. Wainwright, and E. Yarnold, S.J., eds. (New York: Oxford University Press, 1978), pp. 297-301.

7. P. T. Forsyth, "The Ideal Ministry," *The British Congregationalist*, Oct. 18, 1906. Quoted in David Hansen, *The Art of Pastoring: Ministry Without All the Answers* (Downers Grove, Ill.: Intervarsity Press, 1994), p. 152.

8. See the survey of this period in Roland H. Bainton, "The Ministry in the Middle Ages," in *The Ministry in Historical Perspectives*, H. Richard Niebuhr and Daniel D. Williams, eds. (New York: Harper and Bros., 1956), pp. 82-109.

9. The foundational, ecumenical statement on ministry is that of the World Council of Churches, "Faith and Order Paper 133" (the "Lima Document"), in *Baptism, Eucharist and Ministry* (Geneva: World Council of Churches, 1982), p. 30, which describes ordination as "in the name of Christ by the invocation of the Spirit and the laying on of hands."

10. See Jones, Wainwright, and Yarnold, eds., *The Study of Liturgy*, p. 333.

11. Because I am United Methodist, permit me this rather long excursus on ordination within my own ecclesiastical tradition, which may help place in context my concerns related to ordination.

Methodism, the inheritance of the brothers John and Charles Wesley, may serve as a case of how the Protestant conception of clergy developed—an example of the ways that the image of clergy changed in the centuries after the Reformation.

John Wesley attempted a lay reform movement within the Church of England, a church where he served as priest until his death in the late–eighteenth century. A major aspect of his reform was his use of dedicated lay preachers who were primarily *preachers*. Methodism (early in the movement, Wesley and his friends were called "Methodists" because they stressed certain spiritual disciplines and methods for cultivating the spiritual life) eventually spread as a new church, a new denomination, throughout North America in the period after the American Revolution. Its spread was due primarily to the efforts of Methodist circuit riders, those traveling preachers who were assigned a circuit of communities by a bishop. Some were ordained, some were not. They were, in the words of Methodist historian Franz Hillebrandt, "not so much 'in' orders as 'under' orders." Up until the mid–eighteenth century, the average tenure for active circuit riding ministry was only about ten years. The men could not survive much longer under such rigorous work. The average age at time of death was twenty-nine. If a circuit rider married, he was forced to "locate," to settle down and retire from the traveling ministry.

When the Evangelical United Brethren (a German-American wing of Methodism) called the roll at their Annual Conference, the bishop would ask, "Are you willing to travel this year?" Until the very end of the nineteenth century, two years was the common length of time for a Methodist pastor to serve a church. They were truly Wesley's "traveling preachers."

Throughout the nineteenth century, these traveling preachers looked much alike. They cut their hair in the same fashion. They all wore the same black suits and referred to one another as "brother" and "sister." In 1856, when a neo-Gothic church was built by a Methodist congregation in Pittsburgh, there was a great debate among Methodists concerning the appropriateness of Methodists, who once built simple "chapels" in England, having such a fine edifice. Methodists were thus countercultural in their first century, clearly having their greatest appeal among the lower social classes of society.

Wesley listed as a "means of grace," "Christian conferencing." The Annual Conference was a distinctive aspect of the Methodist itinerating ministry. A pastor became a member of the Annual Conference before being ordained to serve a local church (a practice that still holds true today among the United Methodists). That yearly gathering of pastors in their Annual Conference referred to their church as "the connection." Only pastors were members of the Annual Conference. Pastors were never members of the congregations that they served. Thus the Wesleyan system tended to stress the collegial nature of the ordained ministry, though they had continuing problems linking the pastor's performance to the mission of the congregation. Though in theory Methodist clergy have most control over the clergy while the laity have an equal voice in the actual governance of the church, the polity has tended to become clergy dominated and directed.

Sad to say, Methodism, which began as primarily a lay renewal movement, has tended to have difficulty recognizing the ministry of the laity. Recently these problems have surfaced with the creation of a permanent "diaconate," which is now described as concerned with "justice" and "outreach." But what does this diaconate mean for the ministry of all Christians? Must all Christians be ordained in order to be committed to justice and outreach? Is the creation of this permanent diaconate but a rebirth of the problem of the proliferation of orders that plagued the medieval church, in which every major church function was presided over by a class of ordained persons, with little left for the laity? In my opinion, we United Methodists continue to struggle with the problems of being a lay renewal movement that became a separate church, and continue to struggle with an adequate theology and practice of ordination. See Albert C. Outler, "The Ordinal," in *Companion to the Book of Worship,* W. F. Dunkle Jr. and J. D. Quillian Jr., eds. (Nashville: Abingdon Press, 1970), pp. 103-33. See also Thomas E. Frank, *Polity, Practice, and the Mission of The United Methodist Church* (Nashville: Abingdon Press, 1997).

12. The great liturgical scholar Max Thurian examines four passages in which he finds an embryonic rite of ordination: Acts 6:3-8; Acts 13:1-4; 1 Timothy 4:13; 2 Timothy 1:6, and concludes that the Holy Spirit is "both the master and the criterion" of the church's choice of candidates for ordination. Cited in Wainwright, "Some Theological Aspects of Ordination," p. 142.

13. The image is well developed by Edward Schillebeeckx, *Ministry: Leadership in the Community of Jesus Christ* (New York: Crossroads, 1981).

14. David Bartlett, *Ministry in the New Testament* (Minneapolis: Fortress Press, 1993), p. 187. See also G. W. H. Lampe, *Some Aspects of the New Testament Ministry* (London: SPCK, 1949).

15. "Ordination, thus, is that act by which the Church symbolizes a shared relationship between those ordained for sacramental and functional leadership and the Church community from which the person being ordained has come. The community is initiated by God, is given meaning and direction by Christ, and is sustained by the Holy Spirit. This relationship is a gift which comes through the grace of God in assurance of the ministry of Christ throughout the world" *(The Book of Discipline of the United Methodist Church* [Nashville: The United Methodist Publishing House, 1992], p. 233).

16. See Oden, *Becoming a Minister,* pp. 32-40 for a good discussion of the twofold call of clergy in classical theological literature. See also Thomas C. Oden, *Pastoral Theology: Essentials of Ministry* (San Francisco: HarperSanFrancisco, 1983), chap. 2.

17. H. Richard Niebuhr, *The Purpose of the Church and Its Ministry* (New York: Harper and Bros., 1956), p. 64.

18. Elizabeth Barnes, "Ordination," in *A New Handbook of Christian Theology,* Donald W. Musser and Joseph L. Price, eds. (Nashville: Abingdon Press, 1992), pp. 337-40.

19. Wainwright, "Some Theological Aspects of Ordination," p. 131.

20. The United Methodists, for instance, preserve this collegial selection of clergy where candidates for ordination are presented to the bishop by a clergyperson who notes that they have been examined by the clergy and are presented for admission as clergy.

21. See Jones, Wainwright, and Yarnold, eds. *The Study of Liturgy,* pp. 306-7.

22. Perhaps because United Methodist ordinations tend to be rather "absolute," that is, detached from service to a particular congregation, I find myself questioning the tendency in contemporary thought on ordination to absolutely condemn "absolute ordination." A leader of the church must hold in some tension service to a particular congregation, with a vision of service to the whole church at all times and places. A purely or simply congregationalist approach to ordination could lead the ordained to a too exclusive focus on the good of an individual congregation, even as a truly "absolute ordination" could lead to neglect of the needs of a specific congregation.

23. The rise of monasticism also had an effect on this story. In the earliest period, monks were laypeople, not priests. The Christian community saw them as the deep realization of the ideal Christian. Yet this perspective shifted during the Gregorian reforms. After the church was adopted and enforced by official decree in the fourth century, and everyone born into that culture was baptized, the boundary between the spirit of Christ and the spirit of the world came to lie mainly with the clergy. In various attempts to reform the clergy during the late–Middle Ages, the model for reform became the celibate monk. Monastic attributes were read on to the clergy. On Sundays, I now wear an alb, originally the street attire for Roman men, later the archaic dress of monks. The cincture, the rope around the waist of my alb, is a monastic symbol of celibacy. Whereas the first clergy could marry (witness the instructions to married ministers in First Timothy), now celibacy became the norm. Priests were to be pure, unspotted, and preserved from the moral compromises of ordinary life.

24. Although writers such as Ignatius Loyola taught that the divine call to the priesthood is "immutable," and "always pure and clean without any admixture of flesh or other inordinate attachments," Luther considered the idea of an indelible mark that prohibits a priest from the possibility of ever becoming a layperson "mere talk and man-made law." See Thomas C. Oden, *Ministry Through Word and Sacrament,* Classical Pastoral Care Series, vol. 2 (New York: Crossroad, 1989), p. 19.

25. Martin Luther, "To the Christian Nobility of the German Nation," *Luther's Works,* vol. 44, trans. Charles M. Jacobs and James Atkinson (Philadelphia: Fortress Press, 1966), p. 129.

26. Martin Luther, "Private Mass and the Consecration of Priests, 1533" as cited in Oden, *Becoming a Minister,* p. 82.

27. Martin Luther, "The Babylonian Captivity of the Church," in *Works of Martin Luther,* vol. 2, trans. A. T. W. Steinhaeuser (Philadelphia: Muhlenberg Press, 1943), p. 279.

28. "Homily 6.1 on Isaiah," in *The Pastor: Readings from the Patristic Period*, in Philip L. Cuthbertson and Arthur Bradford Shippee, eds. (Minneapolis: Fortress Press, 1990), p. 38.

29. Augustine, "On Baptism" in *Later Christian Fathers*, H. Bettenson, ed. (London: Oxford University Press, 1970), p. 242.

30. Alexandre Faivre, *The Emergence of the Laity in the Early Church*, trans. David Smith (New York: Paulist Press, 1990).

31. Edward Schillebeeckx says that "the ministry in the church is essentially collegiality, i.e. solidarity of Christians equipped with different charismata of ministry." *Ministry* (New York: Crossroad, 1981), p. 46.

32. Cyprian, "Epistle" 5.4, in *The Ante-Nicene Fathers*, vol. 5, Alexander Roberts and James Donaldson, eds. (New York: Charles Scribner's Sons, 1907), p. 283.

33. Quoted in James F. White, *A Brief History of Christian Worship* (Nashville: Abingdon Press, 1993), p. 133.

34. Wainwright, "Some Theological Aspects of Ordination," p. 129.

35. Luther criticizes certain creative preachers whom he calls merely "ambitious eccentrics" whose creativity tempts them "to teach more than Christ" so that people "cast admiring glances at them and exclaim: What a preacher!" Luther advises to follow the injunction of Paul to "know nothing but Christ and him crucified." See Oden, *Ministry Through Word and Sacrament*, p. 31.

36. "The Drum Major Instinct" (February 4, 1968), in *I Have a Dream: Writings and Speeches That Changed the World*, James Melvin Washington, ed.; foreword by Coretta Scott King (San Francisco: HarperSanFrancisco, 1992), p. 191.

2. Ministry for the Twenty-first Century

1. Fulton J. Sheen, *The Electronic Christian: 105 Readings from Fulton J. Sheen* (New York: Macmillan, 1979).

2. Harry Emerson Fosdick, *The Living of These Days: An Autobiography* (New York: Harper, 1956).

3. William Sloane Coffin, *Once to Every Man: A Memoir* (New York: Atheneum, 1977).

4. Mark Daniel Epstein, *Sister Aimee: The Life of Aimee Semple McPherson* (New York: Harcourt Brace Jovanovich, 1993).

5. Barbara Brown Taylor, *The Preaching Life* (Boston: Cowley Publications, 1993).

6. Reinhold Niebuhr, *Leaves from the Notebook of a Tamed Cynic* (New York: Meridian Books, 1957).

7. Will D. Campbell, *Brother to a Dragonfly* (New York: Seabury Press, 1977).

8. I have preferred to speak of "images" rather than "models" for pastoral work. Models seem inherently reductionistic. Joseph Hough and John Cobb cite four models for the ordained ministry that have been significant at different times in American history: the pre-nineteenth-century "master"; the nineteenth-century "revivalist-pulpiteer"; the "builder" of the late-nineteenth and early-twentieth century who built grand institutions and congregations; and today, the "manager," who merely manages an efficient organization, caring for the felt needs of its members. Hough and Cobb are quite critical of this contemporary image in their

Christian Identity and Theological Education (Atlanta: Scholars Press, 1985). I have previously cited Jackson W. Carroll's favorite image of the pastor as "reflective leader," the one who combines solid expertise with critical, professional theological and sociological reflectiveness. Carroll, *As One with Authority* (Louisville: Westminster John Knox Press, 1991). For an alternative array of images of ministry, see Donald E. Messer, *Contemporary Images of Christian Ministry* (Nashville: Abingdon Press, 1989).

9. Neil Postman, *Amusing Ourselves to Death: Public Discourse in an Age of Show Business* (New York: Penguin Books, 1986), p. 87.

10. See Martin E. Marty, *The Public Church* (New York: Crossroad, 1981); also James W. Fowler, *Faith Development and Pastoral Care* (Philadelphia: Fortress Press, 1987).

11. J. Philip Wogaman, *Eye of the Storm: A Pastor to the President Speaks Out* (Louisville: Westminster John Knox Press, 1999).

12. See the article on "court preachers" *Concise Encyclopedia of Preaching,* William H. Willimon and Richard Lischer, eds. (Louisville: Westminster John Knox, 1995) pp. 91-93.

13. On the peculiarity of Christian "politics," see chap. 2 of Stanley M. Hauerwas and William H. Willimon, *Resident Aliens: Life in the Christian Colony* (Nashville: Abingdon Press, 1989).

14. See the article on Fosdick's "life situation preaching" in Willimon and Lischer, eds., *Concise Encyclopedia of Preaching,* p. 362.

15. I hope that John Updike was overstating the flaws of seminary in his novel *Roger's Version* (New York: Knopf, 1986) when he had a professor describe what happens to students in seminary: "We get students who are like cabbages—plump, moist, fragrant with the earthiness of an eager faith. By the time we are through with them they are like cole slaw—chopped, diced, sliced and dripping in a sweet and awful dressing." Quoted in Martin B. Copenhaver, Anthony B. Robinson, and William H. Willimon, *Good News in Exile: Three Pastors Offer a Hopeful Vision for the Church* (Grand Rapids: Eerdmans, 1999), p. 84.

16. Thomas Frank notes that the popular Swiss theologian of the 1950s, Emil Brunner, wrote that the Body of Christ "has nothing to do with an organization and has nothing of the character of the institutional about it." And when they translated the Bible, Luther and Tyndale would not even use the word "church" *(Kirche),* but preferred "congregation" *(Gemeinde),* in order to distance themselves from the institutional church. Thomas E. Frank, *The Soul of the Congregation* (Nashville: Abingdon Press, 2000), p. 39.

17. I have been impressed by how many pastors are reading books such as Kenneth H. Blanchard's, *One Minute Manager* (New York: William Morrow, 1982), a book that reduces the vocation of administration to a one-minute technique.

18. Lyle E. Schaller, *Growing Plans* (Nashville: Abingdon Press, 1983), p. 93.

19. E. Brooks Holifield, *The Gentlemen Theologians* (Durham, N.C.: Duke University Press, 1978). See also Holifield, *A History of Pastoral Care in America: From Salvation to Self-Realization* (Nashville: Abingdon Press, 1983).

20. Charles V. Gerkin, *An Introduction to Pastoral Care* (Nashville: Abingdon Press, 1997), p. 37.

21. I realize that I have used the word "pontificate" to describe the demeanor of some social activist pastors. The word comes from the Latin, *pontifex*, literally "bridge builder." The Pope is *pontifex maximus*. Certainly, part of a pastor's calling is to be a bridge builder between the church and the surrounding community. The issue is not, Should a pastor relate to the secular community? The issue is, *How?*

22. Richard Baxter wisely advises that "flocks must ordinarily be *no greater than we are capable of overseeing.* . . . If the pastoral office consists in overseeing all the flock, then surely the number of souls under the care of each pastor must not be greater than he is able to take such heed as is here required." *The Reformed Pastor* (New York: American Tract Society, 1850), p. 136.

23. Leander Keck, *The Bible and the Pulpit: The Renewal of Biblical Preaching* (Nashville: Abingdon Press, 1978).

24. Robert K. Greenleaf, *Servant Leadership: A Journey into the Nature of Legitimate Power and Greatness* (New York: Paulist Press, 1977). See also Robert K. Greenleaf, *The Servant as Leader* (Indianapolis: The Robert K. Greenleaf Center, 1991).

25. Susan Nelson Dunfee, *Beyond Servanthood: Christianity and the Liberation of Women* (Lanham, Md.: University Press of America, 1989).

26. Edward C. Zaragoza, *No Longer Servants But Friends: A Theology of Ordained Ministry* (Nashville: Abingdon Press, 1999). Some of Zaragoza's criticisms of servant leadership seem unfair and overdrawn. He tends to take liberationist criticism of the image more seriously than the biblical, countercultural basis of the servant metaphor. His advocacy of the image of pastor as "friend" is undeveloped and seemingly unaware of the particular difficulties involved in friendship as a metaphor for ministry. One of the most beautiful and thoughtful expositions on ministry as friendship is by Ambrose in his *Duties of the Clergy*, book 3, sec. 131-35, in *A Select Library of the Nicene and Post-Nicene Fathers of the Christian Church*, 2nd series, H. Wace and P. Schaff eds. (New York: Christian Literature, 1887–1900).

27. Dorothy Day, *The Long Loneliness* (San Francisco: HarperSanFrancisco, 1980).

28. Maria Harris as quoted by Lovett H. Weems Jr., *Leadership in the Wesleyan Spirit* (Nashville: Abingdon Press, 1999), p. 36. See also Letty M. Russell, *Human Liberation in a Feminist Perspective: A Theology* (Philadelphia: Westminster Press, 1974).

29. Robert Banks thinks that all preparation for ministry today ought to be reorganized around a "missional" paradigm. See his *Revisioning Theological Education: Exploring a Missional Alternative to Current Models* (Grand Rapids: Eerdmans, 1999).

30. See Darrell L. Guder, ed., *Missional Church: A Vision for the Sending of the Church in North America* (Grand Rapids: Eerdmans, 1998), and George R. Hunsberger and Craig Van Gelder, eds., *The Church Between Gospel and Culture: The Emerging Mission in North America* (Grand Rapids: W. B. Eerdmans, 1996). The foundational book for this new missionary reading of the church in the industrialized West was Lesslie Newbigin, *Foolishness to the Greeks: The Gospel and Western Culture* (Grand Rapids: Eerdmans, 1986).

31. The realization that the church is in a very different cultural situation, calling forth a renewed emphasis upon the classical duties of pastors, especially the duty of catechesis, runs throughout the essays in David S. Schuller, ed., *Rethinking*

Christian Education: Explorations in Theory and Practice (St. Louis: Chalice Press, 1993).

32. When H. Richard Niebuhr proposed the image of "pastoral director" in his classic book on ministry, too many heard this as a baptism of the big operator style of pastoral leadership—a secularized manager. Niebuhr had in mind the monastic spiritual director who was responsible for community formation and direction, the classical *episcopos*, or shepherd who was overseer. *The Purpose of the Church and Its Ministry* (New York: Harper and Bros., 1956).

33. Jackson W. Carroll, *As One with Authority: Reflective Leadership in Ministry*, p. 53.

3. The Pastor as Priest

1. Marva J. Dawn, *A Royal "Waste" of Time: The Splendor of Worshiping God and Being the Church for the World* (Grand Rapids: Eerdmans, 1999).

2. Martin Luther, *Small Catechism* (New York: Concordia, 1943), p. 123, from Luther's explanation of the third article of the Apostles' Creed.

3. From Bard Thompson, ed., *Liturgies of the Western Church* (Philadelphia: Fortress Press, 1980), p. 9.

4. Robert Webber encourages congregations of any denomination to follow a historic fourfold worship pattern that is quite similar to that of Justin Martyr: gathering, Word, thanksgiving, dismissal. The noteworthy thing about this pattern, says Webber, is that it moves us somewhere. "The fourfold pattern of worship is characterized by a narrative quality because it is taking us someplace (the throne room of God's kingdom)." *Planning Blended Worship: Achieving Substance and Relevance in Worship* (Peabody, Mass.: Hendrickson, 1996), pp. 20-21.

5. *The United Methodist Hymnal: Book of United Methodist Worship* (Nashville: The United Methodist Publishing House, 1989), p. 10.

6. Thomas G. Long, after studying a group of vibrant churches, says he found the following characteristics in the congregational life and worship of faithful congregations who:

- Make room, somewhere in worship, for the experience of mystery.
- Are very intentional about showing hospitality to the stranger.
- Have recovered and made visible the sense of drama inherent in Christian worship.
- Emphasize congregational music that is both excellent and eclectic in style and genre.
- Creatively adapt the space and environment of worship.
- Have a strong connection between worship and local mission, and this connection is expressed in every aspect of the worship service.
- Have a relatively stable order of service and a significant repertoire of worship elements and responses that the congregation knows by heart.
- Move to a joyous festival experience toward the end of the worship service.
- Have strong, charismatic pastors and worship leaders.

I think this is a great list, though it does not, in the manner that Long manages in his book, emphasize vital worship as a theological event, a gift of a Christ who seems to enjoy revealing himself to those who dare on Sunday to expose themselves to him. As Long says, "worship is about awe, not strategy." See Thomas G. Long, *Beyond the Worship Wars: Building Vital and Faithful Worship* (Washington, D.C.: Alban Institute, 2001), pp. 30-31.

7. Karl Barth, *Church Dogmatics*, 4.1, G. W. Bromiley and T. F. Torrance, eds. (Edinburgh: T & T Clark, 1956), p. 415.

8. Many of us mainline Protestants began worrying about our membership losses with the publication of Dean Kelly's *Why Conservative Churches Are Growing* (New York: Harper & Row, 1977). Kelly's thesis was not simply that conservative churches were growing because they were strict and conservative (although their relatively high demands upon their members was a positive growth factor), but rather because these churches kept themselves energetically focused on the main business of religion—making meaning for their members. When churches become distracted, seeing themselves as just another volunteer service organization or one more friendly social club, they decline. The business of churches, said Kelly, is meaning in God.

A book by C. Kirk Hadaway and David A. Roozen, *Rerouting the Protestant Mainstream: Sources of Growth and Opportunities for Change* (Nashville: Abingdon Press, 1995), showed the fruit of decades of studies of church growth and decline. As their title shows, Hadaway and Roozen, two distinguished observers of the mainline church, tried to get beyond analysis and more toward positive prescription.

We live in a buyer's market, as far as religion is concerned, say Hadaway and Roozen. And that's not completely bad. Having had a virtual monopoly on American religious life, today's mainline Protestants must now adapt to a consumeristic culture where people shop for a church, where people demand quality, and where people drop their church if it doesn't meet their demands.

Too often those demands are identified as an upbeat worship service, a clean nursery, a big parking lot—which are important factors. However, Hadaway and Roozen highlight a demand that echoes some of Kelly's earlier claims. They say that, when all the factors are studied, "the key issue for churches seems to be a compelling *religious* character . . . not whether the content of that character is liberal or conservative" (p. 69).

In other words, Kelly was right in insisting that it is not so much that conservative churches are conservative, it is that they stick to the business of providing a theological rationale for people's lives. They keep focusing on God.

Earlier, I had said that mainline Protestantism was in trouble because we provided people with the theological rationale not to go to church. We gave them "a theology of secularity." Hadaway and Roozen seem to agree. Church cannot be a sanctified form of Rotary. We must clearly, intentionally, relentlessly be determined to be a place where we meet God, and God in Jesus Christ meets us.

Hadaway and Roozen are explicit: "To grow and to continue growing, it is necessary for each mainstream church to become a vital *religious* institution, vibrant with the presence of God. It must develop a clear *religious* identity, a compelling *religious* purpose, and a coherent sense of direction that arises from that identity and purpose" (p. 86).

A strong sense of identity and a compelling vision are the two essential characteristics for a vibrant congregation. Hadaway and Roozen are critical of Kelly and others who believe that high demands, conservative theology, or strict expectations are the key. The key is theological.

We desperately need theological leaders, say Hadaway and Roozen, who are dissatisfied with decline, who refuse to bow to sociological determinism, who emphasize the distinctive, spiritual, God dimensions of church. Church growth is not the point. The point is vital witness, in word and deed, to the presence of God in our midst. We must get over our liberal dis-ease with the theological rationale for the church. Hadaway and Roozen accuse us of a "don't-ask-don't-tell" policy in regard to God. We replaced "the intensity of religious experience for reasoned civility" (p. 127).

When John Wesley's preachers returned to him enthusiastically speaking of the great numbers at their meetings, of how well people received their sermons, of how many people got a spiritual high, he loved finally to ask them, "But did you offer Christ?" Our great vocation as preachers is not to offer rules for better living, helpful hints for homemakers, or guidelines for self-esteem. We are to help the church be with God.

9. Urban Holmes calls the priest the *theotokos*, the "God-bearer" or "mystagogue," who bears the divine into all human encounters. Holmes built an entire theology of pastoral ministry around the image of pastor as "mystagogue." Urban T. Holmes III, *The Priest in Community: Exploring the Roots of Ministry* (New York: Seabury Press, 1978).

10. In his wonderful book on liturgical leadership, Robert Hovda says, "People need to be made to feel at home . . . without surrendering the worship character of the assembly. It is not merely another gathering, and the space must speak of transcendence as well as welcome." *Robert Hovda: The Amen Corner*, John F. Baldovin, ed. (Collegeville, Minn.: Liturgical Press, 1994), p. 140.

4. The Priest as Pastor

1. Walter Brueggemann, *To Pluck Up and to Tear Down: Jeremiah 1–25* (Grand Rapids: Eerdmans, 1988).

2. See John J. Pilch, *Healing in the New Testament: Insights from Medical and Medieval Anthropology* (Minneapolis: Fortress Press, 2000), for a contrast between "illness" and "disease" in the biblical context.

3. Philip Rieff, *The Triumph of the Therapeutic: Uses of Faith After Freud* (Chicago: University of Chicago Press, 1987), and also Christopher Lasch, *The Culture of Narcissism: American Life in an Age of Diminishing Expectation* (New York: W. W. Norton, 1978). I have always loved Lasch's subtitle. Our problem, from a specifically Christian point of view (according to C. S. Lewis in his *The Weight of Glory* [London: SPCK, 1942]), is not that we desire too much, but that we want too little. We no longer long to be saved; we only want to feel a bit better. We no longer expect a new world; we only hope to be better adjusted to the present world.

4. Robert Bellah, et al., *Habits of the Heart: Individualism and Commitment in American Life* (Berkeley: University of California Press, 1985).

5. Richard Osmer laments the dominance of what he calls a "pastoral ecclesiology" in which pastors forsake their theologically bestowed leadership functions in favor of "an understanding of the church in which the congregation is viewed primarily as a supportive, nurturing community that assists people in times of crisis and forms programs to meet their needs." See Osmer, "Three 'Futuribles' for the Mainline Church," in *Rethinking Christian Education,* David S. Schuller, ed. (St. Louis: Chalice Press, 1993), p. 128.

6. Flannery O'Connor, *The Habit of Being,* Sally Fitzgerald, ed. (New York: Farrar, Straus & Giroux, 1979), p. 81. One pastor told me that in much of his ministry, "I feel like a Saint Bernard. I go out in the storm to somebody stuck in the snow. All I've got to help them with is a swig of beer and some sympathy. Somebody more effective than I will have to pull them out of the snow."

7. In all these comments, I agree with Eugene Peterson's assessment that in our age, "much of the church's leadership is neither pastoral nor theological. The pastoral dimensions of the church's leadership are badly eroded by technologizing and managerial influences. The theological dimensions of the church's leadership have been marginalized by therapeutic and marketing preoccupations. The gospel work of giving leadership to the community of the Christian faithful has been alienated from its source." Eugene Peterson and Marva Dawn, *The Unnecessary Pastor: Rediscovering the Call* (Grand Rapids: Eerdmans, 2000), pp. 60-61.

8. Quoted in David Fisher, *The 21st Century Pastor* (Grand Rapids: Zondervan, 1996), p. 215.

9. Luther speaks of the "miserable man who is dependent on the help of doctors." Although Luther says he does not deny that "medicine is a gift of God and a science," he counters that "a good diet is of great value." Luther, "Table Talk" in *What Luther Says,* vol. 3, E. Plass, ed. (St. Louis: Concordia, 1959), p. 1287.

10. Jerome, "Letter 52," in *The Pastor: Readings from the Patristic Period,* Philip L. Culbertson and Arthur B. Shippee, eds. (Minneapolis: Fortress Press, 1990), p. 160.

11. Seward Hiltner, *Preface to Pastoral Theology* (Nashville: Abingdon Press, 1979; reprint of 1956 edition).

12. Hiltner's image of the "shepherd" has considerably less content than that image as it appears in Scripture. An ancient Syrian pastor, Aphrahat, in his "Demonstration 10: On Pastors," notes how many leaders of Israel first made their living as shepherds:

> 1. Pastors are set over the flock, and give the sheep the food of life. Whosoever is watchful and toils in behalf of the sheep, is careful for the flock, and is the disciple of our Good Shepherd, who gave himself in behalf of his sheep. And whosoever brings not back the flock carefully, is likened to the hireling who has no care for the sheep. Be like, O pastors, those righteous pastors of old. Jacob fed the sheep of Laban, and guarded them and toiled and was watchful, and so received the reward. For Jacob said to Laban, "Lo! twenty years am I with you. Your sheep and your flocks I have not robbed and the males of your sheep I have not

eaten. That which was broken I did not bring to you, but you required it at my hands! In the daytime the heat devoured me and the cold by night. My sleep departed from my eyes." Observe, you pastors, that pastor, how he cared for his flock. He used to watch in the nighttime to guard it and was vigilant; and he used to toil in the daytime to feed it. As Jacob was a pastor, so Joseph was a pastor and his brethren were pastors. Moses was a pastor, and David also was a pastor. So Amos was a pastor. These all were pastors who fed the sheep and led them well.

2. Now, why, my beloved, did these pastors first feed the sheep, and were then chosen to be pastors of people? Clearly that they might learn how a pastor cares for the sheep, and is watchful and toils in behalf of the sheep. And when they had learned the manners of pastors, they were chosen for the pastoral office. Jacob fed the sheep of Laban and toiled and was vigilant and led them well; and then he tended and guided well his sons, and taught them the pattern of pastoral work. And Joseph used to tend the sheep along with his brethren; and in Egypt he became guide to a numerous people, and led them back, as a good pastor does his flock. Moses fed the sheep of Jethro, his father-in-law, and he was chosen from (tending) the sheep to tend his people, and as a good pastor he guided them.

Culbertson and Shippee, eds. *The Pastor,* p. 97. See also Thomas C. Oden, *Pastoral Theology: Essentials of Ministry* (San Francisco: HarperSanFrancisco, 1983), pp. 49-63 on "shepherding as pivotal analogy" for pastoral ministry.

13. See Carl Rogers, *Client-Centered Therapy* (Boston: Houghton Mifflin, 1951), pp. 219-25.

14. John Calvin, *Calvin: Institutes of the Christian Religion,* 1.6.1, John T. McNeill, ed., *The Library of Christian Classics,* vol. 20 (Philadelphia: Westminster Press, 1960).

15. Don S. Browning, *The Moral Context of Pastoral Care* (Philadelphia: Westminster Press, 1976); see also Browning's *Religious Ethics and Pastoral Care* (Philadelphia: Fortress Press, 1983).

16. Browning, *Moral Context,* p. 109.

17. Thomas Aquinas, *Summa Theologica,* vol. 2, pt. II-II, Q. 32, art. 1, English Dominican Fathers, eds. (New York: Benziger, 1947-48), p. 1325.

18. Wayne Meeks, *The Origins of Christian Morality: The First Two Centuries* (New Haven: Yale University Press, 1993), p. 110.

19. See the discussion of the importance of pastoral visitation in Thomas C. Oden, *Crisis Ministries,* Classical Pastoral Care Series, vol. 4 (New York: Crossroad, 1986), pp. 26-29.

20. Richard Baxter, *The Reformed Pastor* (New York: American Tract Society, 1850), p. 255.

21. Jeremy Taylor, in *The Curate of Souls,* John R. H. Moorman, ed. (London: SPCK, 1958), pp. 22-23.

22. Although their theology may be difficult to recognize from a traditional church perspective, Karen Lebacqz and Joseph D. Driskill are concerned with

moving beyond an exclusive focus on counseling to greater stress on a more wholistic and theological "spiritual care." See their *Ethics and Spiritual Care: A Guide for Pastors, Chaplains, and Spiritual Directors* (Nashville: Abingdon Press, 2000).

23. Donna Schaper says that a pastor ought to spend more time preparing the congregation to care, rather than doing all of the care. *Common Sense About Men and Women in the Ministry* (Washington, D.C.: Alban Institute, 1990), p. 24.

24. See Kenneth C. Haugk, *Christian Caregiving: A Way of Life* (Minneapolis: Augsburg Press, 1984).

25. The possibilities and pitfalls of the small group movement have been extensively examined by Robert Wuthnow, *The Restructuring of American Religion* (Princeton, N.J.: Princeton University Press, 1988).

26. See what Richard Sennett calls our "tyranny of intimacy" in his *The Fall of Public Man* (New York: Knopf, 1976).

5. The Pastor as Interpreter of Scripture

1. To the list should also be added lawyers and computer programmers, but who among them reads closely in order to be changed by their reading?

2. Philip H. Pfatteicher, *The School of the Church: Worship and Christian Formation* (Valley Forge: Trinity Press International, 1995), p. 84, says that "the point is not to have a Bible and a liturgy that say what we mean, but to have a Bible and a liturgy that require us to mean what they say."

3. "Westminster Confession," in *Creeds of the Churches*, John Leith, ed. (Richmond, Va.: John Knox Press, 1973), p. 193.

4. Walter Brueggemann, in *The Church as Counterculture*, Michael L. Budde and W. Brimlow, eds. (Albany: The State University of New York Press, 2000), p. 53.

5. David H. Kelsey, *The Uses of Scripture in Recent Theology* (Philadelphia: Fortress Press, 1975), p. 90.

6. Stanley M. Hauerwas and William H. Willimon, *Resident Aliens: Life in the Christian Colony* (Nashville: Abingdon Press, 1989), p. 46.

7. Walter Brueggemann, *Theology of the Old Testament: Testimony, Dispute, Advocacy* (Minneapolis: Fortress Press, 1997).

8. "When there is a question about the true and full sense of any Scripture (which is not manifold, but one), it must be searched and known by other places that speak more clearly. The Supreme Judge, by which all controversies of religion are to be determined, and all decrees of councils, opinions of ancient writers, doctrines of men, and private spirits, are to be examined, and in whose sentence we are to rest, can be no other but the Holy Spirit speaking in the Scripture." "Westminster Confession," in Leith, *Creeds of the Churches*, p. 196.

9. Martin Luther, "An Order of Mass and Communion for the Church at Wittenberg" (1523), *Luther's Works*, vol. 53, Ulrich S. Leupold, ed. (Philadelphia: Fortress Press, 1965), p. 19.

10. See David Bartlett's excellent critique of historical criticism, from a homiletical point of view, in *Between the Bible and the Church: New Methods for Biblical Interpretation* (Nashville: Abingdon Press, 1999), pp. 138-51.

11. The image of our work "in front of the text" is from Paul Ricoeur. See Bartlett's discussion of Ricoeur in *Between the Bible and the Church*, pp. 39-40.

12. Robert Alter, *The World of Biblical Literature* (New York: Basic Books, 1991), p. 91.

13. Biblical fundamentalism and literalism certainly owes more to modernity and its lust for absolute certain knowledge than to classical Christian modes of interpretation. See John W. Yolton, *John Locke and the Way of Ideas* (Oxford: Oxford University Press, 1956), for a striking presentation of the way modern interpretive modes of certitude were born.

14. David Bartlett says, "When we are in conversation with Scripture, Scripture is still the senior partner in that conversation." *Between the Bible and the Church*, p. 13.

15. Robert McAfee Brown, *Unexpected News: Reading the Bible with Third World Eyes* (Philadelphia: Westminster Press, 1984), pp. 13-14.

16. Erich Auerbach, *Mimesis: The Representation of Reality in Western Literature*, Willard R. Trask, trans. (Princeton: Princeton University Press, 1968), p. 118.

17. Karl Barth, *The Epistle to the Romans* (London: Oxford University Press, 1960), p. 122.

18. Stanley Hauerwas reminds us that it is a fundamental Christian claim that the language of Scripture actually envisages the world as it is. *Vision and Virtue* (Notre Dame: University of Notre Dame Press, 1974), p. 46.

19. William C. Placher, "Is the Bible True?" *The Christian Century* 112 (Oct. 11, 1995): 924-28.

20. Origen, in a sermon on the book of Numbers, asked what good it would do us if we knew the precise place where the children of Israel encamped in the wilderness. "What use would that be to me, or what progress could it afford to those who read and mediate on the Law of God day and night?" Homily XXVII on Numbers, quoted by Thomas C. Oden in *Ministry Through Word and Sacrament*, Classical Pastoral Care Series, vol. 2 (New York: Crossroad, 1989), p. 49.

21. Peter J. Gomes, *The Good Book: Reading the Bible with Mind and Heart* (Boston: Bard, 1998). Walter Brueggemann says that one of our pastoral roles is "nurturing folk into new metaphors." "Covenanting as Human Vocation," *Interpretation* 33 (1979): 115-29.

22. Walter Brueggemann, in his *Old Testament Theology: Testimony, Dispute, Advocacy* (Minneapolis: Fortress Press, 1997).

23. Flannery O'Connor, *Mystery and Manners*, Sally and Robert Fitzgerald, eds. (New York: Farrar, Straus & Giroux, 1961), pp. 111-13. Karl Barth noted that the watchword of the Enlightenment, a product of Kant, was *Sapere aude!* that is, "dare to understand," or as Barth put it, have the courage to use your own understanding with a determination not to be instructed by anyone else. I agree with Barth that it is precisely this Enlightenment-engendered stress upon understanding as exclusively self-understanding that is the greatest impediment to modern interpretation of Scripture. Karl Barth, *Protestant Thought: From Rousseau to Ritschl* (London: SCM Press, 1959), p. 152.

24. As Barth says, "Scriptural exegesis rests on the assumption that the message which Scripture has to give us, even in its apparently most debatable and least

assimilable parts, is in all circumstances truer and more important than the best and most necessary things that we ourselves have said or can say." *Church Dogmatics,* 1.2, G. W. Bromiley and T. F. Torrance, eds. (Edinburgh: T & T Clark, 1956), p. 719.

25. My friend Stanley Hauerwas would subordinate Scripture to the church, or at least contend that Scripture must be read in the manner that it was created— communally, corporately. I agree with him to a point. See his *Unleashing the Scripture: Freeing the Bible from Captivity to America* (Nashville: Abingdon Press, 1993). Yet as a preacher, I have too often experienced Scripture as something set against the church to exchange my Protestant *sola scriptura* for his *sola ecclesia.* With Calvin, I see the institution as subordinate to the text and interpreted by the text, not vice versa. See Wesley A. Kort's review of Calvin on this in his *Take, Read: Scripture, Textuality, and Cultural Practice* (University Park: Pennsylvania State University Press, 1996), chap. 1. Some postmodern critics have stressed the way in which we readers project and insinuate ourselves onto the text. True, eisegesis is always a risk of any reading. Yet I am impressed, as a preacher, with the sheer otherness of the biblical text and the way the text keeps assaulting the church. The major proponent of this reader-dominated theory of reading, and a major influence on Hauerwas at this point, is Stanley Fish, *Is There a Text in This Class? The Authority of Interpretive Communities* (Cambridge: Harvard University Press, 1980).

26. Barth, *Church Dogmatics,* 1.2, p. 718.

27. George Lindbeck, *The Nature of Doctrine: Religion and Theology in a Postliberal Age* (Philadelphia: Westminster Press, 1984), p. 118. "To become a Christian involves learning the story of Israel and Jesus well enough to interpret and experience oneself and one's world in its terms" (p. 34).

28. David Bartlett also praises African American preachers for their unashamed use of typology in their biblical interpretation and preaching. Typology sees one figure of Scripture (Moses) as prefiguring another (Jesus). Typology has received much criticism from modern biblical critics, but it has an honored tradition and may be an imaginative means of the church's proclamation of Scripture. *Between the Bible and the Church,* p. 31.

29. Jackson W. Carroll notes how many of the rapidly growing fundamentalist churches quite explicitly attempt to form an all-encompassing world for their members with a plethora of small groups, weekly activities, and recreational and educational opportunities that offer members a coherent and alternative world to that of their lives outside the church. *Mainline to the Future: Congregations for the 21st Century* (Louisville: Westminster John Knox, 2000), pp. 21-25. Carroll is critical of the way that the alternative world of the fundamentalist churches sometimes provides an escape for their members. The alternative world of the church has as its function the transformation of the world rather than escape from it.

30. John Calvin, *Calvin: Institutes of the Christian Religion,* John T. McNeill, ed., *The Library of Christian Classics,* vol. 20 (Philadelphia: Westminster Press, 1960), 1.61 and 1.14.1.

31. Auerbach, *Mimesis,* pp. 14-15.

32. Walter Brueggemann, *Interpretation and Obedience: From Faithful Reading to Faithful Living* (Minneapolis: Fortress Press, 1992).

33. As cited by Richard Baxter in *The Reformed Pastor* (New York: American Tract Society, 1850), p. 120.

34. Karl Barth, "The Doctrine of Reconciliation," in *Church Dogmatics*, 4.2, G. W. Bromiley, trans. (Edinburgh: T & T Clark, 1958), pp. 124-25.

35. Hans Urs von Balthasar has said that a saint's whole life can be seen as the living out of just one little verse of Scripture to the fullest. Noted in David F. Ford, *The Shape of Living: Spiritual Directions for Everyday Life* (Grand Rapids: Baker Books, 1997), p. 74.

36. Jean Leclercq, O.S.B., *The Love of Learning and the Desire for God: A Study of Monastic Culture*, Catharine Misrahi, trans. (New York: Fordham University Press, 1961). Erasmus says that we ought to prepare for Scripture reading as if preparing ourselves for a meal, "with washed hands, that is, with the greatest purity of mind." "The Handbook of the Christian Soldier" (Enchiridion militis christiani) in *Collected Works of Erasmus*, John W. O'Malley, ed. (Toronto: University of Toronto Press, 1988), 66:34.

37. Jerome, "Letter 52," in Philip L. Culbertson and Arthur B. Shippee, eds., *The Pastor: Readings from the Patristic Period* (Minneapolis: Fortress Press, 1990), pp. 154-55. In the Liturgy of the Hours, there is a petition: "Wisdom of God, be with me, always at work in me."

38. Thus Luther says that the test of our ministry is "not whether many or few people believe or do not believe, are damned or saved," but rather fidelity to the Word of God. As cited in *Sermon on Matthew*, vol. 3, E. Plass, ed. (St. Louis: Concordia, 1959), p. 1208.

39. Michael Casey, *Sacred Reading: The Ancient Art of Lectio Divina* (Liguori, Mo.: Triumph Books, 1996). See also, John S. Dunne, *Reading the Gospel* (Notre Dame, Ind.: University of Notre Dame Press, 2000).

40. Barbara Brown Taylor, *The Preaching Life* (Cambridge, Mass.: Cowley Publications, 1993), p. 47.

41. The Interlude is adapted from William H. Willmon, "Postmodern Preaching: Learning to Love the Thickness of the Text," *Journal for Preachers* 19, no. 3 (Easter 1996): 32-37.

42. I suppose it was Wittgenstein who was among the first modern to notice that biblical texts appear to be almost intentionally opaque. Why is it that the biblical authors want to communicate, yet also want to be difficult? Might it be that the authors want to do something to the texts' readers (hearers) through the very difficulty of the texts? Ludwig Wittgenstein, *Culture and Value*, G. H. Von Wright, ed., trans. Peter Winch (Oxford: Blackwell, 1980).

43. G. K. Chesterton, *Orthodoxy* (London: John Lane, 1908), p. 151.

44. See Walter Brueggemann's wonderful, "Preaching As Reimagination," *Theology Today* 52 (October 1995): 313-29, for a wonderfully concise rendering of his continuing quarrel with historical criticism.

45. In his now notorious defense of historical criticism in *The Interpreter's Dictionary of the Bible*, vol. 1 (Nashville: Abingdon Press, 1962), p. 431, Krister Stendahl contended that we preachers must answer to the objective, dispassionate, honest work of the not-necessarily-believing-anything "descriptive biblical theologian." Fortunately, James Sanders corrected Stendahl's hermeneutical

naïveté in his article "Hermeneutics" in *The Interpreter's Dictionary of the Bible: The Supplementary Volume* (Nashville: Abingdon Press, 1976), pp. 402-7, in which Sanders drops the pretense to scientific objectivity, urging us to approach the text with humility and humor.

46. Susan Handelman's *The Slayers of Moses* (Albany: State University of New York Press, 1982) praises the traditional rabbinical methods of biblical interpretation that relished the endlessness of interpretive possibilities and that loved certain biblical texts precisely because they were so impervious to "right" readings.

47. William C. Placher, *Narratives of a Vulnerable God: Christ, Theology and Scripture* (Louisville: Westminster John Knox Press, 1995), p. 88.

48. Alas, much of the "hermeneutics of suspicion," particularly the type practiced by feminists such as Elisabeth Schüssler Fiorenza [*In Memory of Her: A Feminist Theological Reconstruction of Christian Origins* (New York: Crossroad, 1983)], is not nearly suspicious enough of its own subservience to the epistemologies of the Enlightenment. A reductionistic reading of texts in favor of "liberation" or some other unifying prior principle can be an unwarranted coercion of the odd voice of the text. It is easier to see the cultural conditioning of the text than to acknowledge our own.

49. Placher recalls the remarkable story of Bishop Theodoret's suppression (A.D. 423) of Tatian's *Diatessaron*. The book was Tatian's attempt to harmonize the four Gospels into one. Despite the way Theodoret went about it, the bishop was right in defending the diversity and difficulty of interpretation represented by our having four Gospels rather than one (*Narratives of a Vulnerable God*, pp. 86-87).

50. Frank Kermode, *The Genesis of Secrecy: On the Interpretation of Narrative* (Cambridge, Mass.: Harvard University Press, 1979), pp. 49-73.

51. I believe that something like this is being claimed by Donald McCullough in his diatribe against the way in which modern American Christianity tends to deflate and dishonor the holiness of God. *The Trivialization of God: The Dangerous Illusion of a Manageable Deity* (Colorado Springs: NavPress, 1995).

52. See David J. Bryant, *Faith and the Play of Imagination: On the Role of Imagination in Religion* (Macon: Mercer University Press, 1989).

53. Surely this is what Luther meant by his otherwise absurd claim that, "he who has only one word of the Word of God and cannot preach a whole sermon on the basis of this one word is not worthy ever to preach." Scripture is, by its nature, so thick that just one word of it can provide the preacher all that is needed for a whole sermon! *What Luther Says*, vol. 3, E. Plass, ed. (St. Louis: Concordia, 1959), p. 1110.

6. The Pastor as Preacher

1. Luther says that the preacher "should not be silent or mumble, but testify without being frightened or bashful. He should speak out candidly without regarding or sparing anyone, let it strike whomever or whatever it will. It is a great hindrance to a preacher if he looks around and worries about what people like or do not like to hear." "The Sermon on the Mount," in *Luther's Works*, vol. 21, J. Pelikan and H. T. Lehmann, eds. (St. Louis: Concordia, 1967), p. 9. Luther recalls

that Ambrosius, after admonishing his congregation to come hear a good sermon, was told, "The truth is, dear pastor, that if you were to tap a keg of beer in church and call us to enjoy it, we would be glad to come." Quoted in Thomas C. Oden, *Ministry Through Word and Sacrament*, Classical Pastoral Care Series, vol. 2 (New York: Crossroad, 1989), p. 32.

2. Søren Kierkegaard, *Provocations: Spiritual Writings of Kierkegaard*, Charles E. Moore, ed. (Farmington, Pa.: The Plough Publishing House, 1999), p. 35.

3. This section is indebted to Wilhelm Pauck, "The Ministry at the Time of the Continental Reformation," in *Ministry in Historical Perspectives*, H. Richard Niebuhr and Daniel D. Williams, eds. (New York: Harper and Bros., 1956), pp. 110-48.

4. As quoted in Wilhelm Pauck, "The Ministry in the Time of the Continental Reformation," in *The Ministry in Historical Perspectives*, p. 110.

5. Ibid., 114.

6. As expressed in the Helvetica Posterior.

7. Thomas G. Long, *The Witness of Preaching* (Louisville: Westminster John Knox, 1989), p. 45.

8. Leander E. Keck, *The Bible in the Pulpit* (Nashville: Abingdon Press, 1978).

9. Dietrich Bonhoeffer, *Life Together* (New York: Harper and Bros., 1954), pp. 97-98.

10. This emphasis upon the sermon as an event in time, something that moves from crisis to equilibrium or resolution, has been the seminal insight of Eugene L. Lowry in his books *The Homiletical Plot: The Sermon As Narrative Art Form* (Atlanta: John Knox Press, 1980), and *Doing Time in the Pulpit: The Relationship Between Narrative and Preaching* (Nashville: Abingdon Press, 1985).

11. Herman Melville, *Moby Dick* (New York: W. W. Norton, 1967), pp. 43-44.

12. See Elizabeth Achtemeier, *Preaching Hard Texts of the Old Testament* (Peabody, Mass.: Hendricks, 1998).

13. David L. Bartlett has a concise survey of interpretive methods for preachers in his *Between the Bible and the Church: New Methods for Biblical Preaching* (Nashville: Abingdon Press, 1999).

14. John Chrysostom, *On the Priesthood*, chap. 5, sec. 2-3, in The *Nicene and Post-Nicene Fathers*, vol. 9, Philip Schaff, ed. (Grand Rapids: Eerdmans, 1989), pp. 70-71.

15. St. Jerome, Letter 22 (n.p., n.d.).

16. Luther advises his fellow ministers to "heap together all manner of books indiscriminately and think only of the number and size of the collection," but then he says it is important, in a pastor's reading, to "discard all such dung" as will be unprofitable to a preacher's growth. Still, even the works of pagans help us become more appreciative of "the marvelous works of God." Cited in Thomas C. Oden, *Becoming a Minister*, Classical Pastoral Care Series, vol. 1 (New York: Crossroad, 1987), pp. 161-62.

17. Eugene H. Peterson, *Under the Unpredictable Plant: An Exploration of Vocational Holiness* (Grand Rapids: Eerdmans, 1992), p. 56.

18. Richard Lischer, *The Preacher King: Martin Luther King, Jr. and the Word that Moved America* (New York: Oxford, 1995), pp. 69-71.

19. Phillips Brooks, *Lectures on Preaching: The Yale Lectures on Preaching, 1877* (Grand Rapids: Baker, 1978), p. 5.

20. As quoted by Gary Wills, *Saint Augustine* (New York: Penguin Putnam, 1999), p. 69.

21. Jean Leclercq, *The Love of Learning and the Desire for God: A Study of Monastic Culture* (New York: Fordham University Press, 1961), pp. 21-22.

22. David H. Kelsey, *The Uses of Scripture in Recent Theology* (Philadelphia: Fortress Press, 1975), p. 91.

23. P. T. Forsyth, *Positive Preaching and the Modern Mind* (London: Independent Press, 1907), p. 53. Quoted in *Preaching in the Witnessing Community*, Herman G. Stuempfle Jr., ed. (Philadelphia: Fortress Press, 1973), p. viii.

24. From "Words We Tremble to Say Out Loud," Barbara Brown Taylor, 1990, in *Concise Encyclopedia of Preaching*, William H. Willimon and Richard Lischer, eds. (Louisville: Westminster John Knox Press, 1995), p. 512.

25. This interlude is an adaptation of my article, "Eyewitnesses and Ministers of the Word: Preaching in Acts," *Interpretation* 42, no. 2 (April 1998): 158-70. Adapted with permission.

26. Stanley M. Hauerwas, *Vision and Virtue* (South Bend: Fides Publishers, 1974), p. 46.

7. The Pastor as Counselor

1. I find it interesting that Clebsch and Jaeckle did not list teaching as an aspect of care. This section follows my survey of the history of pastoral care in William H. Willimon, *Worship as Pastoral Care* (Nashville: Abingdon Press, 1979), pp. 32-37.

2. William A. Clebsch and Charles Jaeckle, *Pastoral Care in Historical Perspective* (Englewood Cliffs, N.J.: Prentice-Hall, 1964) pp. 34-66. Seward Hiltner in *Preface to Pastoral Theology* (Nashville, Abingdon Press, 1958), pp. 89-172, first discussed the first three historic functions of pastoral care.

3. Clebsch and Jaeckle, *Pastoral Care*, p. 30.

4. Ibid., p. 13; see also Mary Catherine O'Conner, *The Art of Dying Well: The Development of the Ars Moriendi* (New York: Columbia University Press, 1942).

5. J. A. Jungmann, S.J., *Pastoral Liturgy* (New York: Herder & Herder, 1962), p. 380.

6. Richard Baxter, *The Reformed Pastor*, Hugh Martin, ed. (London: SCM, 1956; Richmond, Va.: John Knox Press, 1963), p. 49.

7. Anton Boisen, *Out of the Depths* (New York: Harper & Row, 1960), pp. 143-97.

8. Thomas C. Oden, *Pastoral Counsel*, Classical Pastoral Care Series, vol. 3 (New York: Crossroad, 1989), p. 7.

9. Tertullian repeatedly advises, "Trust your soul." Tertullian, "Testimony of the Soul," chap. 6, in *Fathers of the Church*, R. J. Deferrari (Washington, D.C.: Catholic University Press, 1947), p. 141.

10. "When the people see that you unfeignedly love them, they will hear any thing and bear any thing from you. . . . We ourselves will take all things well from one that we know entirely loves us. We will put up with a blow that is given us in

love sooner than with a foul word that is spoken to us in malice or in anger." Thomas Aquinas, quoted in Oden, *Pastoral Counsel*, p. 29.

11. Ambrose, in *Duties of the Clergy*, asks, "Who seeks for a spring in the mud?" arguing that self-knowledge is essential for those who are called to offer counsel to others. "Am I to suppose that he is fit to give me advice who never takes it for himself?" (bk. 2, chap. 12, sec. 62, 2, *A Select Library of the Nicene and Post-Nicene Fathers of the Christian Church*, vol. 10, H. Wace and P. Schaff, eds. (New York: Christian, 1887–1900), p. 53.

12. I listed humor as an essential pastoral virtue in my book *Calling and Character: Virtues of the Ordained Life* (Nashville: Abingdon Press, 2000).

13. Quoted in Rebekah Miles, *The Pastor as Moral Guide* (Minneapolis: Fortress Press, 1999), p. 76.

14. Jeremy Taylor advised seventeenth-century English pastors: "A minister must not stay till he be sent for; but, of his own accord and care, go to them, to examine them, to exhort them to perfect their repentance, to strengthen their faith, to encourage their patience, to persuade them to resignation, to the renewing of their holy vows, to the love of God, to be reconciled to their neighbours, to make restitution and amends." *The Curate of Souls*, John R. H. Moorman (London: SPCK, 1958), p. 23.

15. Richard Baxter, *The Reformed Pastor* (New York: American Tract Society, 1850), p. 255.

16. In *The Preaching Life*, Barbara Brown Taylor says that "the church's central task is an imaginative one." (Cambridge, Mass.: Cowley Publications, 1993), p. 39.

17. Quoted by Oden, *Pastoral Counsel*, p. 8.

18. John Patton, *Pastoral Counseling: A Ministry of the Church* (Nashville: Abingdon Press, 1983), pp. 107-8.

19. See John Patton, *Pastoral Care in Context: An Introduction to Pastoral Care* (Louisville: Westminster John Knox, 1993), pp. 223-26.

20. Gregory Nazianzen, Oration II.28-33, as quoted in Oden, *Pastoral Counsel*, p. 110.

21. Much prudence and discretion is called for in this early stage of definition of the particular problem that is in need of care. Invoking Gregory of Nazianzus "of revered memory has taught, one and the same exhortation is not suited to all, because they are not compassed by the same quality of character. Often, for instance, what is profitable to some, harms others . . . herbs which nourish some animals, kill others; gentile hissing that calms horses, excites young puppies; medicine that alleviates one disease, aggravates another." Gregory the Great, *Pastoral Care*, part 3, prologue, *Ancient Christian Writers*, vol. 11, J. Quasten, J. C. Plumpe, and W. Burghardt, eds. (New York: Paulist Press, 1984), p. 89.

22. For a more detailed, yet succinct description of the challenges of the counseling session, see Philip Culbertson, *Caring for God's People: Counseling and Christian Wholeness* (Minneapolis: Fortress Press, 2000), pp. 256-76.

23. Patton, *Pastoral Counseling*, p. 171.

24. Ibid., pp. 184-85.

25. Though Patton does not put the matter this way, I would say that we pastors must resist transference by a continual reminder to ourselves that we are not

God. We are servants of God, but not God, not the Messiah, not the one who is able to work miracles in someone's life. Only God can do that. We are also sinners. True, we are sinners attempting to care for other sinners, but sinners nevertheless. That means that we are capable of the same projection, transference, and fantasy that we observe in our counselees.

26. Virginia Satir, *Conjoint Family Therapy* (Palo Alto, Calif.: Science and Behavior Books, 1983).

27. Edwin Friedman, *Generation to Generation: Family Process in Church and Synagogue* (New York: Guilford, 1985).

28. Rebekah Miles, *The Pastor as Moral Guide* (Minneapolis: Fortress Press, 1999).

29. Clebsch and Jaekle, *Pastoral Care,* pp. 49-56.

30. E. E. Shelp quoted in Miles, *The Pastor as Moral Guide,* p. 81.

31. Luther, "An Open Letter to the Christian Nobility," in *The Works of Martin Luther,* vol. 2 (Philadelphia: Muhlenberg Press, 1943), p. 161.

32. Miles, *The Pastor as Moral Guide,* p. 5.

33. Gregory the Great exhorts pastors that "the hale are to be admonished in one way, the sick in another. The hale are to be admonished to employ bodily health in behalf of mental health. Otherwise, if they divert the favour granted them of their good condition to the doing of evil and thus become the worse for the gift, they will merit punishment." Quoted in Thomas C. Oden, *Crisis Ministries,* Classical Pastoral Care Series, vol. 4 (New York: Crossroad, 1986), p. 51.

34. Martin Luther, *Letters of Spiritual Counsel,* Theodore G. Tappert, ed. and trans., Library of Christian Classics, vol. 18 (Philadelphia: Westminster Press, 1955), p. 27.

35. All references to St. Augustine's *Confessions* are from the translation by Henry Chadwick (Oxford: Oxford University Press, 1991). Used by permission.

36. From *Shadowlands,* William Nicholson's screenplay about C. S. Lewis. Quoted by John S. Dunne, *Reading the Gospel* (Notre Dame, Ind.: University of Notre Dame Press, 2000), p. 1.

37. As quoted by Garry Wills in his *Saint Augustine* (New York: Penguin Putnam, 1999), p. 72.

38. Anne Lamott, *Traveling Mercies: Some Thoughts on Faith* (New York: Pantheon, 1999).

39. William A. Beardslee, *Literary Criticism of the New Testament* (Philadelphia: Fortress Press, 1970), p. 76.

40. Here might have been a good place for a digression on the role—on the need—for mentors in our reading of Scripture. Theological education, at its best, is apprenticeship in the disciplines of ministry. The word *mentor* comes from the name of that guide who led young Telemachus in the *Odyssey.* The indebtedness of Augustine to Ambrose at this crucial point in his odyssey suggests the essential role of mentoring in Christian growth.

41. See pp. 376-81 of Allan D. Fitzgerald, O.S.A., ed., *Augustine Through the Ages: An Encyclopedia* (Grand Rapids: Eerdmans, 1999) for a discussion of Augustine and the book of Genesis.

42. Garry Wills quite successfully calls this Augustine's *testimony* in his *Saint Augustine* (1999).

43. See Brian Stock, *Augustine the Reader: Meditation, Self-Knowledge, and the Ethics of Interpretation* (Cambridge, Mass.: Harvard University Press, 1996).

8. The Pastor as Teacher

1. Anselm of Canterbury, *Proslogion,* by Jasper Hopkins and Herbert Richardson, eds. and trans. (New York: Mellen Press), 1974, p. 93.

2. Robert Bellah, et al., *Habits of the Heart: Individualism and Commitment in American Life* (Berkeley: University of California Press, 1985), pp. 220-21.

3. Cited in Jackson W. Carroll, *Mainline to the Future: Congregations for the 21st Century* (Louisville: Westminster John Knox, 2000), p. 34.

4. The Greek word for disciple, *mathetes,* shares the same Greek root as the word for learning, *manthano.*

5. Clement of Alexandria has a wonderful treatise on Christ as teacher, a continuing educational presence in our lives. "Christ the Educator," bk. 1, chap. 1, sec. 23 in *Fathers of the Church,* R. J. Deferrari, ed. (Washington, D.C.: Catholic University Press, 1947), pp. 3-8.

6. Peter L. Berger, *A Rumor of Angels: Modern Society and the Rediscovery of the Supernatural* (Garden City, N.Y.: Doubleday, 1969), p. 43.

7. The Greek word for "conversion" is *metanois,* made from *meta,* "change," "transform," and *nous,* "mind." Conversion is best defined as that lifelong process where we go through that metamorphosis, that great change of heart and mind whereby we belong to Christ rather than the powers that be.

8. Loren Mead, *The Once and Future Church: Reinventing the Congregation for a New Mission Frontier* (Bethesda, Md.: Alban Institute, 1991).

9. Lesslie Newbigin, *Foolishness to the Greeks: The Gospel and Western Culture* (Grand Rapids: Eerdmans, 1986); and *The Gospel in a Pluralist Society* (Grand Rapids: Eerdmans, 1989).

10. George A. Lindbeck, *The Nature of Doctrine: Religion and Theology in a Postliberal Age* (Philadelphia: Westminster Press, 1984).

11. Lesslie Newbigin speaks of the necessary "cultural bilinguality" of the Christian life in which we are forced to know one language (the Christian faith) while living with another (secular speech). *Gospel in a Pluralist Society* (Grand Rapids: Eerdmans, 1989), pp. 55-65.

12. Thus Edward Farley refers to theology as *habitus,* "a habit, an enduring orientation, and dexterity of the soul." *Theologia* (Philadelphia: Fortress Press, 1983), p. 35.

13. In Philip L. Culbertson and Arthur B. Shipee, *Pastor: Readings from the Patristic Period* (Minneapolis: Fortress Press, 1990), pp. 157-58. Much the same is said by Chrysostom in *On the Priesthood,* chap. 5, sec. 6, in *The Nicene and Post-Nicene Fathers,* vol. 9, Philip Schaff, ed. (Grand Rapids: Eerdmans, 1989), p. 8.

14. See William H. Willimon and Stanley M. Hauerwas, *Preaching to Strangers* (Louisville: Westminster John Knox, 1992), pp. 1-13.

15. "It is easy to get religion; it is something else to hold on to [it]," Robert L. Wilken, *Remembering the Christian Past* (Grand Rapids: Eerdmans, 1995), p. 23.

16. The catechetical implications of the various aspects of the church's liturgy are explored in John. H. Westerhoff III and William H. Willimon, *Liturgy and Learning Through the Life Cycle*, rev. ed. (Akron, Ohio: OSL Publications, 1994). See also Phillip H. Pfatteicher, *The School of the Church: Worship and Christian Formation* (Valley Forge: Trinity Press International, 1995), especially chap. 6.

17. *The Church Today: Insightful Statistics and Commentary* (Glendale, Calif.: Barna Research Group, 1990), pp. 24-25.

18. This insight is strongly developed by Richard Robert Osmer, *A Teachable Spirit: Recovering the Teaching Office in the Church* (Louisville: Westminster John Knox Press, 1990).

19. Rodney Clapp, "Practicing the Politics of Jesus," in Michael L. Budde and Robert W. Brimlow, eds., *The Church as Counterculture* (Albany: State University of New York Press, 2000), p. 29.

20. For a discussion of the practices of Christian formation, see Margaret Miles, *Practicing Christianity: Critical Perspectives for an Embodied Spirituality* (New York: Crossroad, 1988) and Dorothy Bass, ed., *Practicing Our Faith: A Way of Life for a Searching People* (San Francisco: Jossey-Bass, 1997).

21. Walter Brueggemann, *The Creative Word* (Minneapolis: Fortress Press, 1982), p. 27.

22. The great need, as well as the great desire for Christian instruction and formation, is documented by the results of a massive national study among five mainline denominations in North America. See Peter L. Benson and Carolyn H. Eklin, *Effective Christian Education: A National Study of Protestant Congregations—A Summary Report on Faith, Loyalty, and Congregational Life* (Minneapolis: Search Institute, 1990). This study is a basis for Eugene C. Roehlkepartain's book on congregational involvement in Christian education, *The Teaching Church: Moving Christian Education to Center Stage* (Nashville: Abingdon Press, 1993).

23. Dean Kelley, *Why Conservative Churches Are Growing* (New York: Harper & Row, 1972).

24. C. Ellis Nelson in his *How Faith Matures* (Louisville: Westminster John Knox Press, 1989) stresses that the whole congregation is the agency of Christian education (p. 199).

25. Westerhoff and Willimon, *Liturgy and Learning Through the Life Cycle*.

26. Ronald Heifetz, *Leadership Without Easy Answers* (Harvard: Belknap Press, 1994), p. 187.

27. Donald A. Luidens, Dean R. Hodge, and Benton Johnson, "The Emergence of Lay Liberalism Among Baby Boomers," *Theology Today* 51 (July, 1994): 249-55. Reprinted with permission.

28. Ibid., p. 252.

29. Ibid., pp. 253, 254.

30. Ibid., p. 254.

31. See Robert L. Wilken, *The Christians as Romans Saw Them* (New Haven: Yale University Press, 1984), pp. 88-91.

32. Heifetz, *Leadership*, p. 187.

33. Janet Fishburn believes that the emergence of the Sunday school in the nineteenth century as a vast lay movement accounts for the decline of the pastor as the

lead Christian educator. The educational task was given over to laypersons in the Sunday school setting, or (later) to "professional" Christian educators who inappropriately relieved the pastor of this leadership role. See Fishburn's chapter in C. Ellis Nelson, ed., *Congregations: Their Power to Form and Transform* (Louisville: Westminster John Knox Press, 1988).

34. Paul J. Achtemeier works this theme well in his commentary on Mark, *The Gospel of Mark* (Philadelphia: Fortress Press, 1975).

35. For an engaging account of how *Disciple* influenced the life of a congregation, see Daniel V. Olson, "Fellowship Ties and the Transmission of Religious Identity," in Jackson W. Carroll and Wade Clark Roof, eds., *Beyond Establishment: Protestant Identity in a Post-Protestant Age* (Louisville: Westminster John Knox, 1993), pp. 32-53.

36. Samuel D. Proctor and Gardner C. Taylor, *We Have This Ministry: The Heart of the Pastor's Vocation* (Valley Forge: Judson Press, 1996), p. 20.

37. Eugene Peterson says, "If you have any desire or aptitude toward teaching, embrace the life of pastor. The vocation of pastor is the best of all contexts in which to teach." Peterson, with Marva Dawn, *The Unnecessary Pastor: Rediscovering the Call* (Grand Rapids: Eerdmans, 2000), p. 128.

9. The Pastor as Evangelist

1. This chapter is a reworking of my chapter, "Suddenly a Light from Heaven," which appeared in Kenneth Collins, *Conversion in the Wesleyan Tradition* (Nashville: Abingdon Press, 2001).

2. Beverly R. Gaventa, *From Darkness to Light: Aspects of Conversion in the New Testament* (Philadelphia: Fortress Press, 1986). A good collection of Christian conversion narratives is Hugh T. Kerr and John M. Mulder, eds., *Conversions: The Christian Experience* (Grand Rapids: Eerdmans, 1983).

3. Paul does not seem to know how to describe what happened to him on the Damascus Road. Was it death or birth? It felt like both at the same time. I am fascinated by the parallels between conversion and the near-death experiences that Raymond Moody has recorded. For instance, a major theme that runs through the literature on near-death experiences (the experience of having had a sense of almost dying and returning to life) is "transforming aftereffects" that cause "renewed dedication to the values of empathetic love, lifelong learning, and service to others. For some, these positive effects are accompanied by difficulties in adjusting to normal life." Carol Zaleski, *The Life of the World to Come: Near Death Experience and Christian Hope: The Albert Cardinal Meyer Lectures* (Oxford: Oxford University Press, 1996), p. 19.

4. C. S. Lewis, *Surprised by Joy* (New York: Harcourt, Brace & Co., 1955), p. 211.

5. Theodore Jennings dismissed Aldersgate as a "non-event." "John Wesley Against Aldersgate," *Quarterly Review* 8, no. 3 (fall 1988): 7. Those who are reasonably well situated in this world as it is have a stake in denying the possibility of radical change. For an informed critique of anticonversionist literature in Methodism, see Kenneth J. Collins, "Other Thoughts on Aldersgate: Has the

Conversionist Paradigm Collapsed?" *Methodist History* 30, no. 1 (October 1991): 10-25.

6. In his *Small Catechism* (St. Louis: Concordia, 1943), Luther says that baptism with water signifies, "that the Old Adam in us should, by daily contrition and repentance, be drowned and die with all sins and evil lusts and, again, a new man daily come forth and arise" (p. 178). *Daily.* See William H. Willimon, *The Bible: A Sustaining Presence in Worship* (Valley Forge: Judson Press, 1981), pp. 66-67.

7. Conversion, dislodgment, is a threat to the establishment, the powers that be, particularly when it occurs among the dispossessed and the poor, among those who have the least to lose by having their world rocked. See the dramatic accounts of conversions among African American ex-slaves in *God Struck Me Dead: Voices of Ex-Slaves,* Clifton H. Johnson, ed. (Boston: Pilgrim Press, 1993).

8. The accounts of Paul's "conversion" are more properly interpreted as stories of vocation rather than conversion. To be called, according to Paul, is to be changed, transformed, converted. To be converted is to be called. See William H. Willimon, *Acts: Interpretation* (Atlanta: John Knox Press, 1988), pp. 73-83. As Karl Barth stressed repeatedly, to be called is "to be given a task." Barth, *Church Dogmatics,* 4.3.2, p. 573.

9. John Wesley characterized sanctification as the progressive, lifelong aspect of conversion. Sanctification, according to Wesley, is "carried on in the soul by slow degrees, from the time of our first turning to God." *Forty-Four Sermons* (London: Epworth Press, 1944), p. 523.

10. *Vatican Council II: The Conciliar and Post Conciliar Documents,* Austin Flannery, O.P., ed. (Collegeville, Minn.: Liturgical Press, 1975). Wesley frequently spoke of the Lord's Supper as "a sanctifying and a justifying ordinance." See William H. Willimon, *The Service of God: How Worship and Ethics Are Related* (Nashville: Abingdon Press, 1983), pp. 124-29.

11. John Calvin, *Calvin: Institutes of the Christian Religion,* 3.3.9, John T. McNeill, ed., *The Library of Christian Classics,* vol. 20 (Philadelphia: Westminster Press, 1960), p. 601.

12. Wade Clark Roof, *Spiritual Marketplace: Baby Boomers and the Remaking of American Religion* (Princeton: Princeton University Press, 1999).

13. In their study of American churches, Finke and Stark present this market-place mentality as the driving force in American religious life—a force that they seem to feel accounts for the vitality and diversity of that life. Roger Finke and Rodney Stark, *The Churching of America, 1776–1990: Winners and Losers in Our Religious Economy* (New Brunswick, N.J.: Rutgers University Press, 1992). I join those who take a more critical view of this marketplace metaphor. See James L. Street and Philip Kenneson, *Selling Out the Church: The Dangers of Religious Marketing* (Nashville: Abingdon Press, 1997). Such marketing of Christ is not new for American religious life. See R. Laurence Moore, *Selling God: American Religion in the Marketplace of Culture* (New York: Oxford University Press, 1994).

14. David Steinmetz, "Reformation and Conversion," *Theology Today* 35 (April 1978): 25-32.

15. Jim Wallis, *Call to Conversion* (New York: Harper & Row, 1982). See the use of the conversion as a metaphor for what needs to always happen in the church in

Darrell L. Guder, *The Continuing Conversion of the Church* (Grand Rapids: Eerdmans, 2000).

16. Calvin, *Institutes*, 3.3.9, p. 601. "Viewing Wesley's doctrine of salvation through the interpretive lens of John Calvin will render the former's doctrines of justification and grace, at least in some respects, remarkably clear." Kenneth J. Collins, *The Scripture Way of Salvation: The Heart of John Wesley's Theology* (Nashville: Abingdon Press, 1997), p. 206.

17. Robert Wuthnow, *After Heaven: Spirituality in America Since the 1950s* (Berkeley: University of California Press, 1998).

18. Hans J. Mol, *Identity and the Sacred* (New York: Free Press, 1977), pp. 45-53.

19. James W. Fowler, *Stages of Faith* (San Francisco: Harper & Row, 1981); Donald Capps, *Life Cycle Theory and Pastoral Care* (Philadelphia: Fortress Press, 1983).

20. Karl Barth, *Church Dogmatics*, G. W. Bromiley, ed. (Edinburgh: T & T Clark, 1962), 4.3.2, sec. 71.2, pp. 504-6.

21. Ibid., pp. 505-6.

22. After discussing the limits of the organic, developmental notions of "faith development" in Fowler and Capps, Craig Dykstra says that any faithful account of the Christian faith must include room for the free activity of God: "The tradition's emphasis on the priority of the activity of God as the source of faith and on the nature of faith as response to God in history makes it wary of organic metaphors which suggest that faith is a structure built into human beings that undergoes evolutionary or developmental transformation. . . . The tradition has usually been hesitant to place too much emphasis on progress in the life of faith or to stake out any stages by which such progress might be marked . . . hesitant to define or describe maturity in faith and in the life of faith too exactly." *Growing in the Life of Faith: Education and Christian Practices* (Louisville: Geneva Press, 1999), p. 36.

23. John Calvin defines faith, this way: "We shall possess a right definition of faith if we call it a firm and certain knowledge of God's benevolence toward us, founded upon the truth of the freely given promise in Christ, both revealed to our minds and sealed upon our hearts through the Holy Spirit." *Institutes*, 3.2.7, p. 551.

24. If I were to indicate the main way that contemporary heirs of Wesley deviate from Wesley's anthropology, it would be in our inadequate assessment of human sinfulness. The late Thomas Langford, a wonderful Wesleyan theologian, once told me that he conducted a survey of twentieth-century theological writings by Methodists, and was struck by how few of them even mentioned the word *sin*. Perhaps this omission of sin is one of the reasons we no longer speak much of prevenient, justifying, and sanctifying grace. Who needs the grace of God when we are basically good people capable of progress?

25. Richard Heitzenrater, *Wesley and the People Called Methodist* (Nashville: Abingdon Press, 1995).

26. Ibid., p. 192.

27. Ibid., p. 138.

28. Robert Wuthnow, *Sharing the Journey: Support Groups and America's New Quest for Community* (New York: Free Press, 1994), pp. 357-58.

29. Jackson W. Carroll, *Mainline to the Future: Congregations for the 21st Century* (Louisville: Westminster John Knox, 2000), pp. 90-94.

30. Stanley Hauerwas and I attempted to stress the centrality of Christian practice for Christian holiness in *Where Resident Aliens Live: Exercises for Christian Practice* (Nashville: Abingdon Press, 1996).

31. Essential to sanctification is the cultivation of the disciplines necessary to be in the world as Christians, which is our chief ministry to the world. The great challenge for the heirs of Wesley has been to keep together the instantaneous element that relates to justification by God and the participatory, practical element that is our response to the initiatives of God upon our lives. Kenneth Collins has noted Wesley's unique "conjunctive theology." In church life, Wesley managed to be rich, tensive, evangelical *and* catholic, conversionist *and* sanctificationist, stressing the triumph of the justifying *and* sanctifying grace of God in Christ. Methodists seem not to know how to speak of the movement that God wrought through the Wesleys, except through conjunctions. Because of its richness and depth, few of us have been able to do justice to its conjunctive quality, but we ought to try. Collins, *The Scripture Way of Salvation,* p. 207.

32. A conversionist faith enables us to admit that education as transformation involves relinquishment, divestment, a sort of death. Something is gained in growth, but something is lost as well. Thus Wesley A. Kort stresses transformative reading of Scripture as a process of "divestment." To Augustine we owe this deep sense, developed also in Calvin *(Institutes,* 3.12.8), that a right understanding of Scripture involves letting go of ourselves. Kort, *Take, Read: Scripture, Textuality, and Cultural Practice* (University Park: Pennsylvania State University Press, 1996), pp. 28-30.

33. Hans Küng, *The Church* (Garden City, N.Y.: Doubleday, 1976), p. 438.

34. A frequent theme that runs through Bill Hybels's story of the dramatic birth of Willow Creek Church is that, in the dull, boring, predictable churches of the mainline, "Surprises—in terms of programs or sermons or policies or life transformations—seldom occur, and a sense of the miraculous is an outdated notion" (p. 47). In my own estimation, part of the power of the new "seeker-sensitive churches" like Willow Creek is that they stress the transformative power of God to work change—though it remains for these churches (as for any church) to demonstrate that the transformation being worked is transformation into the living Christ, rather than just another aspect of adaptation to American culture. Lynne Hybels and Bill Hybels, *Rediscovering Church: The Story and Vision of Willow Creek Community Church* (Grand Rapids: Zondervan, 1995). For a rather scathing Evangelical critique of Willow Creek that accuses Bill Hybels of "obsequiously prostrating himself before baby boomers, a generally self-centered, relativistic, unloyal generation" in his efforts to evangelize, see David Wells, *No Place for Truth, or, Whatever Happened to Evangelical Theology?* (Grand Rapids: Eerdmans, 1993), pp. 144-45. See Donald E. Miller, *Reinventing American Protestantism: Christianity in the New Millennium* (Berkeley: University of California Press, 1997), for a dramatic testimonial to the place of the conversionist perspective in the life of the "new paradigm churches."

35. Fred Hobson, *But Now I See: The White Southern Racial Conversion Narrative* (Baton Rouge: Louisiana State University Press, 1999).

36. Anne Braden, *The Wall Between* (New York: Scribner's, 1958), pp. 27-28. In language that supports the thesis of this interlude, Braden writes, "Race prejudice being an emotional thing cannot be removed by intellectual arguments alone. There must be some real emotional experience" (p. 51).

37. William Martin, *A Prophet With Honor: The Billy Graham Story* (New York: William Morrow, 1991).

38. Barth does not approve of making much of biblical "conversion" stories, preferring rather to stress them as call or vocation stories. *Church Dogmatics*, 4.3.2, p. 573.

39. John Donne, "Holy Sonnet 14," in *The Norton Anthology of English Literature* (New York: W. W. Norton, 1975), p. 611.

40. See Douglas Sloan's account of the ways in which secular, naturalistic ways of knowledge essentially closed American higher education to the witness of the gospel in his *Faith and Knowledge: Mainline Protestantism and American Higher Education* (Louisville: Westminster John Knox Press, 1994).

41. David Bosch, *Transforming Mission: Paradigm Shifts in Theology of Mission* (Maryknoll, N.Y.: Orbis, 1991), p. 390.

42. Darrell L. Guder, *The Continuing Conversion of the Church* (Grand Rapids: Eerdmans, 2000).

43. Richard Hays, "Ecclesiology and Ethics in 1 Corinthians," *Ex Auditu* (1994): 2.

44. Lesslie Newbigin, *The Open Secret: Sketches for a Missionary Theology* (Grand Rapids: Eerdmans, 1978), p. 40.

45. George Hunsberger contrasts the church as "a people sent or a vendor of religion" in *Missional Church: A Vision for the Sending of the Church in North America,* Darrell Gruder, ed. (Grand Rapids: Eerdmans, 1998), p. 83.

46. Gerhard Lohfink, *Jesus and Community: The Social Dimension of the Christian Faith,* J. P. Galvin, trans. (Philadelphia: Fortress Press, 1984), p. 28.

47. Allen Verhey, *The Great Reversal* (Grand Rapids: Eerdmans, 1984), p. 74.

48. Barth, *Church Dogmatics,* 4.3.2, p. 555.

49. Marva Dawn contends that the church makes a mistake in confusing evangelism with worship. I think that her main concern is using Sunday morning worship primarily for reaching the unchurched so that it becomes more anthropocentric rather than theocentric. Like it or not, on Sunday morning, in saying and showing what we believe, Christ is making his appeal through us. "One of the primary and irreplaceable ingredients in evangelism is the quality of worship in the Christian community," William J. Abraham, *The Logic of Evangelism* (Grand Rapids: Eerdmans, 1989), p. 168. "Not all evangelization is worship, but all worship is evangelization," Darrell L. Guder, *The Continuing Conversion of the Church,* p. 157. Evangelism is not the point of Sunday worship, but an aspect of the point of worship—the praise of God in Christ.

50. "Solomon's Porch," in *The Church as Counterculture,* Michael L. Budde and Robert W. Brimlow, eds. (Albany: State University of New York, 2000), pp. 109-10.

51. "The Church," in *Keeping the Faith*, Geoffrey Wainwright, ed. (Philadelphia: Fortress Press, 1988), p. 193.

52. This dated point of view is criticized and countered in Robert A. Chestnut, *Transforming the Mainline Church: Lessons in Change from Pittsburgh's Cathedral of Hope* (Louisville: Geneva Press, 2000).

53. Walter Brueggemann, "Always in the Shadow of the Empire," in Budde and Brimlow, eds., *The Church as Counterculture*, p. 43.

54. William H. Willimon, *The Intrusive Word: Preaching to the Unbaptized* (Grand Rapids: Eerdmans, 1994), pp. 1-3.

10. The Pastor as Prophet

1. Reinhold Niebuhr, *Leaves from the Notebook of a Tamed Cynic* (New York: Meridian, 1960), p. 74.

2. Joseph Blankinsopp, *A History of Prophecy in Israel* (Philadelphia: Westminster Press, 1983).

3. Mohandas K. Gandhi, *An Autobiography, or the Story of My Experiments with Truth* (Ahmedabad, India: Navajivan Press, 1927).

4. Even a fine historian and theologian such as Robert Wilken, who has spent his life helping to clarify and to define orthodox Christian belief, can say, "It's believing that counts, not *what* one believes." The tenets of this faith are known by the lives they are able to produce. Robert L. Wilken, *Remembering the Christian Past* (Grand Rapids: Eerdmans, 1995).

5. Augustine, "Letters XXIX, To Alypius, A.D. 395," sec. 6-8, in *A Select Library of the Nicene and Post-Nicene Fathers of the Christian Church*, vol. 1, H. Wace and P. Schaff, eds. (New York: Christian, 1887–1900), p. 255.

6. Stanley M. Hauerwas and William H. Willimon, *Resident Aliens* (Nashville: Abingdon Press, 1989), pp. 117-27.

7. Ibid., p. 123.

8. Charles Williams, *The Descent of the Dove* (New York: Meridian, 1956), p. 205.

9. Quoted by Rodney Stark, *The Rise of Christianity: A Sociologist Reconsiders History* (Princeton, N.J.: Princeton University Press, 1996), p. 87.

10. Phillip Hallie, *Lest Innocent Blood Be Shed: The Story of the Village of Le Chambon and How Goodness Happened There* (New York: HarperPerennial, 1979). Christian educator Craig Dykstra calls Haillie's book "a singularly important book for Christian educators," *Growing in the Life of Faith: Education and Christian Practices* (Louisville: Geneva Press, 1999), p. 57.

11. Hallie, *Lest Innocent Blood Be Shed*, p. 3.

12. Ibid., p. 283.

13. Ibid., p. 110. If courageous, prophetic resistance is most impressive as a non-heroic act, then complicity with evil is also nonheroic. Alongside the story of Pastor Trocme and Le Chambon, we ought to read Victoria J. Barnett's *Bystanders: Conscience and Complicity During the Holocaust* (Westport, Conn.: Greenwood Press, 1999). She writes, "In the long term, Nazism was powerful not just because of the numbers of party stalwarts, but because millions of Germans were prepared to inform on one another, obey orders, and remain passive while others became vic-

tims" (p. 83). On the "ordinariness" of evil in the Holocaust, see also Christopher Browning, *Ordinary Men: Reserve Police Battalion 101 and the Final Solution in Poland* (New York: HarperCollins, 1992), and Daniel J. Goldhagen's, *Hitler's Willing Executioners: Ordinary Germans and the Holocaust* (New York: Knopf, 1996). That so many had so little ability to resist the evils of Nazism is testimony to the importance of ordinary prophetic formation in the church.

14. Harold Bloom, *The American Religion: The Emergence of the Post-Christian Nation* (New York: Simon & Schuster, 1992).

15. Martin Luther, *Exposition on the Third and Fourth Chapters of John,* 1538, Weimar ed., 47, 1.10, p. 193; my translation.

16. See, for instance, chapters 1 and 2 of Stanley M. Hauerwas, *Christian Existence Today: Essays on Church, World, and Living in Between* (Durham, N.C.: Labyrinth, 1988).

17. Stanley M. Hauerwas and William H. Willimon, *Where Resident Aliens Live: Exercises for Christian Practice* (Nashville: Abingdon Press, 1996), pp. 27-28.

18. Quoted in E. Plass, *What Luther Says*, vol. 1 (St. Louis: Concordia, 1959), p. 303.

19. Stark, *The Rise of Christianity*, p. 87.

20. Wayne A. Meeks, *The First Urban Christians* (New Haven, Conn.: Yale University Press, 1983), p. 71.

21. The role of eschatology in Christian ethics is highlighted strongly in Richard B. Hays, *The Moral Vision of the New Testament* (San Francisco: HarperCollins, 1996), pp. 19-27, 85-88, 179-81.

22. Elisabeth Schüssler Fiorenza, highlights the place of widows in the social strata of the early church in *In Memory of Her: A Feminist Theological Reconstruction of Christian Origins* (New York: Crossroad, 1983), p. 140.

23. Walter Brueggemann, *The Prophetic Imagination* (Philadelphia: Fortress Press, 1978), p. 13.

24. In these contentions I am indebted to John Howard Yoder, *The Politics of Jesus* (Grand Rapids: Eerdmans, 1994).

25. William H. Willimon, *Sighing for Eden: Sin, Evil, and the Christian Faith* (Nashville: Abingdon Press, 1985). See also William H. Willimon, "A Peculiarly Christian Account of Sin," *Theology Today* 50, no. 2 (July 1993): 220-28.

26. M. Scott Peck, *People of the Lie: The Hope for Healing Evil* (Simon & Schuster, 1983).

27. See Randy Frame, "Christian Children's Fund Practices Questioned," *Christianity Today* 38 (Nov. 14, 1994): 71.

28. The former Benedictine priest, Matthew Fox, has made much of his claim that the orthodox Christian teaching on sin is rooted in, and a product of a sense of self-loathing and little more. Matthew Fox, *Original Blessing: A Primer in Creation Spirituality in Four Paths, Twenty-Six Themes, and Two Questions* (Santa Fe: Bear Press, 1983).

29. Quoted in Jeffrey Burton Russell, *Mephistopheles: The Devil in the Modern World* (Ithaca, N.Y.: Cornell University Press, 1986), p. 80. Actually, I understand that Baudelaire said it first. See Flannery O'Connor, *Mystery and Manners*, Sally and Robert Fitzgerald, eds. (New York: Farrar, Straus & Giroux, 1961), p. 112.

30. See Carl E. Braaten and Robert W. Jenson eds., *Sin, Death, and the Devil* (Grand Rapids: Eerdmans, 2000).

31. Will Campbell, *Brother to a Dragonfly* (New York: Seabury Press, 1977), p. 98.

32. Will Campbell, *Forty Acres and a Goat* (Atlanta: Peachtree Publishers, 1986), p. 5.

33. John Egerton, *A Mind to Stay Here: Profiles from the South* (New York: Macmillan, 1970), pp. 15-31.

34. Campbell, *Brother to a Dragonfly*, p. 97.

35. Ibid., p. 241.

36. Will Campbell, *Race and the Renewal of the Church* (Philadelphia: Westminster Press, 1962), pp. 46-47.

37. Campbell, *Brother to a Dragonfly*, p. 201.

38. Campbell, *Forty Acres and a Goat*, p. 270.

39. *Book of Common Prayer* (New York: Church Hymnal Corporation, 1979), pp. 62-63.

40. Fred Hobson, *But Now I See: The White Southern Racial Conversion Narrative* (Baton Rouge: Louisiana State University Press, 1999), p. 73.

41. One of the purposes of Reinhold Niebuhr's *The Nature and Destiny of Man* (New York: Scribner's, 1964) was "to relate the biblical and distinctively Christian conception of sin as pride and self-love to the observable behavior of men." Sin is a universal attribute that all people display as a result of their awareness of their finitude. Feminists have criticized Niebuhr's view of sin as culture bound, perhaps gender determined rather than biblically derived. See particularly Judith Plaskow, *Sex, Sin and Grace: Women's Experience and the Theologies of Reinhold Niebuhr and Paul Tillich* (Washington, D.C.: University Press of America, 1980), pp. 62-72.

42. Karl Barth, "Evangelical Theology in the 19th Century," *Scottish Journal of Theology Occassional Papers* 8 (1959): 58. Quoted in W. Stephen Gunter, *Resurrection Knowledge: Recovering the Gospel for the Postmodern Church* (Nashville: Abingdon Press, 1999), pp. 31-32.

43. Gunter, *Resurrection Knowledge*, p. 31.

44. Karl Barth, *Church Dogmatics*, 4.3.1, G. W. Bromiley, ed. (Edinburgh: T & T Clark, 1957), p. 359.

45. Karl Barth, *Dogmatics in Outline* (New York: Harper & Row, 1959), p. 122.

46. James W. McClendon Jr., "Sin," in *A New Handbook of Christian Theology*, D. W. Musser and J. L. Price, eds. (Nashville: Abingdon Press, 1992), pp. 446-47.

47. See *Sighing for Eden*, pp. 183-90, for my thoughts on the implications of a doctrine of original sin for the practice of Christian ministry.

50. "Ash Wednesday," in *The United Methodist Hymnal: Book of United Methodist Worship* (Nashville: The United Methodist Publishing House, 1989), p. 353.

11. The Pastor as Leader

1. Karl Barth, *Church Dogmatics*, 4.3.2, G. W. Bromiley, ed. (Edinburgh: T & T Clark, 1957), p. 743.

2. Gerhard Lohfink, *Jesus and Community: The Social Dimension of the Christian Faith,* trans., J. P. Galvin (Philadelphia: Fortress Press, 1984), p. 28.

3. Stanley M. Hauerwas, *A Community of Character: Toward a Constructive Christian Social Ethics* (Notre Dame, Ind.: University of Notre Dame Press, 1981), p. 49.

4. See Aaron Wildavsky's intriguing book on situational leadership, *The Nursing Father: Moses as a Political Leader* (Tuscaloosa: University of Alabama Press, 1984).

5. See Gary Wills, *Certain Trumpets: The Call of Leaders* (New York: Simon & Schuster, 1994).

6. James MacGregor Burns, *Leadership* (New York: Harper Colophon, 1978).

7. John Kotter highlights the transformative nature of leadership by making this distinction between managers and leaders: "management is about coping with complexity," whereas "leadership is about coping with change." As quoted by George G. Hunter III in *Leading and Managing a Growing Church* (Nashville: Abingdon Press, 2000), p. 25.

8. Mark Twain, "Old Times on the Mississippi," *Atlantic Monthly* 35, no. 209 (March 1875): 283-84.

9. Ron A. Heifetz, *Leadership Without Easy Answers* (Cambridge, Mass.: Harvard University Press, 1994). Management theorist Peter Drucker says, "The business of a corporation is to satisfy them." Quoted in Kirk Hadaway, *Behold I Do a New Thing: Transforming Communities of Faith* (Cleveland: Pilgrim Press, 2001), p. 11.

10. Heifetz notes the essential role of the leader as intentional troublemaker within any organization that wants to grow and change. The adaptive leader, "Rather than fulfilling the expectation for answers, . . . provides questions; rather than protecting people from outside threat, . . . lets people feel the threat in order to stimulate adaptation; instead of orienting people to their current roles, . . . disorients people so that new role relationships develop; rather than quelling conflict, . . . generates it; instead of maintaining norms, . . . challenges them." *Leadership,* p. 126.

11. Ibid., p. 14.

12. Loren B. Mead, *Five Challenges for the Once and Future Church* (Washington, D.C.: Alban Institute, 1997).

13. Donald E. Miller, *Reinventing American Protestantism: Christianity in the New Millennium* (Berkeley: University of California Press, 1997). See also Rick Warren, *The Purpose-Driven Church: Growth Without Compromising Your Message and Mission* (Grand Rapids: Zondervan, 1995), pp. 384-85, for a firsthand account of leadership in a "new paradigm church."

14. Robert L. Wilson and I criticized the tendency of our own denomination to elevate "managers rather than leaders." See chapter 5 in *Rekindling the Flame: Strategies for a Vital United Methodism* (Nashville: Abingdon Press, 1987). In this we built upon the classic work of Warren Bennis, who said, "The problem with many organizations, and especially the ones that are failing, is that they tend to be over-managed and underled." Warren Bennis and Burt Nanus, *Leaders: The Strategies of Taking Charge* (New York: HarperBusiness, 1986), pp. 19-20.

15. Some years ago, when Samuel Blizzard surveyed Protestant clergy, he found that they reported spending more than half of their time in administrative and

organizational duties. This compared with only 18 percent of their time expended in preaching, and 5 percent as teacher. *The Protestant Parish Minister: A Behavioral Science Interpretation*, Society for the Scientific Study of Religion Monograph Series, vol. 5 (Storrs, Conn.: Society for the Scientific Study of Religion, 1985), p. 100.

16. James E. Dittes, "Administration vs. Ministry," in *Re-Calling Ministry*, Donald Capps, ed. (St. Louis: Chalice Press, 1999), pp. 107-22.

17. Some of Mead's themes are confirmed in Jackson W. Carroll's book on pastoral leadership, *As One with Authority: Reflective Leadership in Ministry* (Louisville: Westminster John Knox, 1991). Carroll describes three core tasks of pastoral leadership:

1. Meaning Interpretation—Pastors work with the congregation "to reflect on and interpret their life, individually and corporately, in light of God's purpose in Jesus Christ." A pastor is an intellectual leader who helps people to read their lives through the peculiar lens of the story of Jesus Christ.

2. Community Formation—As we have said earlier, pastors are uniquely "community persons," who keep concerning themselves with the character and the contours of the Christian community. The gospel is about the creation of a community. In pastoral work, we become embodiments of that gospel dynamic of family formation through the Word and work of God in Christ.

3. Empowering Public Ministry—Christians are to share in Christ's work in the world. The church is called not only to "make disciples," but also to "go into all the world" doing what Christ did in the world so that the world might come to know itself as under the judgment and redemption of God.

18. Anthony B. Robinson, "Leadership That Matters," *Christian Century* 116 (December 15, 1999): 1228-31.

19. Dittes, *Re-Calling Ministry*, p. 15.

20. Dietrich Bonhoeffer, *The Cost of Discipleship*, trans. R. H. Fuller (New York: Macmillan, 1963), p. 99.

21. Ibid., p. 98.

22. Ibid., p. 54.

23. Raymond E. Brown, "The Gospel According to John (I-XII)," in *The Anchor Bible* (New York: Doubleday, 1966), p. 295.

24. James Dittes argues, quite convincingly, that one reason pastors neglect preaching is because preaching is that pastoral activity that is most frequently prone to failure. In preaching, results are uncertain at best, negative reaction is always a possibility, and there are so few indications that our preaching "works." Dittes, "Preaching As Risky Investment," in *Re-Calling Ministry*, pp. 123-37.

25. "Homily 14.1-5 on Jeremiah," in *The Pastor: Readings from the Patristic Period*, Philip L. Culbertson and Arthur Bradford Shippee, eds. (Minneapolis: Fortress Press, 1990), p. 40.

26. Walter Hooper, ed., *The Business of Heaven: Daily Readings from C. S. Lewis* (San Diego: Harcourt Brace Jovanovich, 1984), p. 84.

12. The Pastor as Character

1. This chapter is, to a great extent, a reworking of material from my book *Calling and Character: Virtues of the Ordained Life* (Nashville: Abingdon Press, 2000).

2. Richard Baxter as quoted by Thomas C. Oden in *Ministry Through Word and Sacrament*, Classical Pastoral Care Series, vol. 2 (New York: Crossroad, 1989), p. 43.

3. Walter Brueggemann in *The Church as Counterculture*, Michael L. Budde and Robert W. Brimlow, eds. (Albany: State University of New York Press, 2000), p. 40.

4. David Bartlett, *Ministry in the New Testament* (Philadelphia: Fortress Press, 1993), p. 183.

5. See Philip L. Culbertson and Arthur B. Shippee, eds., *The Pastor: Readings from the Patristic Period* (Minneapolis: Fortress Press, 1990).

6. Ibid., pp. 202-3.

7. Cited by Oden in *Ministry Through Word and Sacrament*, p. 116.

8. James F. Keenan and Joseph Kotva, eds., *Can There Be Ethics in Church Leadership?* (Franklin, Wis.: Sheed & Ward, 2000) stresses clergy ethics as a matter of character.

9. St. Anthanasius, *The Incarnation of the Word of God* (New York: Macmillan, 1946), p. 96. Quoted in Stanley M. Hauerwas, *A Community of Character: Toward a Constructive Christian Social Ethic* (Notre Dame, Ind.: University of Notre Dame Press, 1981), p. 36. In his now classic essay, Nicholas Lash says that "the fundamental form of the *Christian* interpretation of scripture is the life, activity, and organization of the believing community." *Theology on the Way to Emmaus* (London: SCM Press, 1986), p. 42.

10. *Readings in Classical Rhetoric*, Thomas Benson and Michael Prosser, eds. (Bloomington: Indiana University Press, 1969), p. 136.

11. *The Preaching of John Henry Newman*, W. D. White, ed. (Philadelphia: Fortress Press, 1969), p. 28.

12. Historian Brooks Holifield documents the tendency of clergy to be subsumed into the culturally dominant images of success in *A History of Pastoral Care in America: From Salvation to Self-Realization* (Nashville: Abingdon Press, 1983).

13. Stanley Hauerwas, "Clerical Character," in *Christian Existence Today: Essays on Church, World, and Living in Between* (Durham, N.C.: Labyrinth Press, 1988), p. 144.

14. The word *seminary* means literally "seed bed," a place where masters cultivate new seedlings for future growth and development. On the significance of seminary as a place of clerical moral formation, see Richard Neuhaus, ed., *Theological Education and Moral Formation* (Grand Rapids: Eerdmans, 1992).

15. Stanley Hauerwas says that "our seminaries have no more important function than to direct those preparing for and in the ministry to reflect on those lives that have honored their calling as ministers." "Clerical Character," in *Christian Existence Today*, p. 145. For this reason I enjoy having seminarians read autobiographies and biographies of ministers.

16. John Chrysostom, *Treatise Concerning the Christian Priesthood*, book 3, trans. W. R. W. Stephens, *A Select Library of Nicene and Post-Nicene Fathers of the Christian Church*, vol. 9, Philip Schaff, ed. (Grand Rapids: Eerdmans, 1956), p. 49.

17. John C. Harris, *Stress, Power, and Ministry* (Washington, D.C.: Alban Institute, 1977), p. 125, speaks of the need for pastors to cultivate "a healthy disenchantment" from our congregations. Only when we have some distance from our people and their expectations can we truly be there for them as a caring leader, says Harris.

18. Chrysostom, *Treatise Concerning the Christian Priesthood*, book 3, p. 52.

19. Ambrose, "Letters," "Letters to Priests," *Fathers of the Church*, vol. 26, R. J. Deferrari, ed. (Washington, D.C.: Catholic University Press, 1947–.), pp. 347-48.

20. Søren Kierkegaard, *Provocations: Spiritual Writings of Kierkegaard*, Charles E. Moore, ed., (Farmington, Pa.: The Plough Publishing House, 1999), p. 350.

21. Ibid.

22. Ibid., p. 354.

23. Cited in Geoffrey Wainwright, "Some Theological Aspects of Ordination," *Studia Liturgica* 13, nos. 2-4 (1979): 139.

24. Aristotle, *Nichomachean Ethics*, 2.1, trans. Martin Oswald (Indianapolis: Bobbs-Merrill, 1962), p. 34.

25. Alasdair MacIntyre, *After Virtue* (Notre Dame, Ind.: University of Notre Dame Press, 1981), p. 175.

26. Marie M. Fortune, "The Joy of Boundaries," in *Boundary Wars: Intimacy and Distance in Healing Relationships*, Katherine Hancock Ragsdale, ed. (Cleveland: Pilgrim Press, 1996), p. 86.

27. Rebekah L. Miles, "Keeping Watch Over the Shepherds by Day and Night," *Circuit Rider* 23, no. 3 (May/June 1999): 14. See also Rebekah L. Miles, *The Pastor as Moral Guide* (Minneapolis: Fortress Press, 1999).

Carter Heyward has argued that the notion of "boundaries" is an inappropriate metaphor that clergy uncritically borrowed from other professions. She believes that the argument for boundaries is "patriarchal" and that there are times when therapists and pastors must attempt to be friends and colleagues with those under that care. Despite her arguments, I still feel that the notion of learned and carefully followed boundaries has a place in pastoral practice. *When Boundaries Betray Us: Beyond Illusions of What Is Ethical in Therapy and in Life* (San Francisco: HarperSanFrancisco, 1993).

28. Miles, "Keeping Watch Over the Shepherds by Day and Night," p. 15.

29. Naturally, with his dependence upon Aristotle (*Ethics*, vi. 10), Aquinas stresses prudence as chief among pastoral virtues, those right actions applied to right situations that are not simply susceptible to rules. *Summa Theologica*, vol II, pt. II-II, Q. 47-49, English Dominican Fathers, eds. (New York: Benziger, 1947–48). For Aquinas, the chief gift of the sacrament of ordination is prudence, the sacramental remedy for ignorance.

30. Miles, "Keeping Watch Over the Shepherds by Day and Night," p. 15.

31. Ambrose, *De Officiis Ministrorum* in *The Nicene and Post-Nicene Fathers*, second series, vol. 10 (New York: Christian Literature, 1896), 2.12.60.

32. Walter Brueggemann, *The Covenanted Self: Explorations of Law and Covenant* (Minneapolis: Fortress Press, 1999), p. 10.

33. "Finally we must ask of those in ministry whether they are capable of joy; if they are not they lack a character sufficient to their calling. For a person incapable

of joy will lack the humor necessary for the self-knowledge that that character requires." Hauerwas, "Clerical Character," p. 143.

34. John Dominic Crossan, *The Dark Interval: Towards a Theology of Story* (Niles, Ill.: Argus Communications, 1975).

35. Charles V. Gerkin, *The Living Human Document* (Nashville: Abingdon Press, 1984), chap. 8.

36. "Holy Eucharist I" in *Book of Common Prayer* (New York: Church Hymnal Corporation, 1979), p. 321.

13. *The Pastor as Disciplined Christian*

1. These factors are retrieved from my book *Clergy and Laity Burnout*, Creative Leadership Series, Lyle E. Schaller, ed. (Nashville: Abingdon Press, 1989). In that book I was indebted to John A. Sanford, *Ministry Burnout* (New York: Paulist Press, 1982), and to my interviews with dozens of pastors who had called it quits in ministry, as well as counselors who work with pastors who quit.

2. See Lloyd Rediger's *Clergy Killers: Guidance for Pastors and Congregations Under Attack* (Louisville: Westminster John Knox, 1997).

3. Kierkegaard said that a pastor must "be able to put up with all the rudeness of the sick person without letting it upset him, any more than a physician allows himself to be disturbed by the curses and kicks of a patient during an operation." Quoted by David Hansen, *The Art of Pastoring: Ministry Without All the Answers* (Downers Grove, Ill.: Intervarsity Press, 1994), p. 39.

4. Sanford, *Ministry Burnout*, p. 128.

5. Richard Baxter, *The Reformed Pastor*, 1656, John T. Wilkinson, ed. (London: Epworth Press, 1950), pp. 113-14.

6. Thus Luther confessed that "it would not be surprising if I threw the keys at the Lord's feet and said: Lord, do your own preaching. No doubt You are able to do better; for we have preached to them, but they will not listen to us. But God wants us to stand fast in our calling." Quoted in Thomas C. Oden, *Ministry Through Word and Sacrament*, Classical Pastoral Care Series, vol. 2 (New York: Crossroad, 1989), p. 28.

Elsewhere Luther laments, "I often become so angry and impatient with our peasants, townsfolk, and nobility that I think that I never want to deliver another sermon; for they carry on so shamefully that a person is inclined to be disgusted with life. Besides this, the devil does not stop plaguing me without and within. Therefore I would almost like to say: Let someone else be a preacher in my place." Oden, *Ministry Through Word and Sacrament*, p. 13. See also Archibald D. Hart, *Coping with Depression in the Ministry and Other Helping Professions* (Waco, Tex.: Word Publishing, 1984).

7. Thomas Aquinas, *Summa Theologica*, vol. II, pt. II-II, Q. 32, art. 1, English Dominican Fathers, eds. (New York: Benziger, 1947–48), p. 1325.

8. It is striking, in the classical literature on clergy, how often money is depicted as the chief pastoral temptation. See Oden, *Ministry Through Word and Sacrament*, pp. 205-8.

9. Wade Clark Roof and William McKinney, *American Mainline Religion: It's Changing Shape and Future* (New Brunswick, N.J.: Rutgers University Press, 1987), p. 233.

10. Gerard Egan, *The Skilled Helper: A Model for Systematic Helping and Interpersonal Relating* (Monterey, Calif.: Brooks-Cole, 1975), pp. 17-18.

11. See G. Lloyd Rediger, *Fit to Be a Pastor: A Call to Physical, Mental, and Spiritual Fitness* (Louisville: Westminster John Knox Press, 2000).

12. Baxter notes a pastoral temptation that inclines some pastors to focus upon "superfluities" rather than "necessities." *The Reformed Pastor,* p. 114.

13. See the research on five thousand women pastors in fifteen denominations by Barbara Brown Zikmund, Adair T. Lummis, and Patricia M. Y. Chang in *Clergy Women: An Uphill Calling* (Louisville: Westminster John Knox, 1999).

14. Quoted by Parker J. Palmer, *Let Your Life Speak: Listening for the Voice of Vocation* (San Francisco: Jossey-Bass, 2000), p. 17.

15. Dietrich Bonhoeffer, *Psalms: The Prayer Book of the Bible* (Minneapolis: Augsburg Press, 1970), pp. 64-65.

16. Norma Cook Everist, ed., *Ordinary Ministry, Extraordinary Challenge: Women and the Roles of Ministry* (Nashville: Abingdon Press, 2000), p. 124.

17. Quoted in *The Pastor: Readings from the Patristic Period,* Philip L. Culbertson and Arthur Bradford Shippee, eds. (Minneapolis: Fortress Press, 1990), p. 75.

18. Eugene H. Peterson lists prayer, contemplative reading of Scripture, and the practice of spiritual direction as essential to keeping integrity in ministry. *Working the Angles: The Shape of Pastoral Integrity* (Grand Rapids: Eerdmans, 1987).

19. I agree with Eugene H. Peterson when he says that "spiritual leadership vocations in America are badly undercapitalized. Far more activity is generated by them than there are resources to support them." Therefore, we need constant attentiveness to the nurture and restoration of our sense of vocation. *Under the Unpredictable Plant: An Exploration of Vocational Holiness* (Grand Rapids: Eerdmans, 1992), p. 3.

20. Stanley M. Hauerwas and William H. Willimon, *The Truth About God: The Ten Commandments in Christian Life* (Nashville: Abingdon Press, 1999), chap. 3.

21. See the fascinating history of the American Sunday by Alexis McCrossen, *Holy Day, Holiday: The American Sunday* (Ithaca, N.Y.: Cornell University Press, 1999).

22. Gregory the Great, *Pastoral Care,* in Ancient Christian Writers Series, vol. 11.4, J. Quasten, J. C. Plumpe, and W. Burghardt, eds. (New York: Paulist Press, 1954), p. 234.

23. See Lyle E. Schaller, *The Multiple Staff and the Larger Church* (Nashville: Abingdon Press, 1980).

24. Edwin Friedman, the family systems theorist, complains of the pastor's need to play the hero in the congregation and, in Friedman's word, "overfunction." The pastor's overfunctioning leads the laity, as well as the rest of the church staff, to underfunction. See Edwin Friedman, *Generation to Generation: Family Process in Church and Synagogue* (New York: Guilford Press, 1985), p. 210.

25. After surveying a number of contemporary novels on ministry, James P. Wind notes that nearly all of them appear to regard the church as a negative

resource for pastors in trouble. Always, in these novels, the church "appears as problem, burden, inhibitor, complicator." "Clergy Ethics in Modern Fiction," in *Clergy Ethics in a Changing Society,* James P. Wind, et al., eds. (Louisville: Westminster John Knox Press, 1991), pp. 99-113.

26. Martin Luther, *Treatise on Good Works,* as cited by Oden in *Ministry Through Word and Sacrament,* p. 101.

27. T. S. Eliot, from "East Coker" in *Four Quartets* (New York: Harcourt Brace, 1971), p. 31.

INDEX OF NAMES

SCRIPTURE INDEX

SUBJECT INDEX

Great (best?) story: evangelism 246 ff

Sabbath section 328+